de Gruyter Studies in Organization 21
The Third Sector: Comparative Studies of Nonprofit Organizations

de Gruyter Studies in Organization

Organizational Theory and Research

This de Gruyter Series aims at publishing theoretical and methodological studies of organizations as well as research findings, which yield insight in and knowledge about organizations. The whole spectrum of perspectives will be considered: organizational analyses rooted in the sociological as well as the economic tradition, from a socio-psychological or a political science angle, mainstream as well as critical or ethnomethodological contributions. Equally, all kinds of organizations will be considered: firms, public agencies, non-profit institutions, voluntary associations, inter-organizational networks, supra-national organizations etc.

Emphasis is on publication of *new* contributions, or significant revisions of existing approaches. However, summaries or critical reflections on current thinking and research will also be considered.

This series represents an effort to advance the social scientific study of organizations across national boundaries and academic disciplines. An Advisory Board consisting of representatives of a variety of perspectives and from different cultural areas is responsible for achieving this task.

This series addresses organization researchers within and outside universities, but also practitioners who have an interest in grounding their work on recent social scientific knowledge and insights.

The Third Sector: Comparative Studies of Nonprofit Organizations

Editors
Helmut K. Anheier and Wolfgang Seibel

Walter de Gruyter · Berlin · New York 1990

Editors

Dr. Helmut K. Anheier is Assistant Professor of Sociology at Rutgers University, New Brunswick, USA
Dr. Wolfgang Seibel is Professor of Political Science at the University of Konstanz, Federal Republic of Germany

Library of Congress Cataloging-in-Publication Data

The Third sector : comparative studies of nonprofit organizations / editors, Helmut K. Anheier and Wolfgang Seibel.
    XIV, 414 p. 15,5 × 23 cm. — (De Gruyter studies in organization ; 21)
    Includes bibliographical references.
    ISBN 0-89925-486-1 (U.S. : alk. paper)
    1. Corporations, Nonprofit. I. Anheier, Helmut K. II. Seibel, Wolfgang, 1953—, III. Series.
HD2769.15.T45   1990
658'.048—dc20   90-3292
                                                          CIP

Deutsche Bibliothek Cataloging in Publication Data

The third sector: comparative studies of nonprofit organizations / ed. Helmut K. Anheier and Wolfgang Seibel. — Berlin ; New York : de Gruyter, 1990
New York : de Gruyter, 1990
    (De Gruyter studies in organization ; 21 : Organizational theory and research)
    ISBN 3-11-011713-2
NE: Anheier, Helmut K. [Hrsg.]; GT

⊗ Printed on acid-free paper.

Printed in Germany
Typesetting: Arthur Collignon GmbH, 1000 Berlin 30. — Printing: Gerike GmbH, 1000 Berlin 36. — Binding: Heinz Stein, 1000 Berlin 30. — Cover design: Johannes Rother, 1000 Berlin 21.

Preface

This is a volume which could not have been written a few years ago, for it represents the coming of age of a completely new field of policy research.

The systematic investigation of the non-profit sector in the United States began less than two decades ago, although of course traditional studies of charity, social welfare and cognate subjects had long existed. For a variety of reasons, most significantly deriving from the retreat from Great Society social programs, U.S. scholars of the 1970's began to identify the behavior of non-profit organizations as crucial to understanding socio-political behavior. They quickly came to locate the space occupied by a wide variety of organizations operating outside of both the political and commercial spheres.

The question for research thus became how to identify "non-profit" behavior and how to conceptualize its significance in U.S. social behavior. Scholars from a wide variety of disciplinary backgrounds began to work in the emerging field — from economics, political science, history, sociology, anthropology, psychology, education, law, social work. A number of paradigms for interpreting the role of what came to be called either the "third sector" of the "independent sector" were put forward, while at the same time empirical researchers described the sector and began to test the paradigms. By the late 1980's, it was clear that non-profit scholars had created a new field of study in the United States. The field grew and became institutionalized in university-based centers, academic departments and think-thanks. In Europe, the study of organizational forms located between the state and the commercial world predates American efforts in this area. However, it took place in the context of distinct national scholarly traditions and specialized communities. Comparative and international research questions were rarely asked. As the field in America grew, U.S. scholars very naturally began to wonder about cognate behaviors in other national cultures. National comparison research began, first in economics and then sociology and political science, in an effort to locate the culturally specific aspects of the U.S. system. Not surprisingly, Americans discovered that disciplinary colleagues abroad were exploring similar or cognate problems. They also discovered that U.S. paradigms were not necessarily appropriate in foreign contexts.

So began a series of international scholarly conferences, of which the Bad Honnef meeting was one of the earliest and best. The papers deriving from this conference constitute the core of the volume in hand, and represent the most important exemplar of current international work on non-profit organization in different countries and internationally. The essays cover a wide range of subjects, disciplinary approaches and national cultures, and thus provide the most important approach to the national and international study of non-profit organizations published to date.

This in itself would be enough to recommend the volume, but the tumultuous events of late 1989 in Eastern Europe and the Soviet Union illuminate an aspect of the subject which was not yet fully apparent in Bad Honnef. The "transition from socialism," or whatever the democratization of Eastern Europe is to be called, immediately demands fresh thinking about the organizational alternatives to the administrative state. It may well be (and there is already evidence available) that non-profit models will prove extremely useful in the emergence of socio-political organizations poised between capitalism and socialism. If so, we shall feel grateful to the intrepid scholars who have already begun to chart the course.

The study of non-profit organizations has thus emerged as a central task of policy research for social scientists. The Anheier-Seibel volume demonstrates how much has already been accomplished by the growing international community of scholars — and it also provides an indication of how much important work remains to be done.

New York, 20 March 1990   *Stanley N. Katz*

Contents

Contents

Contents

Contents XIII

Introduction

Helmut K. Anheier and Wolfgang Seibel

During the past few years, a substantial research agenda has begun to develop around the topic of nonprofit organizations, private voluntary organizations, philanthropic and operating foundations — in short, on those organizational forms located between the private, for-profit world and the government. We will refer to this intermediary organizational universe as the *Third Sector*. Research shows that the third sector performs important social, economic, and political functions in Western societies. In many European countries, researchers have begun to examine how nonprofits provide social services, contribute to the arts, research, and education, and, increasingly, help shape and formulate policies at local, regional, national, and even international levels. Other scholars have found that nonprofit organizations are playing an increasingly important role in the development of Third World countries. Indeed, nonprofit organizations exist in virtually all societies. Recently, eastern European countries like Hungary, Poland, and the Soviet Union have allowed, to varying degrees, the private, nonprofit provision of quasi-public goods.

When theories of nonprofit organizations were first introduced in the 1970s, the organizational universe of North America provided the background for their development. Theories either highlighted "market failure" or "government failure" or some combination of private and public deficiencies in the delivery of quasi-public goods as the reason behind the emergence of nonprofit organizations.

By the end of the 1970s, changing political and economic tides led to a reconsideration of the division between "private" and the "public" in many European countries and elsewhere. Researchers and policy-makers have begun to reexamine decentralization and privatization and to consider the third sector as a possible remedy for the "crisis of the welfare state." In England, there is concern about the trend towards transferring social services from the government to the non-statutory sector; in France, the "associational" movement is being widely discussed; in Germany, the role of the larger welfare organizations, political foundations, and the smaller self-help organizations is under consideration. In many European countries, an increased interest in foundations and individual philanthropy is being discussed against the background of a restrictive tax structure.

Recently, researchers into the third sector have begun to compare the role — both historical and current — of nonprofits in European, Asian,

African and Latin American countries. Major questions that have been asked include: Why do different countries make different choices about the public — private division of responsibility for providing quasi-public goods and services? Why and under what conditions has the nonprofit organization developed as an institutional form? Under what circumstances does it have comparative advantage over government and profit-maximizing organizations? How do nonprofits and government bureaucracies compare with respect to quantity, quality, cost, efficiency, and distribution of services? To what extent can fees and donations replace tax revenues for financing these goods? Is private funding a desirable alternative to higher government budgets? What are the implications (for efficiency and equity) of relying on private funding versus government subsidy for the provision of quasi-public goods? What kinds of regulations are needed to mitigate the less desirable effects of privatization? What is the relationship between traditional voluntary associations, churches, and the new grassroots movements in most European countries? Can third sector organizations avoid bureaucratization and competitive entrepreneurship?

One of the major results of recent research has been the acknowledgement of the complex interdependencies between the public and the private sectors in all industrialized countries. Concepts such as "third party government," "neo-corporatism," or "private interest government" suggest that the distinction between government and third sector has become increasingly blurred. Moreover, analysis of the evolution and current state of the third sector tells the history of the country, and the way in which societies "choose" to govern themselves.

Estelle James was among the first to present comparative theories of nonprofit organizations. Her theory predicts a strong and positive relationship between a society's religious heterogeneity and the size and importance of its third sector. Countries with a diversity of religious groupings such as the Netherlands develop a large third sector, while homogeneous countries like Sweden are characterized by a small third sector. While differentiated demand, based on religious preferences, explains the size of the third sectors in developed countries, excess demand for public and semi-public goods — combined with donor preferences and religious competition among suppliers — explains differences in third sectors in the Third World.

Yet despite recent advances in theories on nonprofits, many central aspects of the subject have still not been covered. Comparative research on the third sector faces several problems. Studies of the third sector differ from one country to another, according to different histories, traditions, and developments of these countries. Most European countries have accumulated a varied and broad literature on specific forms of third sector organizations, cooperatives, and firms offering public services. However, until recently, the broader scope suggested by the term third sector or nonprofit sector has been absent from the European debate. The first editor of this volume, Helmut K. Anheier, has attempted to stimulate international exchange and collaboration among researchers by producing the *International Directory of Research on Non-Profit Organizations*, compiled for the Yale Program on Non-Profit Organizations in 1985–6. The Directory lists more than 200 researchers from more than 40 countries worldwide.

In 1986, a group of researchers from Europe and the United States formed a *"Planning Committee for the 1st European Conference on the Nonprofit Sector and the Modern Welfare State"* (members were Professors Estelle James [State University of New York, Stony Brook], Ralph Kramer [University of California, Berkeley, and Hebrew University, Jerusalem], Christoph Sachsse [University of Kassel], and the editors Anheier and Seibel). The Committee identified a group of some 50 scholars from 12 European countries, the United States, and Israel, who were each asked to propose a paper for presentation at the conference. From these the planning committee selected 30 papers for presentation. The 1987 conference aimed to draw up a list of research needs and activities which would enhance comparative as well as country-specific studies of nonprofit organizations. The conference, funded by the Stiftung Volkswagen (Volkswagen Foundation), took place in Bad Honnef, West Germany, in June 9–12, 1987. The 30 papers presented at the conference served as the matrix for the present volume.

How to Use this Book

The book offers a survey of international research on the third sector. It does not claim to be exhaustive but incorporates the major issues of third sector research from nine countries and various academic disciplines. The study of the third sector has emerged as a truly interdisciplinary field of the social sciences. In each part of our book, we have included an introductory chapter designed to bridge the various disciplines and so assist the specialist and non-specialist reader alike. These chapters by Anheier (Part 2), Rose-Ackerman (Part 3), and Bauer (Part 4) give an overview and orientation.

Part 1 offers a general introduction to the study of the third sector. The following two parts deal with key theoretical and empirical aspects of third sector research: the question of institutional choice and organizational behavior (Part 2), and the problems of efficiency, resource dependencies, and organizational autonomy (Part 3). Finally, Part 4 presents several country studies and offers a general profile of the third sector (or special industries) in Hungary, France, Japan, Switzerland, Spain, and the Federal Republic of Germany. The chapter on Africa deals with the role of third sector organizations in the developing world.

Acknowledgements

This book owes much to the efforts of others. It is more than a formal obligation if we express our appreciations to all those who, in one way or another, contributed. As the first editor, I would like to express my gratitude to John Simon and Paul DiMaggio of the Yale Program on Non-Profit Organizations for their intellectual guidance and support. Jürgen Reese of the University of Kassel, West Germany, and the Arbeitsgruppe Verwaltungs-forschung he assembled have made the "Third Sector" known to the West German scholarship and inspired much of what resulted in the present book project.

We were particularly glad to have been able to count on Estelle James's advice and encouragement. We would also like to thank the Salzburg Seminar for American Studies who brought many of us together at Schloss Leopolds-kron in June 1986. The hospitality and support of the Salzburg Seminar allowed us to concentrate on comparative research on the third sector for two weeks, and to plan the Bad Honnef conference a year later. We wish to thank Christoph Sachße and Ralph Kramer as members of the planning committee. Our thanks also go to the Stiftung Volkswagen which funded the conference and to its Secretary General, Rolf Möller. For Wolfgang Seibel the stimulating atmosphere of the Institute for Advanced Study at Princeton provided a perfect environment during the final editing of this volume.

Producing an edited volume on a relatively new and emerging research area with authors from various countries and disciplines proved a major logistical and intellectual task. Several people were of great assistance in this respect. Bianka Ralle from De Gruyter's has carefully managed our novice editorship, and has patiently tolerated more than one delay in delivering the final manuscript. Sioban Gibbons, graduate student in sociology at Rutgers, carefully read the manuscripts and helped reduce some of the stylistic and grammatical Babel created by authors of seven different mother tongues.

We would also like to thank Maria Muschong of the University of Konstanz for preparing the name and subject index for this volume.

Last but not least, we wish to thank the authors of this volume. They patiently attended to the repeated and sometimes bothersome objections, suggestions, revisions, and modifications expressed by the editors. Together, we hope that this book will contribute to comparative research on the third sector and will help stimulate cooperation amongst researchers in this field.

Part I
The Third Sector Between the Market and the State

1.1
Sociological and Political Science Approaches to the Third Sector

Wolfgang Seibel and Helmut K. Anheier

1. Introduction

Few countries use the American terms *"nonprofit sector"* to describe the set of organizations located between the private, for-profit, and the public sector. While the term "nonprofit sector" refers to a relatively well-defined organizational universe in the United States and perhaps in the United Kingdom, the term seems less precise when used to distinguish such sectors in most European countries (Anheier 1988). For comparative purposes, it seems useful to adopt the term *"third sector"* to designate all organizations which are neither profit-oriented businesses nor governmental agencies or bureaucracies. We assume that despite considerable differences in history, legal treatment, organizational activities, and composition, the French *"économie sociale,"* the British *"non-statutory sector,"* or the German *"gemeinnützige Organisationen"* and *"gemeinwirtschaftliche Unternehmen,"* and the American *"nonprofit sector"* share many central features.

The term "third sector" was first used by several U.S. scholars (Etzioni 1973; Levitt 1973; Nielsen 1979) and the influential *Filer Commission* (1975), and it is now increasingly applied by European researchers (Douglas 1983; Reese 1987; Reese et al. 1989; Reichard 1988; Ronge 1988). The term has both normative and strategic roots. For Etzioni (1973), the term "third sector" suggested elements of the then widely discussed convergence thesis. "Third sector" was intended to express an alternative to the disadvantages associated with both profit maximization and bureaucracy by combining the flexibility and efficiency of markets which the equity and predictability of public bureaucracy.

Due to the more visible impact of the market and the state — which together provided 97.8% of U.S. GDP in the 1970s (Rudney 1987: 56) —, discussion of the third sector was somewhat neglected by policy-makers and social scientists alike. Aware of this neglect, the *Filer Commission*, initiated by John D. Rockefeller in 1973, applied the term "third sector" as a pragmatic convention and useful shorthand to draw public and scholarly interest to these organizations. The term exists also in West Germany and Austria, where "third sector" is applied to all those organizations which, for one reason or another, do not readily fit into the dichotomy of for-profit sector versus public sector.

It is perhaps not surprising to find that such pragmatic and apparently ideologically neutral approaches also contain normative elements. The "discovery" of a "third sector" occurred at a time when politicians and policy-makers in most Western societies began to reconsider the division of labor between the public and the private sectors, and to examine ways of reducing state responsibilities. This intensified interest in the third sector was sup-ported not only by conservative political forces but also by others from across the political spectrum. The reasons for this new, or − in some countries − rediscovered, interest in the third sector are complex and can be only partially conveyed by catchwords such as *"new solidarity,"* *"sociabilité,"* *"private initiative,"* *"self-reliance,"* *"alternative to both market and state,"* and *"reduction of big government."* The broad range of economic and social attributes which exist under the term "third sector" allow politici-ans to support those parts or aspects of the third sector which seem to support their own critique and interpretation of the "welfare state in crisis."

The ideological shift of the mid-1970s coincided with growing national and international economic difficulties. The public sector and expectations of what it could or should achieve moved to a more central place in the political agenda. U.S. and European scholars approached this discussion of the third sector from very different angles: Whereas U.S. social scientists − as Hall (1987) argued − viewed the third sector as an essential ingredient of a civil, liberal society, many European scholars emphasized its historical importance in conservative political scenarios (Bauer 1987; Heinze and Olk 1981). While U.S. researchers refer to de Tocqueville's observations in *"Democracy in America"* on the role of voluntary associations in a liberal and democratic society, Europeans are quick to point to the conservative goals served by the third sector in the nineteenth century, and agree with the founder of an influential Protestant welfare association, *Wichern*, that charity organizations are the *"armed daughter of the church"* for combatting atheism and socialism. Finally, whereas it took a "crisis of nonprofit sector scholar-ship" (Hall 1987) to make researchers realize that they had to acknowledge fully the importance of the state in order to understand the third sector in the United States, researchers in Europe found it difficult to see the third sector as an organizational universe of its own.

But does the term "third sector" signify a substantive concern that goes beyond current political debates? To what extent is the term conceptually justified? What are the major theoretical approaches used by political scien-tists and sociologists to understand an organizational universe which is neither market nor state? What are the criteria which differentiate the third from the other sectors? We will briefly address these questions in the following pages.

In reviewing the available literature, we can identify three major sets of criteria that are used to differentiate the third sector from both the for-profit world and the state (Ronge 1988): institutional characteristics of organizations; the different rationales for social and economic action in the three sectors; and, finally, the institutional functions served by the organizations.

2. Institutional Characteristics and Classifications

The first set of criteria — institutional characteristics of third sector organiza-tions — appear plausible at first; yet, as already mentioned above, they fail to encompass cross-cultural variations. By applying the dual criteria "private, not for-profit" and "non-governmental," we may distinguish a core set of organizations across different countries. But we will also exclude those types of organizations which cannot be easily classified under these headings, as such: autonomous public enterprises and administrative units, types of cooperatives, corporations of public law, quasi non-governmental organiza-tions, state churches, certain types of foundations, and nonprofit organiza-tions legally established as for-profit businesses.

Difficulties in classifying organizations by applying institutional character-istics such as "nonprofit" versus "for-profit" or "private" versus "public" are, to a large degree, the result of continuous shifts in what societies define as private and public, for-profit and nonprofit. We are reminded by Kramer (1981) and Kaufmann (1986) that sectoral boundaries are far from constant and have become increasingly blurred. Moreover, authors like Wuthnow (1988) and Watt (1988) argue that "private" and "public" produce a mislead-ing dichotomy which gives the false impression of a zero-sum game between the two sectors.

Political scientists have conceptualized the third sector as an intermediary zone between market and state, and have analyzed the way in which third sector organizations act as mediators between the organized economic inter-ests of market firms, labor, and the political interests of state agencies and their constituencies on the other (Berger 1981; Lehmbruch and Schmitter 1982; Schmitter and Lehmbruch 1979). Whereas most non-political science research on the third sector is in the tradition of either micro-economics or organizational analysis, political science research tends to describe the third sector's macro-political functions. However, political science research in general deals with the third sector's mediating role, and gives little attention to analysis of the sector's service-providing organizations.

The third sector mediates between special and general interests. The central characteristic of mediating organizations in this sector is their ability to combine aspects of social and political integration with economic objectives. Several scholars demonstrate this duality in a variety of cases: Bauer (1978) links the development of voluntary welfare agencies to the emergence of social and political movements in Germany. Kramer (1981) has similar conclusions in the case of the United States and Israel. Karl and Katz (1987) suggest that large foundations in the United States served as ideological shelters for business interests.

Anheier (1988; see also chapter 4.5 in this volume) demonstrates that some European societies such as West Germany do not apply the for-profit versus nonprofit criterion with the same consistency with which they apply the public versus private dichotomy. In legal, fiscal, and administrative terms, the West German organizational universe is primarily divided along the *"commercial"* versus *"non-commercial"* line (cf. Hansmann 1980). The distinction "profit versus nonprofit" is less important in West German classification than both the "public—private" and the "commercial—non-commercial" distinctions. West German national accounts tend to recognize only the non-commercial provision of services as part of third sector GNP; however, they tend to exclude commercial for-profit and nonprofit service-provision as well as interest-mediation groups.

Few countries treat the third sector as a separate category in national account statistics (see also chapter 4.4 by Wagner); and those who do rarely report in the same detail as the for-profit and the public sector. Systems of national accounts in Italy, the United Kingdom, France, and West Germany treat the third sector in many ways as a residual category necessary to correct the GDP contributions of public and for-profit sectors, and private households. Consequently, GNP data are not directly comparable from one country to another. Moreover, only in recent years have official statistics begun to pay more attention to the employment provided by the third sector. For example, in France, the SIRENE data base system (*Système d'identification pour le répertoire des entreprises et de leurs établissements*) includes all operative organizations with at least one employee (see chapter 4.3 by Archambault; Kaminski 1987). In West-Germany, the 1970 and 1987 employment census included data on the number of third sector organizations, the type, income, number of employees, and salaries for all those which employ at least one person.

Following Venanzoni (1981), we can use data from the 1970 employment census to put the German third sector into perspective. With about 52,000 organizations, 582,000 employees, and a payroll of DM 5,8 billion, the third sector contributed about DM 7,966 billion or 1.15% to GDP, a similar contribution to that of the insurance business. The comparison with the insurance industry, however, cannot be taken too far. Insurance companies are relatively large corporations with detailed, complete, and homogeneous accounting systems; they represent a mature industry and operate in a relatively well-defined oligopolistic market. By contrast, the third sector is composed of many small organizations which often have only rudimentary accounting and reporting procedures and operate in a highly heterogeneous field of diverse constituencies.

In some European countries, the heterogeneity of the third sector has encouraged the study of one or two particular types of nonprofit organizations rather than of the third sector as a whole. This is particularly the case in countries where the cooperative movement produced a well-developed system of cooperative enterprises, such as in Scandinavian countries, Austria, West Germany, and France. In Germany, for instance, the study of public service enterprises (*Gemeinwirtschaftslehre*) has long occupied a prominent place in the social sciences (Thiemeyer 1970).

In countries where the division of labor and spheres of influence between secular and religious powers are regulated by state law and/or contract (*concordat*), the political and legal study of religious organizations and churches looks back on a long tradition (Weber 1983). In Germany, research shows that two factors led to a well-defined sharing of responsibilities and to a complex division of labor between the state and the third sector (Rinken 1971). First, governments had active control over the early emergence of private welfare organizations in the late nineteenth and early twentieth centuries. Second, legal and financial autonomy of the welfare organizations has consistently grown by a process which, although it came late, stressed compromise rather than confrontation. As a result, in West Germany's "decentralized state and centralized society" (Katzenstein 1987), the government and large parts of the third sector are "walking hand in hand," neither very quickly nor dynamically, but smoothly and without excitement.

However, this neo-corporatist arrangement is not without its price. When, as part of the economic crisis of the 1970s, the social security system began to experience difficulties, new social movements challenged the harmony within the welfare state. Reluctantly, the neo-corporatist arrangement between the state and the traditional welfare organizations had to accommodate and incorporate the claims of the new social movements.

A comparison between the German and the French situation highlights the development of distinct national styles in the third sector (see chapter 2.5 by Hood and Schuppert). In France, the third sector was only recently discovered when the term *"économie sociale"* entered political discourse in the 1980s (see chapter 4.3 by Archambault). At that time, the third sector seemed to offer for the socialist government an alternative to both capitalist and public bureaucracy, and thus fitted well into the government's approach to decentralization. A quasi-official *"Conseil pour la vie associative"* was initiated by the government in 1982, and was followed by the appointment of a secretary of state responsible for the *"économie sociale."*

3. Organizational Rationales

Although it seems impossible to distill the immense body of literature on cooperative societies, public service organizations, and religious organizations into a single basic theme, we can, nevertheless, discern a common concern: how do cooperatives, autonomous public organizations, and church-related bodies fit into the dichotomy of state versus market? Can we find distinct organizational cultures and rationalities in church-related charities, independent public service corporations, or rural savings associations?

It is here that we confront a basic issue: If we assume that cooperatives, churches, charities, autonomous public organizations, or any organization located between the market and the state must operate efficiently in allocating goods and services, and obey the same rational dictum as for-profit enterprises and state bureaucracies, on what grounds can third sector organizations be distinct (see Horch 1988)? And, if they are distinct from both state and market organizations, is it this distinction that justifies their special status — for example, in tax treatment — or is it something else? More concretely, what differentiates *Crédit Agricole* or *Raiffeisenbank*, a transnational cooperative society, from giant corporations such as *Crédit Lyonnais* or *Deutsche Bank*?

One answer to these questions has been suggested by classical theorists, such as Franz Oppenheimer (1896) in the case of cooperatives, and Robert Michels (1911) in the case of political parties. Oppenheimer's law of transformation and Michels's "iron law of oligarchy" predict a general convergence and assimilation of organizational types. Similarly, Max Weber argued that bureaucracy may evolve as the ubiquitous organizational type of modern society. Since then, organizational theory has largely modified the general statements by classical theorists and has begun to consider organizational fields and environments (Hannan and Freeman 1977, 1983). DiMaggio and Powell (1983) argue that the processes of institutional isomorphism and differentiation account for the convergence as well as the divergence of organizational types.

What are the underlying rationales which form the basis of the third sector? Reichard (1988) suggests that this basis consists of four variables: means rationality, formality, solidarity, and type of exchange. Thus, third sector organizations tend to be characterized by lower degrees of means rationality and formality, and higher degrees of solidarity and direct exchange. Moreover, third sector organizations are defined by a higher degree of autonomy in relation to these aspects than either state agencies or for-profit firms. Therefore, third sector organizations are different in relative, not in absolute terms: they may be less means-rational and less formal, and they may put more emphasis on solidarity and direct exchanges than do organizations in other sectors.

To some extent, Reichard's view is a more general formulation of Powell and Friedkin's (1987) assertion that, in contrast to for-profit firms, nonprofits tend to be loosely coupled and characterized by multiple goal structures and heterogeneous, often conflicting, constituencies. Moreover, the informality of social relations within and between third sector organizations is described by Boorman (1981) and Boorman and Levitt (1982) who argue that acquaintance networks and the availability of informal resource allocation and distribution channels are the true human capital of this sector. Similar claims are made by Horch (1983) and Winkler (1988).

Solidarity and altruism as independent components are far less accepted by scholars. Following Olson (1965), micro-economic research suggests that solidarity and altruism may be interpreted as elements of individual utility maximization (Derlega and Grzelak 1982). As Boorman's work (1981) demonstrates, the often observed informality of inter-organizational relations among nonprofits rests on means-rational behavior to maximize utility, and not, as it is sometimes asserted, on notions of solidarity or altruism. Moreover, in a study on the motives of founders of foundations and philanthropic trusts, Odendahl (1987) reports that altruistic motives played, at best, a minor part.

4. Sectoral Functions

The third general approach to the third sector does not analyze underlying organizational rationales nor does it investigate the *modus vivendi* of third sector organizations; rather it examines their functions and contributions to resource allocation and social welfare. For example, which third sector organizations achieve results and supply goods and services that cannot be provided by other sectors, including households?

Two broad orientations emerged from this approach. The first is represented by the American micro-economic school which views the third sector either as a combination of market and state failure within the framework of institutional choice, or as an institutional option to reduce transaction costs (see chapter 1.2 by James and Chapter 2.2 by Badelt in this volume for an overview; Rose-Ackerman 1986). Weisbrod (1977, 1988), for example, sees the third sector as compensating for the state's failure to meet minority demands for public or semi-public goods. According to Hansmann (1980, 1987), however, nonprofit organizations arise as a response to market failure, such as information asymmetries between producer and consumer. In this case, Hansmann argues, nonprofit organizations appear more trustworthy since they have fewer incentives to downgrade quality in order to increase profits.

Micro-economic approaches have been extensively criticized on various grounds (see chapters 1.2 and 2.2 by James and Badelt). For comparative purposes, their greatest deficiency is, as James argues, that they cannot explain cross-national variations in third sector size and composition, without introducing variables external to the micro-economic model, such as social, ethnic, and ideological heterogeneity. Going one step further, Salamon (1987, and chapter 3.4 in this volume) and Badelt (see chapter 2.2) argue that neither the market failure nor the state failure thesis can explain why a third sector is needed to compensate for failures in the first place. Why do market and state not compensate each other's shortcomings, as assumed in classical political economy, instead of resorting to a third sector?

Neo-corporatist theories represent the second functional approach. From this perspective, the third sector offers a buffer zone between state and society and mitigates social tensions and political conflicts. Third sector organizations take on functions which the state, for various reasons, cannot fulfill or delegate to for-profit firms (Heinze and Olk 1981; Hilbert 1988; Streeck 1983). Consequently, Seibel (1987, 1989, and chapter 2.6) argues that an essential function of the third sector is the institutionalization of organizational responses to "unsolvable" problems. Finally, Reese (1987) approaches the delegation of functions to the third sector from a different angle. He asserts that voluntary associations compensate for functions no longer fulfilled by the family which finds itself less able to integrate individuals into society and to provide services for them (Becher and Pankoke 1981; Gross 1982; Offe and Heinze 1986).

5. Research Strategies

We suggest two avenues for research. First of all, it seems useful to disaggregate research problems. Taking up an approach first suggested by Hansmann (1987), DiMaggio and Anheier (1990) differentiate between two major research strategies: the first tries to explain the existence of nonprofit organizations in organizational, sectoral, and societal terms, while the second shows the effects of nonprofit organizations on selected variables. Thus, the first strategy uses "nonprofit" as a dependent variable, and the second uses it as an independent variable. Together, this yields six main research questions:

The first three questions refer to "nonprofit" as a dependent variable: (1) Why are some organizations nonprofit? (2) How do we explain the division of labor among sectors, their industries, and branches? (3) Why does the prevalence of nonprofits and their organizational forms vary from one society to another? The second set of questions address "nonprofit" as an independent variable: (4) Do nonprofits behave differently from for-profit firms and public organizations? (5) How do predominantly for-profit, public, and nonprofit industries and branches differ? (6) What is the impact of nonprofits at the national level, and are societies with a well-developed third sector in a better position to face social, political, and economic challenges than societies with a small third sector?

The second avenue for research is to abandon strict sectoralization and to proceed instead from the observation that all three sectors — for-profit, nonprofit, and public — contain fluid institutional arrangements. Population ecology, structural analysis, the theory of organizational niches (see Hannan and Freeman 1977; see Seibel's chapter 2.6), and inter-sectoral relations (Gronbjerg 1987) offer good starting points for understanding and measuring sectoral morphologies and boundaries.

With this in mind we can then focus on the exchange and adaptation processes that occur between the third sector and the for-profit and public sectors. DiMaggio and Powell (1983: 149), paraphrasing Schelling (1978: 14), observe that organizations "respond to an environment that consists of other organizations responding to their environment, which consists of organizations responding to an environment of organizations." Though some of these responses are reactions to market and political influences, we can argue that third sector organizations are less subject to market and political pressures, if we assume that means rationality is not as prevalent there as in the for-profit and public sectors. The third sector has only partial access to mechanisms of correction comparable to that of the ballot box for the public sector and that of the market for the for-profit sector.

A consequence of this is that third sector organizations, once established, may be less challenged and threatened in their survival than for-profit organizations which are subject to market considerations, or public agencies which are subject to various forms of majoritarian control. Although they may not actively seek niches, third sector organizations may carve out niches for themselves in the course of their organizational life cycle.

These niches, in turn, increase the probability of survival. In fact, few organizations in Europe are older than the foundations, and few a more stable than those linked to the Catholic church. The remarkable longevity of third sector organizations is further demonstrated by foundations in Germany, a country where few public and private organizations can look back on a history spanning more than two generations: yet about 20% of the existing German foundations were created in the nineteenth century, 10% between the sixteenth and the eighteenth centuries, and about 100 predate 1500 (Neuhoff, Schindler, and Zwingmann 1983).

Seibel (1989) shows that the survival of third sector organizations seems remarkably independent of their performance criteria. Some welfare organizations and nonprofit ambulance and emergency services continue to operate unchallenged despite serious shortcomings and failures. The value rationality of third sector organizations makes permanent failures more likely (Meyer and Zucker 1989). Since means-rational considerations are relatively less important, members of nonprofit organizations may find it easier to divorce performance from goals. This built-in characteristic of nonprofit organizations is at one and the same time their greatest weakness and their greatest strength. It makes third sector organizations suitable candidates for "functional dilettantism," a "mellow weakness" which can be utilized by political bodies to project the illusion that "at least something is being done" (see chapter 2.6 by Seibel, and Seibel 1989).

However, the third sector, though having distinct features, is by no means independent of the government and the for-profit sectors. This interdependency is not only based on subsidies and other financial transfers. Hall (1987: 17) uses several striking examples to show the overlap between the three sectors in terms of executive career patterns. To give just one example: Robert McNamara's career brought him from the Harvard Business School, to the Ford Motor Company, to the Defense Department, and to the presidency of the World Bank, while he also served on the board of directors for the Ford Foundation, the Brookings Institution, and the California Institute of Technology (Hall 1987: 17).

Public and nonprofit sectors also overlap in the area of policy formulation. Whether at local, regional, national, or international levels, governments seem to find it increasingly difficult to formulate policies on their own. Third sector organizations, foundations, and "think tanks" in particular, serve as policy-formulating and consulting institutions for political bodies. Analyzing sectoral dependencies (Gronbjerg 1987) will most likely lead to a more explicit consideration of inter-sectoral powers and influences, and will help to explain why the third sector, despite continuing to be relatively insignificant economically, has achieved a visible and prominent status.

References

Anheier, H. K. (1988): "The Public Sector and the Private: Organizational Choice and the Third Sector in Europe," in *1988 Spring Research Forum*, (Ed.), Washington, D.C.: The Independent Sector, 558–573.

Bauer, R. (1978): *Wohlfahrtsverbände in der Bundesrepublik*, Weinheim und Basel: Beltz.

Bauer, R. (1987): "Intermediäre Hilfesysteme personenbezogener Dienstleistungen in zehn Ländern. Eine Einführung," in *Verbandliche Wohlfahrtspflege im internationalen Vergleich*, R. Bauer and A.-M. Thränhardt (Eds.), Opladen: Westdeutscher Verlag, 9–32.

Becher, B. and E. Pankoke (1981): "Sozialadministration und selbstaktive Felder. Neue Relationsprobleme kommunaler Sozialpolitik," *Archiv für Wissenschaft und Praxis der sozialen Arbeit* 12, 219–239.

Berger, S. (1981): *Organizing Interests in Western Europe. Pluralism, Corporatism, and the Transformation of Politics*, Cambridge and London: Cambridge University Press.

Boorman, S. A. (1981): "Network Matching," Seminar-Paper "Legislation," Yale Law School, New Haven.

Boorman, S. A. and P. R. Levitt (1982): "The Network Matching Principle," *Economic Letters* 10, 1–7.

Derlega, V. J. and J. Grzelak (Eds.) (1982): *Cooperation and Helping Behavior. Theories and Research*, New York and London: Academic Press.

DiMaggio, P. J. and H. K. Anheier (1990): "Sociological Conceptualization of Nonprofit Organizations and Sectors," *Annual Review of Sociology* (forthcoming).

DiMaggio, P. J. and W. W. Powell (1983): "The Iron Cage Revisited: Institutional Isomorphism and Collective Rationality in Organizational Fields," *American Sociological Review* 48, 147–160.

Douglas, J. (1983): *Why Charity? The Case for a Third Sector*, Beverly Hills and London: Sage.

Etzioni, A. (1973): "The Third Sector and Domestic Missions," *Public Administration Review* 33, 314–323.

Filer Commission [Commission on Private Philanthropy and Public Needs] (1975): "The Third Sector," in *America's Voluntary Spirit. A Book of Readings*, Brian O'Connell (Ed.), New York: The Foundation Center 1983, 299–314.

Gronbjerg, K. A. (1987): "Patterns of Institutional Relations in the Welfare State: Public Mandates and the Nonprofit-Sector," *Journal of Voluntary Action Research* 16, 64–80.

Gross, P. (1982): „Der Wohlfahrtsstaat und die Bedeutung der Selbsthilfebewegung," *Soziale Welt* 3, 26–48.

Hall, P. D. (1987): "Abandoning the Rhetoric of Independence. Reflections on the Nonprofit-Sector in the Post-Liberal Era," *Journal of Voluntary Action Research* 16, 11–28.

Hannan, M. T. and J. Freeman (1977): "The Population Ecology of Organizations," *American Journal of Sociology* 82, 929–964.

Hannan, M. T. and J. Freeman (1983): "Niche Width and the Dynamics of Organizational Populations," *American Journal of Sociology* 88, 1116–1145.

Hansmann, H. B. (1980): "The Role of Nonprofit Enterprise," *Yale Law Journal* 89, 835–898.

Hansmann, H. B. (1987): "Economic Theories of Nonprofit Organizations," in *The Nonprofit Sector. A Research Handbook*, W. W. Powell (Ed.), New Haven and London: Yale University Press, 27–42.

Heinze, R. G. and Th. Olk (1981): "Die Wohlfahrtsverbände im System sozialer Dienstleistungsproduktion. Zur Entstehung und Struktur der bundesrepublikanischen Verbändewohlfahrt," *Kölner Zeitschrift für Soziologie und Sozialpsychologie* 33, 94–114.

Hilbert, J. (1988): "Die Rolle der organisierten Sozialparteien bei der Produktion des öffentlichen Gutes 'berufliche Bildung'," Beitrag zum *Workshop "Der Dritte Sektor zwischen Markt und Staat"* auf dem 17. Wissenschaftlichen Kongreß der Deutschen Vereinigung für politische Wissenschaft (DVPW), Darmstadt, 12.−16. September 1988 [unpublished conferenced paper].

Horch, H.-D. (1983): *Strukturbesonderheiten freiwilliger Vereinigungen. Analyse und Untersuchung einer alternativen Form menschlichen Zusammenarbeitens,* Frankfurt a. M. and New York: Campus.

Horch, H.-D. (1988): "Kommerzialisierung und Politisierung. Finanzsoziologische Probleme freiwilliger Vereinigungen," in *Soziologie wirtschaftlichen Handelns,* K. Heinemann (Ed.), Opladen: Westdeutscher Verlag, 216−233.

Kaminski, P. (1987): "Des chiffres pour l'économie sociale: où en est-on en 1987"? Contribution au colloque *Batir le compte satellite de l'économie sociale − approches régionales, approches nationales,* ADDES [Association pour le Développement de la Documentation sur l'Économie Sociale], Nanterre, 17 juin 1987 [conference paper, mimeo].

Karl, B. D. and S. N. Katz (1981) "Foundation and Ruling Class Elites," *Daedalus* 11, 1−40.

Katzenstein, P. (1987): *Policy and Politics in West Germany. The Growth of a Semi-sovereign State,* Philadelphia: Temple University Press.

Kaufmann, F.-X. (1986): "The Blurring of the Distinction 'State versus Society' in the Idea and Practice of the Welfare State," in *Guidance, Control and Evaluation in the Public Sector,* F.-X. Kaufmann, G. Majone, and V. Ostrom (Eds.), Berlin and New York: de Gruyter, 127−138.

Kaufmann, F.-X., G. Majone, and V. Ostrom (Eds.) (1986): *Guidance, Control and Evaluation in the Public Sector,* Berlin and New York: de Gruyter.

Kramer, R. M. (1981): *Voluntary Agencies in the Welfare State,* Berkeley, Los Angeles, and London: University of California Press.

Lehmbruch, G. and Ph. C. Schmitter (Eds.) (1982): *Patterns of Corporatist Policy Making,* London and Beverly Hills: Sage.

Levitt, T. (1973): *The Third Sector. New Tactics for a Responsive Society,* New York: Amacom.

Meyer, M. D. and L. G. Zucker (1989): *Permanently Failing Organizations,* Beverly Hills and London: Sage.

Michels, R. (1911): *Zur Soziologie des Parteiwesens in der modernen Demokratie. Untersuchungen über die oligarchischen Tendenzen des Gruppenlebens,* Stuttgart: Kröner.

Neuhoff, K., A. Schindler, and H. J. Zwingmann (1983): *Stiftungshandbuch,* Baden-Baden: Nomos.

Nielsen, W. A. (1979): *The Endangered Sector,* New York: Columbia University Press.

Odendahl, T. (1987): *America's Wealthy and the Future of Foundations,* New York: The Foundation Center.

Offe, C. and R. G. Heinze (1986): "Am Arbeitsmarkt vorbei. Überlegungen zur Neubestimmung 'haushaltlicher' Wohlfahrtsproduktion in ihrem Verhältnis zu Markt und Staat," *Leviathan* 14, 471−495.

Olson, M. (1965): *The Logic of Collective Action,* New York: Schocken Books.

Oppenheimer, F. (1896): *Die Siedlungsgenossenschaft,* Jena: Gustav Fischer.

Powell, W. W. and R. Friedkin (1987): "Organizational Change in Nonprofit Organizations," in *The Nonprofit Sector. A Research Handbook,* W. W. Powell (Ed.), New Haven: Yale University Press, 180−194.

Reese, J. (1987): "Die gesellschaftliche Bedeutung des Dritten Sektors," *Der Dritte Sektor zwischen Markt und Staat*, Kongreß vom 30. 9. bis 2. 10. 1987 in Kassel, AG Verwaltungsforschung (Ed.), Tagungsband [unpublished conference volume], 1 – 16.

Reese, J. et al. (Eds.) (1989): *Zwischen Markt und Staat. Der gesellschaftliche Beitrag von Organisationen des Dritten Sektors*, Baden-Baden: Nomos.

Reichard, C. (1988): "Der Dritte Sektor. Entstehung, Funktion und Problematik von 'Nonprofit'-Organisationen aus verwaltungswissenschaftlicher Sicht," *Die Öffentliche Verwaltung* 41, 363 – 370.

Reichard, C. (1989): "Abgrenzung, Typisierung und Deskription des Dritten Sektors," in *Zwischen Markt und Staat. Der gesellschaftliche Beitrag von Organisationen des Dritten Sektors*, J. Reese et al. (Eds.), Baden-Baden: Nomos, in print.

Rinken, A. (1971): *Das Öffentliche als verfassungstheoretisches Problem, dargestellt am Rechtsstatus der Wohlfahrtsverbände*, Berlin: Duncker & Humblot.

Ronge, V. (1988): "Theorie und Empirie des 'Dritten Sektors'," in *Jahrbuch zur Staats- und Verwaltungswissenschaft* 2, Th. Ellwein et al. (Eds.), Baden-Baden: Nomos, 113 – 148.

Rose-Ackerman, S. (Ed.) (1986): *The Economics of Nonprofit Institutions. Studies in Structure and Policy*, New York and Oxford: Oxford University Press.

Rudney, G. (1987): "The Scope and Dimensions of Nonprofit Activity," in *The Nonprofit Sector. A Research Handbook*, W. W. Powell (Ed.), New Haven: Yale University Press, 55 – 64.

Salamon, L. M. (1987): "On Market Failure, Voluntary Failure, and Third Party Government: Toward a Theory of Government – Nonprofit Relations in the Modern Welfare State," *Journal of Voluntary Action Research* 16, 29 – 49.

Schelling, T. C. (1978): *Micromotives and Macrobehavior*, New York: Norton.

Schmitter, Ph. C. and G. Lehmbruch (Eds.) (1979): *Trends Toward Corporatist Intermediation*, Beverly Hills and London: Sage.

Seibel, W. (1987): "Der Staatsstil für Krisenzeiten. 'Selbststeuerung' öffentlicher Aufgabenträger und das Problem der Kontrolle," *Politische Vierteljahresschrift* 28, 197 – 219.

Seibel, W. (1989): "The Function of Mellow Weakness. Nonprofit Organizations as Problem Nonsolvers in Germany," in *The Nonprofit Sector in International Perspective. Studies in Comparative Culture and Policy*, E. James (Ed.), New York and Oxford: Oxford University Press, 177 – 192.

Streeck, W. (1983): "Die Reform der beruflichen Bildung in der westdeutschen Bauwirtschaft 1969 – 1982. Eine Fallstudie über Verbände als Träger öffentlicher Politik," Wissenschaftszentrum Berlin (WZB), International Institute of Management – discussion papers, III/LMP 83-23.

Thiemeyer, Th. (1970): *Gemeinwirtschaftlichkeit als Ordnungsprinzip. Grundlegung einer Theorie gemeinnütziger Unternehmen*, Berlin: Duncker & Humblot.

Venanzoni, G. (1981): "Private Organisationen ohne Erwerbszweck im europäischen System volkswirtschaftlicher Gesamtrechnung," Untersuchung im Auftrag des Statistischen Amtes der Europäischen Gemeinschaft, Rom.

Watt, D. H. (1988): "The Public Sphere and the Third Sector," Paper delivered at the *Symposium on Religion and the Independent Sector*, Princeton University, June 9 – 10, 1988.

Weber, H. (1983): "Gelöste und ungelöste Probleme des Staatskirchenrechts," *Neue Juristische Wochenschrift* 36, 2541–2554.

Weisbrod, B. A. (1977): *The Voluntary Nonprofit Sector. An Economic Analysis*, Lexington, Mass.: Lexington Books.

Weisbrod, B. A. (1988): *The Nonprofit Economy*, Cambridge, Mass.: Harvard University Press.

Winkler, J. (1988): *Das Ehrenamt. Zur Soziologie ehrenamtlicher Tätigkeit dargestellt am Beispiel der deutschen Sportverbände*, Schorndorf: Karl Hofmann.

Wuthnow, R. J. (1988): *The Restructuring of American Religion: Society and Faith since World War II*, Princeton: Princeton University Press.

1.2
Economic Theories of the Nonprofit Sector: A Comparative Perspective

Estelle James

In recent years, social scientists and policy-makers have paid increasing attention to the possibility of providing quasi-public goods through private rather than public organizations. Quasi-public goods yield both social and private benefits and can be funded from either private or social sources. Common examples are health care, education, cultural activities, and social services. These are major services associated with the modern welfare state. Nonprofit organizations (NPOs) are also the major private providers of these services. Therefore, when we consider the private provision of welfare state services, we are also discussing the role of the nonprofit sector in a society. Some of the questions economists ask are: What factors determine the size of the nonprofit sector? How do nonprofits behave when they bear key responsibility for providing public services? If we shift some of the responsibility for these services from the government to the private nonprofit sector, would this make matters better or worse in terms of variables such as quantity, quality, cost, efficiency, and distributional equity?

Let me start with a brief definitional comment, which has substantive implications as well. In the U.S., the term "nonprofit organization" is commonly used and refers to a set of organizations that qualify for tax exemption and for tax-deductible donations. However, in other countries, the term nonprofit organization is much less common, and tax privileges often don't apply. Similar organizations exist, however, and are called by many other names: non-governmental organizations (NGOs), private voluntary organizations (PVOs), or community associations, for example. The characteristic they all share in common is that they do not have owners who are entitled to receive the profits of the organization in the form of dividends or capital gains. These organizations may earn profits, but may not distribute them. Instead, all earnings must remain with the organization, and used to further the purposes of the organization.

This important characteristic of NPOs has led to the development of several economic theories that help explain which goods will be produced by the nonprofit sector (for a comprehensive survey of these theories see James and Rose-Ackerman 1986; also see Rose-Ackerman 1986). One important set of theories draws the boundary line between private NPOs and private PMOs (see Easley and O'Hara 1983 and 1986; Fama and Jensen 1983a and 1983b; Hansmann 1980 and 1986; Krashinsky 1986; Nelson and Krashinsky 1973; Thompson 1980). They stress that NPOs will be found in situations where consumers don't have enough information to evaluate the quality of a product and therefore must place their trust in the enterprise that is producing it. In such situations, consumers may be more willing to trust nonprofits, because profit-maximizing managers would have an incentive to downgrade quality, but this incentive is weakened in nonprofits by the non-distribution constraint. The basic idea is that if managers cannot benefit financially by receiving profits, they will be less likely to cheat consumers; therefore nonprofits are more trustworthy. For similar reasons, potential donors (of money or of volunteer labor) are more willing to donate to NPOs because nonprofits are more likely to use donations for the intended purpose. Thus, nonprofits develop where trustworthiness is important, because many small customers or donors do not have adequate information about the product. Examples are frequently given from the fields of education and health services where consumers clearly have problems in measuring quality.

While the non-distribution constraint is thus said to make nonprofits more trustworthy, another line of theory suggests it also makes them less efficient. If no one has a "property right" in the residual, no one has an incentive to keep the organization free from sloth and waste. This tendency toward inefficiency is the other side of the coin of the tendency toward trustworthiness, implied by economic theory (see Alchian and Kessel 1962; Alchian and Demsetz 1972; Clarkson and Martin 1980; Leibenstein 1966; Steinberg 1986). Nonprofit managers may also divert excessive revenues to staff and emoluments (see Williamson 1964, for a discussion of expense preference); and may downgrade the quality of one good in order to cross-subsidize another which he or she prefers (James 1978, 1983, 1986a; James and Neuberger 1981).

While these theories based on consumer information and the non-distribution constraint may help explain the American situation, where private fees and donations are a major source of nonprofit revenues, they do not help us with many of the questions we would like to answer about other countries. Three such questions are particularly important for our purposes. (These questions, as well as answers based on international experience, are also discussed in James 1988b.)

First, theories based on the American experience alone ignore the fact that NPOs in many countries are in competition with government, not with for-profit firms. Therefore, we need to draw the line between government and NPOs, to explain why government is used in some cases, nonprofit provision in others. This is the question we must address, in particular, when we are considering the best way to provide public services in the modern welfare state.

Second, we observe that, while government is a substitute for NPO's in production, it is usually a complement in financing. Indeed, from a worldwide point of view, private philanthropy is insignificant while government subsidies are a crucial source of funds to nonprofit organizations, particularly in countries where the nonprofit sector is large. Therefore, we need to explain why governments contribute resources to NPOs which may be competing with them. And we also need to explore some of the problems that this creates.

Third, these theories do not explain why the nonprofit sector varies so widely from one country to another.

Weisbrod's work (1977, 1980) provides a starting point for the answers to some of these questions. Weisbrod views nonprofit organizations, particularly those financed by donations, as providers of goods with "external" benefits, i. e. quasi-public goods, in situations where government does not produce as much service or the precise kind of service that people demand. My own work provides empirical evidence that nonprofit provision has emerged as a market response to excess demand or differentiated demand. Using education as an example, many private schools exist in developing countries because the public school capacity is not large enough to enroll everyone who wants to attend. If the private rate of return is high, people are willing to pay for a privately produced service. In modern societies, private schools exist as a result of differentiated tastes, often stemming from deep-seated cultural (religious, linguistic) heterogeneity. The more heterogeneous the society, the larger we would expect the private sector to be, and empirical work I have done confirms this expectation (see James 1984, 1986b, 1986c, 1987a, 1987b; James and Rose-Ackerman 1986).

My work also shows that the entrepreneurship for nonprofit provision of education, health, and social services, historically, has come from religious (or other ideological) groups. It is important to note that service-providing nonprofits are typically started not by individual entrepreneurs, but by religious or other ideologically motivated organizations; by providing education, health, and other vital social services, they hope to maximize faith or adherents rather than profits. Thus, we would expect to find nonprofits concentrated in areas with strong independent religious groups competing for clients — currently or in the recent past. Again, my empirical research confirms this expectation (see James 1982, 1984, 1986b, 1986c, 1987a, 1988a; also see Rose-Ackerman 1982, 1983a, 1983b).

As mentioned above, the funding for NPO services, especially in modern welfare states, comes primarily from the government. While philanthropy plays an important role in the American nonprofit scene, and private fees are important in developing countries, in most advanced industrial states, government subsidies are the major source of revenue (see James 1987b, 1987c, 1988b). (Even in the U.S., recent evidence indicates that subsidies are large, especially when implicit tax subsidies are taken into account; see Hodgkinson and Weitzman 1984; Salamon 1981, 1987; Smith and Rosenbaum 1981.) Thus, when we describe the division of responsibility between the state and the nonprofit sector for providing welfare state services, we must distinguish between production responsibility and funding responsibility. Funding responsibility is usually retained by the government, even when the private sector carried out production.

The important question then becomes: Why does the government sometimes delegate production of public goods rather than producing itself, and what differences does this make? The work that I as well as other social scientists have been doing suggests some of the answers (see Anheier 1988; Hills 1988; James 1982, 1988b; Kramer 1981; Seibel 1988; Smith 1988). First, if policy-makers prefer (or face pressure) to provide services differentiated by language, religion, etc., delegation of production responsibilities to NPOs is one way to achieve this objective. In some instances, especially in modern societies, the religious organizations that wish to provide these services are politically powerful enough to obtain subsidies. One consequence of providing education, health, and other social services through NPOs in this case is the segmentation of the population along religious (and sometimes linguistic or ethnic) lines. Some people may consider this desirable, others may consider it very undesirable, indeed dangerous to the cohesion of a society (see James 1984, on the Dutch case).

Second, private organizations can more easily charge fees for services, so the government's share of total cost is reduced when production responsibility is delegated to them; more people can be served for the same public expenditures. For example, private schools in many countries, especially in developing countries, charge tuition which covers part of their costs, and governments in modern welfare states may also wish to pass on some of the burden to private sources (although this may, in fact, turn out not to be possible) (see James and Benjamin 1988 on the case of Japan).

Third, private organizations may also generate lower costs than government institutions, especially for labor. This is partly because such organizations do not face civil service wages and other constraints, and partly because, historically, they have benefitted from voluntary donations of time as well as money. Both these factors lead private service suppliers to pay lower wages than public on average, hence to have lower costs (see James and Benjamin 1988; Knapp 1988).

It is not clear, however, whether these lower costs imply lower quality or greater efficiency. This is what we would very much like to know but find it hard to determine because it requires us to measure the value added by the organization. Public and private schools, public and private hospitals often deal with different kinds of customers (students with different back-grounds and prior learning, patients with different diagnoses), so if they obtain differential results, we don't know whether this is due to consumer differences *ex ante* or to the differential value added by the institution. This is a very fertile area for research, and some studies along these lines are included in this volume. Nevertheless, despite our inability to measure value added or quality, subsidies to lower-cost private producers enable the government to increase output with less taxes and are therefore tempting.

It is ironical that the subsidies, in turn, lead the private organizations to become regulated, higher cost, and therefore similar to the public sector in many respects. In many countries I have studied, these regulations pertain to inputs, rather than outputs. For example, they require salaries and working conditions that are equivalent to those in the civil service. They lead to the use of paid credentialed labor rather than volunteer labor. These rules and consequences eliminate the initial cost advantage that nonprofits may have had.

Controls extend, too, over the distribution of service, e. g. the criteria for selecting recipients and the price that can be charged, etc. The rationale is that if government is providing the funds it also wants to influence the distribution of benefits from these services, and therefore satisfy diverse political constituencies.

One of the most interesting regulations concerns the decision-making process in NPOs. For example, in some countries, NPOs must share decision-making authority with workers and consumers. This is one way to retain public accountability and control while delegating production responsibilities. It follows from this discussion that, while "private nonprofit" may remain an unambiguous legal category, the public—private breakdown of funding and management is much more mixed and continuous. In reality, NPOs are a public—private hybrid which makes the analysis of these organizations very complex. And in some cases, the public funding and regulations proceed to a point where nonprofits are virtually indistinguishable from government organizations; in effect, the nonprofits have been "nationalized," not by a hostile "takeover" of assets but by the "gift" of subsidies, which inevitably go together with controls (e. g. the voluntary schools in the U.K., and the religious schools in Holland) (see James 1984 for the Dutch case; for a detailed discussion of government subsidies and the controls that accompany them in a sample of 35 countries, see James 1987c).

Does the delegation of production responsibility to nonprofits increase the variety and choice available to consumers, raise the quantity and quality of services, and decrease their costs, thereby improving the situation, or does it mean more waste, less accountability and equity, thereby making matters worse? If subsidies are given, thereby implying tax revenues are being used to support nonprofits, should the nonprofits correspondingly be subject to social controls over their activities, and if so, what form should these controls take? What are the probable economic consequences of alternative public policies toward nonprofits? These questions are at the forefront of current research on the nonprofit sector.

References

Alchian, Armen A. and Harold Demsetz (1972): "Production, Information Costs, and Economic Organization," *American Economic Review* 62 (December), 777−795.

Alchian, Armen A. and Reuben Kessel (1962): "Competition, Monopoly, and the Pursuit of Pecuniary 'Gains'," in *Aspects of Labor Economics*, National Bureau of Economic Research Report (Ed.), Princeton: NBER, 156−186.

Anheier, Helmut K. (1989): "Private Voluntary Organizations and Development in West Africa: Comparative Perspectives," in *The Nonprofit Sector in International Perspective: Studies in Comparative Culture and Policy*, Estelle James (Ed.), New York: Oxford University Press, 339−357.

Clarkson, Kenneth and Donald Martin (Eds.) (1980): *The Economics of Nonproprietary Organizations*, Greenwich, Conn.: JAI Press.

Easley, David and Maureen O'Hara (1983): "The Economic Role of Nonprofit Firms," *Bell Journal of Economics* 14 (Autumn), 531−538.

Easley, David and Maureen O'Hara (1986): "Optimal Nonprofit Firms," in *The Economics of Nonprofit Institutions: Studies in Structure and Policy*, S. Rose-Ackerman (Ed.) New York: Oxford University Press, 85−94.

Fama, Eugene and Michael Jensen (1983a): "Agency Problems and Residual Claims," *Journal of Law and Economics* 26 (June), 227−250.

Fama, Eugene and Michael Jensen (1983b): "Separation of Ownership and Control," *Journal of Law and Economics* 26 (June), 301−326.

Hansmann, Henry (1980): "The Role of Non-Profit Enterprise," *Yale Law Journal* 89 (April), 835−898. (Reprinted in S. Rose-Ackerman (Ed.), (1986): *The Economics of Nonprofit Institutions: Studies in Structure and Policy*, New York: Oxford University Press, 57−84.)

Hansmann, Henry (1987): "Economic Theories of Nonprofit Organizations," in *Between the Public and the Private: The Nonprofit Sector*, W. Powell (Ed.) New Haven: Yale University Press, 27−42.

Hills, John (1989): "The Voluntary Sector in Housing: The Role of British Housing Associations," in *The Nonprofit Sector in International Perspective: Studies in Comparative Culture and Policy*, Estelle James (Ed.), New York: Oxford University Press, 245−266.

Hodgkinson, Virginia and M. Weitzman (1984): *The Dimensions of the Nonprofit Sector*, Washington, D.C.: Independent Sector.

James, Estelle (1978): "Product Mix and Cost Disaggregation: A Reinterpretation of the Economics of Higher Education," *Journal of Human Resources* 13, 157−186.

James, Estelle (1982): "The Nonprofit Organization in International Perspective: The Case of Sri Lanka," *Journal of Comparative Economics* 6 (June), 99−122.

(Reprinted in E. James (Ed.) (1988): *The Nonprofit Sector in International Perspective: Studies in Comparative Culture and Policy*, New York: Oxford University Press, 289−318.)

James, Estelle (1983): "How Nonprofits Grow: A Model," *Journal of Policy Analysis and Management* 2 (Spring), 350−365. (Reprinted in S. Rose-Ackerman (Ed.) (1986): *The Economics of Non-Profit Institutions: Studies in Structure and Policy*, New York: Oxford University Press, 185−195.)

James, Estelle (1984): "Benefits and Costs of Privatized Public Services: Lessons from the Dutch Educational System," *Comparative Education Review* 28 (December), 605−624. (Expanded version reprinted in Daniel Levy (Ed.) (1986): *Private Education: Studies in Choice and Public Policy*, Oxford University Press.)

James, Estelle (1986a): "Cross Subsidization in Higher Education: Does it Pervert Private Choice and Public Policy?" in *Private Education: Studies in Choice and Public Policy*, Daniel Levy (Ed.), New York: Oxford University Press, 237−258.

James, Estelle (1986b): "The Private Nonprofit Provision of Education: A Theoretical Model and Application to Japan," *Journal of Comparative Economics* 10 (September), 255−276. (Reprinted in E. James (Ed.), (1988): *The Nonprofit Sector in International Perspective: Studies in Comparative Culture and Policy*, New York: Oxford University Press, 61−84.)

James, Estelle (1986c): "Differences in the Role of the Private Educational Sector in Developing and Modern Countries," International Conference on the Economics of Education, Dijon. (Also distributed as World Bank Discussion Paper.)

James, Estelle (1987a): "The Public/Private Division of Responsibility for Education: An International Comparison," *Economics of Education Review* 6, 1−14. (Reprinted in T. James and H. Levin (Eds.) (1987): *Comparing Public and Private Schools: Institutions and Organizations*, vol. I, London: Falmer Press, 95−127.)

James, Estelle (1987b): "The Nonprofit Sector in Comparative Perspective," in *The Nonprofit Sector: A Research Handbook*, W. Powell (Ed.), New Haven: Yale University Press, 397−415.

James, Estelle (1987c): "Public Policies Toward Private Education," World Bank Discussion Paper and *Journal of International Educational Research*, 1990.

James, Estelle (1989a): "The Private Provision of Public Services: A Comparison of Sweden and Holland," in *The Nonprofit Sector in International Perspective: Studies in Comparative Culture and Policy*, E. James (Ed.), New York: Oxford University Press, 31−60.

James, Estelle (Ed.) (1988b): *The Nonprofit Sector in International Perspective: Studies in Comparative Culture and Policy*, New York: Oxford University Press.

James, Estelle and Gail Benjamin (1988): *Public Policy and Private Education in Japan*, London: Oxford University Press.

James, Estelle and Egon Neuberger (1981): "The Academic Department as a Non-Profit Labor Comparative," *Public Choice* 36, 585−612. (Reprinted in M. J. Bowman (Ed.), *Collective Choice in Education*, The Hague: Martinus Nijhoff, 207−235.)

James, Estelle and Susan Rose-Ackerman (1986): *The Nonprofit Enterprise in Market Economies*, a monograph in *Fundamentals of Pure and Applied Economics*, J. Lesourne and H. Sonnenschein (Eds.), London: Harwood Academic Publishers.

Knapp, Martin (1989): "Inter-Sectoral Differences in Cost Effectiveness: Residential Child Care in England and Wales," in *The Nonprofit Sector in International Perspective: Studies in Comparative Culture and Policy*, E. James (Ed.), New York: Oxford University Press, 193–216.

Kramer, Ralph (1981): *Voluntary Agencies in the Welfare State*, Berkeley: University of California Press.

Krashinsky, Michael (1986): "Transactions Cost and a Look at the Nonprofit Organization," in *The Economics of Nonprofit Institutions: Studies in Structure and Policy*, S. Rose-Ackerman (Ed.), New York: Oxford University Press, 114–132.

Leibenstein, Harvey (1966): "Allocative Efficiency vs. 'X-Efficiency'," *American Economic Review* 56 (June), 392–415.

Nelson, Richard and Michael Krashinsky (1973): "Two Major Issues of Policy: Public Subsidy and Organization of Supply," in *Public Policy for Day Care of Young Children*, D. Young and R. Nelson (Eds.), Lexington, Mass.: D. C. Heath, 9–21.

Rose-Ackerman, Susan (1982): "Charitable Giving and 'Excessive' Fundraising," *Quarterly Journal of Economics* 97 (May), 195–212. (Reprinted in Rose-Ackerman (Ed.), (1986): *The Economics of Nonprofit Institutions: Studies in Structure and Policy*, New York: Oxford University Press, 333–346.)

Rose-Ackerman, Susan (1983a): "Unintended Consequences: Regulating the Quality of Subsidized Day Care," *Journal of Policy Analysis and Management* 3 (Fall), 14–20.

Rose-Ackerman, Susan (1983b): "Social Services and the Market," *Columbia Law Review* 83 (October), 1405–1438.

Rose-Ackerman, Susan (1986): *The Economics of Nonprofit Institutions. Studies in Structure and Policy*, New York: Oxford University Press.

Salamon, Lester M. (1981): "Rethinking Public Management: Third-Party Government and the Changing Forms of Public Action," *Public Policy* 29, 255–275.

Salamon, Lester M. (1987): "On Market Failure, Voluntary Failure and Third Party Government: Toward a Theory of Government-Nonprofit Relations in the Modern Welfare State," *Journal of Voluntary Action Research* 16 (Spring), 29–49.

Seibel, Wolfgang (1989): "The Function of Mellow Weakness: Nonprofit Organizations as Problem-Non-Solvers in Germany," in *The Nonprofit Sector in International Perspective: Studies in Comparative Culture and Policy*, E. James (Ed.), New York: Oxford University Press, 177–192.

Smith, Brian (1989): "More Than Altruism: The Politics of European International Charities," in *The Nonprofit Sector in International Perspective: Studies in Comparative Culture and Policy*, E. James (Ed.), New York: Oxford University Press, 319–338.

Smith, Bruce and Nelson Rosenbaum (1981): "The Fiscal Capacity of the Voluntary Sector," paper prepared for the Brookings Institution National Issues Seminar, Washington, D.C., December 9.

Steinberg, Richard (1986): "Nonprofit Organizations and the Market" in *The Nonprofit Sector: A Research Handbook*, Walter Powell (Ed.), New Haven: Yale University Press, 118–138.

Thompson, Earl A. (1980): "Charity and Nonprofit Organizations," in *The Economics of Nonproprietary Organizations*, K. Clarkson and D. Martin (Eds.), Greenwich: JAI Press, 125–139.

Weisbrod, Burton (1977): "Toward a Theory of the Voluntary Nonprofit Sector in a Three-Sector Economy," in *The Voluntary Nonprofit Sector*, B. Weisbrod (Ed.), Lexington, Mass.: D. C. Heath, 51–76. (Reprinted in S. Rose-Ackerman (Ed.) (1986): *The Economics of Nonprofit Institutions: Studies in Structure and Policy*, New York: Oxford University Press, 21–44.)

Weisbrod, Burton (1980): "Private Goods, Collective Goods: The Role of the Nonprofit Sector," in *The Economics of Nonproprietary Organizations*, K. Clarkson and D. Martin (Eds.), Greenwich: JAI Press, 139–179.

Williamson, Oliver (1964): *The Economics of Discretionary Behavior: Managerial Objectives in a Theory of the Firm*, Englewood Cliffs: Prentice-Hall.

1.3
Modern Welfare State Policy Toward the Nonprofit Sector: Some Efficiency—Equity Dilemmas

John G. Simon

The idea that claims of efficiency often conflict with claims of equity is far from novel. Versions of it appear in *Antigone*, in the Book of Matthew (16:26), and in twentieth Century social science literature (Okun 1975). The efficiency—equity clash, however, has not received the attention it deserves in analyses of the role and legal status of the nonprofit sector in the modern welfare state. In these pages, I discuss several of the equity—efficiency dilemmas that such a welfare state must confront when it legislates or otherwise makes policy affecting nonprofit institutions. I also point to some of the research questions that are raised by this discussion.

Before getting into trouble with colleagues from other disciplines, I hasten to say that I have given an expansive meaning to "efficiency" and "equity." Efficiency refers not only to the economists' notions of productive or Pareto efficiency, but also, more generally, to effective ways of achieving various social purposes. Equity refers not only to horizontally or vertically equal treatment, but also to fairness in the way an institution relates to other individuals and groups.

Three overarching questions arise when the modern welfare state considers legal policies affecting the nonprofit sector:

(1) What roles are appropriate for the nonprofit sector to perform?
(2) What methods should the state use to encourage the nonprofit sector to perform such roles?
(3) What regulatory controls should be placed on nonprofit sector relations with the governmental and business sectors and with charitable donors?

These issues overlap a great deal. For example, the question of whether a certain mission is appropriate for nonprofit organizations may be difficult to answer without evaluating the pro's and con's of the methods (such as subsidy) that may induce nonprofits to undertake such a mission. Similarly, issues of subsidy and issues of regulation are not easily separated: In the United States, many of the rules that are imposed on nonprofits as a condition of receiving a tax or other subsidy have an important regulatory impact. In the cause of brevity, however, I will try to deal separately with these three questions.

Space constraints will also preclude discussion of another overlap well known to all nonprofit scholars: the fact that the "sectors" are very far from being watertight compartments and that, in truth, all organizations are, to a greater or lesser extent, hybrids. For the most part, I will also put to one side another overlap: the fact that it is possible to build equity into the concept of efficiency by defining equity as one of the objectives of an organization or a society and then examining the efficiency with which this objective is pursued.

We turn now to the efficiency – equity aspects of the three overarching issues, drawing heavily on the American experience for precedents and examples, but with some suggestions about the implications for other modern welfare states.

1. Appropriate Roles for the Nonprofit Sector

Could Italy encourage the growth of a private nonprofit sector in higher education, or Belgium reduce the degree of its reliance on private universities? Should the United States seek to make the for-profit, not the nonprofit, hospital the dominant form of organization in the hospital industry (Clark 1980), or to transfer adoption services from the nonprofit sector exclusively to the government, or to force all for-profit nursing homes to convert to nonprofit status? Each of these questions has been explored by scholars or practitioners because of dissatisfaction with existing role allocations among the three sectors. In considering these questions, and scores more that could be asked, the first of our efficiency – equity conflicts is presented.

There is evidence suggesting that, controlling for quality, some services may be more cheaply provided by nonprofits than by governmental or for-profit organizations.[1] Sometimes this is the result of the superior ability of nonprofits to attract contributions of volunteer labor of workers accepting

---

[1] Martin Knapp, Julia Montserrat Codorniu, and Robin Darton reported at the 1987 *International Symposium on The Nonprofit Sector and the Modern Welfare State* that "[i]n both Catalunya and England, the nonprofit social care sector appears to provide [old people's home] services at significantly lower cost than the public sector" (unpublished paper distributed at the meeting). Estelle James has made similar findings about the lower cost of private, nonprofit schools and hospitals, as compared to public entities, in several countries (James 1987).

lower wages (James and Rose-Ackerman 1985). Sometimes it results from the ability of nonprofits to enforce internal cross-subsidization of one class of users at the expense of another class of users (e. g. when undergraduate tuition payments subsidize graduate research, or when fees paid for inexpensive hospital services subsidize more costly services [James 1982]). And sometimes the cheaper nonprofit performance may result from the avoidance of bureaucratic constraint that attaches to much governmental activity (James and Rose-Ackerman 1985).

There are, of course, counter-arguments, concerning *in*efficiencies attributable to the nonprofit form, as compared to for-profits and sometimes governmental bodies as well. For present purposes, however, let us assume the validity of the efficiency propositions. The point is that they beget countervailing equity objections. Thus, for example, the voluntary labor attracted to a private school will come from relatively affluent parents who do not need a second income — thus providing the children attending these schools with an advantage not usually available to public school children. A different kind of equity objection is lodged against internal cross-subsidization: that it imposes, without majoritarian legitimacy, a "tax" on one class of persons for the benefit of another class of persons, even though the taxed class may be more affluent that the beneficiary class (Clark 1980; discussed in James 1982). Finally, the bureaucratic constraints imposed on governmental programs may derive from an insistence on policing these programs to ensure that they serve all elements of the population — in the service of equity.

Although these equity arguments tilt against the nonprofit sector, there are also equity arguments that can be raised in *support* of the nonprofit sector, countering arguments of inferior nonprofit efficiency. (Thus, nonprofit nursing homes probably offer more widespread access than proprietary homes, even if efficiency factors favor the latter.) These controversies cannot be resolved here; my point is simply to "flag" some of these efficiency — equity conflicts — and to note research agenda items that flow from them, including the following:

(1) When is it the case that the nonprofits produce in a more efficient manner than government? Thus, if the evidence points that way in the case of elderly homes in Catalunya and England (see footnote 1), does it point that way in the case of family services in New York City? Would it apply to the provision of nonprofit firefighting services in, say, Japan? And would it apply in any of these cases after we have properly controlled for quality (as variously defined), access, and other variables? To make a comparison with the for-profit sector: if, as has been suggested (Clark 1980), federal tax policy were to encourage the use of the for-profit form in the hospital industry, would the resulting growth in proprietary hospitals result in lower hospital costs for the country?

(2) With respect to equity, what is the evidence as to access? If opera companies were state instrumentalities in California, as they are in most of Europe, would the result be free tickets for the poor? If higher education in Western Europe became the responsibility of private nonprofit institutions, would the cost to students be higher than the cost of public education, after taking into account scholarship and loan assistance?

To this point, I have been discussing equity in terms of impacts on consumers or beneficiaries. It can also be considered as a matter of governance. When the French city of Beauvais accepted an indoor swimming pool from a wealthy citizen in 1978, its mayor publicly complained that the residents were "giv[ing] ourselves over to patronage, consigning our fates to the powerful and the rich ..." (Kandell 1978). (This example, it will be noted, involves a private philanthropic contribution to a public sector (municipal) body; the hybrid nature of the arrangement was itself the trigger to governance objections.) And when a New York municipal hospital delegated management functions to a nonprofit hospital, there were complaints that majoritarian political controls were being evaded. Both of these cases, and others that could be cited, raise questions of "Who Governs?" (Dahl 1961) that scholars could usefully study. What are the realities of control in these settings? Would the voice of the people be more faithfully honored were the nonprofit hospital out of the New York picture, or the wealthy donor out of the Beauvais picture?

2. Methods to Encourage Nonprofit Performance

In several different ways, the American legal system provides a hospitable environment that encourages a high level of nonprofit sector activity. Perhaps the most salient method is "subsidization," through the tax system and through direct grants. (My reason for putting subsidization in quotation marks will appear shortly.) These subsidy methods raise the question of efficiency: How can the government most effectively help nonprofit organizations to obtain the funds they need from donations or from income earned on capital? And the subsidies raise issues of equity: How consistent are these measures with norms of equal treatment and distributive justice?

Several different forms of tax subsidy are available to American nonprofit organizations under federal and state legislation. One type of subsidy applies to most nonprofit organizations, both those that Bittker and Rahdert (1976) call "public service" groups (educational, religious, scientific, cultural, and other charitable entities — often called "charitable organizations" or "charities" in the aggregate) and those that are called "mutual benefit" groups, serving the private interests of their members (e. g. labor unions, social clubs, veterans' organizations, trade associations, political parties). The subsidy that applies to *both* categories is the exemption of the nonprofit's income from federal income tax. The subsidies that, for the most part, apply only to the "charities" are deductibility from federal income tax of charitable contributions made by individuals and companies,[2] deductibility from federal estate (death) tax of charitable bequests, and exemption from state and local property taxes of real estate owned by charitable organizations.

The efficiency — equity issues raised by these forms of subsidy include the following:

- Should *all* taxpayers be permitted to deduct their charitable contributions from taxable income? Several tax deductions, in addition to charitable deductions, are available to American taxpayers, including deductions for medical expenses, state and local taxes, and miscellaneous quasi-business payments. If a taxpayer has a large amount of these deductible expenses, in relation to total taxable income, it will be advantageous for him or her to "itemize" them — to list and deduct them separately instead of taking an overall, flat percentage "standard" deduction. Only the "itemizers" can derive a tax benefit from their charitable contributions. (A law that permitted non-itemizers to claim a charitable deduction, on top of the standard deduction, expired in 1986.) As of 1987, itemizers represented approximately 20% of all taxpayers; this group was, on average, significantly wealthier than the 80% who took the standard deduction. These facts lead to the equitable argument that it is not fair to allow only the more affluent contributors to enjoy a tax benefit from their gifts. On the other hand, this arrangement is considered efficient, because the charitable deduction does not appear to have a strong incentive effect for lower-income, non-itemizing taxpayers; it is sometimes called a "wasted" deduction.
- Should owners of property that has increased in value be able to give that property to charity and take an income tax deduction for the full amount? Under the American tax code, taxpayers who are not subject to a special "alternative minimum tax" can claim this deduction for gifts to most charities. Not only do they deduct the full amount of the property from their other taxable income, but the capital gain that is embedded in this property escapes the tax that would have been paid, had the donor first sold the property and then given the proceeds to charity. Many tax reformers call this a double tax benefit — one that violates equitable

[2] Contrary to the assumptions of many Americans, deductions for charitable contributions are available in almost all Western European countries (Sweden is the exception), although in a more limited form than the United States version (Schuster 1986).

principles, particularly because property donors tend to be the wealthier taxpayers. Yet this "double benefit" is probably efficient, for it appears to encourage an increased amount of giving to charity on the part of the affluent — although the research on this point is incomplete. On the other hand (turning back to equity), the institutions that receive most of these property-gifts are private universities and cultural institutions, which are said to benefit affluent citizens proportionately more than do other charities. (This is yet another topic for investigation.)

— A third example involves the deduction system itself. Let us assume that all taxpayers are "itemizers." Even so, the taxpayer who gave $100 to charity in 1987 and who was in a 38.5% tax bracket (the top bracket for 1987) ended up, after taxes, paying only $61.5 for the gift. A less affluent taxpayer who was in the 15% bracket had to pay $85 for the gift. A person too poor to have any income tax liability at all paid $100 for the gift. The equity problem is obvious. But because the upper income taxpayers seem to be more responsive to tax incentives than lower income taxpayers, we have an efficiency claim. Indeed, I have argued that the impact of the increased giving may be beneficial for lower income groups in a way that substantially mitigates the equity problem (Simon 1978).

— Finally, what about the *objects* of the tax subsidy system? Should certain kinds of charity be ineligible for tax benefits? Some years ago, the Connecticut Supreme Court ruled that certain elite private schools did so little to help the poor, offered so few scholarships, that they should no longer be exempt from local property taxes.[3] These court rulings were effectively overruled by the state legislature, but the problem continues to arise in other contexts. The Internal Revenue Service, for example, refuses to confer exemption on nursing homes for the elderly that evict their patients when they become too poor to pay their bills — even though that is, from the institution's point of view, a fairly efficient policy. And occasionally one hears it said that the federal and state tax authorities should refuse to give an exemption to such an institution as the Metropolitan Opera, which for some productions sells no tickets cheaper than $18 — even though that may be efficient pricing.

These subsidy issues generate important research challenges — both empirical and theoretical. First, we do not fully understand the incentive effects of tax subsidies, because we do not really know much about motivations for charitable giving and volunteering. There are excellent econometric studies (Clotfelter 1985), but very few behavioral scientists or sociologists have looked at the dynamics of the giving and volunteering process so as to explain, in behavioral terms, why some charities appeals succeed and some

[3] Pomfret School v. Town of Pomfret, 105 Conn. 456 (1927); Female Academy of the Sacred Heart v. Darien, 108 Conn. 136 (1947).

do not: or to explain the enormous volatility from year to year in charitable giving by the wealthy, even when controlling for every variable one can imagine; or to explain the enormous disparity in generosity among individual donors, even when all income and wealth variables are held constant (Auten and Rudney 1987).

Second, what is a subsidy? Several times I have used the word "subsidy" to refer to the way the tax system helps nonprofit organizations. There is a respectable body of scholarly opinion that contends that none of the exemptions or deductions I have been talking about are really subsidies at all. They simply reflect more accurate ways of defining what is taxable income, of defining what is taxable wealth, or of defining what is taxable property. In other words, under this interpretation, what are called subsidies are, instead, mechanisms that implement the fact that certain kinds of revenue or certain kinds of property were never meant to be part of the "tax base" in the first place. Elsewhere, I have discussed these contentions, and rebuttals to them, in some detail (Simon 1987). Here I do no more than point out that if one accepts those contentions, the nature of the equity—efficiency claims changes dramatically. For example, equity claims take on a different tone if one is no longer able to refer to "subsidizing the rich." Accordingly, a further scholarly effort to resolve the subsidy vs. tax-base-defining debate is very much in order.

It will be observed that we have not discussed the aspect of "subsidies" involving the legal conditions that must be met to take advantage of a subsidy. As noted earlier, these legal conditions have a regulatory impact. To the issues of regulation we now turn.

3. Regulation of Nonprofit Relations with Government and Business Sectors and with Donors

The regulatory system for American nonprofits, as noted above, is conducted partly through the tax system, using special penalty taxes or conditions on tax exempt status; it is also conducted outside the tax system, largely through restrictions accompanying federal grants and regulations imposed by the 50 states on nonprofits operating within their borders. Much of this regulation applies to *intra*-organizational matters, relating to the manner in which trustees and officers of the organization discharge the duties of care and loyalty they owe to the institution. A great deal of regulation, however, involves the external affairs of a nonprofit: the ways in which is relates to the government and business sectors and to the donor population. With respect to all three of these intersections, efficiency—equity issues arise.

The first two of these intersections involve what I have called "border patrol" (Simon 1987) — the set of rules, largely found in the federal tax code, that tend to restrain charitable organizations from wandering outside of their own territory to exercise influence or play an active part in the governmental or business sectors. There are several dimensions of this border patrol (some of which have particular relevance to private foundations), but here we will focus on those issues having the widest application.

3.1 The Business Border

The past decade has been an era of fiscal constraint for American nonprofits, caused by expanded responsibilities (partly the result of a smaller federal social role), reduced government support of nonprofits, and a failure of private giving to match cost increases. In response, nonprofits have increasingly employed "earned income" strategies in order to stay healthy, and even to survive. Efficiency is claimed for this approach: when a nonprofit university rents out its computers, its dining halls, its athletic stadium; when a museum runs a gift shop or book shop on its premises; when a nonprofit television station starts accepting commercial advertising; then these organizations are producing a return from otherwise "underutilized" resources.

Yet equitable objections have been widely and bitterly raised against such commercial practices. The charge is one of "unfair competition" with for-profit competitors, which do not have tax exemption, favorable postal rates, an aura of nonprofit "trustworthiness," and other benefits attributed to nonprofit status.

These competing claims have led to a robust debate — probably the greatest controversy now raging with respect to American nonprofits, a controversy that has spilled over into federal and state courts and legislatures, where opponents of nonprofit business activity have brought about some legal restrictions and seek a variety of additional measures. Protagonists on both sides of this debate can cite some pertinent research regarding both the efficiency and equity claims (see, generally, Center for Entrepreneurial Studies 1988). For example, one scholar (Hansmann 1989) has cast doubt on the assumption that certain forms of nonprofit commercial activity represent efficient behavior, although another economist supports some of the efficiency claims (Steinberg 1988). Evidence appearing to support claims of unfair competition has been challenged on empirical grounds (Dale 1988) or as a matter of micro-economic analysis (Rose-Ackerman 1982). A great deal of work remains to be done, however, before we can speak confidently about either the equity or efficiency claims relating to nonprofit commercial activity.[4]

[4] In addition to the restrictions on business involvement applied to all charities, private foundations are subject to a further prohibition: They are not permitted to own controlling interests in business enterprises. Opponents of this ban, passed by Congress in 1969, argued that, by preventing the donation of business interest to

3.2 The Governmental Border

Much of the work that nonprofits do depends for its fruition upon government action: for example, housing groups lobby for new legislation on the subject and for increased appropriations, pro and anti-abortion groups battle in court for judicial support and seek the election of sympathetic candidates, and civil rights groups press for stronger executive enforcement. Such efforts to obtain governmental action — legislative, judicial, or executive — appear to be efficient ways for an organization to work toward the achievement of its charitable goals.

Yet much of this activity is severely restricted by federal tax law, which limits the amount of lobbying that can be undertaken by tax-exempt charitable organizations, and which absolutely prohibits a charity from assisting the electoral campaign of a candidate for executive or legislative office (even where the sole reason for supporting the candidate is to advance the charity's programs and policies). One of the rationales for these restrictions is an unfairness point somewhat similar to the "unfair competition" complaint discussed under "the business border." It is contended that the nonprofit enjoys an unfair advantage over other participants in the political process, which do not have tax-exempt or tax-deductible funds at their disposal. I have questioned this contention (Simon 1973), noting that often the nonprofit's opponents are also using tax-deductible funds, but further pointing out that this and other aspects of the "government border" issue require empirical investigation — a research task that remains to be done.

These issues of "border patrol" involving the governmental and business sectors arise in other countries as well. Thus, both the British courts and Charity Commissioners have wrestled with the question of whether charities can seek to influence legislative action (Corson and Hodson 1973), and new regulations have been issued regulating commercial activity on the part of Hungary's growing population of private foundations and civic associations (Marschall 1989; see also Marschall's chapter in this book).

Before leaving "border patrol," it is important to note that the issue of whether tax exemption or tax deductibility represents a subsidy has a bearing on the "unfairness" claims that arise when nonprofits are active in the governmental and business sectors. In part, the unfairness argument is based on the notion that the tax system is "subsidizing" one party to a commercial or political contest. If it is plausible to say that no subsidy is involved, for reasons mentioned earlier, then this aspect of "unfairness" recedes. The

foundations, the legislation would reduce total charitable giving — and would, in this sense, be inefficient (Simon 1987). Proponents supported the legislation partly on the equitable ground that foundation-owned businesses had an unfair competitive advantage over other businesses.

"subsidy" issue, therefore, remains a significant area for further scholarly pursuit.

We turn now to another set of relationships — the intersection between a nonprofit organization and its donors.

4. Relations with Donors

Two aspects of a nonprofit's relations with its donors provoke regulatory activity and raise efficiency — equity issues: the organization's response to donor restrictions and the organization's use of the donor's gift for fundraising rather than programmatic purposes.

4.1 Response to Donor Restrictions

Managers of charitable organizations frequently find that donor restrictions on contributed funds preclude what the managers regard as efficient use of these resources. When they seek to escape from these restrictions, they are met with a form of equitable argument: the claim that it would be unfair to the donors, who no longer control these funds (and, indeed, may no longer be alive), to disobey donor instructions.

Courts in the United States and England have developed a mechanism known as the *cy pres* proceeding for resolving this particular version of the efficiency — equity conflict. Where the implementation of the donor's instructions has become illegal, impossible, or impractical and where the donor is deemed to have had a general charitable intention, courts will authorize an alternative use of the funds which is as close as possible to the donor's original specification. In Norman French, used by the early English courts, "as close as possible" is *"cy pres comme possible"* (*si près* in modern French); hence the name *cy pres* given to this proceeding.

A particularly dramatic and controversial *cy pres* case arose recently in California involving the Buck Fund. Beryl Buck died in 1975; her will bequeathed shares of oil company stock to a community foundation, The San Francisco Foundation, organized to serve the five counties of the San Francisco Bay area. Mrs. Buck's will provided that her fund should be used only in Marin County, the smallest and wealthiest of the five counties, indeed the second richest county in America with a population of over 50,000. As of the time of her death, the oil stock that comprised the fund was valued at approximately $ 10 million. Within four years, however, as a result of the turbulent history of the oil industry, the stock was worth approximately $ 250 million. Early in 1984, when the assets of the Buck Fund were worth approximately $ 340 million, the governing committee of the San Francisco Foundation determined that it could not make efficient use of this fund in so small and affluent a county; that there were opportunities for more effective grant-making in other parts of the Bay area; and that, therefore, the foundation could discharge its responsibilities in a more "efficient" manner if it were given permission to spend Buck Fund money in the other four counties served by the foundation. The foundation petitioned a California court for a *cy pres* order to this effect.

The result was an enormous outcry from Marin County, whose officials claimed that it was not illegal, impossible, or impractical to spend the fund in Marin County; that inefficiency was not the same thing as impracticability. Moreover, they argued that a *cy pres* order would be an inequitable breach of faith with the deceased Mrs. Buck. The foundation responded, *inter alia*, that impracticability included inefficiency and that there would be no breach of faith with Mrs. Buck, for had she known the true size of her benefaction, she would have wished to do what every other major philanthropist in modern times has done: to spread the benefaction over a broader realm.

After several months of trial, the case was settled. 20% of the fund was to be spent on national or international projects based in Marin County, but not by the foundation; it consented to be removed as the administrator of the Buck Fund. The settlement meant that there was no final adjudication of the various efficiency and quity claims that reverberated throughout California for several years (see, generally, Simon 1988).

The dilemma presented in peculiarly dramatic form by the Buck case has been a familiar one in England and America for several years; changed circumstances have often caused charitable trustees to resist "dead hand" control in the interests of effective performance. As levels of private giving increase in other modern welfare states, their legal systems will have to cope with this difficult set of questions.

4.2 Fundraising Limitations

The issue of fair dealing with the donor arises not only in connection with explicit restrictions, as in the Buck case, but also in connection with what might be considered *implicit* restrictions. Some charities spend high percentages of total revenues on fundraising (advertising, promotional mailings, etc.). It is quite frequent for these costs to equal 25 to 30% of total expenditures, sometimes 50%, occasionally much higher. Partly on the assumption that "excessive" fundraising outlays violate the wishes of donors — in effect, violating an implicit set of donor restrictions —, many state legislatures have passed laws imposing a "cap" on these expenditures.

Efficiency considerations may point the other way. New charities may require high fundraising expenditures in the early years in order to achieve viability (Rose-Ackerman 1986). With respect to older organizations, if an extra dollar of fundraising expense produces more than a dollar of extra revenue, then, from the organization's perspective, the added dollar is efficiently spent, regardless of the overall percentage of fundraising expense. Indeed, from this perspective, cultural, educational, and welfare organizations appeared in the 1970s to be spending at inefficiently low levels in several regions of the United States (Steinberg 1983).

A supervening set of events appears to have diverted attention from the task of resolving the efficiency – equity claims on fundraising expense. In three successive decisions, the U.S. Supreme Court has held that legislation directly or indirectly imposing a fundraising "cap" is unconstitutional.[5] The Court reasoned that fundraising appeals are one method by which charities communicate with the public on issues of social importance, and that restrictions on these communications violate the free speech clause of the First Amendment. In a sense, the Court has made a point about the efficiency of fundraising activity, not as a producer of revenue but as a vehicle for dissemination of messages.

Further research tasks are suggested by the fundraising question. It would be well to know more about the dollar efficiency of fundraising, more about donor attitudes toward fundraising levels, and more about the accuracy of the Supreme Court's assumption concerning the message content of fundraising.

The values of equity and efficiency, however, are surely of great importance for policy-makers. Accordingly, the research community will do well to undertake the theoretical, analytical, and empirical work without which efficiency and equity will remain abstractions worthy of respect but terribly difficult to apply.

References

Auten, G. and G. Rudney (1987): "The Variability of the Charitable Giving of the Wealthy," Yale University, Program on Nonprofit Organizations Working Paper, No. 126.

Bittker, B. and G. Rahdert (1976): "The Exemption of Nonprofit Organizations from Federal Income Taxation," *Yale Law Journal* 85, 299 – 358.

Center for Entrepreneurial Studies (1988): "Research Conference on the Commercial Activities of Nonprofits," Working Papers, New York: New York University.

---

[5] Village of Schaumburg v. Citizens for a Better Environment, 444 U.S. 620 (1980); Sec'y of State of Md. v. J. H. Munson Co., 467 U.S. 947 (1984); Riley v. Nat'l Fed'n of the Blind of N.C., 108 S. Ct. 2667 (1988).

Clark, R. C. (1980): "Does the Nonprofit Form Fit the Hospital Industry?" *Harvard Law Review* 93, 1416−1489.

Clotfelter, Ch. (1985): *Federal Tax Policy and Charitable Giving*, Chicago: University of Chicago Press.

Corson, J. J. and H. V. Hodson (Eds.) (1973): *Philanthropy in the 70's: An Anglo-American Discussion*, New York: Council on Foundations.

Dahl, R. (1961): *Who Governs? Democracy and Power in an American City*, New Haven: Yale University Press.

Hansmann, H. (1989): "Unfair Competition and the Unrelated Business Income Tax," *Virginia Law Review* 75, 805−835.

James, E. (1982): "Cross-Subsidization by Nonprofit Organizations: Theory, Evidence and Evaluation," Yale University, Program on Nonprofit Organizations Working Paper No. 30.

James, E. (1987): "The Nonprofit Sector in Comparative Perspective," in *The Nonprofit Sector: A Research Handbook*, W. Powell (Ed.), New Haven: Yale University Press, 397−415.

James, E., and Susan Rose-Ackerman (1985): "The Nonprofit Enterprise in Market Economies," Yale University, Program on Non-Profit Organizations Working Paper No. 95.

Kandell, J. (1978): "Private Charity Going out of Style in West Europe's Welfare State," *The New York Times* (June 30) 1, 4.

Marschall, M. (1988): "The Nonprofit Sector in Hungary," Yale University, Program on Nonprofit Organizations, unpublished mimeo.

Okun, A. M. (1975): *Equality and Efficiency: The Big Tradeoff*, Washington, D.C.: The Brookings Institution.

Rose-Ackerman, S. (1982): "Unfair Competition and Corporate Income Taxation," *Stanford Law Review* 34, 1017−1039.

Rose-Ackerman, S. (1986): "Charitable Giving and 'Excessive' Fundraising," in *The Economics of Nonprofit Institutions: Studies in Structure and Policy*, S. Rose-Ackerman (Ed.), New York: Oxford University Press, 333−346.

Schuster, J. M. D. (1986): "Tax Incentives as Cultural Policy in Western Europe," in *Nonprofit Enterprise in the Arts: Studies in Mission and Constraint*, P. J. DiMaggio (Ed.), New York: Oxford University Press, 320−360.

Simon, J. (1973): "Foundations and Controversy: An Affirmative View," in *The Future of Foundations*, F. F. Heimann (Ed.), Englewood Cliffs: Prentice-Hall, 58−100.

Simon, J. (1978): "Charity and Dynasty Under the Federal Tax System," *The Probate Lawyer* 5, 1−92.

Simon, J. (1987): "The Tax Treatment of Nonprofit Organizations: A Review of Federal and States Policies," in *The Nonprofit Sector: A Research Handbook*, W. Powell (Ed.), New Haven: Yale University Press, 67−98.

Simon, J. (1988): "American Philanthropy and the Buck Trust," *University of San Fransisco Law Review* 21, 641−679.

Steinberg, R. (1983): "Economic and Empirical Analysis of Fundraising Behavior by Nonprofit Firms," Yale University, Program on Nonprofit Organizations Working Paper No. 76.

Steinberg, R. (1988): "Fairness and Efficiency in the Competition Between For-Profit and Nonprofit Firms," Yale University, Program on Nonprofit Organizations Working Paper No. 132.

Part II
Organizational Theory and Behavior

2.1
Institutional Choice and Organizational Behavior in the Third Sector

Helmut K. Anheier

The following contributions address two central issues of third sector research: First, how can we explain the existence of nonprofit organizations?
Second, what factors influence their organizational behavior? It is well worth
considering briefly the complexity and bewildering cross-national variety of
institutional choices. Curative and preventive health services are a good
example. Hospitals can be public, for-profit, or nonprofit. In West Germany,
each sector accounts for about one third of the hospitals (see chapter 4.5 by
Anheier), while in the social democracies of Scandinavia, the great majority
of hospitals are public. In Sweden, only about five nonprofit hospitals exist
(Elmer 1987: 199).

Rural fire services and lifeboat services in three countries are used as
another example by Hood (1984). In Britain, lifeboat services are provided
by voluntary organizations, while rural fire services are the responsibility of
the local authorities. In Sweden, lifeboat services are state organizations,
whereas rural fire services are run by voluntary organizations. In West
Germany, both services are in the nonprofit sector.

While administrative or national style might explain some of the cross-
national variations of institutional choice, there remain many cases which
do not fit: How can we explain that there are more private nonprofit hospitals
in the German Democratic Republic (47 according to Goeckel 1988: 217)
than in Sweden? Yet, as Salamon's third party government thesis implies (see
chapter 3.4 in this volume), the financing of nonprofit organizations also
contributes to the puzzle: Whereas services in the few Swedish nonprofit
hospitals are not covered by public medical insurance, nonprofit hospitals
are fully supported by the state in the German Democratic Republic. As this
example suggests, a theory of institutional choice would have to differentiate
between ownership (private versus public), distribution of surpluses (for-
profit versus nonprofit), and the predominant mode of financing.

Thus, in terms of institutional choice, we must identify and separate
various factors which influence the distribution of organizational forms
(public, for-profit, nonprofit). First of all, there are basic institutional processes as described in the various economic theories of nonprofit organizations. Here we have the median voter thesis to explain the public versus

nonprofit choice, and the trustworthiness thesis, based on the mismatching of information between suppliers and clients, to explain the for-profit versus nonprofit choice. Secondly, there are national dispositions and styles of organizing. Here, we differentiate between the influences of regulatory regimes (liberal, conservative, social democratic) and legal traditions (common law, Roman law). Finally, institutional inertia and historical contingencies have an impact on institutional choice. The following contributions demonstrate the progress which has been made in separating the various factors and in identifying crucial variables. They also point to the next step of comparative analysis: to a study of how basic institutional processes, national styles, and institutional inertia interact to produce the organizational fields which are populated by nonprofit organizations.

Badelt (chapter 2.2) offers a *critique* of institutional choice approaches in economics. He distinguishes between the *failure performance approach* and the *transaction cost approach* in explaining the existence of nonprofits. The failure performance approach sees the nonprofit sector as an institutional response to market and state failures. The transaction cost approach, like the trustworthiness thesis mentioned above, suggests that nonprofits emerge as an institutional response to informational asymmetries between supply and demand.

While Badelt identifies several limitations and shortcomings of each approach, he suggests that it may be too ambitious to expect that a theory of nonprofit organizations could become a general theory of institutional choice. Not only may such a theory attempt to achieve too much (for-profit versus nonprofit, for-profit versus public, and public versus nonprofit), but such a general theory may ultimately take the form of a model of hierarchical or sequential choices that runs the danger of remaining both unfounded and intestable. Badelt's essay can be interpreted as a plea to pay more attention to the empirical aspects of institutional choices. He argues for a closer link between the political economy of institutional choices and the formal modeling of such choices. Badelt's suggestion to pay more attention to the political economy of institutional choices is addressed in the contributions by Hansmann (2.3), Pestoff (2.4), Hodd and Schuppert (2.5) and Seibel (2.6).

Hansmann (chapter 2.3) deals with the problem of commercial nonprofit organizations in the United States. He recalls the categorization of nonprofit organizations which he suggested in an earlier article (Hansmann 1980). There he distinguishes nonprofit organizations by two characteristics: source of income (donative or commercial) and organizational control (mutual or entrepreneurial). Together they yield four ideal types of nonprofit organizations: mutual-donative (common cause associations), mutual-commercial (country clubs), entrepreneurial-donative (charities), and entrepreneurial-commercial (hospitals).

While the asymmetric information theory seems widely accepted in the case of donative nonprofit organizations, it is more controversial when applied to commercial-entrepreneurial associations organized as nonprofits (see also chapters by Seibel and Anheier (1.1), James (1.2) and Badelt (2.2) in this volume). Can the diversity of organizational forms in fields like child care, medical care, services for the elderly, or the banking industry be explained by the non-distribution constraint, i. e. the protection of consumers from opportunistic organizational behavior?

In the case of the savings bank industry, Hansmann suggests that the emergence of commercial nonprofits is primarily a response to contract failure. In the early nineteenth century, for-profit banks were too untrustworthy, and nonprofit savings banks offered the only saving opportunity for middle- and low-income clients. Only with the progressive introduction of federal and state regulations, which increased the trustworthiness of for-profit banks, did the institutional mix of for-profit and nonprofit organizations develop in the same industry.

Hansmann's analysis emphasizes the need to explore the institutional history of organizations populating the same industries and organizational fields. By adding a historical dimension to the problem of institutional choice, and by acknowledging the decisive influence of third parties (like state policies and legislation) on the development of particular industries, it becomes possible to disentangle the contract failure factor from the impact of institutional inertia and other factors such as taxation and subsidies.

Pestoff's analysis (chapter 2.4) of consumer organizations in Sweden also demonstrates the importance of studying the interaction of variables like information asymmetries with external factors such as the role of the government. Like the savings associations in Hansmann's case, Pestoff shows how the consumer unions became increasingly embedded in an emergent organizational field. However, unlike savings banks in the United States, the Swedish consumer associations did not become irrelevant, nor did they slowly decline. Pestoff shows how, as a result of the social democratic government's active support, consumer associations became a countervailing power mediating between producers and consumers. From the period of wartime rationing (when the government engaged consumer associations for economic and political reasons) to the 1980s, governmental support has meant that consumer associations have played a more powerful role in policy-making than would be the case otherwise.

The prominence of consumer associations stands in contrast to the negligible role nonprofit organizations play in the provision of health services. This, however, is in accordance with two characteristics of social democratic policy: First, the "decommodification" of health and welfare services, by which goods and services are turned into rights; and second, the use of non-market associations in market systems as a means of mediating and resolving conflicts. Whereas the first characteristic necessarily leads to the public sector virtually monopolizing welfare and social services, the second emphasizes what Pestoff in reference to Hirschman (1970) calls the "general voice-option" of social democracies.

Hood and Schuppert (chapter 2.5) focus on para-government organizations, defined as independent agencies providing public and semi-public goods. They formulate the institutional choice problem at two levels: First, why are different organizational forms used for different tasks and goals? Second, how can we explain the general trend towards the increased use of para-governmental organizations in different countries? Hood and Schuppert argue that an acceptable institutional choice theory should be able to answer both questions.

They present and discuss three approaches. First, they consider the national style approach, a version of historical institutional analysis which tries to explain choices by reference to the unique historical circumstances of societies and cultures. Hood and Schuppert criticize the national style approach: They point out that while it may explain cross-national differences, it is much less useful in explaining similarities in the ways in which different countries use para-government organizations.

In a second step, they discuss the administrative dilemmas approach, which assumes that contradictory organizational principles are at the root of institutional choice processes. For instance: a government, finding it cannot provide all the services needed by its citizens, faces such a dilemma. It can lighten the burden by off-loading some tasks onto non-governmental organizations — but only by losing some of its direct influence. Again, Hood and Schuppert identify several shortcomings. Most significantly, they argue that, since all governments face such decisions, the administrative dilemmas approach — taken to its logical conclusion — would give a picture of a far more even distribution of para-government organizations from one country to another than is in fact the case. In other words, this approach may explain cross-national similarities, but it is less useful in explaining differences.

The third approach, advocated by Hood and Schuppert, is a more general formulation of the transaction cost approach discussed by Badelt and Hansmann. In reference to Rose (1976), they offer a task-contingency theory, maintaining that the salience of the policy area, service, or product affects institutional choice.

Seibel (chapter 2.6) presents a functional analysis which tries to link aspects of the behavior of nonprofit organizations to their macro-political contribution. The analysis moves away from the economic and sociological reasoning of organizational studies and discusses the political rationale of third sector organizations in functional terms. He argues that nonprofits provide the public sector (and, *inter alia*, the for-profit sector) with unique opportunities to discharge *insoluble* social problems which may prove politically risky, such as poverty alleviation or the reintegration of the handicapped. Thus, the nonprofit sector frees both society and the state from unwanted responsibilities.

The primary function of the nonprofit sector is political risk-reduction for the state and the for-profit sector, and not the efficient and responsive provision of services. Assuming this, efficiency and responsiveness — the conventional parameters of organizational survival — become virtually irrelevant for nonprofit organizations. Thus, Seibel argues that nonprofit organizations survive not because they meet organizational objectives — they survive because of their inefficiency and lack of responsiveness. Thus, the third sector presents an arrangement of de-modernized niches in the context of a modern, means-rational organizational culture.

The last two contributions in this section deal with aspects of organizational behavior. Saxon-Harrold (chapter 2.7) reports on a study of 75 voluntary organizations in the United Kingdom. She refutes the assumption that nonprofit organizations necessarily pursue passive strategies focussing on cooperation rather than on competition. She demonstrates that strategies selected by nonprofit organizations depend on their organizational environment. The environment can be described as a "tangled web" of funding flows. A nonprofit organization assumes its strategy according to the structure of the "web" and its position in that structure. Overall, Saxon-Harrold finds that variations in this organizational environment are more likely to influence nonprofit organizations than are external factors such as critical resource dependencies.

Leat (chapter 2.8) presents an essay on accountability, a requirement which has partially resulted from the resource dependency of many nonprofit organizations in the United Kingdom. She distinguishes various types of accountability and argues that the term implies far more than financial reporting to funding agencies. The "problem of accountability" is based on the multiple, often conflicting, constituencies of nonprofit organizations. Thus, as Middleton (1987) and Young (1987) have pointed out, in terms of organizational behavior, nonprofit organizations are confronted with sometimes radically different expectations, methods of evaluation, and accountability standards.

References

Elmer, A. (1987): "Wohlfahrtspflege in Schweden," in *Verbandliche Wohlfahrtspflege im internationalen Vergleich*, R. Bauer and A. M. Thränhardt (Eds.), Opladen: Westdeutscher Verlag, 195–203.

Goeckel, R. F. (1988): "Church and Society in the GDR," *International Journal of Sociology* 18 (4), 210–228.

Hansmann, H. (1980): "The Role of Nonprofit Enterprises," *Yale Law Journal* 89, 835—901.

Hirschman, A. O. (1970): *Exit, Voice and Loyalty*, Cambridge, Mass.: Harvard University Press.

Hood, C. (1984): "The Hidden Public Sector: The World of Para-Government Organizations," University of Strathclyde, Centre for the Study of Public Policy, Working Paper 133.

Middleton M. (1987): "Nonprofit Boards of Directors: Beyond the Governance Function," in *The Nonprofit Sector: A Research Handbook*, W. Powell (Ed.), New Haven: Yale University Press, 141—153.

Rose, R. (1976): "On the Priorities of Government: A Developmental Analysis of Public Policies," *European Journal of Political Research* 4, 247—289.

Young, D. (1987): "Executive Leadership in Nonprofit Organizations," in *The Nonprofit Sector: A Research Handbook*, W. Powell (Ed.), New Haven: Yale University Press, 167—179.

2.2
Institutional Choice and the Nonprofit Sector

Christoph Badelt

Economics is usually defined as a discipline which seeks to explain human choices under scarcity. While every elementary textbook applies this definition to the choice of resources by producers and to the choice of commodities by utility-maximizing consumers, other choices have not received comparable examination. A case in point is the "institutional choice" decision: Why are certain goods and services provided by suppliers who operate with particular ownership structures rather than other suppliers who use alternative structures?

Whenever institutional choices are investigated, nonprofit organizations (NPOs) present one of several possible solutions.[1] The goal of this paper is to review "institutional choice" approaches and their potential to explain the nonprofit sector.

1. Issues of "Institutional Choice"

Economics usually focuses on a limited subset of institutions in an economy. The "market failure" versus "governmental failure" literature has dominated the discussion of institutional alternatives — if these matters are investigated at all. Yet, this literature ignores the existence of other institutions outside the "public" — "private" dichotomy, for example, the private nonprofit organizations. Moreover, the literature implies an implicit judgement in that market failure is automatically cured by government institutions, and vice versa.

In contrast, the conceptual basis of a theory of institutional choice is much broader. Institutions are generally defined by objective functions and constraints, all of which are expressed in particular ownership structures. The theory, then, comprises at least three elements: (1) a description of the range of possible institutions which may exist to meet a certain goal in society, (2) an explanation of how institutions are formed, and (3) a comparative analysis of the performance of different institutions.

---

[1] Thus, the fact that the nonprofit sector is still not a very popular research topic in economics appears as a logical consequence of the meager attention economists pay to institutional choice questions in general.

Range of Choice: A theoretical understanding of institutions is based on a typology of institutions. A good starting point is to differentiate at least three elementary types: (a) Private Market Organizations (PMOs), which operate on a profit-oriented basis, (b) Government Organizations (GOs), which can be established on various administrative levels, and (c) Nonprofit Organizations (NPOs), which are privately owned and characterized by the non-distribution constraint. Moreover, particular attention should be given to *hybrid forms* of institutions and to those outside the traditional government and business sectors — for example, private nonprofit and joint government — private ventures.

Formation of Institutions: A theory of institutional choice has to explain why specific institutional patterns exist and why they change over time. At an abstract level, a theory would explain the formation of new forms of institutions, competition between institutions, and their equilibrium over time. A complementary approach might examine concrete institutional patterns in their historical, economic, regional, and legal context.

Comparative Analysis: A fundamental element of a theory of institutional choice is the specification of an institution's objective function. Since the relative weights of social goals such as efficiency, equity, social security, or full employment vary, a general theory will have to analyze the broad list of criteria which may be used to evaluate and compare the behavior of alternative institutions.

While numerous studies examine and compare specific aspects of institutional behavior, most of them concentrate on the differences between public and private enterprise sectors. "X-efficiency" considerations on both theoretical and empirical levels are central to the debate about whether private or governmental institutions are superior. Other institutional forms, in particular those involving the private nonprofit sector, are not analyzed as thoroughly as the traditional private market and government forms, although the recent literature — particulary from the United States — raises interesting hypotheses (for a recent overview, see James and Rose-Ackerman 1986).

This brief agenda for research suggests that a theory of the nonprofit sector be conceptualized as a special problem in the wider context of "institutional choice." In practice, however, examination of the nonprofit sector has often advanced our knowledge of institutional choices in general.

2. The Nonprofit Sector as a Result of "Institutional Choice" Considerations

"Institutional choice" is not a clear-cut paradigm but a rather eclectic set of approaches with different backgrounds and partially overlapping arguments. Without simplifying too much, two particular groups of economic theoreticians can be identified who contribute to an explanation of the nonprofit sector in an institutional choice setting:

The first group is usually referred to as "economics of NPOs" (for recent overviews, see James and Rose-Ackerman 1986; Rose-Ackerman 1986; Weisbrod 1988). Here, the existence of NPOs is explained by the failure of other institutional arrangements; in particular, the failure of markets and/or governments. We will call this line of reasoning the *"failure performance approach."*

The second group is often associated with the term "new institutional economics" (for example, Krashinsky 1986; Schenk 1988; Williamson 1985). Here, the starting point is more general: Institutions are explained by the costs of alternative contractual arrangements (transaction costs). Moreover, this approach has also broader concerns; for example, it explains which kind of transactions should be organized within organizations and which ones could be handled on markets. As will be shown later, institutional economics provides a tool to explain the nonprofit sector as a special institutional type. This will be called the *"transaction costs approach."*

Conceptually, the two approaches follow paths which are quite different. While the *failure performance approach* is implicitly based on a hierarchy of institutions (NPOs as a result of a failure of other institutions), the *transaction costs approach* is grounded in contract theory: Alternative institutional arrangements are compared in quasi-preconstitutional situations, irrespective of actually existing institutional settings.

In practice, however, the results of the two approaches overlap to a substantial degree, particularly because of the role informational problems play in most theories of the nonprofit sector. As we will show later, informational asymmetry and the resulting costs of information are crucial to an understanding of NPOs in both approaches.

2.1 The "Failure Performance Approach"

The "failure performance approach" assigns a particular role to each type of institution. Quite often a distinction is made only between private market organizations (PMOs), government organizations (GOs), and private nonprofit organizations (NPOs). Roles of institutions are conceptualized in a sequential order, with PMOs and market failure at the beginning, and NPOs at the end.

2.1.1 Main Arguments

Market failure in an allocative or distributive sense leads to the emergence of GOs as financing sources or providers of goods and services. In this approach, GOs are the typical providers of collective goods; − in toto, a traditional way of rationalizing market failure.

Weisbrod's (1977) theory of the voluntary nonprofit sector develops the first argument for NPOs as alternatives to government provision of collective goods. NPO provision occurs when some people are dissatisfied with the services provided by government. This "undersupply" may have a quantitative or qualitative character;[2] it may be caused either by informational problems between political decision makers and consumers and/or by the objective function[3] of political decision makers. In any case, it will produce a "niche" into which NPOs can settle and act as alternative (or additional) supplier.

While Weisbrod makes an important contribution, this theory cannot explain the whole variety of institutions which exist. In particular, it does not clarify why the "niches" are not populated by PMOs. Moreover, Weisbrod's theory does not explain the provision of private goods by NPOs, although the argument appears to have explanatory power in such cases. Both shortcomings can be solved by analyzing the relationship between PMOs and NPOs.

A number of authors (for example, Hansmann 1980, 1987; Weisbrod 1988) analyze the line between NPOs and PMOs by stressing the problems of informational asymmetry ("contract failure").[4] Whenever the quantity or quality of a service cannot be equally observed or measured by producers and consumers, market failure may occur. NPOs, which by definition must not distribute profits, are seen as a more "trustworthy" alternative by consumers. Therefore, they prefer services provided by NPOs rather than PMOs. Again, the implication is not the only one conceivable, since one could imagine that GOs might also be seen as trustworthy. However, looking at the "undersupply" side of the "triangle" of institutions partially helps to explain the existence of NPOs (Figure 1).

Informational asymmetry also explains why the undersupply by GOs does not necessarily lead to a niche populated by PMOs. If collective goods are provided outside the government sector, the financing of the production needs donations (of time and/or money). Because of their trustworthiness, NPOs have a comparative advantage over PMOs in raising donations.

The logical structure of the literature on NPOs can be summarized in a "triangle" of institutions (Figure 1) (Badelt and Weiss 1988).

---

[2] The qualitative aspect has been investigated in another context as well: Club theoretical research has always stressed the "sorting out of people with like preferences" into specific groups to provide collective goods (starting with Buchanan 1965). However, the institutional form such a club may take was not fully analyzed.

[3] As has been shown in public choice theory, political decisions are often oriented toward the preferences of the median voter, which leaves subgroups of the population "undersupplied."

[4] Also the "principal agent" approach would fall under this category (Fama and Jensen 1983).

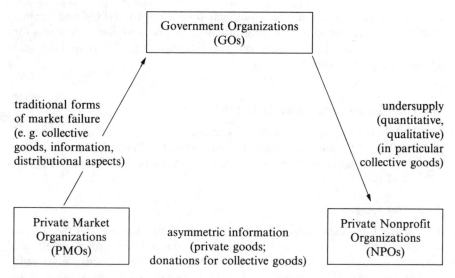

Figure 1: Institutional Triangle

2.1.2 Problems

In the context of general institutional choice analysis, the "failure perform-ance approach" raises several problems. First, the line of arguments is biased toward explaining NPOs. This criticism might sound curious, given that explaining NPOs is an explicit goal. Yet, the bias may lead us to ignore important aspects. For example, while this approach discusses failures of GOs and PMOs, "failures" of NPOs are hardly studied (but see Salamon 1987: 38 – 43) in a way that other organizational forms would be rationalized. Although several behavioral models of NPO activities have been developed (see James and Rose-Ackerman 1986: 31 – 77), "institutional consequences" (i. e. consequences which try to explain the existence of GOs or PMOs out of NPO-failure) are rarely drawn. This, however, can only be achieved by a theory which seeks to explain institutional choices in a general sense.

Second, the implicit normative bias which explains GOs and NPOs by the failure of PMOs (which means that PMOs are not challenged if no market failure is involved) may lead to a misperception of institutional arrangements which dominate in European welfare states. To a large degree, goods and services are designated as *merit goods* in which political decisions are taken to finance them, quite often even to provide them through the government sector. Examples of merit goods are educational institutions and services to elderly or handicapped. Political value judgements may even include a posi-tive or negative preference towards non-governmental institutions in cases where goods or services are provided outside the public sector: In practice, this means that there may be a political preference for NPOs and against PMOs which may lead to licensing practices or protectionistic measures for NPOs.[5] Consequently, a theory of "institutional choice" has to take into account political decision making.

2.2 The "Transaction Costs Approach"

The "New Institutional Economics" explain institutions mainly by costs of alternative contractual arrangements. Although the "New Institutionalists" are not a homogeneous group, they can be represented by Williamson (1975, 1985) and his predecessors.

2.2.1 Main Arguments

The transaction costs approach conceptualizes the formation and the change of institutions in a contract-theoretical way: the members of a society are assumed to make deliberate choices concerning the institutions they would like to establish. This general pattern has been applied to a number of different institutions such as groups (Buchanan and Tullock 1974), hierarchical firms (Alchian and Demsetz 1972), and the state itself (Buchanan 1975).

The work of Williamson and others has transformed these ideas into a theory of the (hierarchical) firm. Transaction costs are defined as costs which occur in preparing and monitoring economic transactions, in particular information costs, decision-making costs, and costs of control. Assuming that alternative institutions could provide commodities with comparable production costs, differences in transaction costs determine the institutional choices.

Furthermore, Williamson posits that transaction costs are determined by the characteristics of both the decision-makers and the market (1975: 86; 1985: 43). Individuals are characterized by bounded rationality and opportunistic behavior. The most relevant "environmental conditions" of institutional choice decisions are (a) the complexity of decisions and transactions; (b) uncertainty of decision-makers concerning important aspects of a transaction; (c) the number of transactions of individuals; and (d) the size of investments for transactions (sunk costs).

The "environmental conditions" are the source of a specific form of market failure. If one of these conditions applies, markets may involve higher transaction costs than alternative contractual arrangements, particularly if

---

[5] To give an example, in several Austrian provinces, social services like "Meals on Wheels," visiting services, transport services to handicapped are contracted out by the government to NPOs. The respective governments do not want private persons "to make profits with these services" and therefore prevent PMOs from entering the markets.

transactions are performed in a hierarchical organization. Williamson concludes that in these cases the vertical integration of transactions — organized by a traditional enterprise — would be the most economical way to arrange production. However, the argument does not consider whether enterprises will necessarily have to be profit-oriented. It is here that the role of the nonprofit sector enters the discussion. To illustrate this point, it should be mentioned that various forms of nonprofit firms have been developed for reasons which are very similar to those Williamson points out. Cases in point are various forms of cooperatives and also a number of modern self-help voluntary organizations.

The transaction costs approach in the Williamson tradition emphasizes the degree of uncertainty contained in transactions (1985: 56), which is seen as the dominant cause for the development of non-market institutions. It is not difficult to see the affinity of this approach to that of informational asymmetry in Arrow (1963) and Hansmann (1980). While Williamson locates informational problems in *transactions*, the latter associate informational problems — in particular, asymmetric information — with the characteristics of *commodities*. Therefore, it is not surprising to see that Williamson's analysis of "organizational failure" comes to conclusions analogous to Hansmann's "contract failure": as markets and PMOs fail, other institutions, especially NPOs, have comparative advantages in transaction costs.

The application of transaction costs considerations to NPOs has been elaborated beyond the basic notion of Hansmann's "contract failure." One fruitful development was to differentiate between the informational problems which exist between producers and consumers, and those which occur between consumers (Krashinsky 1986).

However, the "contract failure" argument primarily concerns transaction costs between producers and consumers (and possible donors of time and/or money). While we should note the difficulties PMOs (and markets) have in handling the supply of commodities the output of which is difficult to monitor, it is not at all obvious why NPOs should be the only alternative. In addition, monitoring the nonprofit status of a firm is costly as well, so that choosing an NPO might only shift transaction costs into the public sector instead of actually saving them (for example, Krashinsky 1986: 117 and 122). Thus, the problem of the *incidence* of transaction costs needs more attention.

Transaction costs between consumers become a relevant problem in the case of joint consumption of collective goods. In this case, as is often pointed out, NPOs constitute a good example of a "club" (Buchanan 1965) which may be established to economize on transaction costs following from potential "free-riding" behavior (see, for example, Krashinsky 1986: 119). This, however, is a wrong perception of club theory, since the basic principle of clubs can be put into practice in various institutional forms (see, for example, Sandler and Tschirhart 1980: 1497). In other words, this aspect of public choice theory cannot serve as a sufficient theoretical explanation for the formation of nonprofit organizations (NPOs).

In summary, informational problems may explain NPOs, but, strictly speaking, information is only an explanation of non-market institutions in cases where output is difficult to monitor, or where similar problems of uncertainty occur. This conclusion follows both from Hansmann's "contract failure" and from Williamson's "organizational failure" model.

There are, however, other informational problems which are ignored in these lines of reasoning (Badelt 1985: 112–138). When these other problems occur, the nonprofit sector, then, exhibits many disadvantages: for example, producers have to incur search costs in order to find potential customers and discover their preferences; other search costs would have to be incurred by "club" members seeking others with the same preferences. These search costs put a heavy burden on a non-market institution which tries to offer services. By contrast, PMOs selling services get quick information via the price mechanism — a channel of information rarely available to NPOs. Experience indicates that these kinds of problems may lead to various distortions which may challenge the role of the nonprofit sector. Thus, other non-price forms of communicating information have to be established by NPOs, a strategy which by itself leads to higher costs.

Finally, while many problems of transaction costs may be traced back to informational problems, this is not true for *all* transaction costs. A good example are decision-making costs. It is hard to generalize on whether decision costs are higher in NPOs than in other institutions. Yet it is fair to assume that decision costs strongly depend on the internal organization of an institution which often varies with the ownership structure. Many forms of NPOs (for example, cooperatives, voluntary organizations, etc.) have an ownership structure in which more collective decisions have to be made than in PMOs or government organizations. Since collective decisions involve higher costs than hierarchical ones, it is unlikely that NPOs have comparative cost advantages in this respect.

2.2.2 Problems

A brief summary of the transaction costs arguments indicates that NPOs may have comparative advantages in some respects. But some asserted advantages of NPOs are neither exclusive to NPOs nor do they refer to all forms of transaction costs. Consequently, predictions on the basis of the theories in the Williamson tradition are to a certain degree ambiguous. Econometric tests are hard to find, because transaction costs are difficult to measure in a comparative institutional setting.

Empirical work on transaction costs usually relies on case studies, biographies of institutional changes, and similar material (see Williamson 1985 for an overview). These methodologies are more likely to be used as a tool of *ex-post facto* rationalization of existing institutional structures than traditional econometric tests which compare the *behavior* of alternative institutions. Moreover, the borderline between *ex-post* rationalization and hidden value judgements is not always clear.

The difficulty in measuring transaction costs is closely related to conceptual problems inherent in transaction costs analysis. Differences in production costs are either excluded from the domain of institutional choice analysis, or it is simply assumed that the *sum* of production costs and transaction costs is decisive for the institutional choice (Williamson 1975: 248, 1985: 92–95). In both cases, the theory implies that transaction costs and not production costs are the key to institutional choices.

For empirical analysis and political discourse, the viewpoint is quite different: Production costs are in the center of interest, because the politically relevant question concerns the X-efficiency (production efficiency) of alternative institutions. To give an example: In many countries, the cost differences between public and private hospitals are heavily debated. Obviously, the political interest focuses on the production costs (X-efficiency) of alternative institutional providers, while transaction costs analysis is of purely academic interest. Therefore, empirical tests also concentrate on the broader cost issue. To put it in a nutshell: Institutional choice theory of the transaction costs kind emphasizes aspects which are not appreciated very much on the applied level, and vice versa.

3. Problems Common to Both Approaches

Both the "failure performance" and the "transaction costs" approaches assume that institutions emerge as a result of choice processes. While, in their analysis, they offer details of this choice process, they have one problem in common (see Badelt and Weiss 1988): The question of who actually makes the choice is hardly touched. In a purely imaginative preconstitutional world, it suffices to assume that "individuals" decide on their contractual arrangements. Yet, in reality, there are suppliers of goods and services, and customers with different interest; and it is too simplistic to assert that these groups negotiate on the institutional form in which commodities are provided and transferred between economic agents. The validity of this assertion depends on the market conditions in which transactions take place.

Institutional choice theories, therefore, have to investigate thoroughly the demand and supply aspects of institutional choices. This requires the formulation of demand and supply functions by specifying those variables which determine the supply and demand of institutions. These functions have to be integrated into a structural model; i.e. in a next step, the coordination of supply and demand plans have to be modelled. At this stage, assumptions concerning market conditions become relevant.

Most existing theories of institutional choices seem to treat the process of choice as a typical free-market process. Consequently, they interpret the results of these choices as equilibrium solutions. Since these assumptions are only implicit, the theories do not make clear, whether it is the consumer who can make a choice, whether the producer has options as well, or whether both choices have indirectly entered the equilibrium. Therefore, the theories do not explicitly comment on the supply and/or demand aspects of institutional choices.

As long as the assumption of perfect competition is valid, the missing specification of the demand and the supply side does not make empirical testing impossible, since reduced form models can be estimated. However, institutional choices involving NPOs are often made in industries where imperfect competition prevails. In these cases, the "short cut" of existing theories causes severe problems. It is not possible to derive predictions as to which market side will be rationed, or — more simply — on whether the suppliers of goods or services can impose their preferences concerning institutions on the consumers, or vice versa.

In practice, this is one of the politically most relevant questions in the context of institutional choice. Do patients actually have the power to determine the institutional type in which hospital services take place? Is it the politician or the voter who decides whether transportation services are provided by PMOs or GOs? Questions of this kind serve to illustrate the practical relevance of modelling supply and demand sides of institutional choices in markets where perfect competition does not exist.

These examples and the theories of institutional choice indicate that government organizations are often directly or indirectly involved in institutional choice decisions. The popular undersupply model of Weisbrod can serve as a case in point. Whenever institutions are created for primarily political reasons, the question of who takes institutional choice decisions leads to explanations of political decisions and to a broader theory of institutional choice which has been extended toward a "political economy."

"Political economy" in this sense means that even *economic* models of institutional choice cannot ignore political decision variables. For example, it is naive to assume that, in a European welfare state, decisions on the institutional type for social services provision only consider (transaction) cost issues. Political preferences (like a positive or negative attitude toward government intervention) also play an important role. Further theoretical developments of institutional choice, therefore, must incorporate structural models containing supply and demand functions. Modelling the political sphere of institutional choices in a way which reflects the specific political and institutional landscape of European welfare states thus becomes an important challenge for further research.

References

Alchian, Armen A. and Harold Demsetz (1972): "Production, Information Costs, and Economic Organisation," *American Economic Review* 62, 5, 777 – 795.

Arrow, Kenneth (1963): "Uncertainty and the Welfare Economics of Medical Care," *American Economic Review* 53, 941 – 973.

Badelt, Christoph (1985): *Politische Ökonomie der Freiwilligenarbeit, Theoretische Grundlegung und Anwendungen in der Sozialpolitik*, Frankfurt, New York: Campus.

Badelt, Christoph and Peter Weiss (1988): "Institutional Choice in the Social Services – Preliminary Empirical Evidence for Austria," paper presented at the European Public Choice Society Meeting, Bergen (Norway) (mimeo).

Buchanan, James (1965): "An Economic Theory of Clubs," *Economica* 72, 1 – 14.

Buchanan, James (1975): *The Limits of Liberty, Between Anarchy and Leviathan*, Chicago, London: University of Chicago Press.

Buchanan, James and Gordon Tullock (1974): *The Calculus of Consent*, (5th edition) Ann Arbor: University of Michigan Press.

Fama, Eugen and Michael Jensen (1983): "Agency Problems and Residual Claims," *Journal of Law and Economics* 26 (June), 250 – 327.

Hansmann, Henry (1980): "The Role of Nonprofit Enterprise," *Yale Law Journal* 89 (April), 835 – 898.

Hansmann, Henry (1987): "Economic Theory of Nonprofit Organisations," in *The Nonprofit Sector, A Research Handbook*, Walter Powell (Ed.), New Haven: Yale University Press, 27 – 42.

James, Estelle and Susan Rose-Ackerman (1986): *The Nonprofit Enterprise in Market Economics*, London, Chur: Harwood Academic Publishers.

Krashinsky, Michael (1986): "Transaction Costs and a Theory of the Nonprofit Organisation," in *The Economics of Nonprofit Institutions*, S. Rose-Ackerman (Ed.), New York, Oxford: Oxford University Press, 114 – 132.

Rose-Ackerman, Susan (Ed.) (1986): *The Economics of Nonprofit Institutions*, New York, Oxford: Oxford University Press.

Salamon, Lester M. (1987): "Of Market Failure, Voluntary Failure, and Third Party Government: Toward a Theory of Government – Nonprofit Relations in the Modern Welfare States," *Journal of Voluntary Action Research* 16, 1 – 2, 29 – 49.

Sandler, Todd and John T. Tschirhart (1980): "The Economic Theory of Clubs: An Evaluative Survey," *Journal of Economic Literature* 18 (December), 1481 – 1521.

Schenk, Karl E. (1988): *New Institutional Dimensions of Economics*, Berlin: Springer.

Weisbrod, Burton A. (1977): *The Voluntary Nonprofit Sector, An Economic Analysis*, Lexington, Mass.: D. C. Heath.

Weisbrod, Burton A. (1988): *The Nonprofit Economy*, Cambridge: Harvard University Press.

Williamson, Oliver (1975): *Markets and Hierarchies: Analysis and Antitrust Implications*, New York: Free Press.

Williamson, Oliver (1985): *The Economic Institutions of Capitalism*, New York: Free Press.

2.3
The Economic Role of Commercial Nonprofits: The Evolution of the U.S. Savings Bank Industry*

Henry Hansmann

1. Introduction

In previous work, I and others have argued that nonprofit firms in general tend to arise as a response to problems of asymmetric information facing consumers — or, as I termed it in my earlier work, "contract failure" (Hansmann 1980). The notion, simply put, is that individuals prefer to deal with nonprofit firms rather than for-profit firms when they have difficulty policing the quality or quantity of the goods or services that the firm offers or provides. Under such circumstances, nonprofit firms — which operate under a "non-distribution constraint" that prohibits the distribution of the firm's net earnings to anyone who exercises control over it (such as its directors, officers, or members) — hold the promise of behaving less opportunistically than would for-profit firms toward the individuals who patronize them, since those who control the firms cannot profit directly from opportunism and thus have less incentive to engage in it.

This theory is persuasive, and indeed seems to be widely accepted, for donative nonprofits — that is, nonprofits that rely upon gifts or grants for a significant portion of their income. Here the "customers" who have a contract failure problem are the organization's donors, and the nonprofit form is undoubtedly employed in large part to provide them with a degree of fiduciary protection. The theory is more controversial, however, in the case of those nonprofits that I have elsewhere termed "commercial" nonprofits (Hansmann 1980). These are nonprofit organizations that receive little or no income from donations, but rather derive all or nearly all of their income from prices they charge for the goods and services they produce and sell. Such commercial nonprofits are becoming increasingly common in the United States today. For example, they account for most of the nation's hospital care, and also have large shares of other important service industries such as nursing care for the elderly, day care for children, and primary medical

* I wish to thank Eric Rasmusen for helpful comments on an earlier draft.

care.[1] It is not obvious that, in industries such as these, consumers are at such an informational disadvantage that the crude protection from opportunism afforded by the non-distribution constraint could be very important. As a result, many analysts, myself included, have wondered whether we should look elsewhere for an explanation of the development of commercial nonprofits (Hansmann 1987a).

One alternative theory is that commercial nonprofits are just historical anachronisms. This seems like a persuasive theory where hospitals are concerned, for example. Nonprofit firms first came to dominate the hospital industry in the United States when it was entirely charitable and all the nonprofit firms in it were donatively supported. Health technology and financing techniques have since changed, however, in ways that have now rendered donative funding of hospitals largely unnecessary. Yet the nonprofit firm has survived in this industry, perhaps just through institutional inertia; hospitals that were formerly donatively supported institutions have simply evolved into commercial nonprofits.

Another theory is that commercial nonprofits are often just a response to tax exemption and other implicit and explicit subsidies that give them artifical cost advantages over their for-profit competitors: take away the subsidies, and eventually the commercial nonprofits would largely disappear.

There have been some efforts by economists in recent years to test these different theories empirically. For example, in an effort to provide a direct test of the asymmetric information theory, Burton Weisbrod and his students have sought to determine whether there are discernible differences in the quality of services provided by nonprofit and for-profit firms in service industries containing both types of firms (e. g. Weisbrod and Schlesinger 1986). Similarly, there have been efforts to determine empirically the extent to which commercial nonprofits in particular industries are simply a response to tax exemption (Hansmann 1987b). But, in general, this work has not yet provided us with a clear answer as to whether, and to what degree, the asymmetric information theory helps explain the role of commercial nonprofits in many, or even any, industries.

I now believe, however, that we can discern at least one industry in the United States in which commercial nonprofits clearly arose, from the beginning, primarily as a response to contract failure. And that is the savings bank industry. I shall explore the evolution of that industry in some detail

---

[1] In primary medical care, nonprofits appear in the form of firms of doctors organized as group practices — commonly termed health maintenance organizations — that sell their services on a prepaid basis. Such firms are also often organized on a for-profit basis.

here, both as an illustrative case study in the role of nonprofit enterprise and in an effort to explain in otherwise puzzling diversity of organizations that populate the banking industry today.[2]

2. The Origins of the Savings Bank Industry

Nonprofit firms appear in the banking industry in the United States in the form of so-called mutual savings banks. Although the term "mutual" suggests that these banks are consumer cooperatives that are owned by their depositors, this is not the case. The depositors in a mutual savings bank have no voting rights or other means of exercising direct control over the organization, and thus are not members or owners in any proper sense. Instead, control over mutual savings banks lies in the hands of a self-perpetuating board of directors that holds the bank's assets in trust for its depositors. "The term 'mutual' only indicates that all distributed earnings must be shared by the depositors" (Teck 1968: 13). (In addition, depositors in mutual savings banks arguably have the right, upon dissolution of the organization, to share among themselves the organization's accumulated surplus.[3]) Thus, mutual savings banks are appropriately classified as true nonprofit organizations rather than as cooperatives.[4] In this respect, they should not be confused with mutual savings and loan associations, which are also common in American banking and — as discussed further below — are (at least formally) true consumer cooperatives that are owned by their depositors collectively.

Mutual savings banks arose in the United States early in the nineteenth century, following earlier English models. The first mutual savings bank was chartered in Massachusetts in 1816; by 1849, 87 mutual savings banks were

---

[2] After writing an earlier draft of this paper I discovered a paper by Eric Rasmusen, since published (1988), that makes much the same argument about the historical role of mutual savings banks.

[3] See Teck (1968: 13–14). The term "arguably" is used here, because depositors' rights to the distribution of surplus upon dissolution are a bit unclear; see *In re Dissolution of Cleveland Savings Society*, Ohio Ct. Com. Pls. (1961); *Morristown Institute for Savings v. Roberts*, 42 N.J. Eq. 496, 8 A. 315 (1887).

[4] In classifying nonprofits, I have elsewhere (Hansmann 1980) distinguished between "mutual" nonprofits, in which control of the organization is in the hands of the class of patrons for which the organization is a fiduciary, and "entrepreneurial" nonprofits, in which control is vested in a board of directors that is self-perpetuating or appointed by third parties. Within this scheme, mutual savings banks, despite their name, are appropriately classified as entrepreneurial rather than mutual nonprofits.

in operation, primarily in urban centers in the northeastern and mid-atlantic states (Teck 1968: 8, 16). They were typically founded as philanthropic institutions, with their initial capital donated by wealthy businessmen. The founders' motivation, it is said, was to help prevent pauperism, and relieve the burden on public charity, by encouraging thrift among the working class (Welfling 1968: 17).

Given this early history, one might conclude that mutual savings banks were established simply as a vehicle whereby the rich could provide charitable services to the poor, in the form of subsidized interest on the latter's savings. Indeed, this is the conventional view. These banks would then have assumed the nonprofit form, rather than being established as proprietary organizations, for the same reasons of contract failure that lead donative institutions in general to be formed almost universally as nonprofits: in order to provide some degree of fiduciary protection for the organization's donors, who otherwise would have little assurance that their contributions were being used for the purposes they intended rather than simply going into the pockets of the organization's proprietors.

Yet this theory seems unsatisfying for several reasons. To begin with, although hard data seem to be lacking, the amounts of capital contributed by the founders were probably inadequate to yield more than a trifling subsidy per individual depositor. Thus, it seems implausible that mutual savings banks were established merely as charitable intermediaries through which the rich could redistribute some of their income to the poor, or even to the frugal poor. Likewise, the subsidy per investor must surely have been too small to provide any important incentive in itself for saving, and thus to encourage noticeable changes in the savings behavior of the working classes.

Further, and more important, commercial banks at the time did not serve as places where individuals could deposit their savings. Although commercial banks were numerous in the early nineteenth century — there were over 300 in the United States in 1820 (Polakoff 1970: 68) —, they did not accept small deposits from individuals (Gup 1980: 137). Rather, they generally dealt only with businesses. They served primarily a monetary function, creating money in the form of bank notes, which were then the principal circulating currency (Polakoff 1970: 17). These bank notes were issued in exchange for notes from merchants, which the bank purchased at a discount.

"... neither the merchant, nor the saver, [of the early nineteenth century] thought of banks in connection with deposits. A bank ... meant primarily a place of discount for his notes. He owed bills ... [but] [h]is own note would not suffice to pay those bills, even though his credit were excellent, because it would not pass acceptably from hand to hand. But if he exchanged it for the note of some bank, paying for the privilege, through a discount, he would obtain something which would pass acceptably" (Bennett 1924: 20–21).

Commercial banks obtained their working capital not through deposits, but through sale of stock in the banks. And the savings that went to purchase this stock were, presumably, large sums accumulated by wealthy merchants, not the meager weekly savings of the working class.

In the early nineteenth century, then, there was no convenient vehicle through which persons of modest income could invest. Thus, the mutual savings banks were not founded simply to provide a place where the working poor could get a more attractive rate of return on their savings; they were founded as the *only* place where such people could deposit their savings at all. To understand the role of the early mutual savings banks, therefore, we have to understand why it was that there were no commercial savings banks until well into the nineteenth century. That is, why did the commercial banks not take deposits from individuals, and consequently obviate the need for the mutual savings banks?

The principal reason, it seems, is that commercial banks were too untrustworthy to serve as a repository for the savings of persons of modest means. That is, the problem was probably not on the supply side but on the demand side. If individuals had been willing to entrust their savings to commercial banks, the latter might well have taken them; but willing depositors were probably too few to make the activity worthwhile.

The reason that commercial banks were so untrustworthy in the early nineteenth century is that they were then largely unregulated; they did not have to maintain minimum levels of reserves, and there were no restrictions on the ways in which they could invest their assets. Commercial banks therefore had both the incentive and the opportunity to behave opportunistically toward their depositors. In particular, they had an incentive to invest depositors' savings in highly speculative ventures that would pay off handsomely if successful, but that ran a substantial risk of not paying off at all. If the bank was lucky in such investments, it would earn a large profit. And if it was unlucky, it would go bankrupt, leaving its depositors to bear most of the losses. Further, commercial banks had an incentive to maintain only very small reserves. That way, if the bank's investments went sour, only a minimum of the owners' assets would be exposed; most of the losses would fall on the depositors.[5]

Depositors would, of course, have had an incentive to try to bind banks by contract to maintain adequate reserves and not to undertake excessively speculative investments with their savings (and banks, in turn, would have

---

5 Similar incentive problems are now well recognized as a limitation on the feasible debt/equity ratios for business corporations (Jensen and Meckling 1976). And they also go far toward explaining why mutual firms dominated the life insurance business in its early days in the first half of the nineteenth century (Hansmann 1985).

had an incentive to bind themselves in this way in order to attract more business). But, under the circumstances, it was probably impossible to draft a contract of this type that was both effective and enforceable.

In short, consumer deposit banking was characterized by a high degree of asymmetric information (contract failure) in its early years: depositors could not know, or control, what commercial banks were doing with their funds.

Indeed, the early commercial banks often engaged in speculation, and not infrequently behaved opportunistically toward holders of their notes (for example, by making it difficult for them to be redeemed in specie) (Scoggs 1924). And they were, in fact, highly risky ventures: nearly 50% of all commercial banks formed between 1810 and 1820 closed by 1825, and the same proportion of banks formed between 1830 and 1840 failed before 1845 (Trescott 1963: 19). For these reasons, commercial banks were popularly viewed with distrust during the first half of the nineteenth century (Clain-Stefanelli 1975: 51). Individuals would, with reason, have been very hesitant to permit such institutions to hold their life savings for any length of time. Thus the commercial banks confined themselves to short-term transactional services, such as discounting notes, that exposed their customers to only limited losses in case the bank failed.

There was, consequently, a demand for savings banks that would provide a higher degree of fiduciary protection for depositors than commercial banks could offer. This demand grew particularly strong in the early nineteenth century, when for the first time there was a large class of urban industrial workers who received their income in the form of wages rather than in kind, and who lacked the traditional supports of the farm communities to tide them through periods of unemployment (Welfling 1968: 5). The mutual savings banks met this need. They obtained their seed capital — a problem for nonprofits in general, since they cannot obtain equity capital — from wealthy philanthropists. The mutual (nonprofit) form thus served the useful purpose of providing a degree of fiduciary protection both to the depositors and to the donors.[6] But, unlike other types of donative nonprofits (such as

---

[6] Although commercial banks did not take consumer savings deposits until the middle of the nineteenth century, there did exist before then a number of commercial trust companies that administered private and charitable trusts. Why did these commercial trust companies develop and survive in this period, while commercial savings banks did not? The answer presumably lies in the size of the individual trusts and the method of remuneration devised for trust managers. The trust companies, then as now, took a percentage of the total assets as their form of compensation. This reduced their incentive to behave opportunistically; indeed, it essentially made each individual trust into a small nonprofit firm. The trust managers could not keep any fraction of the gains from speculating irresponsibly with the trust assets, so they had little incentive to engage in such activity. In a savings

traditional redistributive charities), mutual savings banks were evidently not established as nonprofit rather than proprietary firms primarily to protect donors. Rather, the mutual savings banks sought donative financing *because* they were nonprofit, and they were nonprofit to protect their "commercial" customers, the depositors. Confirming this, donative financing seems to have been largely confined to the initial formation of mutual savings banks; once established, they tended to become purely commercial nonprofits.

3. The Development of Commercial Savings Banks

The mutual savings banks grew rapidly throughout the nineteenth century, reaching their peak in number of banks around 1900, when there were 652 such banks with a total of $ 2.1 billion in deposits (Teck 1968: 13). By the turn of the century, however, commercial banks had begun actively entering the savings field. In 1900, commercial banks held only $ 600 million in savings deposits; by 1915, this had increased to $ 3 billion (Welfling 1968: 58 – 59). By 1983, total deposits at commercial banks were roughly ten times those at mutual savings banks (FDIC 1983: Table 1).

Why did the commercial banks begin entering the savings account business late in the nineteenth century? A likely explanation is that the advent of

account, the depositor receives a fixed rate of return on his savings, and the bank keeps all profits (or absorbs all losses) that result from its investment of these funds. Thus the incentive for the bank to behave opportunistically is much higher than in the case of a trust account.

Of course, the banks could have arranged a method of remuneration for savings accounts that looked more like that of trusts. An individual savings account is generally too small to permit a bank to segregate and account separately for the investments it makes with the amounts deposited in the account; the funds from a number of such accounts must be pooled for efficient administration. Nevertheless, a bank could simply have confined itself to a fixed rate of compensation for the entire pool of savings, such as a percentage of the total assets. All earnings beyond this would be returned pro rata to the depositors as interest on their accounts. Yet this approach would essentially turn the bank into a nonprofit entity. Such a method of compensation makes the bank a trustee of the depositors' funds. The pool of assets administered by the bank would be held by it in trust for the beneficial owners, who are the depositors. In effect, this is the type of contractual relationship that was established between the managers of the mutual savings banks and their depositors. (Alternatively, the pooled assets could be owned by the depositors as a group not just beneficially, but directly; acting as a group, they would then simply hire the bank's management. This is the arrangement employed in the mutual savings and loan associations.)

state and federal banking regulation did what private contractual mechanisms could not — namely, make commercial banks a relatively safe place for members of the general public to deposit their savings. Prior to 1860, there was relatively little regulation of banks in general, and the regulation that existed was directed almost exclusively at protecting holders of the banks' notes rather than depositors. A number of states passed legislation during this period that required banks to maintain reserves of some kind.

Massachusetts was evidently the first to act, in 1829, and the movement toward such legislation accelerated rapidly after the banking crisis of 1837 (Dewey 1915: 155; Sharp 1970). Typically, this legislation limited note issues by a bank to some stated multiple of the amount of specie or other reserves held by the bank. Absent from most of this legislation, however, was any provision for a reserve requirement against deposits, whether demand deposits or time deposits. Louisiana was the first state to enact a reserve requirement against deposits as well as notes, in 1842. Prior to 1860, it was followed in this only by Massachusetts, which enacted a reserve requirement covering both deposits and notes in 1858 (Sharp 1970: 112–113).

In 1863 and 1864, however, the federal government, in response to the financial pressures created by the Civil War, passed legislation providing for federally chartered banks. This legislation required that banks chartered under it maintain a specie reserve of 25% against both notes and deposits. Many states copied this chartering system after the Civil War, and thus laws requiring reserves against deposits as well as notes became common (Rodkey 1934). This legislation, by limiting the ability of banks to act opportunistically toward their depositors, was probably a critical precondition for the increasingly strong role that the commercial banks played in savings banking in the latter part of the nineteenth century. On the other hand, such legislation still provided something less than complete protection to depositors. The reserve requirements were often rather lax; most states, for example, permitted banks to keep a substantial portion of their reserves in the form of demand deposits at other banks (Rodkey 1934: 393). Thus it is not surprising that the mutual savings banks continued to grow during this period, and at the end of the century still held in aggregate far more savings deposits than did commercial banks.[7]

A further decisive step in banking regulation took place in 1933, however, when the federal government passed legislation establishing federal deposit insurance that provided complete insurance for savings deposits at commercial banks (and mutual savings banks as well). This insurance essentially

---

[7] It should be noted, however, that other factors, such as governmental regulation of the types of investments that could be made by commercial banks and mutual savings banks, respectively, probably also contributed to the relative shares of the savings deposit business held by these two types of institutions.

eliminated the problem of contract failure between depositors and commercial banks; mutual savings banks could, therefore, no longer offer a higher degree of protection for savings deposits than could commercial banks. Thus, mutual savings banks quite suddenly lost whatever remaining efficiency advantage they had over commercial banks.

Yet the mutual savings banks did not disappear after 1933. Although virtually no new mutual savings banks have been established since then, many of the preexisting ones have remained in business. This presumably reflects the fact that there has been, at least until recently, no easy way for capital to leave the mutual savings bank industry. The managers and directors of the savings banks, having no claim on the banks' net assets, have little incentive to liquidate the banks — a step that could threaten their jobs. Yet nobody else has any control. Thus, so long as the mutual savings banks are not so inefficient relative to commercial banks as to waste away their capital, they tend to remain in business even though they are anachronistic. Only recently have large numbers of mutual banks begun to convert to the stock form (i. e. to commercial banks) through transactions that are brokered and promoted by investment banks (which take substantial remuneration from the transaction) and that secure the approval of the existing management through a bit of self-dealing in which they acquire some of the stock in the newly formed commercial bank at a bargain price (and perhaps keep their jobs in the bargain).

4. Mutual Savings and Loan Associations

Mutual savings banks have a close cousin in the form of mutual savings and loan associations (MSLAs), which have also played an important role in savings banking. Unlike the mutual savings banks, however, MSLAs are not nonprofits, subject to a strict non-distribution constraint, but rather are true cooperatives: their depositors have formal voting control over the organization as well as the sole claim to residual earnings. Although space precludes extensive discussion of these institutions here, a few words about their role may be appropriate, for purposes of comparison with mutual savings banks.

MSLAs first began to be formed in the United States in the 1830s. They originally arose as institutions in which small groups of working people would pool their savings, and from which they would then take loans, by turns, with which to finance the construction or purchase of a house. In the early stages of their development, an MSLA would be dissolved once all of its original members had acquired a house; subsequently, they became perpetual

undoubtedly had better information with which to determine which of their
friends and fellow workers would be good risks, and thus should be permitted
to join the mutual, than a commercial bank would have had. Further, when
times are hard, a borrower is likely to be less inclined to default when he
knows that his friends and neighbors will bear the loss than when he knows
that the owners of a commercial bank will bear it.

Thus mutual savings and loan associations had the potential of solving
two different problems, where the mutual savings banks only solved one.
Whether for this or other reasons, mutual savings banks never took root in
those sections of the country where MSLAs developed — which were essentially those parts of the country (the South and West) where development
occurred primarily after the 1830s.[8]

5. Conclusion

Commercial nonprofits are the great puzzle of the nonprofit sector today.
The historical experience with mutual savings banks throws some important
light on the possible roles that commercial nonprofits can play, and on the
patterns of evolution that characterize them.

To begin with, the experience with mutual savings banks shows that
nonprofit firms can play an important role in the early stages of purely
commercial industries that are characterized by severe problems of asymmetric information. In effect, they offer a form of consumer protection. But
that experience also indicates that public regulation is likely, in the long run,

---

[8] For further discussion of the role of cooperative enterprise, and of the way in which
it compares and contrasts with the role of nonprofit enterprise, see Hansmann
(1988).

to be more effective than the nonprofit form as a means of dealing with problems of asymmetric information in commercial enterprise. Regulation can make for-profit firms viable; and for-profit firms, with better access to capital than nonprofit firms, and better incentives for customer responsiveness and cost efficiency as well, are then likely to begin to take over the industry. Yet, nonprofit firms, once established, tend to become embedded and do not quickly leave an industry, even after the conditions to which they initially responded have long disappeared. And thus we see that mutual savings banks have survived for more than half a century after they became anachronistic.

Nursing care and day care are arguably two other industries that have evolved along paths similar to that followed by mutual savings banks. When, several decades ago, these industries were new, consumers might reasonably have been wary of trusting commercial firms to provide the sensitive services involved, and therefore preferred nonprofit providers. Yet, as public regulation of these industries became tighter, as consumers became more knowledgeable, and as for-profit firms developed stronger reputations, the need, and hence the special demand, for the nonprofit form of organization presumably diminished. Nevertheless, the already established nonprofits still occupy a substantial market share in these industries, and may continue to for some time to come.

References

Bennett, Frank P. (1924): *The Story of Mutual Savings Banks*, Boston: Frank P. Bennett & Co.

Clain-Stefanelli, Elvira and Vladimir (1975): *Chartered for Progress: Two Centuries of American Banking*, Washington, D.C.: Acropolis Books.

Dewey, Davis Rich (1915): *Financial History of the United States*, New York: Longmans Green & Co.

Federal Deposit Insurance Corporation, Division of Accounting and Corporate Services, Bank Statistics Branch (1983): *Banks and Branches Data Book: Summary of Accounts and Deposits in all Commercial and Mutual Savings Banks and Domestic Branches of Foreign Banks, 1983*, Washington, D.C.: FDIC.

Gup, Benton E. (1980): *Financial Intermediaries: An Introduction*, Boston: Houghton Mifflin Co.

Hansmann, Henry (1980): "The Role of Nonprofit Enterprise," *Yale Law Journal* 89, 835–901.

Hansmann, Henry (1985): "The Organization of Insurance Companies: Mutual Versus Stock," *Journal of Law, Economics, and Organization* 1, 125–153.

Hansmann, Henry (1987a): "Economic Theories of Nonprofit Organization," in *The Nonprofit Sector: A Research Handbook*, Walter Powell (Ed.), New Haven: Yale University Press.

Hansmann, Henry (1987b): "The Effect of Tax Exemption and Other Factors on the Market Share of Nonprofit Versus For-Profit Firms," *National Tax Journal* 40, 71–82.

Hansmann, Henry (1988): "Ownership of the Firm," *Journal of Law, Economics, and Organization* 4, 267–304.

Jensen, Michael and William Meckling (1976): "Theory of the Firm: Managerial Behavior, Agency Costs, and Capital Structure," *Journal of Financial Economics* 3, 305–360.

Polakoff, Murray E. (1970): *Financial Institutions and Markets*, Boston: Houghton Mifflin Co.

Rasmusen, Eric (1988): "Mutual Banks and Stock Banks," *Journal of Law and Economics* 31, 395–422.

Rodkey, Robert (1934): *Legal Reserves in American History*, Ann Arbor: University of Michigan Press.

Scoggs, William D. (1924): *A Century of Banking Progress*, Garden City, N.Y.: Doubleday.

Sharp, James Roger (1970): *The Jacksonians Versus the Banks*, New York: Columbia University Press.

Teck, Alan (1968): *Mutual Savings Banks and Savings and Loan Associations: Aspects of Growth*, New York: Columbia University Press.

Trescott, Paul B. (1963): *Financing American Enterprise: The Story of Commercial Banking*, New York: Harper & Row.

Weisbrod, Burton and Mark Schlesinger (1986): "Ownership Form and Behavior in Regulated Markets with Asymmetric Information," in *The Economics of Nonprofit Institutions: Studies in Structure and Policy*, Susan Rose-Ackerman (Ed.), Oxford: Oxford University Press.

Welfling, Weldon (1968): *Mutual Savings Banks*, Cleveland, Oh.: Case Western Reserve University Press.

2.4
Nonprofit Organizations and Consumer Policy: The Swedish Model

Victor A. Pestoff

1. Introduction

Since 1940, the Swedish government has encouraged nonprofit organizations to participate actively in consumer policy, first as an interlocutor for private business, and then as a countervailing force against business. This development was facilitated primarily by the use of political, rather than monetary resources. The government gave the nonprofit organizations access to official consumer agencies by providing them with seats on the governing bodies of consumer authorities, and thereby endowed them with official status and influence, rather than providing them with direct financial assistance. As a result, consumers were organized and institutionally pitted against producers and business in order to resolve, through negotiations, their many conflicting interests.

This paper, therefore, explores the changing role of nonprofit organizations in the formulation and implementation of Swedish consumer policy since the end of World War II. How were traditional hurdles to consumer organizing overcome? What policy has the Swedish government pursued to augment the influence of consumers? What do recent governmental proposals for decentralizing consumer policy imply for the future success of this policy?

2. Theoretical Concerns and Systemic Considerations

Four theoretical concepts are important in order to understand Swedish consumer policy and the role attributed to nonprofit organizations. These are exit and voice, collective action, countervailing power, and integrated participation. These concepts, which are related to certain basic properties of Swedish markets and politics, have influenced the options facing policy-makers in Sweden.

2.1 Exit and Voice

Hirschman (1970) analyses the typical economic and political responses to decline of firms, organizations, and states in terms of exit and voice. For instance, deterioration in product quality normally results in the exit option, that is, some customers may cease buying the firm's products, or some members may leave the organization. Alternatively, the firm's customers or the organization's members may express their dissatisfaction by protesting, that is, they may exercise their voice option. Voice is "any attempt at all to change, rather than escape from, an objectionable state of affairs" (Hirschman 1970: 30). It can function both as a complement to and an alternative to exit (1970: 33−40). Compared with exit, however, voice is costly and conditioned by the influence and bargaining power customers can bring to bear on the firms from which they buy (1970: 40). Customers must first find an employee who is willing to listen to their complaints and then explain why they are dissatisfied. Employees must in turn understand these complaints and be willing to relay them to the management. Voice, nevertheless, provides much more qualified information than exit behavior.

2.2 Collective Action

Olson (1965) explores a dilemma inherent to the second important concept, that of collective action. He notes that large groups which would benefit substantially from organizing to promote their common interests, notoriously fail to do so. But small, narrowly defined groups tend to succeed in organizing and advancing their own interests, usually at the expense of the broad based groups. Consumers are an example of a broad group, while business firms constitute a narrowly focused one. Olson explains this dilemma in terms of individual or personal calculus. He introduces the problem of "free-riding" and its solution through selective incentives. Rational self-interests, thus, pose a major economic obstacle to mass consumer organizations.

Olson discusses various alternatives to creating new organizations. The enormous inputs of time and money required for starting and running new movements can be minimized if existing organizations can adopt additional or new goals corresponding to the interests of these unorganized broad groups. Thus, in our case, the government might be inclined to persuade existing organizations to play an active role in consumer policy, thereby encouraging the development of indirect consumer organizations. Although started for and primarily pursuing other purposes, they may also promote the interests of their members as consumers.

2.3 Countervailing Power

Galbraith (1952) coined the term "countervailing power" in his classic book on *American Capitalism*. He argues that competition is no longer the driving force of advanced capitalist economies, given its monopolistic and oligopolistic tendencies. Instead, he argues the "countervailing power" of various interests has emerged to challenge, and even to equal, the power of oligopolies and monopolies. In the United States, for example, some "organized consumers," such as giant retail chains, are as influential as any manufacturer (1952). As concentration intensified, new power configurations replaced competition as the fundamental constraint on private power. However, they are not on the same side of the market, among competitive producers, but rather in the other arenas — among customers or suppliers (1952: 125).

"The development of countervailing power requires a certain minimum capacity for organization ... If the large retail buying organizations had not developed the countervailing power which they have used, by proxy, on behalf of the individual consumers, consumers would have been faced with the need to organize the equivalent of the retailer's power" (1952: 140).

He points out that the labor movement provides the clearest and most fully developed example of countervailing power in an American market, where trade unions augment the power of the suppliers of labor (1952: 128). Galbraith indicated that countervailing power has also been achieved by consumer cooperatives in Scandinavia, for instance, the Swedish *Kooperativa Förbundet's* (KF) historical struggle against the cartels (1952: 140). However, despite Gailbrath's assertion of the decline in importance of competition, it continues to constrain the influence of the members of Swedish consumer cooperatives and reduces cooperatives' efficiency (Pestoff 1988). Thus, they face the dilemma of balancing the interests of members and employees against market forces and authorities.

2.4 Integrated Organizational Participation in Public Policy Making

Heckscher (1946) described Sweden as an "organizationally saturated" society, and he also distinguished between totalitarian corporatism in Italy and "free" or democratic corporatism in Sweden. Today, organizational participation in Swedish public policy making extends throughout Swedish society and permeates the whole of it (Pestoff 1984a). Organizations are integrated into the policy process through both formal and informal channels. Their participation is often highly visible and permanent owning to the many *ad hoc* parliamentary commissions, the *remiss* system of remitting written answers to the proposals of the former, and lay representation on the governing boards of central administrative agencies.

However, in general, consumers stand out among those groups facing severe organizational difficulties (Galbraith 1952; Olson 1965; Pestoff 1984b; and Schmitter 1984). Moreover, collective action constitutes the only means whereby individual consumers and citizens can obtain an audible and permanent voice in a relatively centralized market economy and an organizationally saturated socio-political system. Individual consumers' and citizens' voices are normally too weak or indistinct to be heard and understood: they either drown each other or all disappear in the din. Only collective action can provide consumers' and citizens' voices with the necessary amplification to achieve permanent voice in markets and politics. It could therefore be argued that consumer organizations become as essential to the well-being of small, open, yet oligopolistic market economies as political parties are to democratic systems.

3. The Origin and Development of Consumer Influence in Sweden

In the post-World War II period, Swedish consumer policy has attempted, among other things, to mitigate the lack of organized consumer spokespeople by encouraging various existing organizations to assume an active role in the articulation, protection, and promotion of consumers' interests. Thus, Olson's idea of engaging existing organizations for additional activities rather than establishing new organizations gained official sanction in Swedish consumer policy. Ultimately, these official efforts attempted to establish a countervailing power, similar to that conceived by Galbraith, in order to offset the power of industry and commerce on behalf of consumers.

The following presentation discusses one major aspect of institutional negotiations between consumers and producers. This is an overt legitimization of consumer organizations, which is made possible by balancing the tripartite governing bodies of public consumer authorities, as part of the rules of the game of institutionalized social bargaining in Sweden. We will focus on changes in the overall composition of these governing bodies as well as the changing representation of legitimate consumer spokespeople. Another important aspect of Swedish consumer policy is how direct negotiations between consumers and producers helped to develop new products, determine food prices, influence market practices, or facilitate product complaint and redress procedures, etc. They are dealt with elsewhere and will not be repeated here (Pestoff 1989).

Swedish consumer policy can be divided into five phases. They are the initiation, expansion, consolidation, retrenchment, and decentralization phases.

3.1 Initiation Phase, 1940—1953

During the Second World War, both producers and consumers were encouraged to economize on scarce resources. But in order to achieve effective implementation, the government had to obtain consumers' cooperation in spreading and securing acceptance of these wartime rationing drives. In 1940, at the request of several women's organizations, the Bureau for Active Housekeeping (*Aktiv hushållning*) was established, under the Department of (Wartime) Economic Planning (*Hushållningsdepartementet*). The Bureau collaborated with many women's groups, such as the women's sections of political parties, the Women's Guild of the Consumer Cooperatives, and the Home-Economics Teachers' Associations. The Population Commission, under the leadership of Tage Erlander, made a grant to establish the Institute of Home Research (HFI), in order to institutionalize the collaboration between these women's associations. However, the grant required that business match the public funds and continue to provide matching funds for HFI's financing in the future. Thus, in 1944, HFI started operations as a quasi-public body. From 1944—1953, during the initial phase of Swedish consumer policy, it became the principal consumer authority, thereby providing consumers with voice in addition to exit available through traditional market reactions.

Its governing body consisted of 15 representatives from various women's organizations, home-economics teachers, and a few experts. Thus, the official policy accorded with Olson's recommendation to encourage existing organizations to take on supplementary goals rather than starting a new organizations. Manufacturers and entrepreneurs obtained only minority representation on the governing body of HFI, although they repeatedly but unsuccessfully asked for more seats. Business, however, collaborated with HFI on an equal basis in numerous group projects and continued to contribute half of the funds until 1954, after which its share decreased to 15%.

When wartime rationing ended, the government encouraged HFI's founders to become a joint, cohesive, and comprehensive advocate for consumers and to promote their interests against industry and commerce. However, in the changing political climate, once the national (wartime) coalition was replaced by a Social Democratic—Agrarian Party (or red-green) government, the differences between the various founder-members of HFI proved irreconcilable. Growing dissention among the founding-members and the conflicting personal interests of prominent board members eventually prompted both the government to withdraw its political support and industry its financial support. Rather than abandon this effort, the government embarked upon a more ambitious project, one which did not merely shore up consumers' weak market position and provide for an amplification of their voice.

The first indication of the political will to explore a new approach, based on a different constellation of organizations, was gleaned with the establishment of the Swedish Institute for Informative Labelling (*Varudeklarationsnämnden* VDN) in 1951. In addition to representatives of many of the same women's organizations and experts as in HFI, VDN also included representatives nominated by the Trade Union Confederation (*Landsor-*

ganisationen, LO), the Central Organization of Salaried Employees (*Tjänstemännens Centralorganisationen*, TCO), *Kooperativa Förbundet*, and private enterprise.

3.2 Expansion phase, 1954—1971

Many new public consumer authorities were established in the expansion phase, such as the Office of the Competition Ombudsman (*Näringsfrihetsombudsmannen*) and the Competition Council (*Näringsfrihetsrådet*), which came into being in 1954. HFI's governing body was reshuffled in the same year and public financing raised from 50% to 85% of its budget. Three years later, in 1957, the government abandoned HFI and assumed full responsibility for its activities by creating two new public agencies to replace it: the Institute for Consumer Information (*Konsumentinstitutet*) and the National Council for Consumer Goods Research and Consumer Information (*Konsumentrådet*, KR). The National Price and Cartel Office (*Statens pris- och kartellnämnd*, SPK) was also created in the same year. In addition, the Consumers' Delegation of the National Agricultural Marketing Board (*Statens jordbruksnämnd* SJN) was established in 1963 and, from 1967 onward, the price-regulation associations (*prisregleringsnämnder*) included one or more consumer representatives directly appointed by the government. Meanwhile, the Public Merchandise Complaints Board (*Allmänna reklamationsnämnden*, ARN) was started on an experimental basis in 1968, under KR's auspices. Finally, the Competition Council received broader directives and changed its name in 1971 to the Market Court (*Marknadsdomstolen*). The list of nonprofit organizations on the governing bodies of the public authorities during the expansion phase demonstrates a composition different from that seen earlier with HFI. During this phase, the present pattern of consumer representation, that of relying on the two central trade union organizations and the consumer cooperatives (LO, TCO, and KF, respectively) as the legitimate "consumer organizations," took shape.

The National Council for Consumer Goods Research (KR) included a few business representatives, but most were from the trade unions and "consumer groups," such as women's organizations. The Consumers' Institute and the National Price and Cartel Office, on the contrary, both had a balanced representation of consumers and producers. The Trade Union Confederation's Secretary became the KR's first chairman, while the Central Organization of Salaried Employee's Chairman was the first Director General of the Institute for Consumer Information. These appointments clearly indicate the government's new strategy on consumer issues: that of actively engaging the two largest trade union movements in consumer policy at the national level. Together, these broad popular movements could constitute an effective countervailing power for consumers, which the women's organizations of the earlier phase were unable to provide. Furthermore, the strength of the Swedish trade unions also ensured greater volume and unison of voice than was possible with the numerous conflicting women's organizations.

In many of these newly established consumer authorities, a pattern of balanced tripartitism was seen in the organizational representation on their governing boards. Unlike the HFI, in which industry only obtained minority representation, the new consumer agencies included an equal number of industry and consumer representatives, while nominees of the government, *Riksdag*, and the governmental departments comprised the spokespeople for the public interest. Thus a new structure was established during this period, one which required negotiated solutions based on parity and compromise concerning the direction of these consumer agencies.

3.3 Consolidation Phase, 1972—1977

Developments during the consolidation phase continued along lines drawn up in the previous phase, as witnessed by the Letters of Instruction and Letters of Appointment issued by the Departments of Commerce (later Finance) and Agriculture. These Letters assume numerical parity between wage earners and consumers, on the one hand, and business and commerce, on the other, in the composition of public-agency governing boards. Civil servants and MPs form a third group, giving these agencies their tripartite constellation. This balanced tripartite pattern occurs in the Price and Cartel Office, the Market Court, and the Public Merchandise Complaints Board.

The Letter of Instruction or Letter of Appointment for the Consumer Delegation of the Agricultural Marketing Board also mentions consumer representation. The need for such tripartite representation on the National Board for Consumer Policies (*Konsumentverket*, KoV), formed by an amalgamation of VDN, KI, and KR, was discussed in the *Riksdag* prior to its 1973 creation. While the instructions for the Agricultural Marketing Board and the National Food Administration (*Statens livsmedelsverk*) make no mention of consumer or producer representatives, they display the same pattern of tripartite corporatist representation as found in the other bodies mentioned above. The same nonprofit organizations are represented on most of the governing boards of these public consumer agencies. The composition of the governing bodies of the public consumer authorities changed only marginally during the consolidation phase, although the 1976 *Riksdag* election ushered in the first non-socialist government for nearly half a century. Thus, this phase shows the continued endeavor to establish a countervailing power.

The state provided an institutional forum for negotiations between organized consumers and producers in many ways, in addition to the governing bodies of public consumer agencies: it authorized the public consumer agencies designed to oversee a variety of consumer protection legislation and to preside over semi-annual price negotiations between consumers and producers of food stuffs. It also provided an institutionalized means of resolving conflicts between consumers and business over complaints connected with goods and services, and finally, negotiated directly with producers for branch-specific norms in relation to the terms of trade and fair marketing legislation.

3.4 Retrenchment Phase, 1978—1984

The first non-socialist government in almost fifty years inspired many of the changes that occurred in this phase. Substantial changes took place, but in terms of financial priorities rather than of consumer representation. The changes associated with this phase were politically inspired and concern the ambitions and objectives of consumer policy. While no overall revision of consumer policy took place between 1976—1982 and no new goals were overtly defined, nevertheless, numerous marginal changes were introduced which, in combination, effected far-reaching reforms. S. Burenstam-Linder, Secretary of Commerce, professed greater reliance on market forces as the principal instrument for protecting and promoting consumer interests. This implied that exit would be given priority over voice, since in his opinion, public consumer policy was costly and merely raised consumer prices (*Dagens Nyheter*, 12. 03. 81).

The national budget became the main instrument for effecting a change in the direction of consumer policy under the four non-socialist governments. Gone were the automatic annual increases in public funds. Instead, consumer policy was subject to extraordinary curtailments of public appropriations. In addition, voice was made more cumbersome, as the two major public bodies, the National Board for Consumer Policies and the Price and Cartel Office, came under heavy political fire and incurred sharp financial cutbacks (Pestoff 1984b).

Despite of their often repeated belief in the superiority of market forces over public bureaucracy and regulatory legislation, the non-socialist governments did little to affect the balanced tripartitism in consumer authorities. In fact, the Public Merchandise Complaint Board gained permanent status in 1981 plus a balanced tripartite council of its own, which it had lacked during its 13 years of temporary existence.

3.5 Decentralization Phase, 1985—present

The previous activist policies in consumer policy were reinstated by the newly returned Social Democratic Government, when it set up the Parliamentary *ad hoc* Committee on Consumer Policy in 1982. Thus, one of the Committee's responsibilities was to examine the role of popular movements in Swedish consumer policy in order to find ways to increase their participation and strength. This renewed interest in popular movements may be seen in part as a response to the absence of an "independent consumers' movement" in Sweden, and in part, a recommitment to the maintenance of a countervailing power. Thus, the new Social Democratic Government continues to see consumer affairs in adversarial terms, that is, producers versus consumers and markets versus associations.

A special report entitled *Konsumentinflytande och konsumentorganisering — den svenska modellen* (Consumer Influence and Consumer Organization — the Swedish Model) was prepared for the committee. It criticized the growing inertia of the Swedish model and made several suggestions for its revitalization (Pestoff 1984b). This inertia stems from the fact that consumer matters are invariably secondary, or perhaps even tertiary, issues for trade unions and consumer cooperatives, that is, the very organizations presently entrusted with voicing consumer interests. This fact alone is hardly unusual, since most complex organizations have numerous goals of varying status, many of which may conflict. But, given the tensions between consumer interests and the primary goals of these organizations, consumer issues need to be institutionalized and structured in order to preserve and defend their status in relation to the organizations' main goals. Moreover, trade unions and cooperatives in recent years have not been entirely free from the in-fighting which characterized much of the initiation phase. The report also outlines institutional alternatives for improving the status of consumer issues in the internal decision making of Swedish consumer organizations.

More important, however, was the suggestion to extend the number and role of officially recognized consumer organizations to include other nonprofit organizations, such as groups representing women, immigrants, the disabled, pensioners, patients, youth, and environmental groups. Consumer policy in Sweden would thus obtain greater legitimacy and a vital injection of new ideas which could help to revive it and ensure a more dynamic future. By activating the established "consumer organizations" and engaging new ones in consumer matters, the members of such organizations could be mobilized for consumer protection, without significantly increasing public assistance or financing.

A number of these suggestions were reiterated by the Committee in its final report (SOU 1985: 32), which was sent to several nonprofit organizations for written comments, as part of the normal consultative procedure (*remiss*) in Swedish law-making. All but one of these nonprofit organizations favored suggestions of greater involvement on their part.

Another suggestion adopted by the Parliamentary Committee called for the creation of a national umbrella organization for all consumer groups. However, in 1986, KF's Consumer Policy Council (*Konsumentpolitiska råd*) was established as a consumer forum for KF, LO, TCO, and several other consumer cooperative organizations. The government's bill on consumer policy could thus refer to this development in order to justify the lack of any public funds for setting up such a national umbrella organization.

Several new organizations, and some previously involved, have responded positively to these proposals, by engaging some of their elected officials in consumer advisory activities at the local and/or regional level. Thus began the decentralization which was the hallmark of the Committee's proposals. Some groups have started or planned courses for training "consumer ombudsmen" at the local or regional level, such as local trade unions or pensioners' organization. Others are developing their own local consumer policy and consumer-education materials, and yet others have started projects for economic counselling among members. The trained "consumer ombudsmen" are then expected to lead study circles on subjects related to consumer interests. The Stockholm section of the Housewifes' Association (*Husmodersförbundet*) has also developed a consumer program and plans to run its own courses in consumer finance, legislation and other areas of consumer interest. Moreover, Verdandi, an organization for helping alcoholics, recently started providing economic counselling among its members in eight local areas, as a pilot project.

The National Board for Consumer Policies (KoV) and the municipal consumer advisory authorities have encouraged these decentralized activities on the part of nonprofit organizations. KoV supported the role of popular movements by allocating 200,000 Swedish crowns of its 45 million Swedish crowns budget in 1986/87 to them, and by listing such activities as one of its priorities. National and local authorities have also helped to plan and run courses, at times even provided financial support for this renewed interest in consumer issues at the local and/or regional levels. All of these activities, of course, concur with the Committee's suggestions to decentralize responsibility for consumer policy. Although no extra funds were made available for municipalities to improve their consumer advisory activities, cooperation between the authorities and nonprofit organizations at local level may render municipal efforts more effective by extending their scope far beyond that of local civil servants. Thus, implementation of consumer policy may also become more efficient without any significant rise in the input of public resources.

Another important element of the decentralizing momentum is the recent formation of an "independent consumer movement" comprising 500 individual members in a dozen or more localities. Each local consumer association is known as a "consumer group." In addition, a national peak organization — the "Independent Consumers' Forum" — is taking shape. However, the establishment of a new organization from scratch and the creation of a peak organization has proven to be a much more difficult and demanding task than its initiators realized, thus confirming Olson's arguments. Conflicts have also arisen over funding, staffing, control, direction, official recognition, and methods. After an uncertain beginning, it has now entered into a network-like collaboration with numerous alternative and environmental movements and may, perhaps, find the support necessary, both to establish itself at the national level and to extend its activities at the local level. However, as its financial situation was highly precarious until very recently, it is too soon to announce that Sweden has finally acquired its own "independent consumer movement."

Because it commends engaging alternative movements and environmental groups in consumer issues and policy, the National Board for Consumer Policies welcomes the efforts of the Independent Consumers' Forum. However, it remains an open question whether a countervailing power can be achieved and sustained from fragmented and uncoordinated organizational efforts such as these. Rather, there appear to be certain built-in trade-offs between a countervailing power stance and attempting to engage various heterogeneous groups, although the creation of a national consumer network with a peak forum might alleviate some of these problems, as experience from the United Kingdom suggests.

4. Summary and Conclusions

This paper explores the relationship between markets, politics, and nonprofit organizations in Swedish consumer policy. It shows that, while consumer policy does not rest exclusively in the public domain, neither is it simply left to the whims of the market. Rather, its success depends in part on the participation of nonprofit organizations in negotiations between consumers and producers in a variety of contexts. Furthermore, no single omnipotent public agency serves as the watchdog of consumer policy. Instead, a number of agencies provide a forum for "organized consumers" and producers to meet in a corporatist fashion and negotiate about product innovation, consumer protection and redress, and even price levels. A unique combination of historical, political, economical, and organizational factors have made this possible. Most important, however, was the government's active role. Like Swedish developments elsewhere in welfare services (Esping-Andersen and Korpi 1984), in economic policy (Bosworth and Rivlin 1986), and in labor-market policy (Wilensky and Turner 1987), consumer political developments have borne witness to an activist approach under Social Democratic rule, rather than a passive "wait and see" attitude. The government actively sought to create a countervailing power on behalf of consumers in order to facilitate and extend negotiations between consumers and producers.

The tendency for consumer policy to follow overall public policy can also be seen when other countries' consumer policies are compared to their general economic and social policies. Thus, the Social Democratic preference of voice over exit, its pursuit of countervailing power through collective action, and integrated participation in public policy making corresponds by and large with similar Swedish patterns found in welfare services, economic policy, labor-market policy, and industrial relations. However, unlike these other arenas, where both parties (i. e. labor and capital) are well organized, the government must continually oversee and intervene on behalf of consumers, who, in existing monopolistic and oligopolistic conditions, experience an inherent lack of power in the market or in negotiations. By its intervention, the state attempts to shore up consumers' meagre organizational structures and to establish a countervailing power against the well-organized and highly consolidated producers, wholesalers, and retailers. This, however, requires a sustained public effort, which is not always forthcoming, owing to the discretionary nature of consumer policy and the lack of well-organized consumer groups, which constantly call for an active consumer policy. Policy slack — the absence of spokespeople to keep such consumer concerns on the public agenda and to criticize adverse changes in policy goals associated with different governments — illustrates the major disadvantages of this approach. Nevertheless, it still seems likely that such second-best solutions are better than surrendering to unbridled market forces.

Many producers would benefit from a dialogue with "mature and knowledgeable consumers." The problem is how can producers complement market signals with the qualified and rich information that voice bears with it? This can only be done if consumers are able to articulate their needs and desires loudly and clearly. Producers must therefore recognize the need for and the benefits of voice as a complement to exit. Given that the market accentuates producers' power vis-à-vis consumers, a non-market framework must be created to promote a consumer—producer dialogue. Gailbraith's idea of a countervailing power suggests that producers must also be willing to acknowledge these institutions as legitimate and to listen to the message they carry. Some of them of course do, but others perceive the world in black and white terms or long for a return to simpler times when the market was unbridled or its omnipotence remained unchallenged. Such attitudes risk stifling the voice of consumers and squandering its beneficial effects.

Many Swedish businesspeople agree and demonstrate an acute awareness of the benefits of a dialogue with their customers and have taken certain steps to gain fuller and richer information from them. Market research is clearly one expression of this awareness. But, they do not always appreciate the institutional prerequisites for continued access to such information. Thus, while they show a willingness to help finance small "independent" consumer movements, they are also highly critical or existing public and nonprofit consumer institutions. But business-financed consumer organizations would require extensive resources to get started and nevertheless still face the risk of being considered "his master's voice," rather than the true voice of consumers. Olson's recommendation about using existing institutions seems relevant here. Although a lap dog may at times seem preferable, only a watch dog can get the real message across and raise the alarm about intolerable products or conditions.

A greater challenge to the objective of a consumer voice and power is the growing political malaise in Sweden. As Sweden moves farther away from the politics of compromise and consensus and towards a neo-adversarial or non-accommodationalist epoch, the growing political dissent over the rules of social and economic bargaining will intensify. For example, the opportunity for interest organizations to nominate representatives to the governing bodies of central administrative agencies, or "lay representation" (*lekmannarepresentation*), constitutes a pivotal aspect of social and economic bargaining. Recently, however, the two most important peak business interest associations, the Swedish Employers' Confederation (SAF) and the Federation of Swedish Industries (SI), have openly challenged this practice. They suggest that private enterprise should no longer formally participate in implementing public policy, and therefore should not nominate lay representatives to such governing bodies. The organizations representing commerce oppose this change, as does organized labor. Since employers and industrial organizations, through their effective and well-financed lobbying, can help shape private and public opinion (Pestoff 1987), it seems likely that the Conservative Party may join the Liberal Party in condemning lay representation as "corporativism." If private enterprise boycotts the official channels, it would then prove difficult to maintain integrated organizational participation in most arenas of public policy making. Dismantling integrated participation would also effectively end the nomination of official consumer representatives to the tripartite governing bodies of consumer authorities. This, in turn, would imply the *de facto* termination of the active pursuit of countervailing power in consumer policy, though negotiations between consumers and producers in other fora might still be possible.

A second, even more general challenge is posed by the Common Market, which requires a complete harmonization of all laws including consumer protection laws by 1992. Sweden and the EFTA countries will be expected to adopt most of the harmonization and deregulations measures reached by the EEC, even if they remain outside the Common Market. Moreover, the level of harmonization remains subject to negotiations. For example, Sweden might be required to adapt its laws on consumer safety, marketing, contract terms, etc. to a level substantially below its current one. If so, what will happen to the public authorities like KoV, SPK, and SLV which oversee Swedish legislation in their respective areas? Will they be stripped of their funds and powers, or perhaps even disbanded in the name of European harmonization? If so, what will remain of the Swedish model of indirect consumer representation on par with producers? Thus harmonization, if implemented at the level of the lowest common denominator, could also end the policy of countervailing power in Swedish consumer policy.

List of Acronyms Used in This Article

ARN = *Allmänna reklamationsnämnd* — Public Merchandise Complaints Board
HFI = *Hemmens forskningsinstitut* — Institute of Home Research
KF = *Kooperativa Förbundet* — Cooperative Union and Wholesale Society
KoV = *Konsumentverket* — National Board for Consumer Policies
KPK = *Konsumentpolitiska kommitten* — Committee on Consumer Policy
KR = *Konsumentrådet* — National Council for Consumer Goods Research and Consumer Information
LO = *Landsorganisationen i Sverige* — Swedish Trade Union Confederation
SJN = *Statens jordbruksnämnd* — National Agricultural Marketing Board
SPK = *Statens pris- och kartellnämnd* — National Price and Cartel Office
TCO = *Tjänstemännens Centralorganisation* — Central Organization of Salaried Employees
VDN = *Varudeklarationsnämnden* — Institute for Informative Labelling

References

Bosworth, B. and A. Rivlin (Eds.) (1986): *The Swedish Economy*, Washington, D.C.: The Brookings Institution.

Dagens Nyheter, 12.03.1981, Interview with Secretary of Commerce, S. Burenstam-Linder.

Esping-Andersen, G. and W. Korpi (1984): "Social Policy as Class Politics in Post War Capitalism: Scandinavia, Austria and Germany," in *Order and Conflict in Contemporary Capitalism*, J. Goldthorpe (Ed.), Oxford: Clarendon Press, 179−207.

Galbraith, J. (1952 and 1963): *American Capitalism*, Harmondsworth: Penguin Books.

Heckscher, G. (1946 and 1951): *Staten och organisationer*, Stockholm: KF tryckeri.

Hirschman, A. (1970): *Exit, Voice and Loyalty*, Cambridge, Mass.: Harvard University Press.

Hirschman, A. (1980): *Essays in Trespassing*, Cambridge, Mass.: Harvard University Press.

Lane, S. (1983): "The Rationale for Government Intervention in Seller-Consumer Relationships," *Policy Studies Review* 2, 3; 419−428.

Olson, M. (1965 and 1971): *The Logic of Collective Action*, Cambridge, Mass.: Harvard University Press.

Pestoff, V. A. (1977): *Voluntary Associations and Nordic Party Systems*, Stockholm: Studies in Politics.

Pestoff, V. A. (1984a): "The Swedish Organizational Community and its Participation in Public Policy-Making," AASBI RR No. 6, Stockholm: Department of Political Science.

Pestoff, V. A. (1984b): *Konsumentinflytande och konsumentorganisering — den svenska modellen*, DsFi 1984: 15, Stockholm: Department of Finance.

Pestoff, V. A. (1986): *The Politics of Organized Business Interest in Sweden*, Stockholm: Department of Business Administration.

Pestoff, V. A. (1987): "Har folkrörelserna räd att hänga med?" (Can Popular Movements Afford to Keep up?), *Arbetet* 29.04.87.

Pestoff, V. A. (1988): *Co-operatives, Markets and Politics in Sweden*, Stockholm: Department of Business Administration R1988: 11.

Pestoff, V. A. (1989): "Organisationernas medverkan och förhandlingar i svensk konsumentpolitik" (Organizational Participation and Negotiations in Swedish Consumer Policy), in *Forhandlingsøkonomi i Norden* (A Negotiated Economy in the Nordic Countries), K. Nielsen and O. K. Pedersen (Eds.), Copenhagen: DJØF forlag and Oslo: Tano.

Pestoff, V. A. (1990): "Joint Regulation, Meso-Games and Political Exchange in Swedish Industrial Relations," forthcoming (1990) in B. Marin (Ed.), *Generalized Political Exchange*, Frankfurt & New York: Campus & Westview.

Schmitter, P. (1984): "Democratic Theory and Neo-Corporatist Practice," Florence: European University Institute, Working Paper No. 74.

Schmitter, P. and W. Streeck (forthcoming): *Organizing Business Interests*, in print.

SOU (1985: 32): *Hushållning för välfärd. Den framtida konsumentpolitikens inriktning*, Stockholm: Department of Finance.

Wilensky, H. and L. Turner (1987): *Democratic Corporatism and Policy Linkages*, Berkeley: University of California.

2.5
Para-Government Organization in the Provision of Public Services: Three Explanations

Christopher Hood and Gunnar Folke Schuppert

1. Introduction

Why is it that some public services are provided by core or classic public bureaucracies, some by independent public enterprises, and some by organizations constituted as private or independent? And why does there seem to be an administrative "megatrend" (Naisbitt's [1982] term) away from the use of classic public bureaucracies in Western countries, and an explosion of para-government bodies? (See for example, Hood and Schuppert 1988; Sharkansky 1979.)

A good institutional theory should be able to explain *both* institutional patterns (that is, why different types of agency are used for different tasks) *and* the apparent "megatrend" towards para-government organization. But do we have a good institutional theory? This paper looks at three possible candidates. We are not here concerned principally with the normative or justificatory doctrines associated with each of these types, but rather with ways of understanding and explaining institutional patterns.[1]

For the purposes of this paper, core or classic public bureaucracies are defined as enterprises which are legally the embodiment of public officials elected under a general franchise (and thus formally under the direct day-to-day oversight of such officials), or which otherwise owe their origins to a constitutional document or treaty creating an all-purpose organization. Examples are city councils, national government ministries, the "primary" institutions of the European Community, the formal "subjects" of public international law.

---

[1] This paper builds on a small scale research project on para-governmental organizations in selected Western European countries which was conducted between 1984 and 1986 under the auspices of the European Consortium for Political Research and financed by the Anglo-German Foundation and the Fritz Thyssen Foundation: it involved an examination of para-governmental organization at national level, city level, and international level (for details see Hood and Schuppert 1988).

Independent public enterprises are defined as enterprises which are "public" in that they owe their origins to public law or special statute or order and which are "independent" in that they have a legal personality which is distinct from core government enterprises (such that they are not the direct legal embodiment of general elected representatives). Examples are public corporations and boards, public cooperative associations and foundations.

Private or independent enterprises providing public services are defined as enterprises which are not created under public law or special statute, but which formally owe their origin to general enabling laws for private or independent entities — company law, charity law, the general law of trusts, associations, societies. Such enterprises are of a formal type which can be set up by a registration or licensing procedure which is open to anyone who fulfils certain general criteria, relating to matters such as financial viability or charitable purpose. Typically the directorate is formally accountable to some membership, though this does not always apply, for instance in the case of trusts.

Each of these three types of enterprise is familiar to administrative theory and has a distinct brand of doctrine and normative principle associated with it. The justificatory theory for core government bureaucracy was developed in the work of the "classic" theorists of Public Administration in the late nineteenth and early twentieth century (cf. Wilson 1887). Such theories celebrated the merits of core government bureaucracy, in the language of constitutional law and democratic theory. A classic statement of this principle is the 1918 Report of the UK Machinery of Government Committee which attacked "administrative boards" and argued that: "there should be no omission, in the case of any particular service, of those safeguards which ministerial responsibility alone provides" (Cd 9230, 1918: 11).

Doctrines justifying the use of independent public enterprises started to come into prominence in the 1920s and 1930s, and involved a mix of corporatist ideas, ideas of public sector trusts (cf. Keynes 1952), and "managerialist" ideas reflecting the view that public services are often best provided by organizations run on private-business lines and distanced from core government bureaucracy for their everyday operations. A classic statement of the latter view is the "Morrison doctrine," originally formulated in 1933 (Morrison 1933), although similar ideas were formulated before World War I by Francesco Nitti in Italy (see Hood and Schuppert 1988: 109; Nitti 1974: 643 – 653).

Doctrines justifying the use of enterprises constituted as private or independent for public services also involve a mix of ideas: Roman Catholic doctrines of "subsidiarity," especially for welfare state activities (Wegener 1978: 134 – 136), ideas about the advantages of "self help" through communal organization (Illich 1972), and the new institutional economics which developed since the 1950s and challenged the orthodoxy of traditional Public

Administration by highlighting the potential for allocative and x-inefficiency built into core public bureaucracies (cf. Breton 1974; Downs 1967; Niskanen 1971; Tullock 1965).

This paper, however, is concerned with theories purporting to *explain* patterns of institutional choice rather than justificatory theories. The three approaches examined are the "national style" approach (the approach taken by most work on para-government organization to date), the administrative dilemmas approach, and the transactional approach conventionally associated with the new institutional economics.

2. A "National Style" Approach to Explaining Agency Type

It might be argued that the choice of one type of enterprise rather than another to provide a public service could only be understood by a deep and holistic understanding of the individual political system within which those political choices are made. The underlying assumption is that each country is so distinctive in its traditions and political characteristics that we can only understand the institutional structure of each country by reference to its peculiar history and culture (for example, Chapman and Dunsire 1971; de Tocqueville 1954).

In one sense, this is a truism — impossible to deny. It parallels the views of some students of public policy making (such as Richardson 1982), that overarching "national policy styles" can be reflected in all fields of policy within a country. Indeed, the influence of national style might be expected to be rather stronger in matters of formal organizational type than in the substantive content of public policy or decision-making styles. Policy ideas may quickly come into universal currency through imitative diffusion, but institutional design tends to be deeply rooted in tradition, and linked to fundamental constitutional rules and legal assumptions, which themselves change only very slowly.

Most work on para-governmental organization to date has been in a "national style" vein, in the sense that it has been done on a country-by-country basis, and the explanation of institutional patterns has been couched in terms of what are seen or claimed to be distinctive features of each country. In most Western-type countries, discussion of para-governmental organization has up to now been fragmented and parochial. There has been no real recognition that the phenomenon, or analogies to it, can be found at every level of public service provision — city level, national level, and even international level (particularly with the explosion of para-government

organization within the European Community as documented by Hilf 1982).
Since there is no academic forum in which para-government organization at
all of these levels could be discussed as a *common* administrative development,
no attempts have been made to provide an equally general theoretical
explanation.

Hence the "national style" approach to explanation has predominated
almost by default. In fact, in many Western European countries, it was
commonly but wrongly thought until very recently that that country was
unique in the extent to which public business is carried out by organizations
other than core public bureaucracy. That alleged distinctiveness was in turn
often said to relate to the country's own special history and culture — for
instance, traditional religious cleavages in the Netherlands, the Fascist-era
experience in Italy, pragmatism in Scandinavia, the doctrine of an apolitical
higher civil service in the UK. This goes along with various special terms
which are used in each country to denote the phenomenon, such as quangos,
the parastate, indirect public administration.

Accounts of institutional patterns in terms of individual "national culture"
may certainly help us to understand the finer details of variations on the
general theme. It cannot be dismissed altogether. But the national style
approach to explaining institutional choice has two main drawbacks.

First, it does not explain the "megatrend" referred to earlier. It does not
tell us why in so many Western-type countries (including some Eastern
"Western-type" countries, such as Singapore), despite their different traditions and cultures, there is everywhere such a dense network of independent
public enterprises and private or independent enterprises providing public
services, and why there is an apparent trend towards de-glomeration of
public services and away from core government organization.

Second, the "national style" approach does not really explain why analogies to independent public enterprise and private or independent enterprises
can be readily found at international level, in the "grey zone" between
the legal categories of "subjects of public international law" and of non-
governmental organizations, for instance, in the proliferation of semi-inde-
pendent subsidiary units around institutions such as the United Nations
organization and the European Community (cf. Hood and Schuppert 1988:
199—243). Something other than national style is needed to understand this
"megatrend."

3. An Administrative Dilemmas Approach

A second possible way to understand the distribution of public services
among the three different types of organization considered here is to explain
it as the reflection of generic dilemmas in administration. It is commonplace

that institutional design in the public sector more commonly involves dilemmas — choices between alternative packages of benefits and drawbacks involving painful trade-offs between values — single-dimensional choice between alternatives which can be assessed in terms of a single value (Dunsire 1978; Hood 1976; McLaren 1982; Steinbruner 1974).

In principle, this idea can usefully be applied to explaining the choice between core government enterprise and para-government organization. Core government bureaucracy has many well-known potential advantages stemming from its typical structural characteristics. That is, its rigorous clearance rules in principle set up strong pressures to integrate public policy into a single coherent whole; its traditional hierarchical structure brings maximum responsiveness to the day-to-day demands of elected politicians while its tenure and recruitment rules in principle minimize the influence of favouritism and political "pull" in recruitment, dismissal, and promotion, at least below the topmost levels (Perrow 1979). Such advantages, however, are attended by equally well-known disadvantages as concomitant side-effects, typically involving: Long decision delays while the bureaucracy goes through the clearance process; difficulties in evaluating performance against any single or clearly measurable target because of the multiple and ever-changing goals in play; a very risk-averse ethos because punishment for mistakes is more certain than advancement for successes, leading to difficulties in motivating innovative behaviour on the part of bureaucrats in the system.

Independent public enterprises and private/independent enterprises similarly constitute institutional packages in which desirable features go along with often unwanted but unavoidable side effects. Because such forms of organization do not involve such elaborate clearance rules as core public bureaucracies, they lend themselves in principle to quick decision making. Because they can be given defined tasks by statute or other means, their performance can be easier to assess than that of core government bureaucracies. Because they can often hire and fire staff on their own terms, they can employ, on part-time or other special terms, unorthodox and talented people who would never be attracted to orthodox career service in a regular grade in core government bureaucracy. For example, in its early years, OEEC (later OECD) was able to attract to its independent appendages people of the highest talent for short-term appointments on special terms, and this is said to have significantly contributed to the vibrancy and power of the organization at that time (see Hahn 1988: 242−243).

The corresponding disadvantages of using para-governmental organization are equally familiar: lack of pressures to integrate policy with the rest of the public sector; lack of information exchange and perhaps even outright conflict with other public bureaucracies; risks of political favouritism or corruption in recruitment and promotion; incentives to "solve" problems by transforming them into some other form, even if that means creating major problems for other public-service enterprises (as in the familiar case of strict "commercial" approaches to users which create massive social welfare problems in areas such as transport, energy, housing).

Now, if the choice between core government bureaucracy, independent public enterprise, and private enterprise is just another item in the long list of administrative design dilemmas, it would follow that whatever principle institutional designers first use as a basis for creating organization, they will later design arrangements departing from that principle to take advantage of the opposite, contradictory principle. That is, if you base all public services on core government enterprise, with its many well-known advantages, you will soon find yourself creating independent organizations of one kind or another to try to get round the awkward side effects. Equally, the argument goes, if you begin from the opposite principle, basing all public services on independent public enterprises or private/independent enterprises, with *their* well-known advantages, you will soon find yourself creating core government enterprises, at least in those areas where lack of integration can be fatal to the state (such as defence, foreign policy, public order).

The idea of organizational choice as a product of an eternal warring of contradictory principles of organization has at first sight a certain appeal. Just like the development of contradictory legal principles, the development of contradictory bases of organization is a recurring theme in administrative history and is to be found in most developed systems of public administration. Moreover, unlike the national style approach, the dilemmas approach could help us to explain why there should be a general "megatrend," referred to earlier, towards the use of forms of organization other than core government bureaucracies for the provision of public services.

But — and here the problems begin — this approach would *also* lead us to expect a fluctuating or cyclical pattern in the distribution of administrative tasks among types of organization, not a stable one or a one-way trend. We would expect each type of organization to go in and out of favour as instruments of public service provision, and that a boom in public service provision by independent public enterprise or by private/independent bodies would sooner or later be followed by a resurgence of core government.

Up to now, however, that is not what the development of institutional structures has been like. In fact, an administrative dilemmas approach does not explain the continuing increase in the use of non-core government bureaucracies, even when such non-core forms of organization are out of official favour or when their shortcomings have been sharply demonstrated by financial failure or other dramatic debacles. If the use of different institutional forms goes in and out of fashion, as the dilemmas approach would lead us to expect, this seems to happen only, if at all, at very long intervals of a century or so.

4. A Subsidiarity/Transaction Problems Approach

A third approach, which focuses on factors common across all countries rather than on what is distinctive to each, but which does not predict an ebb-and-flow effect like the dilemmas approach, could be drawn from a marriage of the "transactions analysis" approach in contemporary institutional economics with the "subsidiarity principle" in public service provision (Kaufmann, Majone, and Ostrom 1986: 799–802; Wegener 1978: 134–136).

Contrary to what the first two approaches might suggest, it could be argued that there are very often "service imperatives" associated with particular tasks which lead to common organizational forms, and that this often gives us a better way of explaining or predicting institutional choice than either national style or overall administrative dilemmas. To suggest that there are "service imperatives" or organization is to parallel Richard Rose's (1984) argument, which, contrary to the "national style" approach, suggests that there are strong similarities between the nature and dynamics of each individual program area in each country.

But what exactly are organizational "service imperatives," and how could they be understood? A possible basis for such an approach would be the "transactional" approach to institutional analysis, which tries to identify the costs associated with exchange relationships in different decision situations (see Hood 1986; Kaufmann, Majone, and Ostrom 1986: 799–803). This approach has not been applied specifically to the choice of agency types for the provision of public services, but it could be fruitful in explaining such choices.

(1) Defining, resource mobilization, and social functions

Specifically, we suggest that the use of the three main legal/constitutional types of enterprise considered here may to some extent be linked with the different kinds of public service tasks associated with what Rose (1976) terms defining, resource mobilization, and social areas of policy, and that this may to some degree be explained by the transactional problems characteristic of each of these kinds of policy (Table 1).

"Defining" public service are, as the name implies, those which are part of the definition of government — that is, foreign affairs, arms, justice, revenue, and police (in its traditional senses of public health, public order, and the regulation of trade and commerce [Smith 1978: 398]). We suggest that the "hands-on" operation of such services has — at least since the French Revolution — tended to be conducted by core public bureaucracies, with independent public and private enterprises being used mainly for back-up and supply functions.

Resource mobilization functions are those which have to do with physical alteration of the landscape, infrastructural activities, the advancement of

Table 1: Para-Government Organization and Government Functions

Nature of Policy Area	Relative Salience		
	"Core" government enterprise	Independent public enterprise	Enterprise constituted as private or independent
Defining (Operational aspects)	High		
Physical Resource Mobilization		High	
Social			High

agriculture, forestry, fishing, transport, manufacturing, and so on. Such activities are not defining to government, but over the past century, governments everywhere have increasingly chosen to engage in this kind of provision. In practice, the operational aspects of resource mobilization matters are often *NOT* handled by core government enterprises or by bodies constituted as private or independent enterprises. Rather, we suggest, independent public enterprise has traditionally been prominent in this policy area.

Public services termed by Rose as "social" are those aimed at the advancement of citizens' welfare, by means such as income support, provision of housing, health, social work, home care, education, leisure, recreation, and entertainment facilities. Enterprises constituted as private or independent entities are everywhere highly salient in this field, notably in the form of nonprofit enterprises which are financed, encouraged, and in some cases even created by "core" government enterprises. To the extent that the "social" form of public policy has expanded in recent decades in most countries, it would follow that there would be an increase in the incidence of independent or private organizations providing public services in the recent past.

Rose shows, using documentary evidence on the composition of government in 32 Western-type countries, that government growth in the past has involved a long-term shift of emphasis from an original concentration on "defining" functions to greater emphasis on "resource mobilization" functions and then in turn to emphasis on "social functions." If our suggestion about the kinds of enterprise which are likely to be salient in each of these broad classes of public policy is correct, it would follow that over the course of this century institutional development in Western European countries would switch from an original focus on core public bureaucracy to increasing development of independent public enterprise, and then in turn switch to increasing use of private or independent enterprises for public service provision.

(2) The underlying preference for "minimum public power"

If there is a loose association between institutional type and policy area in Rose's schema, how could we explain it? A possible explanation is that such a pattern of institutional development follows from a preference for using the lightest bureaucratic tackle and the minimum amount of public power needed to deal with any specific task in hand. (Public power, of course, is the generic Roman-law term used to denote the special imperative powers of the state, in terms of command, prohibition, permission, and punishment.) If we assume that the administrative culture of Western European states (in the present day, at least) embodies such a preference, the outcome will generally be the pattern that we have described.

The implicit principle involved here is that of using "heavy-gauge" bureaucracy sparingly. This could spring from several possible sources. One is a preference for exercising public powers *civiliter* (that is, in a manner which is least burdensome in those over whom they are exercised), a preference for the least "bureaucratic" form of provision compatible with the task in hand, and for the performance of public tasks at the lowest possible level. The last is the principle of "subsidiarity," which was briefly mentioned earlier. This is central to the traditional Roman Catholic doctrine of the state (dating from the 1892 Papal Encyclical *De Rerum Novarum*) and is embedded in the public law of some Western European countries.

In general, such a preference would lead to a search for alternatives to classic public bureaucracy wherever feasible. This is because classic public bureaucracy tends to be the instrument of the most wide-ranging and rapidly changing use of the public power. Independent public enterprises, by contrast, typically exercise public power in a more restricted form or sphere (for instance, by compelling membership in a membership-controlled body as the least burdensome way of dealing with "holdout" situations without foreclosing choices about the quantity and quality of services to be produced. A case in point, described by Schleicher (1986: 523−525), is the compulsory-membership rule applied to the Ruhr *Wassergenossenschaften* (*Ruhrverband* and *Ruhrtalsperrenverein*) which prevented "holdout" behaviour by the various communities and enterprises involved in the management of the river basin. Enterprises constituted as private or independent have no special public power at their disposal.

A different way of explaining why a preference for the "subsidiarity principle" in public service provision should be built in to modern administration is Dunleavy's (1985) "bureau-shaping" account of bureaucratic behaviour. Dunleavy assumes that the shape of the bureaucracy is to a large degree determined by the preferences of top bureaucrats in central government. Dunleavy assumes that those bureau chiefs are primarily self-interested but, unlike many earlier writers approaching bureaucracy from economics-based methods of analysis, he assumes that most bureau chiefs derive little benefits from many kinds of budgetary and staff expansion in their bureaucracies. Accordingly, if those bureau chiefs are self-interested, they will aim to "shape" their bureaus in ways that may make those bureaus smaller, but re-fashion the bureaus in such a way as to contain more high-status staff and more discretionary budgets. This implies that, if the same reasoning is applied to independent public enterprises, both core government bureaus and independent public enterprises will be "shaped" in ways that shed staff, functions, and budgets to more autonomous forms of organization.

If we assume that Western European states in general prefer to use "minimum public power" in providing public services for one or both of those reasons, it would follow that private or independent enterprises would be preferred to public enterprises (independent or "core") wherever public services could be conveniently provided in that form without serious institu-tional failure: and that, where that is not so, independent public enterprises would be preferred to core public bureaucracies for any task where the risk of serious institutional failure is low. Institutional failure can be defined as high transactional costs (including delay, vexation, dissipation of energy) of arriving at agreements, dealing with "holdouts," breaking deadlocks, making service provision difficult or impossible. It is often associated with externali-ties (spillover costs for which the actor(s) who generate the costs cannot be obliged to pay, or spillover benefits which cannot be fully appropriated by those who create them).

For "defining" public services, problems of institutional failure, without the exercise of general-purpose public power, tend to be serious. Most defining services involve pure public goods. (That is, they confer benefits which could not feasibly be withheld from those who did not choose to pay for them voluntarily, which in their nature must be consumed collectively [whether consumers want them or not] and in which benefits conferred on one user does not necessarily reduce the benefit which is available to other users). This is the extreme point of the "externality" problem. Services like this can only be provided on the basis of taxation, and they may also involve uses of the public power in other ways, especially in emergencies — requisitioning of property and equipment, demands for information, powers of compulsion to order evacuation of dangerous buildings, and the like.

Moreover, most 'defining services' combine very high uncertainty (meaning that it is impossible to foresee and provide for all the possible contingencies in writing a performance contract) with inherently limited numbers of possible providers. If contingencies cannot easily be foreseen in advance, some ca-pacity for direct command is needed in order to deploy organizational forces in the way that seems best at the time.

In Williamson's (1975) analysis of institutional form based on transaction-cost analysis, a mixture of high uncertainty and small-numbers relationships is a circumstance in which direct employment and "hands-on" control from the centre are likely to have clear advantages over performance contracting and/or arms-length relationships. In Olson's (1971) analysis of collective action problems, taxation is the only possible financial basis for providing collective benefits if numbers are large, benefits diffused, and opportunism is widespread.

However, when it comes to services in the "resource mobilization" group, the problems are typically a little different. Many "resource mobilization" services involve some − but not *ALL* − of the features of public goods. That is, they often involve jointness of consumption, indivisibility of benefit, and infeasibility of making beneficiaries pay for what they enjoy − but often not all three things at once. Specifically, in resource mobilization, the factors leading to the use of the public power are typically: markets where competition is limited by substantial first-mover advantages (as in the case of public utility services); free-rider situations requiring compulsory levy powers over a defined group of beneficiaries (such as industrial training or tourist promotion), compulsory membership rules (as in the case of obligations to insure against sickness, unemployment, or legal liabilities to third parties), or regulatory powers of eminent domain (such as gas, electricity, telephones, cable TV, railways, etc.). In such circumstances, some degree of public power will be needed to break the power of holdouts and free riders (see Hardin 1968; Olson 1971; Ostrom 1974).

However, there is in many cases less inherent uncertainty about resources mobilizing services than applies to the "defining" group. Finance from general taxation is not necessarily needed. The need for "hands-on" control from the centre of government is thus weaker than it is for defining services. A preference for "minimum public power" would suggest that the appropriate instrument to deal with these kinds of problems is some form of enterprise which combines a degree of public power with a degree of legal independence from central government.

That way, public power can be exercised without the rigorous clearance rules (and resulting decision delays) associated with direct day-to-day control by government Ministers or other politicians elected on a general franchise, and perhaps without the elaborate audit and accountability rules associated with enterprises financed by periodic block allocations from a general tax fund. Well-known examples are independent statutory transport undertakings, public utilities, compulsory-membership aid-to-industry undertakings and statutory levy-financed boards.

When it comes to "social" functions, in Rose's terminology, the services involved typically do not have *ANY* of the features of public goods − unless we take a very extended view of "externalities." Governments often decide, as a matter of policy, to pay for "social" services in part or whole from general tax revenue. But there is no transactional reason, either in terms of uncertainty or of joint consumption properties, for any special measure of public power in the hands of the service-delivery organization, still less for "hands-on" control by the core of government. In this group, therefore, enterprises constituted as private or independent entities are likely to be able to provide services without institutional failure.

This framework for explaining institutional choice could not be expected to predict every case, particularly with traditional institutions, since the assumption that exercise of "minimum public power" is, consciously or otherwise, the driving force behind institutional choice in Western European countries does not necessarily extend to the distant past. Nor can this scheme get at the "fine grain" of institutional arrangements: the categories are broad and potentially ambiguous at the margin, especially for "resource mobilization" services. But, as a first step in applying the transactional approach to this area of institutional choice, this framework does what neither of the other two approaches reviewed here will do. That is, it will predict under what circumstances one rather than another type of enterprise will tend to be appropriate, and it will also explain why forms of organization other than core public bureaucracies have expanded in an apparently one-way manner in all Western European countries.

5. Conclusion

Where there are general phenomena, there should be equally general explanations. Explaining the distribution of public service provision among different forms of organization in terms of individual national style cannot help us to understand why independent public enterprises and private/independent organizations are such a common workhorse of modern public administration everywhere. Nor does such an approach offer much basis for a theory of agency types which tries to identify circumstances in which core public bureaucracies might be preferred to para-government organizations of one kind or another (or vice versa), or the circumstances in which one kind of para-government organization (a statutory authority, for example) might be preferred to another (such as a company or nonprofit association).

To understand the phenomenon of provision of public services by private or independent bodies properly, we need to discuss this phenomenon as an international — and transnational — phenomenon. We need an analytic approach which enables us to discuss institutional alternatives in general, not country-specific terms. An institutional dilemmas approach might in principle meet this requirement, but, in fact, it does not predict the "boom" in non-core government organization which appears to have developed in Western Europe. Some form of transactional approach, linked to contextual developments, seems a more promising basis for explanation.

References

Breton, A. (1974): *The Economic Theory of Representative Government*, London: Macmillan.

Chapman, R. and A. Dunsire (Eds.) (1971): *Style in Administration*, London: Allen and Unwin.

de Tocqueville, A. (1954): *Democracy in America*, 2 vols, New York: Vintage.

Downs, A. (1967): *Inside Bureaucracy*, New York: Wiley.

Dunleavy, P. (1985): "Bureaucrats, Budgets and the Growth of the State," *British Journal of Political Science* 15, 299–328.

Dunsire, A. (1978): *The Execution Process Vol 2: Control in a Bureaucracy*, Oxford: Martin Robertson.

Dyson, K. (1980): *The State Tradition in Western Europe*, Oxford: Martin Robertson.

Hahn, H. (1988): "PGOs in the OECD," in Hood and Schuppert (Eds.), 1988, 235–243.

Hardin, G. (1968): "The Tragedy of the Commons," *Science* 162 (December), 1243–1248.

Hilf, M. (1982): *Die Organisationsstruktur der Europäischen Gemeinschaften*, Heidelberg: Springer.

Hood, C. C. (1976): *The Limits of Administration*, London: Wiley.

Hood, C. C. (1986): *Administrative Analysis*, Brighton: Wheatsheaf.

Hood, C. C. and G. F. Schuppert (Eds.) (1988): *Delivering Public Services in Western Europe: Sharing Western European Experience of Para-Government Organization*, London: Sage.

Illich, I. (1972): *Deschooling Society*, London: Calder and Boyers.

Kaufmann, F.-X., G. Majone, and V. Ostrom (Eds.) (1986): *Guidance, Control and Evaluation in the Public Sector*, Berlin: de Gruyter.

Keynes, J. M. (1952): *Essays in Persuasion*, London: Macmillan.

Lowi, T. J. (1969): *The End of Liberalism*, New York: Norton.

Marshall, G. (1984): *Constitutional Conventions: The Rules and Forms of Political Accountability*, Oxford: Clarendon.

McLaren, R. I. (1982): *Organizational Dilemmas*, Chichester: John Wiley.

Morrison, A. (1933): *Socialisation and Transport*, London: Constable.

Mueller, D. C. (1979): *Public Choice*, Cambridge: Cambridge University Press.

Naisbitt, J. (1982): *Megatrends: Ten New Directions Shaping Our Lives*, New York: Warner Books.

Niskanen, W. A. (1971): *Bureaucracy and Representative Government*, Chicago: Aldine Atherton.

Nitti, F. (1974): *Discorsi Parlamentari*, Rome: Grafica Editrice Romana.

Olson, M. (1971): *The Logic of Collective Action: Public Goods and the Theory of Groups*, Rev. ed., New York: Schocken Books.

Ostrom, V. (1974): *The Intellectual Crisis in American Public Administration*, Rev. ed., Tuscaloosa, Ala.: University of Alabama Press.

Perrow, C. (1979): *Complex Organizations: A Critical Essay*, 2nd ed., Glenview, Ill.: Scott, Foresman.

Reports of the Machinery of Government Committee (1918): Cd. 9230, London: H. M. Stationery Office.

Richardson, J. (Ed.) (1982): *Policy Styles in Western Europe*, London: Allen and Unwin.

Rose, R. (1976): "On the Priorities of Government: A Developmental Analysis of Public Policies," *European Journal of Political Research* 4, 247–289.

Rose, R. (1984): *Understanding Big Government: The Programme Approach*, London: Sage.

Schleicher, H. (1986): "Building Coordination Structure," in Kaufmann, Majone, and Ostrom (Eds.), 1986, 510–530.

Sharkansky, I. (1979): *Wither the State?* Chatham, N. J.: Chatham House Publishers.

Smith, A. (1978): *Lectures on Jurisprudence*, R. L. Meek, D. D. Raphael, and P. G. Stein (Eds.), Oxford: Clarendon Press.

Steinbruner, J. (1974): *The Cybernetic Theory of Decision*, Princeton: Princeton University Press.

Tullock, G. (1965): *The Politics of Bureaucracy*, Washington, D.C.: Public Affairs Press.

Wagner, R. E. (1973): *The Public Economy*, Chicago: Markham.

Wegener, R. (1978): *Staat und Verbände im Sachbereich Wohlfahrtspflege*, Berlin: Duncker and Humblot.

Wilenski, P. (1986): *Public Power and Public Administration*, Sydney: Hale and Iremonger/RAIPA.

Williamson, O. E. (1975): *Markets and Hierarchies*, London: Collier Macmillan.

Wilson, W. (1887): "The Study of Administration," *Political Science Quarterly* 2, 197–222.

2.6
Organizational Behavior and Organizational Function: Toward a Micro—Macro Theory of the Third Sector

Wolfgang Seibel

1. Introduction*

In recent years, the near-bankruptcy of the union-owned housing corporation "Neue Heimat" has been the most important and most publicized case of nonprofit organizational failure in the Federal Republic of Germany. However, when one reads the two related parliamentary commissions reports (Bürgerschaft der Freien und Hansestadt Hamburg 1986; Deutscher Bundestag 1987) on "Neue Heimat" and its activities, one is struck by its long-lasting organizational well-being despite pervasive mismanagement.

My own inquiries into mismanagement in the "Third Sector" (Seibel 1988, 1989) have illustrated similar paradoxical phenomena: organizational survival despite organizational failure. Obviously, nonprofit organizations can survive, even in the long run, despite a substantial lack of organizational learning and responsiveness.

How can this paradox be explained? Economists may refer to theories on inefficiency of public bureaucracies (Niskanen 1971): Public bureaucracies may fail, yet they will hardly disappear. However, this leads to a theoretical impasse. How can we explain, then, the delivery of public goods by non-public organizations? Either, nonprofit organizations with their part-public — part-private status are simply treated as quasi-public enterprises in which case the assumption of a "Third Sector" would obviously make no sense. Or, the assumption of a "Third Sector" is maintained, and, in that case, the "third" (nonprofit) type of organizations must deliver something else but public goods.

I will argue that there are good reasons to assume nonprofit organizations to survive *not despite* but *because of* their notorious lack of efficiency and responsiveness. This does not mean that nonprofit organizations are

---

* This article had already been completed when Marshall W. Meyer's and Lynne G. Zucker's superb book on "Permanently Failing Organizations" (London/Beverly Hills: Sage 1989) was published. The Mayer & Zucker book provides a broad based microanalytic complement to the present functionalist approach.

inevitably inefficient and irresponsive. Rather, my argument is that part-public—part-private organizations of the nonprofit type exhibit a broader range of inefficiency and irresponsiveness than private for-profit organizations and public bureaucracies, and that this peculiar organizational behavior is a prerequisite for the peculiar social and political function of nonprofit organizations: that is, *to cope with the political risks of organizational efficiency and responsiveness in a democratic society.* The assumption of organizational survival through organizational failure appears so contradictuous to basic dogmas of organization theory that some preliminary remarks on the relatedness of organizational behavior and organizational function are necessary.

2. Organizational Behavior and Organizational Function

The concept of "organizational behavior" is linked with the progression from "classic" to "modern" organization theory (cf. Argyris 1960; March and Simon 1958: 1–11). Especially by the writings of Herbert Simon and his collaborators, the focus of organization theory had shifted from formal structures *of* organizations to decision making *in* organizations. Theoretical prescriptions for rational decision making were replaced by theoretical concepts of *"satisfying decision making"* and limited rationality. Cyert and March argued that every decision is "rational" which maintains or improves the fitness of an organization according to an environment which is basically uncontrolled (Cyert and March 1963: 99–101).

Thus, the concept of *organization-environment* was introduced into organization theory (cf. Aldrich 1979), and the theoretical focus shifted once more from decision-making behavior to organizational behavior in general. By now, however, *evolutionary theory* had also become part of organization theory. If like Darwin's natural beings, organizations are to "survive" in a given environment, they must develop certain behaviors and functions to accord with the demands made by the environment.

3. The Concept of Organizational Isomorphism and Some Vexing Problems in Explaining the Existence of a "Third Sector"

What was really new with Cyert and March's approach to organizational behavior was not the idea that a lack of organizational adjustment to environmental requirements is necessarily "punished" by organizational failure, but rather their focus on the general patterns of the relationship between organization and the environment. Cyert and March and their theoretical imitators *implicitly* assumed *a certain type* of organization-environment relationship. The ideal-type still remained the formal organization with vertically and horizontally differentiated task-structures and professional staff such as can be found in industrial and public bureaucracies. This means implicitly, that this ideal-type of organization is optimally adapted to the environmental requirements both of the market and the administrative state. Max Weber, however, had already made this basic argument about the functions of modern bureaucracy; today scholars call it the concept of *organizational isomorphism* (Hannan and Freeman 1977: 938–939; DiMaggio and Powell 1983), and assume a general trend to isomorphic organizational culture based on the formal type of "bureaucracy" as archetype.

There are widely accepted agreements on the general functions of the modern formalized organization. In Max Weber's view, formal hierarchy and the division of labor along with well-regulated and professionalized organization is the functional prerequisite of organizational stability and responsibility necessary for both the industrial and the public bureaucracies of modern capitalism. Similarly, the economic theory of the firm (cf. Coase 1937; Williamson 1975) assumes that a hierarchical and formal authority shapes a superior type of organization through minimizing transaction costs. Left-wing German jurists and political scientists in the 1920s emphasized the role of formalized public bureaucracies in modern democracies as they saw formal public bureaucracies as the core-mechanism of administration which could inhibit the arbitrary action of bureaucrats (Heller 1934; Kelsen 1925) in a majority rule system.

From these points of view, the modern industrialized society generates a "modern" organizational culture with a more or less homogeneous type of organizational behavior. It is agreed that both industrial and public bureaucracies have not only flexibility in their organizational *responsiveness*, but also rigidity in their organizational *efficiency*. Given this, an equilibrium of organizational behavior and environmental requirements may be assumed. Organizatiohal outputs – production of commodities, social and political integration – and organizational stability, then, are reciprocal requirements.

Today, such rough concepts of organizational function and organizational behavior may raise objections that then take no account of latent organizational functions or even of dysfunctions in the bureaucratic type of organization (cf. Merton 1968: 73–138). However, there is no doubt that the ubiquitous existence of modern bureaucracies in industrialized societies is due to their general ability to reduce market transaction costs, to enhance an allocative efficiency, and to provide both flexible and reliable structures of collective action in an open society with a democratic political system.

The logic of this argument seems to hold in the world of private enterprises and public bureaucracies. But what about a "third" sector? Early European theoreticians argued that even organizations which are neither public nor private cannot resist the adaptive force of the market and/or of the modern administrative state (cf. Michels 1911; Oppenheimer 1896). In this regard, alternatives to the "modern" type of organization found in the private for-profit and the public sphere are seen as a sort of catch-all for arbitrary, accidental, or "monster" forms of organization within a mainly isomorphic organizational culture which can only have a short life cycle. The "deviant" organizational behavior must either disappear in order to conform to the "normal" organizational structures, or the organization itself must disappear. In either case, the designation third *"sector"* would hardly be justified for such short-lived organizations.

Thus, one either assumes (like Oppenheimer and Michels) that long-term organizational behavior in the third sector is similar to that of private enterprises and/or public bureaucracies, because of the functional necessity of organizational responsiveness and efficiency; or, one assumes that organizational behavior in the third sector differs substantially from organizational behavior in the private or the public sector, because of functional necessities *other* than organizational responsiveness and efficiency.

The former hypothesis presupposes organizational isomorphism as an explanatory variable for the third sector, while the latter hypothesis allows for resistance by third sector organizations against the isomorphic pressures of the private-competitive and the public-administrative environment. The first hypothesis asks the question: under what conditions will which type of goods be provided by third sector organizations in a responsive and efficient way? The second hypothesis focuses on the peculiarities of a "deviant" organizational behavior as well as on its special functions. On the one hand, if third sector organizations display behavior identical to private enterprises and public bureaucracies — why posit the existence of another, or "third," sector? On the other hand, if the modern type of formalized organization satisfies optimally the requirements of efficiency and responsiveness in democratic industrial society, how can we explain the survival of a less efficient and responsive type of organizations?

In fact, there are no satisfactory answers to the questions the first hypothesis poses. All the economic models which try to explain the existence of nonprofit organizations argue that nonprofits compensate for either market failure or government failure under certain circumstances of supply and demand (Rose-Ackerman 1986; and James, chapter 1.2 in this volume). For instance, Weisbrod's (1986, 1988) supramedian-demand hypothesis contends that nonprofits have a competitive advantage over public provision in supplying distinctive, collective goods or collective goods in a particular quality. Hansmann (1986) cites the example of information asymmetries where the purchasers and consumers of a service are not identical (for example, old people's homes or day care). In these cases, a special degree of trustworthyness is required which, as Hansmann points out, nonprofits are better able to provide. Both supply-side and demand-side hypotheses agree that nonprofits have competitive advantages in micro-environments where they are supposed to be more responsive and/or efficient than private enterprises or public bureaucracies (cf. Hansmann 1987, and James in this volume).

However, none of these theories present evidence as to why nonprofit organizations *instead of government* should compensate for market failure, or why nonprofit organizations *instead of private firms* should compensate for government failure (Salamon 1987). Nor can we assume that, when market failure *and* government failure coincide, nonprofits will provide the optimum degree of organizational responsiveness and efficiency.

4. The Niche-Phenomenon in Modern Organizational Culture: X-Inefficiency and Population Ecology of Organizations as an Approach to the Third Sector

If nonprofit organizations have no advantage in organizational responsiveness and efficiency, what kind of relationship between organizational functions and organizational behavior must we assume if we wish to theoretically justify the designation "Third Sector"? One characteristic which is in discussion in the *niche theory of organizations* is the resistence that nonprofit (third sector) organizations display vis-à-vis the adaptive pressure of market forces and public bureaucracies.

The economist Harvey Leibenstein as well as the sociologists Michael Hannan and John Freeman critically examined neo-classical economic theory which argues against the survival of badly managed and inefficient enterprises, and sociological theory of organizational isomorphism, which argues against the endurance of "deviant" organizational behavior in a modern organizational culture. The authors confront these basic dogmas of organization theory with the phenomenon of *organizational inertia* which, they assert, reduces adaptability to a given environment. This may cause few problems within a stable environment. However, given changing conditions, any lack of organizational adaptability, according to these theorists, will most likely lead to organizational failure (bankruptcy, dissolution) or (Huntington 1952) organizational marasmus.

Leibenstein in particular observed that organizations survive despite more or less serious inefficiency and reduction in welfare. Clearly, this does not conform to neo-classical economics' assumption of general congruence between allocative efficiency in a competitive environment and organizational efficiency of the firm. Leibenstein, however, insists that stable organizational inefficiency is not inevitably punished by the adaptive pressure exerted by allocative efficiency of the market. This type of efficiency he calls *"X-Efficiency"* resp. *"X-Inefficiency"* (Leibenstein 1966 and 1976).

In pursuing his argument, Leibenstein points out that a firm's inefficiency has repercussions on the market. In an inert market, competitors will observe each other and may evade competition and its uncertain consequences. In addition, these non-competitive and inert firms often will try to influence their environment through, as Buchanan et al. (1980) call it, "rent-seeking" behavior such as claims for legal protection against competitors as well as for public subsidies. The aggregate effect of all this, Leibenstein points out, is the creation of *inert areas*, i. e. reservations or *niches* within the market process, where the adaptive pressure for allocative efficiency is partially suspended.

Hannan and Freeman (1977) deliver a general theory for such organizational niches (independent of Leibenstein). They start from the tension between organizational adaptability and organizational stability. Organizational inertia (such as lack of responsiveness and efficiency) can be treated as the price of stability. Up to a certain point − until a variable threshold of dysfunction is transgressed − organizational inertia constitutes a prerequisite for organizational survival. Any organization should maintain a certain corridor of inertia in order to maintain both flexibility and stability. However, it is not clear how to apply this general theory to the examination of single organizations: it is mainly a theory of *populations of organization*, or organizational fields where different "ecological equilibria" between organization and environment may exist (Hannan and Freeman 1977).

Whereas Leibenstein concludes that organizational "X-Inefficiency" represents a source of welfare losses (i. e. as a type of economic dysfunction), Hannan and Freeman's theory of organizational ecology and ecological *niches* within organizational fields allows us to consider on the *societal functions* of organizational inefficiency. If we cannot definitively explain the existence of a "Third Sector" by the responsiveness and efficiency under certain circumstances of supply and demand, we may wonder whether the environment of the market combined with administrative state can tolerate "ecological niches" for organizations with a lower degree of responsiveness and efficiency — given that excessive inertia and excessive responsiveness *both* carry risks?

I will argue that the so-called "Third Sector" represents such a *niche for organizational behavior with a low degree of responsiveness and efficiency*, because "Third Sector" niche alleviates a *dilemma of legitimacy* in a democratic political system.

5. Organizational Behavior and Political Functionalism: The Third Sector as Response to Legitimacy-Dilemmas in Modern Democracy

It is stated here that the Third Sector *reduces the risks of organizational responsiveness and efficiency without increasing the risk of organizational inertia.* For instance, when market and government failure coincide, private firms and public bureaucracies, whose behavior is based on organizational responsiveness and efficiency, may endanger a market economy and its democratic political system. Thus, in the 1970s, Marxist as well as liberal and conservative scholars argued that the relative loss of public welfare and the government's incapacity to satisfy the increased demand for public goods would lead to a crisis of governability (Crozier et al. 1975; Habermas 1973; Poulantzas 1977).

As a matter of fact, democratic political systems find it difficult to resist increased societal demand for public goods, since majoritarian decision making implies the transformation of societal demand into governmental action and administrative performance. It is precisely government's responsiveness and efficiency which provides the basis for legitimacy in a democratic system. The democratic system must not only deliver the public goods but also conform to the due process of majoritarian decision making.

However, majoritarian decision making may infringe on ideological and political taboos, such as the free market economy, or may extend the government's capacity to provide goods. In other words: responsiveness, which, under other circumstances, is essential for organizational survival, may inhibit the continued existence of democratic government and public administration. This dilemma can, however, be mitigated by a partial suspension of organizational responsiveness and efficiency.

Accordingly, the structural weakening of governmental responsiveness and administrative efficiency is common to all Western democracies. For instance,

in the West German case, a strong sense of common political values, as well
as the influential role of juridicial decision making in politics and policy,
impede both political radicalism and innovation (Katzenstein 1987). However, restrictions of governmental responsiveness cannot be pursued too far,
as it weakens the legitimacy of the political system.

Thus, the potential dilemma of legitimacy means that government is
expected to be both responsive and efficient, yet these same characteristics
may create crises of governability. One way out of this impasse is to alter
general expectations toward reduced public expenditure. But recent experiences in Western democracies (like France or West Germany) indicate the
limited options for this type of political strategy. Given certain expectations
about the level of public expenditures, the reconciliation of responsiveness
with governability can presumably not be achieved within *governmental*
structures of decision making and delivery of public goods.

To resolve the dilemma, what is needed is a type of organization which,
like government organizations, compensates for market failure but, unlike
the government, also provides an extended range of structural irresponsiveness and inefficiency. At the same time, it must not interfere with the
functioning and legitimacy of democratic government. According to the
theory of organizational isomorphism, one could not imagine such a "special
type" of organization which, however, Leibenstein's theory of X-Inefficiency
and Hannan and Freeman's theory of population ecology of organization
allow for the "third sector."

Within their framework, third sector organizations which provide public
goods are, in one way or another, loosely connected with government.
Although the government exerts influence over them, they are not legitimated
by their connection to the government. Thus, the lack of organizational
responsiveness and legitimacy is not only more tolerable than it is in the
public sector, but it is also a structural prerequisite for coping with the
contradictory societal and political demands which, by itself, government
cannot resolve.

6. Patterns of Micro-Behavior and Macro-Functions

As I have illustrated elsewhere (Seibel 1987, 1989), the present "crisis of
the welfare state" is characterized, to a large extent, by such seemingly
unsolvable problems: If, for instance, West German hospital funding is
like a black hole absorbing not only billions of Deutschmarks, but also
the energy of thousands of policy experts and activists — why not use
the structural inertia of the semi-public hospital system as a *cordon*

sanitaire to both disguise and buffer (but definitively not "solve") the initial problem. Another example occurs in the case of handicapped people. Since it is highly unlikely that the beneficiaries of the West German "Gravely Handicapped People Act" (*Schwerbehindertengesetz*) will find an appropriate employment in the present economic crisis — why not establish a semi-public nonprofit day care, called "Workshops for Handicapped People" (*Werkstätten für Behinderte*). These do not solve any problem but are nevertheless welcomed by clergymen and local politicians, who are represented in the workshop's boards, as tools to consolidate networks of mutual support. A final case in point is the battered women's movement. Public money is provided for independently run battered women shelters even though they are often poorly organized and badly run, thus paralyzing the women's movement by a "tyranny of structurelessness" (Freeman 1972) and segregating a social problem from government's responsibility.

But what happens really in these niches for organizational irresponsiveness and inefficiency? What are the patterns of micro-organizational behavior shaping the macro-political function of these third sector arrangements? If we expect third sector organizations to display a lack of responsiveness and efficiency, we have to expand the scope of our analysis.

Alternatives to hierarchical organization, professional management, formal procedures of decision making, and differentiation of competence and responsibility, may be distinguished according to different levels of organizational and personal coordination (cf. Kaufmann 1986: 213):

— inter-organizational coordination,
— intra-organizational coordination,
— inter-individual coordination,
— intra-individual coordination.

The *Weber*ian ideal-type of modern organization assumes *tightly coupled* patterns of inter-organizational coordination, *formal structures* of intra-organizational coordination, *impersonal* patterns of inter-individual coordination, and *non-ideological* patterns of intra-individual coordination. Demodernized patterns of organizational behavior in the niches may be conceptualized as partial or total suspension of the foregoing mechanisms of coordination.

Obviously, loose instead of tight coupling, informal instead of formal organizational structures, personal instead of unpersonal inter-individual relations, and ideological belief systems instead of role distance and empathy influence "modern" organizational behavior of private firms and public bureaucracies as well. In this respect, they are hardly distinct from third sector organizations. However, the existence of a "third" sector beside the private and the public sector may be confirmed theoretically if one assumes a special institutional zone ("niche") of structural elasticity which tolerate a broader span of de-modernized patterns of organizational behavior. These patterns may be classified according to the different levels of organizational and personal coordination (see Table 1).

Table 1: Patterns of De-modernized Organizational Behavior According to Levels of Organizational and Personal Coordination

Levels of coordination[1]	mechanisms of coordination
Inter-organizational	Loose Coupling[2], Interpolable Balance[3], Polyarchy[4], Bargaining[5]
Intra-organizational	'Type Z' Organization[6], X-Inefficiency[7]
Inter-individual	Solidarity[8], Clans[9], "political money"[10], Quasi-Corruption[11]
Intra-individual	Altruism[12], "closed minds"[13], Ideology

In reconsidering the three West German examples of third sector arrangements (cf. Seibel 1989), we may now distinguish more precisely the dialectics of micro-organizational behavior and macro-political function.

In the West German system of *Hospital Funding*, the easing of tensions between institutions could not take place without the *loose coupling* of inter-organizational relations within the *polyarchical* system of government (state level), hospitals (public of private-nonprofit), and insurance companies (private or para-governmental). The continuous *bargaining* processes between these partners stabilize the *interpolable balance* within the polyarchical sys-

[1] Kaufmann 1986: 213
[2] Glassman 1973; Granovetter 1973.
[3] Hood 1986.
[4] Dahl 1978.
[5] Dahl and Lindblom 1953: 272−323.
[6] Ouchi and Jaeger 1978: Ouchi 1981; 71−94.
[7] Leibenstein 1976: 29−47.
[8] Gretschmann 1986; Hegner 1986.
[9] Ouchi 1980.
[10] Coleman 1970.
[11] Rose-Ackerman 1978.
[12] Derlega and Grzelak 1982.
[13] Rokeach 1960.

tem, inevitably leading to inefficient behavior of the hospitals. This economically inefficient behavior, however, becomes tolerable *"X-inefficiency,"* because hospitals inhabit a niche of institutional compromise. In the case of the *Workshops for Handicapped People*, the niche for organizational *X-inefficiency* is formed by *clans* of local elites, using the workshop's board of directors as a market place where *"political money"* becomes a convertible currency for the purchase of influence and power within the process of local social policy making. Thus, the illusion is created that "something is going on," even if hardly anything happens which benefits the handicapped themselves. Finally, the independent *shelters for battered women* are able to survive despite inefficiency, because they inhabit a niche peculiar to *type-z-organizations* (in the Ouchi sense): *solidarity* among women and individual *altruism* are combined into a relatively stable belief system of feminist *ideology*. The resulting *closed minds* make tolerable the hopeless situation of battered women and their helpers and provoke endless and energy-absorbing quarrels with the subsidy-giving municipalities which, consequently, are perceived as the incarnation of patriarchy.

7. Conclusion and Suggestions for Further Research

I have argued that third sector organizations are characterized by an extended variety of organizational options such as irresponsiveness and inefficiency, thus creating an arrangement of *de-modernized niches in modern organizational culture*. This gives rise to questions which should be considered for further research.

Are all types of third sector organization likely to inhabit a de-modernized niche? What kind of social and political problems are likely to be absorbed by those niches? To what can we attribute the persistence of these niches? What about the niche-width for different types of third sector organizations? Who builds and protects the niches and their environment? Is this the government? Volunteers? Influential clans? Are there life cycles particular to third sector organizations? Are there different national patterns of de-modernized niches in organizational culture? What are the dialectics of modernization regarding the three sectors (private, public, third sector)?

While facing these questions, third sector research must also expand present research strategies. Although the crisis of the welfare state has been recognized as the core-issue of the developing third sector research (see James ch. 1.2 and Seibel and Anheier ch. 1.1 in this volume), no systematic inquiries have been undertaken yet into its impact on the intermediary zone between the market and the state. While political scientists have analyzed interest intermediation in the zone between the market and the state (Berger 1981; Lehmbruch and Schmitter 1982; Schmitter and Lehmbruch 1979) without taking into account its micro-organizational conditionality, third sector research itself still prefers micro-analytical approaches without regarding the macropolitical functionalism of service-providing organizations such as non-profit-/non-governmental organization.

In general, economic and socio-political as well as micro- and macro-analytical perspectives must be integrated for an understanding of the third sector's role in the modern welfare state. Given the assumption that the third sector is somewhat like an institutional hinge mitigating the crisis of the welfare state, research must analyze the micro-organizational conditionality of political function. Furthermore, cross-national analyses will illuminate how different countries adapt their institutions to the macro-political requirements of the welfare state in crisis.

References

Aldrich, H. E. (1979): *Organizations and Environments*, Englewood Cliffs, N.J.: Prentice-Hall.

Argyris, C. (1960): *Understanding Organizational Behavior*, Homewood, Ill.: The Dorsey Press.

Badelt, C. (1984): "Institutioneller Wandel in der Bereitstellung Sozialer Dienste," *Jahrbuch für Politische Ökonomie* 3, 122 – 141.

Barnard, Ch. I. (1938): *The Functions of the Executive*, Cambridge, Mass.: Harvard University Press.

Berger, S. (Ed.) (1981): *Organizing interests in Western Europe. Pluralism, Corporatism, and the Transformation of Politics*, Cambridge and London: Cambridge University Press.

Buchanan, J. M., R. D. Tollison, and G. Tullock (Eds.) (1980): *Toward a Theory of the Rent-Seeking Society*, College Station, Texas: Texas A & M University Press.

Bürgerschaft der Freien und Hansestadt Hamburg (1986): "Bericht des Parlamentarischen Untersuchungsausschusses zur Überprüfung der Aufsichtstätigkeit der Behörden gegenüber der Geschäftätigkeit der Unternehmensgruppe Neue Heimat sowie der Geschäftsbeziehungen zwischen der Freien und Hansestadt Hamburg und der Unternehmensgruppe Neue Heimat," Drucksache 11/5900 v. 7. 5. 1986.

Coase, R. H. (1937): "The Nature of the Firm," *Economica* N.S. 4, 386 – 405.

Coleman, J. S. (1970): "Political Money," *American Political Science Review* 64, 1074 – 1087.

Crozier, M. et al. (1975) (Eds.): *The Crisis of Democracy*, New York: New York University Press.

Cyert, R. M. and J. G. March (1963): *A Behavioral Theory of the Firm*, Englewood Cliffs, N.J.: Prentice-Hall.

Dahl, R. A. (1978): *Polyarchy. Participation and Opposition*, 5th pr., New Haven/London: Yale University Press.

Dahl, R. A. and Ch. E. Lindblom (1953): *Politics, Economics, and Welfare. Planning and Politico-Economic Systems Resolved into Basic Social Processes*, Chicago and London: The University of Chicago Press.

Derlega, V. J. and J. Grzelak (Eds.) (1982): *Cooperation and Helping Behavior. Theories and Research*, New York and London: Academic Press.

Deutscher Bundestag (1987): "Beschlußempfehlung und Bericht des 3. Untersuchungs-ausschusses 'Neue Heimat'," Drucksache 10/6779 v. 7.1.1987.

DiMaggio, P. J. and W. W. Powell (1983): "The Iron Cage Revisited: Institutional Isomorphism and Collective Rationality in Organizational Fields," *American Sociological Review* 48, 147–160.

Freeman, J. (1972): "The Tyranny of Structurelessness," *Berkeley Journal of Sociology* 17, 151–164.

Glassman, R. B. (1973): "Persistence and Loose Coupling in Living Systems," *Behavioral Science* 18, 83–98.

Granovetter, M. S. (1973): "The Strength of Weak Ties," *American Journal of Sociology* 78, 1360–1380.

Gretschmann, K. (1986): "Solidarity and Markets," in *Guidance, Control and Evaluation in the Public Sector*, F.-X. Kaufmann, G. Majone, and V. Ostrom (Eds.), Berlin and New York: de Gruyter, 387–405.

Habermas, J. (1973): *Legitimationsprobleme im Spätkapitalismus*, Frankfurt a. M.: Suhrkamp.

Hannan, M. T. and J. Freeman (1977): "The Population Ecology of Organizations," *American Journal of Sociology* 82, 929–964.

Hannan, M. T. and J. Freeman (1983): "Niche Width and the Dynamics of Organizational Populations," *American Journal of Sociology* 88, 1116–1145.

Hannan, M. T. and J. Freeman (1984): "Structural Inertia and Organizational Change," *American Sociological Review* 49, 149–164.

Hansmann, H. (1986): "The Role of Nonprofit Enterprise," in *The Economics of Nonprofit Institutions. Studies in Structure and Policy*, S. Rose-Ackerman (Ed.), New York and Oxford: Oxford University Press, 57–84 (reprinted from: *Yale Law Journal* 89, 1980).

Hansmann, H. (1987): "Economic Theories of Nonprofit Organizations," in *The Nonprofit Sector. A Research Handbook*, Walter W. Powell (Ed.), New Haven and London: Yale University Press, 27–42.

Hegner, F. (1986): "Solidarity and Hierarchy: Institutional Arrangements for the Coordination of Actions," in *Guidance, Control and Evaluation in the Public Sector*, F.-X. Kaufmann, G. Majone, and V. Ostrom (Eds.), Berlin and New York: de Gruyter, 407–429.

Heller, H. [1934] (1970): *Staatslehre*, ed. by Gerhart Niemeyer, 4th pr., Leiden: A. W. Sijthoff.

Hood, C. (1986): "Concepts of Control over Bureaucracies: 'Comptrol' and 'Interpolable Balance'," in *Guidance, Control and Evaluation in the Public Sector*, F.-X. Kaufmann, G. Majone, and V. Ostrom (Eds.), Berlin and New York: de Gruyter, 765–783.

Huntington, S. P. (1952): "The Marasmus of the ICC: The Commission, the Railroads, and the Public Interest," *Yale Law Journal* 61, 467–509.

Katzenstein, P. (1987): *Politics and Policy in West Germany. The Growth of a Semi-Sovereign State*, Ithaca, N.Y.: Cornell University Press.

Kaufmann, F.-X. (1986): "The Relationship between Guidance, Control and Evaluation," in *Guidance, Control and Evaluation in the Public Sector*, F.-X. Kaufmann, G. Majone, and V. Ostrom (Eds.), Berlin and New York: de Gruyter, 211–228.

Kaufmann, F.-X., G. Majone, and V. Ostrom (Eds.) (1986): *Guidance, Control and Evaluation in the Public Sector*, Berlin and New York: de Gruyter.

Kelsen, H. (1925): *Allgemeine Staatslehre*, Berlin: Julius Springer.

Lehmbruch, G. and Ph. C. Schmitter (Eds.) (1982): *Patterns of Corporatist Policy-Making*, London and Beverly Hills: Sage.

Leibenstein, H. (1966): "Allocative Efficiency versus 'X-Efficiency'," *American Economic Review* 56, 392–415.

Leibenstein, H. (1976): *Beyond Economic Man. A New Foundation for Microeconomics*, Cambridge, Mass./London: Harvard University Press.

March, J. G. and H. A. Simon (with the collab. of Harold Guetzkow) (1958): *Organizations*, New York etc.: John Wiley & Sons.

Merton, R. K. (1968): *Social Theory and Social Structure*, 1968 enl. ed., New York and London: The Free Press.

Michels, R. (1911): *Zur Soziologie des Parteiwesens in der modernen Demokratie. Untersuchungen über die oligarchischen Tendenzen des Gruppenlebens*, Stuttgart: Kröner.

Niskanen, W. A. (1971): *Bureaucracy and Representative Government*, Chicago: Aldine-Atherton.

Oppenheimer, F. (1896): *Die Siedlungsgenossenschaft. Versuch einer positiven Überwindung des Kommunismus durch Lösung des Genossenschaftsproblems und der Agrarfrage*, Jena: Gustav Fischer.

Ouchi, W. G. (1980): "Markets, Bureaucracies, and Clans," *Administrative Science Quarterly* 25, 129–141.

Ouchi, W. G. (1981): *Theory Z. How American Business Can Meet the Japanese Challenge*, Reading, Mass.: Addison-Wesley.

Ouchi, W. G. and A. M. Jaeger (1978): "Type Z Organization: Stability in the Midst of Mobility," *The Academy of Management Review* 3, 305–314.

Poulantzas, N. (1977): *L'état, le pouvoir, le socialisme*, Paris: Presse Universitaire de France.

Rokeach, M. (Ed.) (1960): The Open and Closed Mind. Investigation into the Nature of Belief Systems and Personality Systems, New York: Basic Books.

Rose-Ackerman, S. (1978): *Corruption. A Study in Political Economy*, New York, San Francisco, and London: Academic Press.

Rose-Ackerman, S. (Ed.) (1986): *The Economics of Nonprofit Institutions. Studies in Structure and Policy*, New York and Oxford: Oxford University Press.

Salamon, L. M. (1987): "On Market Failure, Voluntary Failure, and Third-Party Government: Toward a Theory of Government–Nonprofit Relations in the Modern Welfare State," *Journal of Voluntary Action Research* 16, 29–49.

Salamon, L. M. and A. J. Abramson (1982): *The Federal Budget and the Nonprofit Sector*, Washington, D.C.: The Urban Institute Press.

Schmitter, Ph. C. and G. Lehmbruch (Eds.) (1979): *Trends Toward Corporatist Intermediation*, Beverly Hills and London: Sage.

Seibel, W. (1987): "Der Staatsstil für Krisenzeiten. 'Selbststeuerung' öffentlicher Aufgabenträger und das Problem der Kontrolle," *Politische Vierteljahresschrift* 28, 197–219.

Seibel, W. (1988): "Der funktionale Dilettantismus. Zur politischen Soziologie von Steuerungs- und Kontrollversagen im 'Dritten Sektor' zwischen Markt und Staat," unpublished book manuscript, University of Kassel, FRG.

Seibel, W. (1989): "The Function of Mellow Weakness. Nonprofit Organizations as Problem Nonsolvers in Germany," in *The Nonprofit Sector in International Perspective. Studies in Comparative Culture and Policy*, Estelle James (Ed.), New York and Oxford: Oxford University Press, 177–192.

Weisbrod, B. A. (1986): "Toward a Theory of the Voluntary Nonprofit Sector in a Three-Sector Economy," in *The Economics of Nonprofit Institutions. Studies in Structure and Policy*, S. Rose-Ackerman (Ed.), New York and Oxford: Oxford University Press, 21–44 (reprinted from: *The Voluntary Nonprofit Sector*, B. A. Weisbrod (Ed.), Lexington, Mass. and Toronto: D. C. Heath & Co. 1977).

Weisbrod, B. A. (1988): *The Nonprofit Economy*, Cambridge, Mass. and London: Harvard University Press.

Williamson, O. E. (1975): *Markets and Hierarchies. Analysis and Anti-Trust Implications. A Study in the Economics of Internal Organization*, New York and London: The Free Press.

2.7
Competition, Resources, and Strategy in the British Nonprofit Sector

Susan K. E. Saxon-Harrold

1. Introduction

Organizations in the voluntary sector have received little attention from researchers in the field of organizational analysis in Britain. In practice, the strategy of organizations in the voluntary sector has been assumed to be passive, concentrating on a cooperative role with other voluntary, commercial, or public organizations. This chapter examines the strategies of 75 voluntary organizations and argues that strategy is less likely to be fashioned by internal organizational factors than from variations in the degree to which the organization is constrained by external critical dependencies in its environment. The chapter focusses on competition and resource dependence as prime interdependencies that have a commensurate effect on strategic decision making.

2. Characteristics of the British Nonprofit Sector

Since the inception of the Welfare State in the 1940s, Great Britain has witnessed an impressive proliferation of voluntary organizations. Increasingly, government relies on the voluntary sector to carry out a variety of public purposes. Voluntary activity has grown substantially from £ 7.9 billion in 1980 to £ 12.6 billion in 1986 (Posnett 1987). In light of this growth, it becomes more important to clarify how voluntary organizations are organized and managed, how they interact with other organizations in their environment, formulate important decisions, and how they shape their overall strategy.

First we need to have some idea of the characteristics of the nonprofit sector. As many authors have noted, it seems that sectors of voluntary activity are amorphous and the boundaries of many nonprofit organizations are blurred. It is much easier to characterize an organization which operates in a commercial market and produces a tangible and measurable product. One reason that makes if difficult to describe the nonprofit sector is because of variation in the fundamental characteristics of organizational structure and administrative frameworks (Child 1972a and 1972b; Pugh et al. 1968).

Throughout this chapter, the terms "voluntary" or "charitable" refer to a broad group of organizations that have paid employees and volunteers and that are entitled to a number of fiscal concessions and support from public funds (estimated to be worth £ 4 billion in 1987). These organizations exist independently of the state, engage in activities of some common concern of members, but which benefit persons beyond their own membership and which are formally controlled by an unpaid board of trustees. This definition includes social welfare, advocacy groups, grant-making trusts, overseas relief, arts, and neighbourhood groups. Of course, the above broad definitions also include all non-state voluntary membership and common purpose organizations such as private schools, cooperatives, and political parties. However, our definition excludes private schools, memberships of a church, a professional association, or a trade union which have already been the focus of study in their own right.

The implications of such wide variations in organizational characteristics are far-reaching for senior managers. Formulating policies and making strategic decisions is likely to be a very different process in a formal, functionally differentiated, complex organization where individuals work within a clearly defined structure than it is in the relatively ill-defined structure of a social movement or pressure group organization (Hickson et al. 1986; Wilson et al. 1985).

3. Strategy in Voluntary Organizations

A large number of approaches to strategy may be found in the literature of organizational analysis (see, for example, Chandler 1962; Hage 1980; Miles 1982; Mintzberg 1979). However, it is not the primary purpose of this present research to examine in theoretical and empirical detail the concept of strategy alone. Rather, the intention is to draw upon and adapt typologies of strategic orientation (originally developed from research examining commercial organizations or public agencies). These typologies can then be used to distinguish in broad terms any strategic differences which may exist between voluntary organizations. The thrust of the chapter is to isolate the various sources of inter-organizational influences and pressures upon strategy formulation rather than to discuss strategy in conceptual depth.

At first sight, the concept of strategy did not seem an appropriate one to apply to the voluntary sector, as no previous research could be found which examined strategic profile in a large group of voluntary organizations. However, funding and marketing strategies for voluntary organizations have been examined (Best 1974; Kotler 1987) in the light of growing funding uncertainty. The examination of funding in voluntary organizations had noted that if long-term finance was not available to voluntary organizations, then they would remain in an insecure position in their environment. Accordingly, the approach that has been used relies heavily upon the process of deducing strategy from a continuing "stream" of decision topics which occur or arise over time within each organization (Bowman 1976; Miles 1984; Miller and Freissen 1984; and Mintzberg 1979).

Three broad strategy types are classified into *innovatory, consolidatory*, and *cooperative* stances toward organizational domain (Thompson 1967). *Innovatory* strategies are pursued by organizations which are domain prospectors. Such organizations typically launch new and old products in both old and new markets. They diversify both outputs and sources of inputs, since prestige and distinctive competence are valued goals of this type of strategy. *Consolidatory* strategies are pursued by domain defenders (Snow and Hrebiniak 1980: 317−337), where typical decisions focus upon goals of securing general administrative and managerial efficiency. Survival and efficiency are the general goals achieved by careful pruning and retrenchment where appropriate. Finally, *cooperative* strategies are pursued by those organizations which largely react to their domain (in comparison to innovatory and consolidatory strategies), and typical decisions focus upon the cooperative nature of inter-organizational relationships. Pfeffer and Salancik (1978: 162−163) suggest that such decisions can bring in previously lacking skills and expertise to the organization, allow representation of external interests, and can sometimes increase the likelihood of gaining external support for organizational activities.

One extension of this typology is to follow Ouchi (1980) and argue that each of the three strategy types broadly corresponds to organizational form. Thus innovatory strategies become the hallmark of commercial organizations, and consolidatory strategies are associated with bureaucracies. Lastly, cooperative strategies are mostly associated with voluntary organizations operating under conditions of uncertainty and exhibiting the norms of trust and goodwill.

Recent research, however, indicates that voluntary organizations in Britain pursue all three types of strategy and are not restricted to the dominantly cooperative mode (Saxon-Harrold 1986; Wilson and Butler 1985).

In order to explain the overall strategy of 75 voluntary organizations, two major themes were identified. One is political, the other is technical. Technical themes concern the central organizational task and the degree of complexity of that task with which a voluntary organization is faced, whereas political factors are based on more macro-issues of interdependencies between organizations. Although both are important determinants of strategic behaviour, it is some political themes that this chapter deals with (see Figure 1).

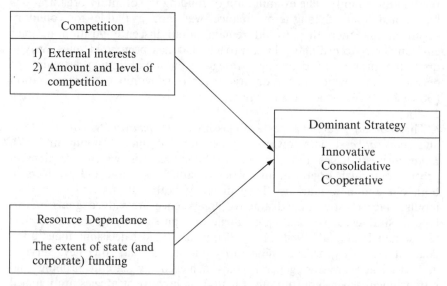

Figure 1: A Theoretical Framework of Strategy in Voluntary Organizations

The political factors have been highlighted in the guise of interdependencies. These are created between individuals and organizations who participate in voluntary organizational strategy and are dependent to some degree on important elements in the environment or within an "organizational field" (DiMaggio and Powell 1983). It has been observed that the maintenance of organizations depends upon some degree of exchange with outside parties. This dependency upon the environment is seen to impose a degree of constraint upon those directing an organization. The environment of an organization cannot be satisfactorily defined without reference to what Levine and White have called "organizational domain" (1961: 597). This consists of the specific goals which organization decision makers wish to pursue and the functions which they cause an organization to undertake in order to implement those goals. With this in mind, writers such as Thompson (1967) and Normann (1969) have distinguished different segments of the environment in terms of their immediacy for the goals and functions ascribed to an organization. An "organizational field" refers to "those organizations, that in aggregate constitute a recognizable area of institutional life: key suppliers, resource and product consumers, regulatory agencies, and other organizations that produce similar services or products" (DiMaggio and Powell 1983: 148). The distinction between several environmental boundaries proceeding "outwards" from an organization implies that decision makers do take positive steps to define and manipulate their own corners of the environment.

Voluntary organizations are dependent for *resources* such as finances or information from key suppliers and consumers. They may face regulatory controls from the external *legitimizing* agencies or face *competitive* pressures from other organizations that produce similar services or products. DiMaggio and Powell (1983) have argued that aspects of organizational change can be explained by "institutional isomorphism," whereby organizations in a field become more similar to one another without necessarily becoming more efficient. They argue that "organizational fields" are marked by increasing "structuration," whereby increased interaction among organizations in a field accelerates the exchange of information, which in turn may lead to the development of structures of prestige and domination within the field. The processes help create institutional self-definition, and organizations not perceived as adhering to "field" norms may lose legitimacy.

These processes and external interdependencies have to be managed by voluntary organizations if they want to be able to manoeuvre in their field of work and not be unduly influences by powerful external bodies. Some interdependent relationships are thought to influence overall strategy, and this chapter focuses upon the amount and level of competition voluntary organizations face from public; commercial; and voluntary bodies, and the degree to which voluntary organizations are resource dependent (i. e. to what extent a voluntary organization is dependent upon the government and commercial organizations for money).

3.1 Competition and Strategy

Another critical aspect of a voluntary organization which may highlight variation in strategic profile is that of competition. Not all voluntary organizations are unique, and organizations operating in the same domain are likely to be highly interrelated (Aldrich 1979: 226). Other competitor organizations could be both public and business organizations as well as other voluntary organizations. Following Child (1972a and 1972b) and Pfeffer and Salancik (1978), some or all of these organizations will constrain the activities of the focal organization and will be seen as powerful in light of controlling certain critical dependencies and manoeuvring in the same domain. An example of this would incluce having access to, and obtaining funds and

facilities. A high degree of competition is seen as especially important in
voluntary organizations when they are trying to obtain financial resources
from givers (Titmuss 1970). It is argued that competition pressures on
organizational decision making are no less apposite to voluntary organizations than to commercial or public organizations (see Astley et al. 1982;
Pettigrew 1973; Wilson 1982).

The greater the degree of similarity of goals and tasks between these
organizations in the domain and the focal organization, the greater the
amount of competition is likely to occur between them, and hence it is
likely that the focal organization's decision making will be impinged upon.
According to resource dependency theory, organizations will, and should,
respond to the demands of groups in the environment that control critical
resources (Pfeffer and Salancik 1978).

3.2 Resource Dependence

As Emerson (1962, 1972) emphasized, the power to influence others stems
from the facility to control those items they value. More recently, Pfeffer
and Salancik (1978) have demonstrated organizations are not internally self-
sufficient requiring resources from the environment. Strategic autonomy is
reduced to the extent that an organization is dependent on other elements
in its domain that provide the most needed forms of support. This kind of
analysis is apposite to the study of voluntary organizations, for a great
number of them receive substantial financial support from individuals and
the state (through E.C., central, and local government funds), and a much
smaller number receive substantial funding from corporate donors and grant-
making trusts.[1]

From the few available studies of inter-organizational dependencies which
examine the funding relationship and its impact upon organizational strategy,

---

[1] Most regular corporate funding of voluntary organizations is mediated through
the Charities Aid Foundation which effectively acts as a banking organization
between firms and voluntary organizations. As we have no data on the extent to
which corporate providers of finance have influence over strategic decision making,
the present chapter focusses solely upon the aspect of state finance. In 1987, British
Petroleum was the largest corporate cash donor to British nonprofits, giving
£ 2,900,000. This is followed by Hanson Trust, Trustee Savings Bank, Barclays
Bank, and I.C.I., all of whom gave in excess of £ 1 million in the same period. The
top 400 corporate donations amounted to £ 72.5 million for 1987. Total company
community involvement amounted to £ 98.2 million in 1987. Central and local
government grants and fiscal concessions amounted to £ 4 billion; households gave
between £ 1.8 – £ 2.7 billion, and the top 400 grant-making trusts £ 204 million
(Charities Aid Foundation 1988).

it is possible to conclude tentatively that financial dependence upon the state erodes strategic autonomy (Mintzberg 1983). Leat, Smolka, and Unell (1981) demonstrated this reduction of autonomy at the level of local government — voluntary organization relationships. They found that where local government gives money to a voluntary organization it demands a commensurate level of influence in what actions are taken and in which ways.

Wortman (1982) indicates that whilst voluntary organizations may attempt strategic planning, such autonomy of goal pursuit is likely to be constrained by the influence of a substantial funding body. Scott (1981: 62) reveals that where the state has the power to increase, withdraw, or reduce funding to voluntary organizations, then acceptance of this funding incurs the penalty of subtle "constraining influence" on organizational actions. Gamm (1983), Tucker (1983), and Sexty (1983) all come to similar conclusions, although their data are drawn from extremely limited samples, often focussing upon just one or one kind of voluntary organization.

In theory, at least, direct state influence should be limited to the exercise of funding policy. Thus, in all other respects, the state should have the facility of direct external control over the strategies of their constituent voluntary organizations. We approach these questions in the light of some selected results from a study of 75 voluntary organizations.

4. Data and Methods

This study presents data from a sample of 75 British nonprofit organizations. Data was collected over a two-year period from 1983—1985. This data collection was guided by and built upon a previous study in which the strategic management of four voluntary organizations was outlined (Wilson and Butler 1985). These intensive strategies informed the present study that a three-way typology of strategy could be identified which could form the analytical basis of a larger, more representative study.

Data was collected from each of the sample organizations concerning the occurrence and the content of strategy that had been made over the previous ten years (including the year of data collection). A postal questionnaire was sent to the director or a senior manager in each organization, and two intensive case studies were undertaken. Both interviews and questionnaires allowed respondents to outline strategic decision making in reply to structured and broad open-ended questions. In this way, both the content and the regularity or frequency of particular decisions could be identified. In addition to interview and questionnaire data, archival documentary data was also used to augment verbal material. The questionnaire and case study interviews collected data on financial dependence, general operating context, organizational history, decision making, competition, and the regulation of charities.

The sample was constructed to be representative of the population to be studied. Given the diversity of organizations in the voluntary sector, this is not easily achieved. However, this study includes both registered charities and non-charitable organizations, and a spread of organizations has been ensured using both the "Charities Digest" and the Charities Aid Foundation's classifications of voluntary activity (such as visually handicapped, aged, or medical research). The sample also includes both large and small established organizations of a variety of ages.

5. Discussion: Resource Dependence and Strategy

From a sample of 75 voluntary organizations, the data indicates that as voluntary organizations become more dependent for money upon central government, the more they are likely to pursue all three strategy types, but that the *cooperative* mode predominates ($r = .235$, $P. < .05$).

This result was surprising because it was expected that voluntary organizations would pursue a cooperative strategy alone. Unfortunately, it was not possible, using this strategy, to discriminate between multiple strategies. Although decision topics which constituted the dominant cooperative strategy were identified, complete data concerning consolidative and innovative strategies was not available. It is not known whether these subsidiary strategies were concerned with inputs (materials, people, and money) or were rather concerned with outputs (services and/or goods).

However, some trends in the data (over a ten-year period) were identified. For, where organizations were hardly resource dependent at all, then they had pursued a single generic strategy (usually innovative) towards inputs, and managing their general domain. However, as resource dependence upon government funds increased, then these organizations adopted multiple different strategies with the cooperative strategy predominating.

The picture drawn from these results indicates that voluntary organizations are either obliged to cooperate with increasing government funding or are directly influenced to do so by the funding body. Kramer (1982) has noted in studies of voluntary organizations in a number of countries that as dependence on a single funding source continues to increase, so the discretion of the donor also increases. However, is it so obvious that dependence on a single funding source is more constraining than dependence on multiple sources of funding?

Data from two case studies and from open-ended responses on postal questionnaires[2] points to two general scenarios. There appears to be a difference between those voluntary organizations which receive a government grant but cannot determine its *level* or amount and those voluntary organizations which receive government money but have the autonomy to decide what proportion of their total income this represents. If a voluntary organization obtains a balance of multiple funding sources, this is probably now more preferable than being dependent on a single source of funding such as a central government grant. The implication being that regulating the level of single source funding will enable voluntary organizations to manoeuvre in the domain. By seeking out multiple sources of funders, voluntary organizations would be able to fend off any conflicting demands made upon them by a particularly influential donor. However, when an influential donor, for example a central government department, determines the level of funding, voluntary organizations are obliged (often quasi-contractually) to cooperate with both state agencies and other voluntary organizations operating in the same domain, and under similar funding circumstances.

Voluntary organizations which receive grant aid, but are able to determine its extent, have a much greater range of strategic discretion. Largely, these organizations only have to adopt a cooperative strategy when they become directly involved with government agencies, which are often providing a similar service, for example in the social services field. When funding becomes difficult, voluntary bodies can pursue a strategy of merger with similar organizations, but this rarely happens as the preservation of its "individualism" and "unique quality" of service will become the priority regardless of whether services are being duplicated. Instead, some voluntary organizations have in the last three years pursued a strategy of "gap filling," that is providing services previously carried out by the state in return for a grant or fees for services rendered. This has been especially prevalent in the fields of mental health and the elderly.

This strategy has been questioned from many quarters as some voluntary organizations feel that they are forced into a "gap filling" role because of inadequate grant funding, but that someone should provide a service even though they believe that it is the state's responsibility to provide services they are asked to replace.

[2] Methodology was a combination of case studies and semi-structured interview schedules. Cases were used to identify and isolate various aspects of the theoretical framework which were then translated into structured and open-ended questions. Respondents in the total sample of 75 organizations were from senior management level and, on average, totalled 2 informants per organization.

Oxfam receives only 8% of total income from government sources and can decide to what extent it receives government money. Oxfam was pursuing a predominantly *innovative* strategy, in particular illustrated by the organization's ventures into education, campaigning, and legal work. However, where government money is deployed to specific projects where Oxfam is involved (such as joint ventures involving the Overseas Development Agency of central government), then Oxfam is placed under pressure to adopt a *cooperative* strategy with government agencies. Often, this results in Oxfam being forced to make decisions which by most criteria are irrational and, certainly, uneconomic. For example, the acceptance of government money by Oxfam brought with it the pressure to purchase only British vehicles for fieldwork operations which were expensive and difficult to service.

At times, it may be considered politically expedient for government to utilize voluntary organizations to provide welfare services. Government can then clearly identify itself as a provider of resources, and voluntary organizations as the receiver of grant aid to carry out their works. It can both accept the appreciation of the public when the services are popular and distance itself a little more when they are controversial, pointing nevertheless to the obvious existence of community support/need for an organization. Government usually will be far more popular for supporting nonprofit sector than for extending its own bureaucracy. Furthermore, organizations that have strong community support may be difficult to bypass without electoral damage.

Graycar (1983) found that agencies which developed so that they had a virtual monopoly of certain resources required by government had a degree of autonomy. Government generally demanded a very low level of accountability, with no one wishing to upset the balance — i. e. "if the government knew more, it would have to pay more." Even so, funding for many voluntary organizations comes on an *ad hoc* basis with limited security. Resource dependence and competition are not the only factors thought to influence overall strategy. Task complexity and variables of external legitimation (number and influence of regulatory bodies) account for some further difference in overall strategy (Saxon-Harrold 1986). In addition, culture and power relationships may also have a bearing.

Income dependent bodies are unlikely to be able to change future strategy and should consider reducing the amount of statutory income received. Future strategy is also likely to be constrained by tasks over which external regulatory bodies have influence, for example, Manpower Services Commission schemes. The implication of this result is that voluntary bodies should contemplate the possible constraining influence of regulators and donors as a consequence of entering such regulated areas as employment and housing. The mere fact of being income dependent on government agencies, corporate donors, or the "public" for funding is not in itself enough to constrain strategic decision making. It is the condition of interdependence or the extent to which the dominant interest groups (government agencies, in the main) use their discretion to intervene or constrain resource allocation and its usage which influences strategic direction.

5.1 Discussion: Competition and Strategy

The degree to which voluntary organizations are vulnerable to influential external interests depends on certain types of exchange voluntary organizations rely on. For example, local and central government agencies are likely to be influential when it comes to funding decisions. In addition, co-opted members from competing voluntary and statutory organizations will be influential in their own areas of expertise. Voluntary organizations will, necessarily, pursue a multiple strategy to cope with, and reduce the influence of external interests.

Prominant external competing interests will have caused the voluntary organizations that they influence to change strategy in the last ten years from a single strategy (usually competitive) to a multiple strategy (cooperative primarily) $r = .239$ (P. < .05). That influence has extended to when strategy should change and what combinations of strategy should be used. Several reasons were forwarded to explain the use of a cooperative strategy primarily. In the main, it is thought that it would be better for voluntary organizations to cooperate rather than attempt to subdue powerful external interests if they did not have the skills to be independent and pursue a single competitive strategy. It has been found that very few voluntary organizations pursue a competitive strategy alone, mainly because of the high cost of obtaining, and the ability to keep injecting, resources into major new services. However, overall strategic direction cannot be wholly attributed to influential external interests or to the "cultural" evolution of the use of a cooperative strategy in the voluntary sector.

Every voluntary organization is embedded in a network of external organizations, and their relationships with these bodies will affect their ability to achieve desired outcomes. Voluntary organizations are no exception, as is further demonstrated by a correlation of $r = .227$ (P. < .05) between total mean influence of external interests and present strategy. This indicates that the greater the mean influence for all external interests, the more likely it is that voluntary organizations will adopt as their current strategic profile multiple strategies, with cooperation as a predominant feature.

Of the external interests, statutory agencies (both from this country and abroad) are perceived to be the most influential. Voluntary organizations indicated 127 bodies (see Table 1) in all from local authorities, the Charity Commission, to central government departments, which together were perceived to have a significant amount of influence over strategic decision making in decisions relating to planning and funding matters.

Table 1: The Relative Influence of State Agencies and Private Associations in Strategic Decision Making*

Mean influence of the Charity Commission	3.0	(n = 55)
Mean influence of the Inland Revenue	1.5	(n = 29)
Mean influence of Local Government departments	1.5	(n = 31)
Mean influence of Central Government departments	4.5	(n = 84)
Total Mean Influence of State Agencies in All Four Categories**	2.6	(n = 199)
Total Mean Influence of Private Associations**	1.2	(n = 61)

   * (Question)
     What are the main regulatory agencies (e. g. central/local government/Charity Commission) which have an interest in, or impinge upon your activities? Please list and circle the degree of influence, on the scale: 1 A little; 2 Some; 3 Quite a lot; 4 A great deal; 5 A very great deal.
  ** Difference between the means significant at p ⩾ .01 using 3-test for sample means.

Increasingly, voluntary organizations are moving into social and personal welfare on an agency or fee-paying basis. The pursuance of a multiple strategy has been made necessary, as increased "linkages" have evolved between voluntary organizations and the state departments involved, and where cooperation rather than competition is promoted between bodies coordinating voluntary activity. Through these linkages, voluntary organizations can gain support for their activities as well as gain legitimation.

The correlations point to competition as being the most important single factor with regard to present strategic profile r = .367 (P. < .05). The amount of competition faced by voluntary organizations explains 16 (%) variation in present strategy and 5.19 (%) of strategic direction. Again, the highest level of competition comes from statutory authorities or other voluntary bodies. It was thought that voluntary organizations may be able to seek a niche in the environment and create a temporary monopoly and reduce the number of competitors in the domain. A few can create a temporary monopoly in the short term, but often find it difficult to consolidate any short-term gains.

However, many voluntary organizations are unable to do this at all because of the "steep learning curve" associated with providing a new service and the high financial cost of building up and holding a leading position in a new field. Therefore, some voluntary organizations may face their environment using a competitive strategy in fundraising, by marketing products and services through advertising, or operating charity shops. This sort of strategy may be used in conjunction with consolidation in order to make internal adjustments to structure, and hence reduce the impact of uncertainty in resource supplies. Other voluntary organizations use cooperation as a strategy, as a means of combining together in joint ventures with others to coordinate facilities and exchange information to reduce dependencies.

Strategies to avoid competition (as well as trading activities) used by overseas relief agencies have included "diversifying" into the research and development of disaster provision such as the provision of high energy biscuits and liquid protein drinks, together with the supply of specialist knowledge on agriculture. These sorts of decisions have been aimed at foreign governments, competitors, and donors in order to secure "distinctive competance" (Miles and Snow 1978) over rival organizations in the domain and to exhibit qualities of flexibility to overseas governments with whom they work.

The correlation between the influence of central government and the pursuit of *cooperative* strategies, r = .289 (P. < .05), tempts an over-simplistic cause and effect relationship. High government influence pressures voluntary organizations to adopt cooperative strategies. Case-study and open-ended data illustrate that an r of 3 does not suggest a simple, direct relationship.

As Thompson (1967: 35) argues, cooperative strategies enable an organization to gain power through the exchange of commitments and hence the reduction of uncertainty for all involved parties. If we examine organizations in the voluntary sector as a whole, it is possible to see that many of them operate in areas of uncertainty or under conditions of high task ambiguity. For example, in sea rescue, the job is done by a charity which would otherwise fall to a government agency. The same kind of government – voluntary organization relationship can be found also in medical and social welfare (and research) voluntary organizations. Whilst the existence of voluntary organizations operating in ambiguous and uncertain environments reduces uncertainty for the state, it equally endows a deal of potential power to the state over the strategies and actions of voluntary organizations.

Yet, one reason for funders not influencing present strategic decision making may well be the divorce between funding arrangements (convincing sponsors) and the quality and relevance of service provision (meeting clients' needs). Voluntary organizations that are resource dependent may be able to continue to convince potential sponsors – statutory agencies, corporate givers, and individuals – that they are doing a good job. This may be regardless of what clients feel or experience, but it is unlikely that anyone will interfere. The degree of control, influence, and accountability which sponsors can reasonably demand will depend on individual voluntary organizations' relationships with funding bodies in terms of the funders expectations and the voluntary organizations' goals. Relevant here is the adoption of both a "public" and a "private" face by voluntary agencies, the raising of funds on one pretext, and using them for other purposes (forming a hidden agenda or developing an emotive appeal base where none is justified).

Government and other outside agencies may well have a policy of "non-interference" in voluntary organizational decision making as a prudent accompaniment to increased use of voluntary bodies as agents of government policy. It is known that voluntary organizations are involved in a large proportion of the state's welfare work already, and this is likely to increase in future. Local authorities have in the past turned to voluntary groups because they can experiment, or provide social care more flexibly, and are better at stimulating people's energy. However, in the last five years, central government has also encouraged the voluntary sector to tackle "new" or difficult health and social problems such as AIDS and drug abuse.

6. Conclusion

The foregoing analysis indicates that pressure from the state to adopt a cooperative strategy will depend not only on what types of voluntary organization we are discussing (e. g. self-help, service provider, or grant-making trust) but also upon the nature of provision. The implication of the analysis is that pressure to cooperate is highest when voluntary organizations are both resource dependent and face competition or are influenced by external interests. Any analysis of resource dependence and aspects of competition in voluntary organizations as an influence upon strategy highlights the role of government policies towards the voluntary sector as a whole. What do voluntary organizations do in light of funding and competitive pressures? The voluntary sector itself is a "tangled web" of funding flows, and for agencies in receipt of multiple sources of income, a change in one source can have dramatic "knock on" effects in their ability to provide or maintain services.

By implication, what voluntary organizations have been doing in response to external pressures is to attempt to secure "new" types of funding. In particular, the last five years has seen the major voluntary organizations competing for company donations and sponsorship monies. Some voluntary organizations have re-organized in the belief that such a strategy would create enough internal efficiency to give them the "edge" over other rival voluntary organizations for company money. This strategy is probably illusory, in that company and sponsorship monies represents only 2.2% of total voluntary income, so voluntary bodies should concentrate more effort on both effectively asking for and obtaining monies from individuals and government.

Recent marked change in economic, social, and fiscal policy in Britain will have ramifications for strategic decision making in voluntary organizations. For example, fiscal concessions that encourage regular giving now enable certain voluntary agencies to take a more proactive role in their domain. Regular gifts would mean they would be more financially secure and able to develop long-term projects and fend off competition. On the other hand, new social policies that change the structuring of welfare benefits may disfavour the establishment or the continued operation of voluntary organizations altogether.

References

Aldrich, Howard (1979): *Organizations and Environments*, Englewood Cliffs, N.J.: Prentice-Hall.

Astley, Graham W., Runo Axelsson, Richard J. Butler, David J. Hickson, and David C. Wilson (1982): "Complexity and Cleavage: Dual Explanations of Strategic Decision Making," *Journal of Management Science* 19, 4, 357–375.

Best, Richard (1974): "Youth Issues," in *Issues in Canadian Public Policy*, G. Doern and V. Wilson (Eds.), Toronto: Macmillan, 137–165.

Bowman, Ernest H. (1976): "Strategy and the Weather," *Sloan Management Review* 17, 2, 49–58.

Chandler, Alfred D. (1962): *Strategy and Structure*, Cambridge, Mass.: MIT Press.

Charities Aid Foundation (1988): *Charity Trends*, Tonbridge, Kent: Charities Aid Foundation.

Child, John (1972a): "Organization Structure and Strategies of Control: A Replication of the Aston Study," *Administrative Science Quarterly* 17, 163–176.

Child, John (1972b): "Organizational Structure, Environment and Performance: The Role of Strategic Choice," *Sociology* 6, 1 (January), 1–22.

DiMaggio, Paul and Walter W. Powell (1983): "The Iron Cage Revisited: Institutional Isomorphism and Collective Rationality in Organizational Fields," *American Sociological Review* 48, 327–336.

Emerson, Ralph E. (1962): "Power-Dependence Relations," *American Sociological Review* 27, 31–41.

Emerson, Ralph E. (1972): "Exchange Theory Part 1: A Psychological Basis for Social Exchange Theory Part 2: Exchange Relations, Exchange Networks, and Groups as Exchange Systems," in *Sociological Theories in Progress, Vol. II*, John Berger (Ed.), Boston, Mass.: Houghton Mifflin.

Gamm, Larry D. (1983): "Interorganizational Relations and the Management of Voluntary Health Organizations," in *Managing Voluntary Organizations*, Mel S. Moyer (Ed.), Toronto: York University Voluntary Sector Program.

Graycar, Adam (1983): "Public and Private in Welfare Services," Working Paper, *Social Welfare Research Centre*, Perth: University of New South Wales.

Hage, Jerald (1980): *Theories of Organizations: Processes and Transformation*, New York: Wiley.

138   Susan K. E. Saxon-Harrold

Hickson, David J., Richard J. Butler, David Gray, Geoffrey R. Mallory, and David
    C. Wilson (1986): *Top Decisions: Strategic Decision in Organizations*, Oxford: Basil
    Blackwell and San Francisco: Jossey-Bass.
Kotler, Philip (1987): *Strategic Marketing for Non-Profit Organizations*, Englewood
    Cliffs, N.J.: Prentice-Hall.
Kramer, Ralph (1982): *Voluntary Agencies in the Welfare State*, Berkeley: University
    of California Press.
Leat, Diana, Gerry Smolka, and Judith Unell (1981): *Voluntary and Statutory Collabor-
    ation: Rhetoric or Reality?* London: Bedford Square Press.
Levine, Stephen and Paul White (1961): "Exchange as a Conceptual Framework for
    the Study of Interorganizational Relationships," *Administrative Science Quarterly*
    5, 583 – 601.
Miles, R. and K. Cameron (1984): *Coffin Nails and Corporate Strategies*, Eaglewood
    Cliffs, New Jersey: Prentice-Hall.
Miller, Danny and Peter Freissen (1984): *Organizations: A Quantum View*, Englewood
    Cliffs, N.J.: Prentice-Hall.
Mintzberg, Henry (1979): "Patterns in Strategy Formation," *International Studies of
    Management and Organization* 9, 3, 67 – 86.
Mintzberg, Henry (1983): *Power in and Around Organizations*, Englewood Cliffs, N.J.:
    Prentice-Hall.
Normann, Richard (1969): "Organizational Innovativeness: Product Variation and Re-
    orientation," *Administrative Science Quarterly* 16, 203 – 215.
Ouchi, William G. (1980): "Markets, Bureaucracies and Clans," *Administrative Science
    Quarterly* 25, 129 – 141.
Pettigrew, Andrew (1973): *The Politics of Organizational Decision Making*, London:
    Tavistock.
Pfeffer, Jeffrey and Gerald R. Salancik (1978): *The External Control of Organizations:
    A Resource Dependency Perspective*, New York: Harper & Row.
Posnett, John (1987): "Trends in the Income of Charities, 1980 – 1985," in *Charity
    Trends 1986/87*, Judith McQuillan (Ed.), Tonbridge, Kent: Charities Aid Founda-
    tion.
Pugh, Derek S., David J. Hickson, Christopher R. Hinings, and C. Turner (1968):
    "Dimensions of Organization Structure," *Administrative Science Quarterly* 23, 1
    (March), 65 – 105.
Saxon-Harrold, Susan K. E. (1986): "Strategy of Voluntary Organizations," doctoral
    dissertation, University of Bradford.
Scott, David (1981): *Don't Mourn for Me — Organise: The Social and Political Uses
    of Voluntary Organizations*, London: Allen and Unwin.
Sexty, Roger W. (1983): "Power Analysis of Management in a Volunteer Organiza-
    tion," in *Managing Voluntary Organizations*, Mel S. Moyer (Ed.), Toronto: York
    University Voluntary Sector Program.
Snow, Christopher S. and Lawrence G. Hrebiniak (1980): "Strategy, Distinctive
    Competence, and Organizational Performance," *Administrative Science Quarterly*
    25, 2, 317 – 337.
Thompson, James D. (1967): *Organizations in Action: Social Science Bases of Adminis-
    trative Theory*, New York: McGraw-Hill.
Titmuss, Richard (1970): *Commitment to Welfare*, London: Allen and Unwin.

Tucker, David (1983): "Environmental Change and Organizational Policy Making," in *Managing Voluntary Organizations*, Mel S. Moyer (Ed.), Toronto: York University Voluntary Sector Program.

Wilson, David C. (1982): "Electricity and Resistence: A Case Study of Innovation and Politics," *Organization Studies*, 3, 2.

Wilson, David C. and Richard J. Butler (1985): "Corporatism in the British Voluntary Sector," in *Private Government and Public Policy*, Wolfgang Streek and Paul C. Schmitter (Eds.), Beverly Hills and London: Sage.

Wortman, Max S. (1982): "Strategic Management and Changing Leadership Roles," *Applied Behavioural Science* 18, 3, 371.

2.8
Voluntary Organizations and Accountability: Theory and Practice

Diana Leat

1. Introduction

In recent years, accountability of voluntary organizations has assumed a new significance. Although it is most often associated with the growth in government funding, this paper suggests that accountability arises from the demands placed upon voluntary organizations by the rise of pluralism, professionalism, and consumerism.

One of the difficulties in discussing voluntary sector accountability is that the concept itself is unclear. As Kramer notes: "The concept of accountability is particularly difficult to grapple with because its popularity in the human services is exceeded only by the lack of agreement about its meanings" (Kramer 1982: 18). Therefore, I will first distinguish the foundations, origins, types, and objects of accountability. These distinctions are then applied in an analysis of the formal complexity of voluntary organization accountability. Finally, I suggest that voluntary organizations are able to manage this complexity, because there are important disjunctions between the theory of accountability and the availability of resources to put accountability into practice.

2. The Rise of Voluntary Sector Accountability: Pluralism, Professionalism, and Consumerism

Voluntary sector accountability has, in large measure, come to be identified with financial accountability to the state and seen largely as a problem of organizational independence. Although these are indeed key issues, other, equally important factors provide the context within which the process of voluntary-statutory accountability is played out. These factors are broadly grouped under three main headings: pluralism, professionalism, and consumerism. Their combined impact has both raised the issue of voluntary sector accountability and, in large part, created the problems or tensions within such accountability.

2.1 Planned Pluralism: External Accountability

I am using "pluralism" as a rather inadequate shorthand for the complex of ideas and practices which suggest and reflect a relatively close relationship between statutory and voluntary agencies, a "mix" of statutory and voluntary provision and activity. Pluralism in this sense has, of course, existed ever since statutory provision was first introduced. The new "planned" pluralism raises the issue of accountability of voluntary organizations most obviously in terms of accountability for funding, but also in a broader form insofar as pluralism implies planned, coordinated variety, rather than merely unrelated co-existence.

From the statutory sector's viewpoint, *"assisted pluralism"* (i. e. voluntary provision by means of statutory grant aid) creates a potential gap between responsibility for provision and provision, between responsibility for public money and its use. One means of closing that gap is by ensuring close accountability both for monies dispensed and for services provided.

From the voluntary sector's viewpoint, statutory funding separates the control of policy from the control of resources. One way of closing the gap between control over policy and control over resources is to delimit the influence of those who control resources by emphasizing the need for independence and autonomy in policy making and management. Another strategy is to diversify control over resources in such a way that the sphere of influence of any one funder is marginal to the total.

2.2 Professionalism: Internal Accountability

With the growth of professionalism in the voluntary sector, responsibility for the overall management and policy has become "separated" from responsibility for policy implementation. Managers and staff are increasingly separated as volunteers and paid workers, employers and employees, and probably in age, social class, and educational background. More fundamentally, professionalism in a voluntary organization creates a situation in which one group of people − elected or selected because they, in some sense, "know best" and then charged with the task of deciding what is best for the organization − employ a worker who professes to "know better."

Once policy making and implementation are separated, and workers are paid (employed) to implement policy, the issue of internal accountability arises. The role of the management committee must be reconciled with claims to professional competence and professional autonomy.

2.3 Consumerism: Client Accountability

Here, consumerism refers to the diverse demands to "take the ordinary person into account." Consumerism has presented to many voluntary (and statutory) welfare organizations a radical challenge. Instead of doing things *for* others, instead of knowing and doing best, many voluntary organizations have been challenged to do things *with* others or even to serve others not in the old paternalist way but in a new relationship in which the user defines and the provider provides.

But, the voluntary sector also has a special relationship with consumerism insofar as it provides a vehicle for the expression and organization or consumerism. One of the many changes in the overall composition of the voluntary sector in the last twenty years has been the growth of both campaigning and specifically consumer-based organizations.

Moreover, accountability to consumers (which is in itself confused, since it may include members of the organization and/or consumers of the organization's services) has come to be identified with the legitimacy of voluntary organizations as such. To some extent, the particular merit or strength of the voluntary sector rests upon client/constituency accountability. Today, there is an emphasis upon a strong voluntary sector as a feature of a democratic society: voluntary organizations are said to be important, because they provide choice (for consumers) and opportunities for participation (for members). Furthermore, voluntary organizations are often said to be more in touch with local and client group needs. Within this new ideology of the merit of the voluntary sector, an expectation of accountability to multiple, segmented, and overlapping constituencies becomes the norm.

3. Accountability and Voluntary Organizations

Accountability becomes an issue when power and resources are delegated. As a social relationship, this delegation implies relative independence, trust, and inequality between those who delegate and those who are delegated to.

3.1 Bases of the Right to Require Accountability

If some have the right to demand that others are accountable to them, what are the possible sources or bases of this right? The right to require accountability may be derived from structures or hierarchies (structural accountability), from particular acts of delegation (delegate accountability), or from more diffuse expectations and allegiances ("communal accountability").

3.2 Types of Accountability

Simey suggests that "to talk of accountability is therefore to talk of control" (Simey 1985). However, such a conceptualization does not reflect the various types of "accountability," and their associated control and sanction mechanisms. It is possible to distinguish between *explanatory accountability* — being required to give an account, to explain; *accountability-with-sanctions* — the right to require an account and to impose sanctions; and *responsive accountability* — the views of those accounted to must be taken into account.

Inadequate though these distinctions may be, they attempt to reflect the variety of everyday use of the term accountability which the definition in terms of existence of sanctions conceals. Finally, the distinctions allow recognition of the way in which there may be informal sanctions attached to accountability, even when no formal sanctions exist. Although these informal sanctions often depend for their force on their perception as such by those who are accountable, they may sometimes be as powerful as those formal sanctions imposed by right.

3.3 Reasons for Delegation

In considering appropriate means of or structures for accountability, it is important to look at why accountability rather than direct control has been chosen. These reasons provide the criteria to assess the adequacy of the means of accountability. Smith and Hague (1971) suggest six reasons for delegation to quangos, and these would seem to be equally applicable to delegation to voluntary organizations:

(1) *Buffer theory*: protecting certain activities from political interference; (2) *Escape theory*: escaping known weaknesses of traditional government departments, independence from financial controls and checks of Parliament and from rulers, regulations and salary scales of the bureaucracy; (3) *"Corson" theory*: put the activity where the talent is; (4) *Participation theory*: spreading power; (5) *Back-double theory*: if governments cannot do what they want within existing structures, then do it outside; (6) *Too many bureaucrats*: a way of extending government activities without increasing the number of government employees.

3.4 Accountability for What?

An individual organization or group may be regarded as accountable for (a) the proper use of money (from whatever source) i. e. fiscal accountability; (b) following proper procedures (whether in a particular project or more generally in acting in accordance with the constitution of the organization) i. e. process accountability; (c) the quality of its work (whether in a particular project or more generally) i. e. programme accountability; and (d) the relevance or appropriateness of (its) work (is it providing the "right" services, doing or saying the right things) i. e. accountability for priorities.

3.5 Accountability and Legitimacy

Although much of the discussion of voluntary organization accountability focusses on financial accountability, there is the broader area of accountability and legitimacy.

There are various means or sources of legitimacy for organizations claiming the right to speak or act in the interest of others. Rein (1975), discussing the search for legitimacy among social planners, identifies three strategies for acquiring legitimacy: elite consensus, rational analysis, and citizen participation. Legitimacy via elite consensus involves endorsement and support (of action/activities) by the leadership of the major institutions in the community. Legitimacy via rational analysis is acquired by presenting actions as rational, coherent, intellectual solutions to the problems that are being dealt with. Legitimacy may also be claimed on the grounds that activities are created, endorsed, or supported by the recipients of the service.

Today, accountability is confused with voluntary sector legitimacy and discussed as though citizen participation were the only adequate or proper source of legitimacy; accountability and legitimacy may be related, but they are not synonymous. An organization may have legitimacy but may be subject to very few, or weak, accountability requirements. Accountability to the people may be one of several sources of organizational legitimacy.

4. The Complexity of Voluntary Organization Accountability

Voluntary organizations are accountable to a number of different, sometimes overlapping, sometimes conflicting, groups. Accountability to each group may be more or less closely related to (a) the organization's legitimacy and (b) the organization's ability to secure resources for its work and ultimately its survival. Fulfilling the accountability requirements of one group may conflict with fulfillment of those of another; by implication, acquiring legitimacy may sometimes conflict with acquiring resources, but in the long term both are necessary for survival.

On paper, the staff and volunteers of an organization are accountable to the organizer or secretary who in turn is accountable to the Executive or Management Committee which in turn is accountable to the membership of the organization. In practice, of course, there are variations and complications. First, it is not clear how far unpaid volunteers using their own time may be regarded as accountable to the organizer. Second, in many voluntary organizations today, the organization is composed of a small core staff and a larger number of people employed on special projects. These special projects may have their own management committees to whom the workers are directly responsible; these committees may then have a more or less strong accountability relationship with the Executive Committee.

In addition to these internal accountabilities, there are various different external groups to which the organization may be accountable for money and projects or provision of services delegated to the organization. These groups may include commercial companies, trusts, quango, various different committees/departments of the local authority, and various different departments of central government (either directly or mediated by the local authority, as in Urban Aid or Inner Area Funding). In addition to delegate accountability for local authority, funded projects/services the voluntary organization may be regarded as more broadly accountable to the local authority for certain types of work with certain client groups which the local authority may or may not fund, but for which it has a responsibility. Within this outer circle of accountability, there may also be the national body of the local organization. Not all local organizations are part of a national body, and where they are, structural relationships, and thus accountability, between the national and local organizations differ.

In addition to external funders, the local organization is accountable in some broad way to the Charity Commissioners (i. e. if the organization is a registered charity).

It may also be regarded, or regard itself, as accountable to "the community," or the general public, either as an expression of communal accountability (discussed above) or, more specifically, as the donor of funds.

The organization may also be regarded, or regard itself, as accountable to clients or users of the organization. Clients/users may, of course, include a wide range of different and sometimes conflicting groups.

For intermediary and other types of local resource agencies, the principle users of the organization are other voluntary groups. However, even for direct service-providing organizations, there may be some measure of accountability to other voluntary organizations either as a result of membership of a specific co-ordinating body or as an expression of "communal solidarity." Communal accountability may also occur in relation to the professional bodies or unions to which staff (including the organizer) may belong.

Identifying the wide range of groups to which any one voluntary organization may be accountable on paper helps to begin to distinguish the different types of bases of accountability involved (i. e. structural, delegate, and communal). It also raises questions about the meanings of accountability involved, in particular the existence of sanctions. It also raises questions about the reasons for delegation and, thus, the different purposes and requirements of accountability (for example, to save time, to avoid bureaucracy, etc.). Consideration of the different types/bases, meanings, and reasons for accountability raises further questions about the processes and the substantive requirements of accountability to the different groups. Consideration also needs to be given to the compatibility of the (differing) accountability requirements of the different groups and to the ways in which organizations manage the conflict (of substance or process) which may arise — when conflicting demands are made upon the organization which group's demands come first?

The answer to the question "which group comes first?," when conflicts of accountability arise, is likely to depend in part upon the power/authority which different groups are able to exert over the organization. In other words, priorities in accountability are likely to depend upon the significance of the sanctions (over the organization) which different groups are able to impose. These sanctions may range from the direct and tangible — such as the withdrawal of grant aid — to the indirect and intangible — such as the withdrawal of support and/or legitimacy. The strength and significance of different groups' accountability demands will, of course, depend upon the particular significance of different types of sanction to different voluntary groups.

So, for example, although the local authority's demands may have priority for many grant-aided voluntary organizations for others, not receiving aid or receiving only a small proportion of income in aid, the authority's demands may be regarded as less significant. For more campaigning organizations, the withdrawal of support or legitimacy by clients may constitute a powerful sanction; for other organizations with other sources of legitimacy, withdrawal of statutory support may be more significant. Thus it seems likely that there is no one hierarchy of groups (to which accountability is owed) for all voluntary organizations but rather a number of different hierarchies related to the different political and resource needs/environments of different types of organization.

Priorities in accountability to different groups are likely to depend not only on the relative significance of the sanctions available to groups, but also on the capacity of any group to "make accountability meaningful." By making accountability meaningful, I refer to the ability of the group to ask the right questions of the organization and assess the adequacy of the answers. Accountability without knowledge and understanding on the part of those to whom the account is presented is an empty gesture. Groups differ in their ability to ask the right questions and assess the adequacy of the answers. Groups working in the same field as the organization are likely to be in a stronger position in this respect than those who lack such professional or detailed knowledge. Appreciation of the significance of knowledge in making accountability meaningful raises questions about the nature of accountability to, say, client groups. Client groups are, of course, experts in their own needs, but very often they are less knowledgeable about other social and political processes, about what is or is not possible or feasible, about costs and likely outcomes, and so on. Indeed, there is a sense in which many groups are disadvantaged precisely because they lack such skills and knowledge.

Lack of the ability to ask the right questions and assess the adequacy of the answers may also affect the accountability of voluntary organizations to otherwise more powerful bodies such as the local authority. One reason why accountability may make few real demands on the voluntary organization is because the authority may have no adequate evaluative framework within which to assess the work of the voluntary organization.

Even within the organization, accountability of staff to the Executive Committee may be affected by "the balance of knowledge" between staff and Committee members. There is now a growing literature on the ways in which staff members may "control" committee members rather than vice versa. This clearly relates to the "problem" of professionalism discussed above.

Thus, meaningful accountability is likely to depend not only on the balance of power (ability to apply significant sanctions) between groups in relation to the accountable organization, but also on the "balance of knowledge" within the organization and between the organization and the groups to which it is accountable.

Managing these differences in power (available sanctions) and knowledge between groups may be one way in which an organization reduces the potential conflicts of multiple accountability.

Before leaving the topic of accountability to different groups, it is important to re-emphasize the distinction between different meanings of accountability. Above, I suggested that groups may vary in the strength and significance (to the organization) of the sanctions they are able to impose on the organization. I have also suggested in an earlier section of this chapter that the concept of accountability does not necessarily imply the existence of sanctions. Even though a group may have no effective ability to require accounts from the organization, it may nevertheless be taken into account in the organization's planning and activities. In other words, in order to understand fully the effects of multiple accountability on voluntary organizations in reality, it may be necessary to recognize the importance of voluntary rather than required accountability. Whilst recognizing the potential significance of voluntary accountability, it is nevertheless important to distinguish such "taking into account" from accountability which requires accounts. Voluntary accountability or responsiveness is something one chooses to provide; required accountability is imposed by others.

Voluntary organizations are not only accountable to a number of different and sometimes conflicting groups, but from within any one group there may be different demands made upon the organization.

As noted above, within any one group to which the organization is accountable, there may be a number of sub-groups, for example, different groups of clients/users, different departments within the local authority. Recognition of groups within groups highlights not only the possibility of conflicting expectations/demands on the organization, but also the possibility that there may be differing emphases within any one group on exactly what the organization is accountable for.

An apparently straightforward and simple example illustrates the point. An organization is accountable to one local authority committee/department for grant aid to provide a particular service. The officers concerned with finance will want the organization to account properly and fully for the money spent (fiscal accountability); the administrators will want the organization to demonstrate that it carried out the project/service in the agreed way, that the staff did what they said they would do (process accountability). The service professionals are, however, likely to want something more than this; they are likely to expect the organization to show that it achieved what it set out to achieve, that it provided a better or more accessible service (programme accountability).

There may, of course, be no conflict between these different demands; problems may arise, however, where one type of accountability acquires very much greater significance than others. For example, it is not uncommon to hear voluntary organizations complain that the Manpower Services Commission's emphasis on fiscal accountability obscures any possibility of discussing programme accountability. The tendency to concentrate on fiscal and process accountability is, of course, no accident. Programme accountability, though arguably the most significant, tends to receive less attention partly because it is so difficult to apply in many areas of work. Even if there are agreed measures for evaluating the success of a project/service, applying these often requires time and resources which are rarely (made) available. Paradoxically, it seems that demands for programme accountability are most likely to come not from funders but from clients/users.

Voluntary organizations may be accountable to different groups for different things (for example, money, services, etc.), to the same group for different things, and to different groups for the same things.

One way of dealing with the problem of multiple accountability might be to clearly separate the lines and "objects" of accountability between different groups, i. e. one would be accountable to one group for, say, money, and to another for, say, quality of service, and so on. The discussion above has highlighted one way in which any one voluntary organization may be accountable to the same group for different things (or for the same thing in different ways). Furthermore, accountability for funding may, of course, be owed simultaneously to several different funders, and indeed several funders may be involved in one piece of work. Funders and clients clearly have overlapping interests in, but perhaps conflicting definitions of, quality of service and thus the organization's accountability for that. It is clear then that careful demarcation is not a solution to the problem of multiple accountability for most voluntary organizations.

Before leaving the issues of "for what" voluntary organizations may be considered accountable, it is worth referring back to the distinctions above between fiscal, process, programme, and "priorities" accountability.

Groups may differ in the extent to which they regard the organization as accountable (to them) for these different things. Some may be interested in only one, others may be interested in all four. Conversely, the organization itself may regard itself as accountable to some groups for only one or two of the four; and to other groups for all four. It should also be noted that insofar as making another accountable involves the ability (knowledge, skill, and legitimacy) to ask the right questions and assess the adequacy of the answer, then groups will vary in that ability in relation to each of the four areas.

The bases of (the right to demand) accountability may differ between the groups to which the organization is accountable; so too may the reasons for delegation (and thus accountability) differ between groups.

As noted above, the bases of (the right to require) accountability may differ between the groups to which the organization is accountable. Unless the different bases of accountability (to different groups) are identified and distinguished, "inappropriate" accountability may be accorded to some groups, i. e. accountability which the accounted-to organization does not have the right to demand. For example, delegate accountability is specific to the tasks/resources delegated; the delegator has the right to require accountability only for those particular tasks/resources. Communal accountability, on the other hand, is more diffuse and, because it usually operates at a higher level of abstraction (i. e. in the realm of norms and values and not at the level of specific tasks and activities), is both broader and less clear. Unless the organization is clear about the bases of its accountability to different groups, then it lays itself open to agreeing to accountability requirements from groups which have no basis (right) for such requirements.

Not only may the bases of accountability differ between groups, but so too may the reasons for delegation (and thus accountability). The initial reasons for delegation set the parameters within which appropriate accountability processes must be formulated. For example, if the funder delegates a piece of work to an organization because it believes this will allow more flexibility in the creation and execution of the work, there is little point in then instituting accountability requirements and processes which effectively destroy or constrain that flexibility. Failure to specify clearly the reasons for delegation may lead to inappropriate accountability requirements and processes which frustrate funder and voluntary organizations alike.

Another reason for inappropriate accountability requirements (i. e. those which either go beyond their basis or which destroy the advantages delegation was intended to achieve) may be recognition of the voluntary organization's other loyalties. Lack of clarity about the nature of the organization's accountability to other groups and the fear that the organization's accountability to this group may be weakened or subverted by the demands of others may lead the group to attempt to exert more control over the organization than is appropriate (either in terms of the basis of accountability or in terms of the reasons for delegation).

Voluntary organizations are not only accountable to a number of different groups, but they are also inevitably caught in "chains of accountability." In other words, voluntary organizations are accountable to (some) groups (for particular things) which are themselves accountable to other groups (for those same things). This may create inappropriate accountability demands as the accountability requirements of one group vis-à-vis another are "passed down the line." Alternatively, of course, it might be argued that there is little time to make those organizations at the end of the line accountable, because those to whom they are accountable are too busy being accountable to those higher up in the line.

It is, of course, also possible that chains of accountability do not have any necessary internal dynamic but may rather provide some organizations with a powerful legitimation for certain demands or actions.

5. The Reality of Voluntary Sector Accountability

Above, I attempted to outline in theory the "problem" of voluntary sector accountability. In essence, the "problem" identified was that of the different meanings of accountability and the multiple groups to which voluntary organizations may be perceived as accountable. In a recent study exploring the reality of voluntary organization accountability (Leat 1988), it became clear that accountability is indeed a problem and probably an increasing one, but perhaps not so significant a problem as the theory suggests. How do voluntary organizations manage multiple accountability and yet still get on with the work? How does an apparently unmanagable system work?

I suggest that at present voluntary organizations, or more accurately the officers/workers of those organizations, manage multiple accountability by working in the spaces between the theory and the practice of accountability.

The system works because funders have little time and often insufficient knowledge to put accountability into practice. The combination of lack of time and other resources, lack of appropriate standards of evaluation, and acceptance of the principle (if not the implications) of risk-taking creates the conditions for a conspiracy of silence. And the silence is only relatively rarely broken because, whatever the theory of pluralism, the reality is that spending on the voluntary sector remains marginal in relation to total departmental expenditure.

Both funders and workers are able to "manage" management committee accountability, because committees are generally composed of people with little time, selected for their interests and skills *outside* the organization. For reasons discussed elsewhere, management committees would seem to have a strong interest in avoiding controversial issues and maintaining a "working consensus" (see, for example, Kramer 1965; Senor 1965).

Accountability to users is "managed" by funders, workers, and committees quite simply because it is difficult to "hear" the voice of users, and when voices are heard judgement must be employed to decide between conflicting demands.

By these means the demands of multiple accountability are "contained" from day to day. However, although the "spaces" permit the containment of these demands, the demands of multiple accountability remain. The problem with containment rather than confrontation of the difficulties of multiple accountability is that voluntary organizations leave themselves open to spasmodic and often unsubstantiated attacks from, for example, MPs and local councillors, to charges of being undemocratic and to challenges to their legitimacy. Workers are often left without appropriate means of support, and the organization is open to more or less appropriate demands to satisfy the accountability requirements of other organizations within one or more chains of accountability.

The "problem" of voluntary sector accountability is unlikely to disappear. The questioning of the role of the state and the growth of "third-party government" — in particular in Britain the increasing reliance upon the voluntary sector as providers of welfare — are likely to emphasize demands for voluntary sector accountability. Demands for greater accountability to the state raise a number of fundamental issues for the voluntary sector, including its ability to reconcile these demands with those of other groups to whom it sees itself, or is seen by others, to be accountable. At a time when the relationship between the state and the voluntary sector is changing on a number of fronts, there is an urgent need for clarity in the bases, meanings, and objects of accountability. Without such clarity, the voluntary sector may destroy or undermine its current sources of legitimacy and defining characteristics.

References

ACC, AMA, NCVO (1981): *Working Together, Partnerships in Local Social Service*, London: Bedford Square Press.

Charities Aid Foundation (1985): *Charity Statistics 1983−4*, London: Charities Aid Foundation.

Gerard, D. (1983): *Charities in Britain, Conservatism or Change?* London: Bedford Square Press.

Harris, M. (1985): "Let's Try Another Route," in *Management Development Unit Bulletin*, No. 5, June, London: NCVO, 15–16.

Kramer, R. M. (1965): "Ideology, Status and Power in Board Executive Relationships," in *Readings in Community Organization Practice*, R. M. Kramer and H. Specht (Eds.), Englewood Cliffs, N.J.: Prentice-Hall, 285–293.

Kramer, R. M. (1982): *From Voluntarism to Vendorism: An Organizational Perspective on Contracting*, PONPO working Paper – 54, Yale University, 2nd Ed., Englewood Cliffs, N.J.: Prentice-Hall.

Landry, C., D. Morley, R. Southwood, and P. Wright (1985): *What a Way to Run a Railroad: An Analysis of Radical Failure*, London: Comedia.

Leat, D. (1988): *Voluntary Organizations and Accountability*, London: NCVO.

Leat, D., S. Tester, and J. Unell (1986): *A Price Worth Paying? A Study of the Effects of Government Grant Aid to Voluntary Organisations*, London: Policy Studies Institute.

Payne, M. (1985): "National Management Committee Week: A Fantasy," *Management Development Unit Bulletin*, No. 5, June, London: NCVO, 17.

Rein, M. (1975): "Social Planning: The Search for Legitimacy," in *Readings in Community Organisation Practice*, R. H. Kramer and H. Specht (Eds.), Englewood Cliffs, N.J.: Prentice-Hall, 307–315.

Rowe, A. (1978): "Participation and the Voluntary Sector: The Independent Contribution," *Journal of Social Policy* 7, 1.

Senor, J. M.: (1963): "Another Look at the Executive Board Relationship," in *Social Work*, 8, 2, April, 19–25.

Simey, M. (1985): *Government by Consent, The Principles and Practice of Accountability in Local Government*, London: Bedford Square Press.

Smith, B. L. R. and D. C. Hague (Eds.) (1971): *The Dilemma of Accountability in Modern Government*, London: Macmillan.

Stanton, E. (1970): *Clients Come Last: Volunteers and Welfare Organizations*, Beverly Hills: Sage Publications Inc.

Stanyer, J. and B. Smith (1976): *Administering Britain*, London: Fontana.

Wagner, G. (1979): *Barnardo*, London: Weidenfeld and Nicholson.

Part III
The Public and the Private:
Efficiency, Funding, and Autonomy

3.1
Efficiency, Funding, and Autonomy in the Third Sector

Susan Rose-Ackerman

Who should control the activities of nonprofit organizations? Do they exist for the benefit of managers, private donors, board members, clients, or funding sources? The papers in this section examine this question in situations where the nonprofit sector is heavily intertwined with government.[1] Those who worry that public money will produce "goal diversion" are met on the other side by those who are concerned that government will abdicate its responsibility to see that general principles of fairness and efficiency govern the spending of public money.[2] The very diversity and responsiveness to local conditions that make nonprofits appear to be attractive providers of services stand in the way of public accountability. Yet attracting private resources can also "distort" an institution's mission. A large gift can skew programs in the direction preferred by the donor; increased fees and charges can change client mix, and entrepreneurial activity designed to raise funds can sap the energies of the professional staff. A sizable government grant or a client population eligible for individual subsidy may be liberating for a charity manager in spite of red tape and regulatory restrictions.

A surprisingly large share of the writing on nonprofits assumes that the charity's professional staff and, perhaps, its board of directors have the "right" values so that any influence exerted by funding sources, clients, or regulatory bodies "diverts" the charity from its proper mission.[3] This perspective, while a natural one for charity managers and professionals, is

---

[1] Salamon (chapter 3.4) in discussing this phenomenon in the United States labels it "third-party government" and provides data on its extent. According to him, the government – nonprofit partnership "forms the core of the human services delivery system in the United States."

[2] Kramer (chapter 3.6), reporting on research on social service agencies, identifies conflicts between autonomy and accountability when nonprofit agencies are heavily dependent on public funds. Knapp, Robertson, and Thomason (chapter 3.3) and Salamon (chapter 3.4) emphasize the same tension.

[3] Lloyd (chapter 3.5) quotes the British National Council for Voluntary Organisations "Code" which states that: "Each voluntary body must regard its freely-chosen aims and objectives as paramount under the law in determining its policy and conduct."

hardly self-evident (Salamon, see chapter 3.4). Nevertheless, I begin by asking: What can be said in support of such a claim?

First of all, individual nonprofit managers are rather special people. Leaving aside the possibility of outright fraud, they obviously cannot be primarily concerned with financial reward, or they would have put their energy and talent to work in the for-profit sector. In large part, they appear to be people who want to reify their ideas. They have beliefs about how children should be educated or theater produced, or the mentally retarded cared for, and they obtain satisfaction from actually putting these ideas into practice (Kramer, see chapter 3.6; Lloyd, see chapter 3.5; Rose-Ackerman 1986 b, 1987; Young 1983, 1985). If the constraints on such people are too stringent, they will simply refuse to found or direct charitable institutions. Under this view, if outside funding sources fail to respect the values of the nonprofit professionals and entrepreneurs, they will be left with no one to support.

Second, one of the things outside supporters are "buying" when they finance nonprofit activities is the diverse set of ideas and ideologies in the nonprofit sector. If the government does not value this diversity and imposes so many constraints that the distinctive features of private provision are lost, then it might as well provide the service in-house. Under such restrictive conditions, nothing will be left of the justification for private nonprofit provision beyond the cynical one that such delegation saves money because charities can get away with paying little or nothing to their workers (Lloyd, chapter 3.5).[4] Thus, when either or both of these conditions holds, it is actually in the interest of government or, indeed, of any outside source of funds to give charity professionals considerable freedom of action.

While this view of the nonprofit sector has widespread validity and should caution resource suppliers against an overly intrusive role, it is surely too utopian. Why should one assume that nonprofit managers and boards have a set of values that corresponds to those of government bodies and private donors? How can one be sure that charities will use untied resources effectively? Even idealists may be sloppy bookkeepers and poor financial planners,[5] and may run rigid, unresponsive organizations (Kramer, chapter 3.6).

---

[4] This is a view that is frequently proved wrong in practice, at least when large-scale public support is involved. Thus low wage hospital workers in the United States improved their positions after the introduction of Medicare and Medicaid. Lloyd (chapter 3.5) reports that voluntary association workers in Britain "are beginning to collectively organize in trades unions to demand the same pay scales as state employees." See also Knapp, Robertson, and Thomason (chapter 3.3).

[5] As Knapp, Robertson, and Thomason (chapter 3.3) point out, the problem for government agencies is that the nonprofits' flexibility and responsiveness often goes along with inconsistency and lack of accountability to public funding sources.

To think about the issue of external control, consider an alternative view of the nonprofit sector in which charitable organizations are viewed as the agents of outside supporters, be they government agencies, private donors, or clients.[6] Then the fact that donors' wishes may be ignored by charity staff is viewed as a problem, not a strength. The first question to ask is how a charity could ever get away with *not* reflecting donors' preferences. There are several ways to answer this question.

In the first place, donors may not *have* any clear preferences beyond a desire to help the needy or to further culture, education, or health care. They are happy to delegate to the charity staff the tasks of articulating a philosophy of service provision and making specific allocational choices. In fact, especially in the public sector, the diversity of approaches itself may be valued independently of their content or efficacy in solving problems (Kramer, chapter 3.6). Nevertheless, nonideological donors are likely to want some sort of financial accountability even if they would be willing to delegate such oversight to a public agency.

Secondly, consider private donors who do have a clearly articulated philosophy that is only imperfectly reflected in the programs of the charities they support. If such mismatches are pervasive, this would seem to leave the way open for charitable entrepreneurs to open new charities or redirect old ones in directions that reflect the preferences of these donors. Such behavior does, in fact, occur with major donors themselves often setting up such institutions and sometimes even managing them. Nevertheless, the match is not perfect, and we need to understand why.

First of all, there are economies of scale in the production of most charitable services. Thus even if managers sought to be the perfect agents of donors, not all donors would be able to find a charity that perfectly matched their own preferences. Some sacrifice in productive efficiency may be made in return for a closer match of donors' and charities' ideologies, but at some point donors can be expected to prefer an optimally scaled provider with a somewhat divergent philosophy to an inefficiently small one that espouses the same beliefs as the donor (Rose-Ackerman 1986a, 1986b). Even an Atheist may give money to an established, well-run Protestant school.

Second, size itself may be valuable to donors. Here we must speculate a bit on the benefits donors receive from giving. If, by their gifts, donors psychologically "buy-in" to the entire range of services provided by the charity, they will prefer large organizations to small ones so long as no part of the organization is actually providing services that are repugnant to them (Rose-Ackerman 1986a). This will increase the entry costs for new charities

---

[6] Writing by economists generally takes this position. See the articles collected in Rose-Ackerman (1986c) and the literature review in James and Rose-Ackerman (1986).

and further reduce the efficient number of charitable firms over and above whatever production economies exist.[7]

Third, the supply of charitable entrepreneurs may not equal the demand. Since financial rewards to risk-taking cannot be used to attract creative people to the nonprofit sector, not enough people may exist who want to put their ideas into concrete form. Furthermore, because the people who do become entrepreneurs are a biased sample of the population, they may poorly reflect the interests of donors most of whom are too busy to be charity entrepreneurs themselves.

In short, for all these reasons, even if all charitable resources came from private donations, charity managers could be expected to have some freedom of action. They would trade off organizational size and financial security against ideological purity, but they would, nevertheless, be left some room to advance their own charitable goals.

Given a gap between the aims of private donors and those of charity professionals, the key issue is whether public money furthers the interests of donors or of charity staff. Thus, if public agencies and private donors have shared goals, the size and visibility of government support may permit it to succeed in modifying the behavior of nonprofits in a way that would be impossible for the mass of individual donors. Managers may cry "goal deflection," but donors may be favorably impressed and increase their support of the charity, both because they are buying into a larger organization, and because they value the type of services provided more higher than before.[8] This can happen even though the marginal social benefit of private gifts may fall when government resources increase. Furthermore, government may be able to impose financial and substantive accountability on an organization more effectively than private donors (Knapp, Robertson, and Thoma-

---

[7] When donors see themselves as buying-in to the charity's entire complement of services, nonprofits must be concerned that some activities do not have negative value for donors. Donors will accept some mismatch between their ideologies and those of the charity in order to give to a large organization, but may withdraw support for all activities if part of the program is repugnant. A conservative graduate may cease contributing to a university that has Communists on its faculty, anti-abortion advocates may not give to hospitals that perform abortions, and peace activists may refuse to donate to otherwise worthy institutions that perform military research.

[8] Lloyd (chapter 3.5) reports on a British study which found that "the more successful a voluntary association was in attracting [government] grant aid, the greater its success in expanding its activities." In fact, nonprofits may welcome the receipt of competitively awarded government grants as representing a seal of approval which assists them in private sector fundraising. In the United States, the National Endowment for the Arts seems to function in this way. See "How One Tiny Theater Snared Harold Pinter," *New York Times* January 8, 1989.

son, chapter 3.3), an action which may also stimulate giving. Thus it is essential to my argument about the impact of public support that nonprofit entrepreneurs and managers are not simple revenue maximizers but, instead, have independent views about charitable behavior. Under that condition, public subsidy can in some cases *increase* a charity's accountability to private donors by reducing the influence of charitable staff.

Conversely, government grants may permit nonprofit managers to run a viable agency with lower levels of private support. Grants may support the managers' own views of how the charity should behave (Lloyd, chapter 3.5, Salamon, chapter 3.4). Managers and professional staff will then eagerly accept public money and may use it to sponsor activities that alienate some private donors (Rose-Ackerman 1987).

Similar ambiguities in the impact of government support arise when we consider private funding sources other than charitable gifts. The most important are fees and charges for mission-related services (fees for hospital care, school tuition payments) and net revenue from projects designed to generate revenue. In the case of fees, the conflict for charities is over the possibility that the client mix required to remain solvent differs from the one mandated by their charitable mission. In the case of commercial activity, the conflict is over whether to pursue strategies that will maximize net revenues but may conflict with other organizational goals and divert staff energies. In both situations, government subsidies can either exacerbate or alleviate these problems.

When public agencies support nonprofits which charge fees, the basic issues are whether the nonprofit has more or less freedom to select its own mix of clients, and if it has less, whether the resulting mixture is preferred to the unsubsidized situation. When fee levels are subsidized, a nonprofit can obviously afford to serve more poor and disadvantaged clients and still break even. However, untied public subsidies will not necessarily produce this result. They may simply permit the nonprofit to be more selective by lowering its prices and obtaining a larger pool of applicants. The nonprofit can then select those clients who fit most comfortably with the interests of its professional staff. Thus, if teachers prefer to teach intelligent students, a generalized subsidy will permit a school to "upgrade" its student body. Of course, some of those selected may be low income students unable to afford the school's tuition, but the broadened economic base of the student body is a by-product of a selection process based on ability, not an explicit attempt to select the most needy. Furthermore, the nonprofit will not necessarily expand in size if the staff's ideology includes a belief in the appropriate size of the organization, be it a school, a day care center, or a home for the developmentally disabled. However, many charitable organizations *do* place a high value on serving the needy and view fees as an unfortunate constraint on that goal. Such organizations would not care if public subsidies were tied to poor clients or generalized. In either case, the client mix would shift in the preferred direction toward disadvantaged individuals.[9]

A large-scale public subsidy program may have a further indirect benefit even for nonprofits that accept no public money. The subsidy may induce the entry of new organizations willing to serve subsidized clients that formerly were cared for by reluctant nonprofits. The charities can now be more selective in choosing clients whose demands mesh closely with those of its professional staff. Sad but uninteresting cases can be shunted to the newly subsidized providers.

Finally, consider activity that is frankly designed to generate revenue. At one level, such activity should interfere least with charity managers' basic goals. Those who use these services, unlike clients, donors, and public agencies, simply want to consume the organization's service. They are making no ideological demands on the organization. Of course, the purest example here is passive investment income. General endowment is the best source of revenue for the ideological manager. Unfortunately, most such managers are not so lucky. Instead, they must actually produce goods or services that paying customers will buy. To obtain a market niche, they may use the reputation of the nonprofit as a marketing ploy. Then they face the risk that commercial activity will dictate the behavior of the nonprofit in other areas. Mission-oriented projects may be chosen with an eye to how they will affect commercial sales. Given the trade-offs between ideological purity and financial solvency present with all sources of funds, however, it is not obvious that the difficulties which arise in commercial activities are necessarily worse than those that exist elsewhere. Nevertheless, the one distinctive feature of this case is the lack of a strong argument for promoting the interests of commercial customers over those of charity professionals. At least in the other cases of conflict, one could claim that the interests of private donors, public agencies, and subsidized clients ought to be given some weight over and above the aims of charity managers and board members.

Paradoxically, the current concern in the United States that commercial activity may deflect nonprofits from their charitable goals seems misplaced. Increasing the share of commercial activity in a nonprofit's revenue base may actually increase the ability of managers to carry out their goals. The losers, however, are the general public whose impact on nonprofits through

---

[9] Salamon (chapter 3.4) presents evidence that this phenomenon has occurred in reverse in the United States, as Federal government support has fallen the 1980s. He and his colleagues found that, outside the health field, where support rose, nonprofits largely substituted fees for grants to make up the shortfall in public money. For social service charities in particular, the result was a less needy client population.

public subsidy and private donation have fallen with the combination of reduced marginal tax rates and lower government support for social services.

The papers which follow fill out the argument sketched here and provide much valuable information on recent experience in the United States, Great Britain, and the Netherlands. Readers from outside the United States should bear in mind that, in spite of the importance of government subsidies and client fees, private giving is a more important source of resources in the United States than elsewhere. This fact necessarily influences the American debate on the role of charitable nonprofits. It may also explain the relative neglect of the role of private donors in the papers by British writers. Thus in comparative work on the nonprofit social service sector, a useful focus might be the relative importance of government support versus both private donations and fees and charges. Can systematic differences in behavior be traced to the sources of funds, or are differences in the ideologies of charity managers sufficient to explain inter-country variations? Such an inquiry, however, would obviously be complicated by the fact that the two variables are not independent. The type of people attracted to the charitable sector may be a function of the role of the state in supporting the services it provides, and, conversely, state support may depend upon the nature of the nonprofit sector. Nevertheless, the tension between ideas and resources can provide a unifying theme for further inquiry.

References

James, Estelle and Susan Rose-Ackerman (1986): *The Nonprofit Enterprise in Market Economies*, Chur, Switzerland: Harwood.

Rose-Ackerman, Susan (1986 a): "Charitable Giving and 'Excessive' Fundraising," in S. Rose-Ackerman (Ed.) (1986 c), 333 – 346.

Rose-Ackerman, Susan (1986 b): "Do Government Grants to Charity Reduce Private Donations?" in S. Rose-Ackerman (Ed.) (1986 c), 313 – 329.

Rose-Ackerman, Susan (Ed.), (1986 c): *The Economics of Nonprofit Institutions: Studies in Structure and Policy*, New York: Oxford University Press.

Rose-Ackerman, Susan (1987): "Ideals versus Dollars: Donors, Charity Managers, and Government Grants," *Journal of Political Economy* 95, 810 – 823.

Young, Dennis R. (1983): *If Not for Profit, for What? A Behavioral Theory of the Nonprofit Sector Based on Entrepreneurship*, Lexington, Mass.: Lexington.

Young, Dennis R. (1985): *Casebook of Management for Non-Profit Organizations: Entrepreneurship and Organizational Change in the Human Services*, New York: Haworth.

3.2
Achievement in Public and Private Secondary Education in the Netherlands[1]

Peter Van Laarhoven, Bart Bakker, Jaap Dronkers,
and Huibert Schijf

1. Introduction

Coleman, Hoffer, and Kilgore (1982) claim that in the United States private high schools are more effective than public high schools. They conclude that private school students learn substantially more than public school students during their last two years in high school, and find that private school attendance is especially favourable for ethnic minority students and those from lower social class backgrounds. Critics content that private schools enroll primarily students of superior academic competence, because of either selection or self-selection. Although Coleman et al., using cross-sectional data, could not distinguish differential sector effectiveness from selection effects, Hoffer, Greeley, and Coleman (1985), using new data on achievement growth, found support for the earlier claims. Willms (1985) and Alexander and Pallas (1985), however, conclude that the benefits of private schooling are much smaller than Hoffer, Greeley, and Coleman claim, and are often statistically insignificant.

Clearly, in comparing different educational practices related to school sector, data are needed to measure the cumulative effect of many years of exposure to the practice in question. Without data on the cumulative impact of school sector on the educational career, it is impossible to estimate the persistence of benefits over time. When a student has received only a few years of schooling within one sector, evaluations are needed over a period of several years to determine effects over time. Conclusions based entirely on short-term effects should never be taken very seriously, since experience has repeatedly shown that long-term effects are far smaller than short-term effects (Jencks 1985: 134).

[1] This research has been made possible by a grant from the Dutch Department of Education and Sciences through the Dutch Foundation of Educational Research and the Educational Research Center of the University of Amsterdam. Address all correspondence to J. Dronkers, Department of Sociology, University of Tilburg, P. O. Box 90153, 5000 LE Tilburg, The Netherlands.

Undoubtedly even the most accurate measure of the sector effect in the U. S. school system will retain some imprecision. The selection problem can not be solved entirely, because in the USA and most other countries the public and private sectors are unequally financed. Thus students in private and public schools differ in at least one respect: the parents of the students in private schools have to pay substantial extra costs. To what extent the willingness to pay for education manifests parents' seriousness about educational outcome or motivation and support for academic achievement will not be elaborated here. The simple fact that students and their parents differ systematically across school sectors on the price they pay for education means that the estimation of the sector effect is biased to some unknown extent.

In contrast to most countries, the Netherlands has an educational system in which public and private education are equally funded (James 1984). It is characterized by a large private sector, existing alongside a public sector, for the most part composed of Catholic and Protestant schools. Although "pillarization" (*verzuiling*) along religious lines has been waning in the last three decades, denominational schools show no sign of losing ground to the public sector. More than 60 % of the school pupils still receive schooling within the private sector. While the government exerts substantial control on curriculum, examinations, and teachers' payment, the non-public schools are still relatively free to hire teachers and to make their own educational programs. Although developed in a quite different historical context than the U. S. system, the Netherlands' educational system offers a good opportunity to test whether school sector effects on achievement can be explained by sector differences in funding.

In Dutch literature on education and "pillarization," several explanations for the prevalence of denominational schools are presented. According to Thurlings (1978), "pillarization" arose originally in those fields of Dutch society which had a large influence on the formation of values and norms. Thus he concludes that pillarization will probably endure in education, especially primary education, even if it disintegrates elsewhere. Van Kemenade (1968) and De Jonge (1978) show that Catholic and Protestant parents value highly a religious upbringing for their children; they prefer denominational schools for the socialization of cherished norms and values.

However, the current participation in Catholic and Protestant education can not be explained entirely by the actual preference of Catholic and Protestant parents. Indeed, in 1979, only 66 % of all Catholic and Protestant parents explicitly preferred denominational education for their children (Social and Cultural Planning Office 1980). Also the percentage of Protestant and Catholic households has dropped far below the percentage of children at denominational schools. Therefore we need to explain why both non-religious and religious parents continue to choose private education.

According to a second explanation, the actual participation in private schools does not reflect parents' preferences but rather their lack of alternatives. When new schools are founded, the current distribution of schools across sectors is commonly taken as a starting point. Moreover, established school boards and their organizations have substantial political power, and they can usually exert enough influence to maintain the existing overrepresentation of denominational schools (Bouhuijs and Boef van der Meulen 1978; Ransdorp and Dronkers 1982). Although many parents may prefer other schools, these may not be available within their neighbourhood or may belong to an undesired sector. This argument, however, does not explain why the relative overrepresentation of private schools has not produced political action to enhance the number of alternatives, as happened when pillarization waned in other fields of Dutch society.

A third possible explanation contends that private schools provide better education than public schools; "better" not necessarily in the sense of superior norms and values but rather in the sense of a fuller development of childrens' faculties. However, it is often impossible for parents to verify whether a particular school has the educational standing they desire. School sector might therefore become a screening device that enables parents to assess the quality of schools. Denominational schools in the Netherlands are, moreover, able to raise some extra school fees (average of Df 200, − , equal to U.S. $100) and, though they cannot use these to pay for extra teachers, higher salaries, or extra books, they can organize more extra-curricular activities than public schools. They can probably also enforce both more effective discipline and stringent educational demands among their teachers and pupils. Finally, they are less sensitive to political pressure.

In the Netherlands, secondary education is divided into hierarchically ordered types of schools. This hierarchy is quite similar to the different tracks that exist in U.S. high schools (college, general, vocational). Before the 1968 educational reform, this hierarchy was: classical grammar school, modern grammar school (for boys and girls), and modern grammar school for girls (vhmo); advanced primary education (ulo); junior domestic science school and junior technical school (lbo); continued primary education (vglo). Within vhmo and ulo, there were two tracks: "A" and "B." Track "A" stood for education which emphasized languages and humanities. Track "B" focussed on mathematics and exact sciences. Track "B" was sometimes accorded higher status, because it offered better opportunities for further education. After 1968, the hierarchy of schools changed into: pre-university education; senior general education; junior general education; junior vocational education. Only the highest level (classical and modern grammar school or pre-university education) provides a direct entry to the university. The other types of secondary education, according to their place in the hierarchy, offer less valued opportunities for further education or jobs.

In an earlier article, we demonstrated a school sector effect in Dutch primary education which enabled denominational primary school students to attain higher levels in the first year of secondary education than public school students (Van Laarhoven et al. 1986). Now we will focus on the differential effects of Catholic, Protestant, and public schools on achievement during secondary education. The analysis is carried out within two levels of education: the grammar school and junior general education.[2] We will examine long-term effects of the educational practices particular to each school sector. However, because of restrictions in the data, our research is limited to the effects on some key-aspects of a pupil's school career: non-promotion, track enrollment, graduation, and continued education after leaving the particular school type. As we also do not have data on school differences which are not related to school sector, we cannot control for these. Our research is, moreover, confined to the generation that completed primary education in 1965, which means that they were at that time approximately twelve years old. This generation completed their school careers in secondary education undergoing the 1968 reform. So some attended the pre-1968 schooltypes, and some the post-1968 ones.

The central question posed by this article can be stated as follows: do Catholic, Protestant, and public secondary schools have differential effects on their pupils' educational achievement, allowing for social background (including gender, region) and characteristics of their previous school careers, including an achievement test score in the sixth grade of primary education.

2. Data, Methods, and Variables

The data include longitudinal information on pupils born around 1953 who left primary education in 1965. From the population of Dutch primary schools, 405 schools were sampled. A stratified sample of 3,042 respondents was taken from the 11,170 sixth grade pupils within this sample of schools. These pupils were interviewed in 1970, 1974, and 1978 (Diederen 1981). A considerable number of students attended more than one level of secondary education. For each pupil, the career within one level of education is considered as a "case." This means that some pupils were examined several times. So the population universe is not the 1965 generation of pupils, but their respective attendances at a certain schooltype.

---

[2] The junior domestic science school and junior technical school are not examined, because the measure of school sector turned out to be unreliable. Continued primary education is left out of the analyses, because there were only 156 observations in the sample.

A major problem with the measurement of contextual effects is how to correct for individual characteristics. Estimating school sector effects, we have to control for initial differences among students entering the different sectors. This is known as the selectivity bias problem: if one school sector enrolls better students than the other, then there will be a selectivity bias in favour of the first. We control for four groups of variables: social background, career in primary education including a scholastic achievement score, previous school career in secondary education (if present), and some present school features.

Our analysis of scholastic achievement in secondary education is confined to some key aspects of the educational career: non-promotion, curriculum track within a particular schooltype, graduation, continued education after leaving the particular schooltype. Non-promotion is also used as a control variable. To meet the methodological criticism of Jencks (1985), we make typologies of school careers of public, Catholic, and Protestant school students. In doing so, we evaluate the long-term effects of educational practices within one school sector: the cumulative effects of several aspects of students' educational careers. Table 1 gives an overview of the variables used. COMPR refers to the possibility that several types of secondary schools were clustered into one multilateral school. We call it a "comprehensive school" when it was such a multilateral school, and a "grammar/junior general school only" when it was not.

We mainly use analysis of covariance (ANOVA, see Nie et al. 1975: 398–433). This technique enables us to examine the relationship between a quantitative dependent variable and quantitative ("covariates") as well as qualitative independent variables ("factors"). ANOVA provides a test of significance for the contribution of each independent variable to the explained variance of the dependent variable. ANOVA also yields estimates for the strength and the direction of the relationships. To investigate if significant interactions are present, we entered interactions as dummy variables in regression analysis. Only if neither interactions with other control variables nor severe deviation of linearity occurred, variables are treated as covariates. When interactions were present in which school sector was not involved, a new control-variable was created which was a full crossing of the original variables. Interactions between school sector and other control-variables are separately presented. For each particular category, we present the grand mean of the dependent variable, and the adjusted mean when both factors and covariates are controlled for.

3. Achievement in Public and Private Grammar Schools

The results of the analyses for public and private grammar schools are presented in Table 2. Achievement in Protestant grammar schools is higher than in either Catholic or public schools. More students in Protestant schools

Table 1: Labels of the Variables Used

Social background	
gender	SEX
father's occupation	FOCC
father's education	FEDUC
mother's education	MEDUC
province of residence	REGION
urbanization of residence	URBAN
religious preference parents	RELI
Career in primary education	
primary school sector	PRISEC
non-promotion	PRINPR
achievement score in sixth grade	PRIACH
teacher's advice on secondary education	PRIADV
Previous secondary school career (if present)	
level of preceding education	PRELEV
Present school features	
type of school within one level	TYPE
grade leaving school	YEARLEA
school sector	SECTOR
comprehensive or grammar/junior general school only	COMPR
extra-curricular activities	EXCUR
participation in extra-curricular activities	EXPART
Achievement in secondary education	
non-promotion	NONPRO
choice of track "B"	TRACK
graduation	GRAD
continued education after graduation	CONGRAD
continued education after leaving school	CONNON
without a certificate to a higher schooltype	FLOWUP

Table 2: Some Key Aspects of Grammar School Career by School Sector, Before (a) and After (b) Controlling for Variables in Table 3

	% NONPRO		% TRACK		% GRAD		% CONGRAD		% CONNON	
	a	b	a	b	a	b	a	b	a	b
Public	43	44	42	40	57	60	66	67	81	81
Catholic	38	38	37	39	61	59	73	74	79	80
Protestant	41	40	45	45	66	65	83	81	83	82
Total	41		41		61		73		81	
(N = 100%)	1116		690		1116		678		438	

study track "B," graduate, and continue education after graduation with or without a certificate. The only exception to this tendency is that students in Catholic schools repeat fewer classes than Protestant school students. In general, the differences between Catholic and public school students are smaller than between Protestant and public schools students.

By controlling for the variables mentioned in Table 3, the school sector effects diminish but are not eliminated, as can be seen in Table 2. The reduction is due largely to sector differences in the distribution of students over subtypes within the grammar school level. The modern grammar school for girls and senior general education can be considered as "easier" (less non-promotion, more assignment to "B"-tracks, more graduation); classical and modern grammar schools are more difficult but usually lead to further enrollment in college and university education. Catholic school students attend these "easier" schooltypes more frequently than either Protestant or public school students. Allowing for social background, primary school career, preceding career in secondary education and present school features leads to an elimination of the difference in graduation in Catholic and public schools, but does not reduce the advantage of Protestant school students.

The variables in the ANOVA-analysis explain from 10 to 39 % of the variance in the several key aspects in grammar school careers (Table 3). The effect of school sector is only significant on the continuation of education after graduation, where it explains 2 % out of 10 % of the variance. The difference between students in public and Protestant schools is large: only 67 % of the public school graduates, against 81 % of Protestant school graduates, enroll in further education.

Five important interaction effects are found in which school sector is involved. In Table 4, we show only the three interaction effects on graduation; the interpretation of the other two is similar. After controls, boys graduate more frequently in denominational schools than girls, whereas this difference is absent in public schools. The school sector effect also varies according to family background of the student. In public schools, there is a non-linear effect of family background: less middle-class students graduate than lower- or upper-class students. In Catholic schools, the upper-class students perform best in this respect, while in Protestant schools, the lower-class students graduate most frequently. Furthermore, high achievement in Protestant schools only occurs in comprehensive schools. Students in non-comprehensive Protestant schools graduate even less frequently than students in non-comprehensive Catholic and public schools.

In Table 5, the results are reconsidered using a typology of school careers in grammar school while allowing for social background, primary school career, preceding career in secondary education, and present school features. The Protestant sector effect leads to relatively high achievement, giving them a considerable advantage over other students. More students study track

Table 3: ANOVA-Estimates of School Sector Effects on Grammar School Careers

	NONPRO	TRACK	GRAD	CONGRAD	CONNON
R^2	.15	.27	.31	.10	.39
attributable to TYPE				.02**	
PRELEV	} .11**	} .15**	} .16**	–	} .14**
NONPRO	–			.04**	
PRIADV	–	–	} .06**	–	–
PRIACH	–	–		–	–
PRINPR	–	–	.00**	–	–
TRACK	–	–	–	.01*	–
COMPR	–	.01**	.04**	–	–
SEX	.01**	.04**	–	–	–
FOCC	.02**	–	–	.01**	.02**
FEDUC	–	.02**	–	–	–
YEARLEA	–	–	–	–	.12**
EXCUR	.00$	–	.00$	–	–
EXPART	.00$	–	.03$$	–	–
SECTOR	.00	.00	.00	.02**	.00
Interactions of SECTOR and	–	COMPR*	COMPR* FOCC* SEX*	FOCC*	

** factor significant with a probability of .01
* factor significant with a probability of .05
$$ covariate significant with a probability of .01
$ covariate significant with a probability of .05

Table 4: Percentage of Graduates by School Sector and Gender, Father's Occupation and Comprehensive or Grammar School Only, After Controlling for Variables in Table 3

		public %	Catholic	Protestant	Total
SEX	– boys	59	62	71	63
	– girls	59	56	59	58
FOCC	– laborers	59	60	72	62
	– small self-employed or lower employees	60	54	61	58
	– middle employees or higher occupations	60	66	67	64
COMPR	– grammar school only	51	50	48	50
	– comprehensive	63	63	71	65

"B," graduate, and continue education after leaving grammar school. Of the Protestant school students, 51 % enroll in college and university education, whereas only 40 % of the public school students and 45 % of the Catholic school students take this decision. Results in public and Catholic schools are much the same, but there seems to be some advantage for Catholic school students (Table 5a).

We found two important interaction effects in the grammar school career. The school sector effect is conditioned by gender. Boys leave Protestant grammar schools more often with an certificate than boys in public or Catholic schools. Protestant grammar school girls do not have such an advantage. While girls in Protestant grammar schools do not enroll in the more advantageous track "B" more often than girls in public or Catholic schools, boys do. As a consequence, there is an 8 % difference in graduation in track "B" among boys of different school sectors, while for girls this difference is nihil (Table 5b).

In Protestant non-comprehensive grammar schools, students are more often assigned to track "B" than in other sectors, but in this track, they graduate less frequently than their comprehensive school colleagues. Comprehensive grammar schools students do not differ in track assignment across sector, but Protestant comprehensives produce more students who attain certificates. Finally, in both categorical and comprehensive Protestant schools, more B-certificates are obtained when compared to public and Catholic schools. When one intends to chose track "B," it seems most advantageous to attend a non-comprehensive Protestant grammar school. When one is not sure about the track assignment, it seems more appropriate to attend a Protestant comprehensive school (Table 5c).

4. Achievement in Public and Private Junior General Schools

Six key aspects in the junior general career are distinguished, which are presented in Table 6. In four of these aspects, Catholic school students achieve better than both Protestant and public school students: they repeat fewer classes, more often enroll in track "B," graduate more frequently, and are more likely to continue their education after graduation. Continuing education without a certificate in modern grammar school, which is an interrupted though successful junior general school career, occurs less frequently in Catholic schools. The effectiveness of Protestant and public schools differs depending on the school career aspect under study. Public junior general school students repeat more classes, less often enroll in track

Table 5: Typology of Grammar School Careers by School Sector (a), by School Sector and Gender (b), and by School Sector and Comprehensive or Grammar School Only (c), After Controlling for Variables in Table 3

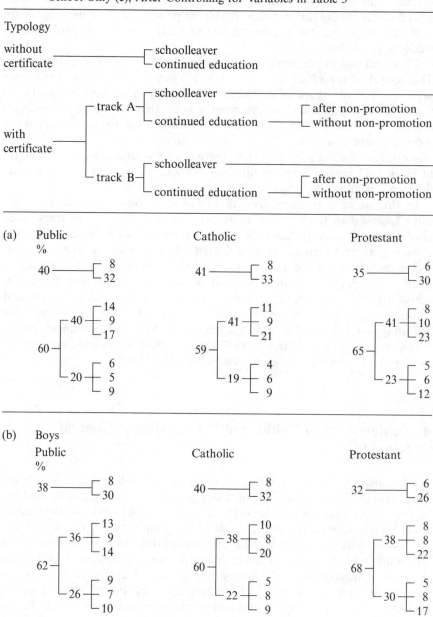

Table 5: (Continued)

Girls

Public %	Catholic	Protestant

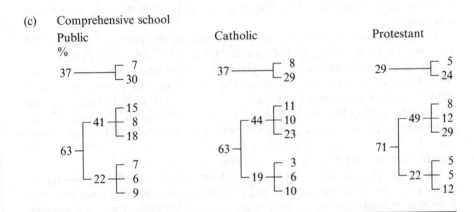

(c) Comprehensive school

Public %	Catholic	Protestant

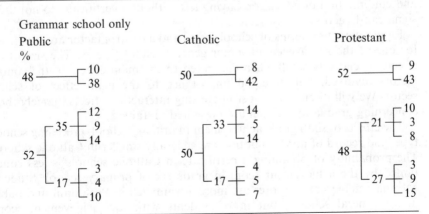

Grammar school only

Public %	Catholic	Protestant

Table 6: Some Key Aspects of Junior General School Careers by School Sector, Before (a) and After (b) Controlling for Variables in Table 7

	% NONPRO		% TRACK		% GRAD		% CONGRAD		% CONNON		% FLOWUP	
	a	b	a	b	a	b	a	b	a	b	a	b
Public	39	38	18	17	61	58	56	57	64	69	26	28
Catholic	32	33	23	22	66	65	67	67	69	67	19	18
Protestant	35	34	21	22	55	58	61	61	72	70	21	22
Total	35		21		61		62		69		22	
(N = 100 %)	1581		971		1581		966		615		423	

"B," and relatively few continue their education after graduation; but they graduate more frequently, and they often enroll in grammar schools without a certificate.

The differences are partially a consequence of the public, Catholic, and Protestant school student population composition (Table 7). Statistical controls of the initial differences in social background and achievement reduce the school sector effect on nearly all the key aspects of the junior general school career. Protestant school students, in particular, seem to have an initial disadvantage, therefore the Protestant school effect is upwardly adjusted. The difference in percentage of graduates between Protestant and public school students is eliminated by allowing for initial differences. Catholic junior general schools still remain the most effective.

However, school sector has a significant effect on the percentage of graduates, the continuation of study after graduation, and enrollment in grammar schools without a certificate. Non-promotion, track assignment, and continuation of education having left without a certificate do not differ significantly across school sector.

Eight interaction terms of school sector and a control factor are significant for one of the key aspects of junior general school careers. The size of the effects is relatively small when compared to the main effects of the control factors involved, but of equal importance to the main effect of school sector. We will discuss the most interesting interaction effects, namely those concerning graduation, which are presented in Table 8.

The effects of sixth grade achievement in primary school, preceding school-type, and record of non-promotion are generally smaller in Catholic schools. The probability of obtaining a certificate in Catholic schools is less conditioned by the achievement score in grade six of primary school. Students with high achievement scores are more advantaged in Protestant and public junior general schools, but more students with low achievement scores

Table 7: ANOVA-Estimates of School Sector Effects on Junior General School Careers

	NONPRO	TRACK	GRAD	CONGRAD	CONNON	FLOWUP
R^2	.10	.07	.25	.13	.40	.35
attributable to TYPE	—	—	.00	—	—	—
NONPRO	—	—	} .02**	.01	} .03**	.02**
PRELEV	.01*	.01**		—		.01*
PRIADV	} .04**	—	.01**	—	.02**	} .12**
PRIACH		—	.01**	.01**	—	
TRACK	—	—	—	.00*	—	—
SEX	.03**	.03**	—	.03**	.04**	—
FOCC	.01**	—	—	.04**	.03**	.05**
FEDUC	—	.01*	—	.01+	.01+	—
MEDUC	—	—	—	—	.01++	.03++
PRINPR	—	—	.01++	—	—	.01++
COMPR	—	.01**	—	—	—	.01++
EXPART	.01++	—	.12++	—	—	—
YEARLEA	—	—	—	.00+	.21++	—
SECTOR	.00	.00	.01*	.01*	.00	.01*
Interactions of SECTOR and	SEX*	FEDUC*	PRIACH* NONPRO* PRELEV*	NONPRO*	PRELEV*	PRIADV*

** factor significant with a probability of .01
* factor significant with a probability of .05
++ covariate significant with a probability of .01
+ covariate significant with a probability of .05

Table 8: Percentage of Junior General School Graduates by School Sector and Achievement Score in Sixth Grade, Level of Preceding Education, and Non-Promotion After Controlling for Variables in Table 7

		Public %	Catholic	Protestant	Total
PRIACH	low	50	64	47	54
	middle	56	65	61	61
	high	70	69	67	68
PRELEV	primary school	55	65	55	59
	lbo, vglo	79	70	81	75
	grammar	44	73	34	55
NONPRO	never	62	67	61	64
	once	50	63	53	56
	twice or more	56	68	52	59

graduate in Catholic schools than in Protestant and public schools. The effect of non-promotion is also smaller in Catholic schools than in Protestant and public schools. Catholic school students who repeated one or more classes do not have less chance in getting a certificate. On the other hand, those who are recruited from grammar schools, and have in fact been downgraded, are more advantaged in Catholic than in public and Protestant schools.

The junior general school careers are again summarized in a typology, which is presented in Table 9. In Catholic schools, the high percentage of graduates and their propensity to continue their study after junior general education combine to channel a relatively high number of students into further education. Approximately 45 % of Catholic school students continue

Table 9: Typology of Junior General School Careers by School After Controlling for Variables in Table 7

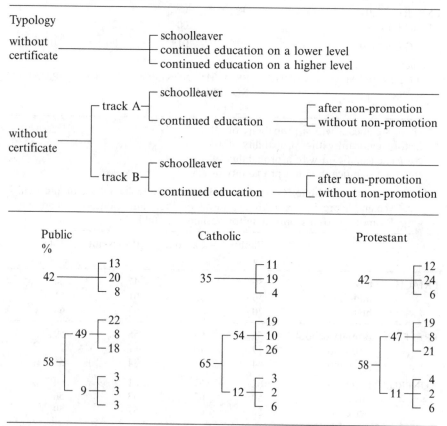

their study as a graduate, compared to only 34 % of public and Protestant school students. Protestant school students graduate nearly as often as Catholic school students in track "B" (11 − 12 %), but the difference is mainly due to graduates in track "A" (54 % − 47 %). The Protestant and public junior general schools do not differ much in overall effectiveness.

5. Conclusions

In this article, we present the Netherlands' educational system as an example of a system in which private and public education are equally supported by the government. Therefore, it offers a good opportunity to test whether school sector effects on scholastic achievement exist in a situation where selection effects due to sector differences in financial funding are absent. The school sector effect is estimated allowing for initial differences in social background, achievement in primary school, preceding secondary school career, and present school features. The estimates for two educational levels are presented separately: grammar and junior general schools.

The analyses provide evidence that in a number of instances students in private schools tend to have higher achievement, and in no instance lower, than students in public schools. The effectiveness of Protestant and Catholic schools relative to each other varies across educational level.

Among grammar schools, Protestant schools are the most effective. The variance in school success accumulates to produce a 10 % difference in college and university enrollment between Protestant and public school students. Catholic grammar schools are slightly more effective than public grammar schools. Among junior general schools, the Catholic schools are the most effective. As in grammar schools, the school sector effect accumulates to create a 10 % difference in further education in favour of Catholic school students. Public and Protestant junior general schools do not differ in effectiveness.

In addition, we also have evidence to indicate that the effect of social class background on educational success differs across school sector. In the Catholic school sector, centripetal forces seem to be active. This is clearest in Catholic junior general schools, where students with an initial disadvantage achieve relatively well: that is to say, social class background does not have an important effect in Catholic junior general schools. In Catholic junior general and grammar schools, non-promotion has a minor effect on school careers in secondary education, while in Protestant and public schools, this effect is substantial. Perhaps, in Catholic schools, non-promotion is not treated as a stigma, but rather as a means of giving students a second chance to attain the highest level of education possible. In the Protestant school sector, however, the social background effect is substantial. The most advantaged Protestant school students are most likely to profit from attending Protestant secondary schools, i. e. those from privileged backgrounds, and those who were formerly high achievers.

Our results cannot be interpreted as evidence that U.S. private schools are more effective than public schools. The different historical settings in which the U.S. and Dutch school systems have developed clearly forbid such a crude generalization. But our research suggests that, when we eliminate the effects of selection and self-selection due to an unequal government support of private and public schools, sector effects remain. As we stated above, one can conclude that in the Netherlands the denominational schools are more effective than public schools. Therefore Hoffer, Greeley, and Coleman's (1985) assertion that the positive effects of private school attendance are more than a methodological artifact becomes more convincing.

Nonetheless, our research still leaves many questions unanswered. So far, we have identified school sector effects as differences in achievement which remain after controlling for initial differences between individual students. But we need knowledge about the processes which produce these effects. For example, to what extent can differences in disciplinary standards and educational demands account for the school sector effect? Furthermore, what prevents the public schools from being similar to private schools in this respect? Another interesting question is the duration of school sector effects. In future research, we shall use the longitudinal data from this study to analyze the effects of school sector on the success of students entering the labor force.

Our data are not sufficient to control for within school sector differences, that is differences within one school sector. However, it is widely accepted that difference within school sectors in the Netherlands do not covary with school sector, thanks to substantial government control over all sectors. Contrary to the United States (Hannaway and Abramowitz 1985), Dutch parents with children in different school sectors do not differ greatly in their interest in education. The choice of a particular school does not coincide with the degree of parental interest, but with their religion, their perception of the school qualities, and their proximity to schools of different sectors.

We demonstrate the presence of a school sector effect in the Netherlands. But the coexistence of public and private sectors and the extensive parental rights with regard to the government-funded establishment of private schools also have their price. This can be seen in the substantial diseconomies of scale which exist in the school system, due to the many small public and private schools. The extra cost because of the small size of the schools has been estimated by Koelman (1987: 227) to be 1,5 to 2 billion Dutch florins, which is 5 to 8 % of the government expenditure on education.

The school sector effect could also explain the enduring quantitative importance of the private school sector in the Netherlands, despite a growing secularization of society. If private schools have better results for nearly the same price, it is a rational decision for parents to send their children to private schools, despite their own religious preferences. If parents are good judges of the quality of schools, or if they use school sector as a screening device for quality, these factors would at least partly explain the persistence of a pillarized educational system in the Netherlands, as well as the importance of denominational education in other European countries well known for their irreligiosity like Belgium, France, and Italy.

References

Alexander, K. L. and A. M. Pallas (1985): "School Sector and Cognitive Performance: When Is a Little a Little?" *Sociology of Education* 58, 115−128.
Bouhuijs, S. J. and S. Boef Van Der Meulen (1978): "Vrijheid van onderwijs en bevoegd gezag," in *Vrijheid van onderwijs*, L. Box et al. (Eds.), Nijmegen: LINK, 111−121.
Coleman, J. S., Th. Hoffer, and S. Kilgore (1982): *High School Achievement*, New York: Academic Press.
De Jonge, J. (1978): "De motivatie voor protestants-christelijk onderwijs," in *Vrijheid van onderwijs*, L. Box et al. (Eds.), Nijmegen: LINK, 122−134.
Diederen, J. (1981): "From Year to Year: The Passage of Young People from Different Social Background Through Dutch Primary and Secondary Education," *Netherlands' Journal of Sociology* 17, 1−22.
Hannaway, J. and S. Abramowitz (1985): "Public and Private Schools: Are They Really Different?" in *Research on exemplary schools*, G. Austin and H. Garber (Eds.), New York: Academic Press, 31−45.
Hoffer, Th., A. M. Greeley, and J. S. Coleman (1985): "Achievement Growth in Public and Catholic Schools," *Sociology of Education* 58, 74−97.
James, E. (1984): "Benefits and Costs of Privatized Public Services: Lessons from the Dutch Educational System," *Comparative Education Review* 28, 605−624.
Jencks, C. (1985): "How Much Do High School Students Learn?" *Sociology of Education* 58, 128−135.
Koelman, J. B. J. (1987): *Kosten van de verzuiling: een studie over het lager onderwijs*, The Hague: VUGA.
Nie, N. H., C. H. Hull, J. G. Jenkins, K. Steinbrenner, D. H. Bent (1975): *SPSS. Statistical package for the social sciences*. New York: McGraw-Hill.
Ransdorp, L. and J. Dronkers (1982): *Verzuiling in het onderwijs en het beleid van een bijzonder schoolbestuur*, Amsterdam: SISWO.
Social and Cultural Planning Office (1980): *Social and Cultural Report 1980*, The Hague: Staatsuitgeverij.
Thurlings, J. M. G. (1978): *De wankele zuil. De Nederlandse katholieken tussen assimilatie en pluralisme*, Deventer: Van Loghum Slaterus.

182   Peter Van Laarhoven, Bart Bakker, Jaap Dronkers, and Huibert Schijf

Van Kemenade, J. A. (1968): *De katholieken en hun onderwijs*, Meppel: Boom.
Van Laarhoven, P., B. Bakker, J. Dronkers, and H. Schijf (1986): "Some Aspects of School Careers in Public and Non-Public Primary Schools," *Tijdschrift voor Onderwijsresearch* 11, 83—97.
Willms, J. D. (1985): "Catholic School Effects on Academic Achievement: New Evidence from the High School and Beyond Follow-Up Study," *Sociology of Education* 58, 98—114.

3.3
Public Money, Voluntary Action: Whose Welfare?

Martin Knapp, Eileen Robertson, and Corinne Thomason

1. Introduction

When the history of British public policy in the 1980s is written, it will probably include half a dozen chapters on re-mixing the economy. The decade has witnessed the reversal of previous public expenditure trends, the posing of penetrating questions about the role of the state, the rediscovery of small business enterprises in areas of social services (such as private residential and nursing homes), the sale of "untouchable" public enterprises like British Airways, British Gas, and British Telecom, and the revival of old quasi-market debates about health insurance, occupational pensions, public housing sales, and student loans.

At the same time, there have been some quite fundamental changes in the role of, and views about, the voluntary sector. We have seen the introduction of payroll donations; the extension of tax advantages for registered charities; the importing of Transatlantic terms such as "purchase of service contracting," "empowerment of mediating institutions," and the "third sector"; the virtual deification of informal carers in some official speeches and reports at a time when researchers were graphically describing the intolerable burdens of care; the arrival of Live Aid and mass philanthropy; some highly critical Parliamentary remarks about the almost non-existent monitoring of charities by central government; and, of course, the sizeable increase in public sector subsidies to voluntary organizations. Voluntary organizations may comprise the *third sector*, but in the 1980s, this has certainly not been the *forgotten* sector.

This paper describes the role of public money in the support of nonprofit organizations. We set out a framework which allows the voluntary or nonprofit sector to be examined within the context of the mixed economy, and then discuss the form of support or funding from the public sector which can be targeted either to the supply side or to the demand side. Some background statistical data give, first, some indication of the extent of public sector funding of the voluntary sector and, second, the voluntary sector's reliance on such sources of income. The assumptions inherent in central and local government support of the voluntary sector are set out, and a number of economic theories of voluntary organizations are explored in an attempt to establish a link between theory and the common assumptions or rationales for public support. Evidence is provided to confront these assumptions and rationales. It also shows how government funding can produce undesirable effects. The problems inherent in the funding relationship for both sectors are considered, and we finally examine who benefits from the encouragement of the mixed economy and the contracting-out (broadly defined) of public sector responsibilities. This paper considers the rationales behind public sector support of the formal voluntary sector. (Informal voluntary action, not channelled through an agency or organization, is not considered.) What justifications lie behind the increase in public support in Britain? What evidence is there to support or refute the beliefs on which this support has been built?

2. The Mixed Economy

The voluntary sector sits in an increasingly complex mixed economy. The variety of producers grows, the funding sources multiply, and different regulatory styles proliferate. Although it is still possible to distinguish four basic *production or supply* varieties — public, voluntary (nonprofit), private (for-profit), and informal —, the margins between them are blurred. Some private agencies disguise themselves as voluntary, some voluntary agencies behave in a manner fully consistent with the maximization of either profits or managers' salaries, and a growing number of public agencies are developing direct labour organizations and all the trappings — but without the benefits — of a commercial enterprise. The *funding or demand dimension* of the mixed economy is no less blurred. For didactic purposes only, we distinguish five varieties of demand:

- *Coerced collective demand*, where the government acts as purchaser on behalf of citizens, mandated by the democratic or electoral process.
- *Non-coerced or voluntary collective demand*, where voluntary organizations use voluntarily donated funds to purchase services. The choice as to precisely what goods or services to purchase, and for precisely whom, is controlled by the organization and not (directly) by individual donors.
- *Corporate demand*, which is interpreted here to mean demand by private sector corporations or firms.
- *Individual consumption*, being payment for goods or services consumed by the payer.
- *Individual donation*, which is payment for goods and services to be consumed by someone else, payments being made directly to suppliers and

not to voluntary organizations as intermediary bodies (the latter being non-coerced collective demand).

It is crucial to maintain a clear distinction between the production and funding dimensions of the mixed economy. For example, the policy assumptions behind supply-side subsidies to the voluntary sector — such as tax exemptions, non-specific grants, or purchase of service contracts — are very different from the assumptions behind demand-side subsidies such as vouchers, food stamps, or social security allowances. Furthermore, if we maintain this distinction, we can cross-classify the sectors of production and forms of funding to parameterize the mixed economy. With our categories,

Table 1: The Mixed Economy: Examples of Production and Patronage Combinations in Britain

Form of Patronage or Demand	Form of Production or Supply			
	Public	Voluntary	Private	Informal
Coerced Collective	National Health Service	Contracted-out day care	Contracted-out school cleaning	Social security payments to encourage family care of disabled
Voluntary Collective	Charities' payments of property taxes (rates)	Federated fund-raising	Charities' purchases of property, goods, and services	Foster family placements by voluntary child care agencies
Corporate	Industrial purchases of water or electricity	Corporate philanthrophy	Inter-firm purchases of resources	Cottage industries
Individual Payments for own Consumption	Charges to consumers of public services	Covent Garden opera tickets or National Trust membership	Coca-Cola, Volkswagen cars, IBM shares	Private childminders and babysitters
Individual Payments for Consumption by Others	Volunteer work within public services, e.g. with elderly	Live Aid, Oxfam donations	Inter-flora and singing telegrams	Intra-family transfers of resources

that representation of a pluralist system becomes a simple 20-celled matrix (Table 1). This is obviously only a highly simplified description of the myriad inter-relationships between demand and supply, but it has the signal virtues of highlighting policy variants and simply describing, for example, the demands or sources of funding for voluntary organizations. It would also be possible to examine the *transaction costs* inherent in any one cell of the matrix (cf. Krashinsky 1986). We have discussed these issues elsewhere (Knapp, Robertson, and Thomason 1987). Open the lid on any one cell and a small library of research reports and ideological treatises will spill out. Obviously our aim in this paper must be modest. Our concern is with government funding of voluntary sector activities (coerced collective demand). First, however, we need to describe the full range of sources of voluntary sector income in order to understand the relevance and impact of government support.

3. Voluntary Sector Revenue and Public Sector Support

3.1 Total Voluntary Sector Income

It is notoriously difficult to estimate the total revenue of the voluntary sector in Britain. The difficulties stem mainly from the absence of any register of voluntary organizations (which would anyway require and imply prior agreement on what was meant by the term). Although all *charities* are supposed to lodge copies of their annual accounts with the Charity Commissioners (or the Inland Revenue in Scotland and Northern Ireland), this information is far from complete. Only 9 % presently do so. The Charity

---

Notes to Table 2:

[1] Deflator based on consumers expenditure element of GDP which is "household expenditure plus final consumption expenditure of private nonprofit making bodies serving persons." *Source:* Central Statistical Office (1986).

[2] Other nonprofit-making bodies not registered as charities. Source of selection not clear.

[3] Includes £ 102 m legacies.

[4] Housing associations and friendly societies.

[5] Added voluntary organizations not registered as charities and excluded charities "predominantly dependent on private fee paying" (Wolfenden 1978: 253). This does not include housing associations or friendly societies.

[6] These areas — social and environmental services — were those upon which the Wolfenden Committee was asked to focus.

[7] CAF estimates are presented as a *minimum* level.

Commissioners' annual report is almost devoid of information, and the House of Commons Public Accounts Committee (1988) has recently been extremely critical of its monitoring practices. Estimates of the incomes of charities have been based on samples drawn from the register but many have employed questionnaire data rather than these lodged accounts.

Table 2: Estimated Total Income of Charities and Other Bodies

Source	Sample	Coverage	Estimated Population Income (£m)	
			Study Year	1985−6[1]
Moyle and Reid (1975)	Charities (purposive)	Eng. & Wales 1970	980	4,771
	Charities + other NPBs[2]	Eng. & Wales 1970	1,111[3]	5,411
	Charities + NPBs + HA + FS[4]	Eng. & Wales 1970	1,074	5,230
Falush (1977)	Charities (estimates)	UK 1975	999	2,683
Austin and Posnett (1977)	Charities	Eng. & Wales 1975	3,615	9,709
	Charities + Univs + Churches	Eng. & Wales 1975	4,159	11,170
Central Statistical Office (1977)	Charities	Eng. & Wales 1975	1,640	4,405
Wolfenden (1978)	Charities	UK 1975	1,563	4,198
	Voluntary organizations[5]	UK 1975	1,200	3,223
	Voluntary organizations − social and environmental[6]	UK 1975	1,000	2,686
Charities Aid Foundation (1979)	Charities (estimates)[7]	UK 1978	1,956	3,618
Charities Aid Foundation (1980)	Charities (estimates)	UK 1979	2,250	3,664
Charities Aid Foundation (1981)	Charities (estimates)	UK 1980	2,643	3,705
Posnett (1984)	Charities (random sample)	Eng. & Wales 1980	7,291	10,222

Previous estimates are summarized in Table 2. The target populations are not radically different; for example, those which have measured the income of charities have all started with the same objective and have differed only in their sampling techniques and the degree of their reliance on accounts already lodged with the Charity Commissioners. What is clear from the figures in the final column of the table are, first, the tremendous variation between the studies — the estimates are (as yet) extremely sensitive to sampling technique — and, second, the marked growth in income over a ten- or fifteen-year period. This is best shown by Posnett (1987) who compared income by source over a ten-year period. His results are shown in Table 3. The data cannot show it, but it appears that the revenues of voluntary organizations — particularly those parts which come from the individual and corporate parts of the economy — tend to move in cycle with the general level of economic activity.

Table 3: Sources of Voluntary Sector Income

From Government (Central, Local, NDPBs)
      lump sum grants
      matching grants
      production cost subsidies
      fees for service
      loans and loan guarantees
      tax exemptions
      "hidden" transfers in kind

From the Voluntary Sector
      grants from trusts and foundations
      charges for service
      federated fund raising
      advice/support services

From the Private Sector
      lump sum donations
      production cost subsidies
      fees for service
      returns on investment and rents

From the Personal Sector (Individuals, Households)
      donations
      bequests and legacies
      membership subscriptions
      charges for services
      other commercial sales and royalties
      volunteer time

3.2 Sources of Voluntary Sector Income

Our mixed economy matrix (Table 1) distinguished five patron or demand groups, each of which makes contributions of cash or kind to voluntary organizations. "Coerced collective" demand comes from central government departments, local authorities, health authorities, and a bewildering variety of quasi non-government organizations (Quangos), now known as non-departmental public bodies (NDPBs). Contributions from individuals and households are received via legacies, street collections, covenants, volunteering, membership subscriptions, and charges for services. The voluntary sector itself can be a major source of revenue; foundations are the obvious examples here. The corporate sector makes a variety of contributions, particularly one-off grants (and, less common, covenants) and aid in kind, such as rent-free office accommodation and equipment. In total, *financial* contributions from the corporate sector amount to about £ 100 million a year, equivalent to rather less than a fifth of individual or household donations (Ashworth 1985). This is tax deductible, and it can be difficult to distinguish between the genuine gift and the promotional event. In addition, some major corporations spend not insignificant amounts advertising their "good works."

The principal sources of voluntary sector revenue are detailed in Table 4. Their relative importance is indicated by returning to Posnett's figures in Tables 3 and the sources of income for the top 200 charities shown in Table 5. By these figures — which may be estimates, but they are the best available — the aggregate income of British charities increased by 95.6 % over the ten years to 1985–86. The most dramatic change was the contribution of fees and charges — a real increase of 248 % and a leap from one-third to nearly two-thirds of aggregate (net) income. This change was particularly marked between 1975 and 1980. This very closely mirrors the US experience of the increasing commercialization of nonprofit organizations, but the underlying reasons are different. A substantial part of the increase in revenue from fees and charges in the UK is accounted for by increased government contracting with voluntary organizations; in the US, the *decrease* in government support has moved nonprofits into new and more important commercial activities with non-governmental purchasers of services. Grants from statutory bodies increased between 1975 and 1985 by 192.6 % in real terms in the UK, but they still represent a small part of total income.

3.3 Public Support for Voluntary Organizations

It is marginally easier to gauge the financial support for the voluntary sector coming from the public sector than to estimate its gross income. It is impossible to do any more than guess at the level of support "in kind." These difficulties stem from the multiplicity of funding agencies and the

Martin Knapp, Eileen Robertson, and Corinne Thomason

Table 4: Trends in Net Income by Source, 1975–76 to 1985–86

	1975–76 £m	%	1980–81 £m	%	1985–86 £m	%	Change in real income (%) 1975–80	1980–85	1975–85
Fund Raising and Donations	683.6	28.4	890.6	12.2	1925.3	15.2	–32.0	54.3	4.9
Fees and Charges	821.5	34.1	4,802.6	65.9	7672.3	60.7	205.2	14.0	248.0
Rents and Investment	523.3	21.7	886.3	12.2	1398.4	11.1	–11.6	12.6	– 0.4
Income									
Grants from Statutory Bodies	175.2	7.3	576.9	7.9	1375.7	10.9	71.9	70.2	192.6
Commercial Activity	205.8	8.5	135.2	1.8	278.4	2.2	–65.7	46.9	–49.6
Other Income									
Total (£m)	2,409.4	100	7,291.6	100	12650.1	100.0	58.0	23.8	95.6

Source: Posnett (1984, 1987).

Table 5: Sources of Income for 200 Largest Charities, 1982–83 to 1985–86

(£m)

	1981–82	1982–83	1983–84	1984–85	1985–86
Covenants	23.5	35.2	35.8	34.5	40.4
Legacies	122.8	143.0	173.8	194.0	236.2
Other Gifts	245.9	267.8	316.9	469.3	444.8
Total Voluntary Income	392.1	446.0	526.5	697.7	721.4

						Real percentage increase 1981–82 to 1985–86
Rents, Investments, etc.	70.3	79.3	88.9	106.4	119.6	
Trading	27.9	27.4	30.2	44.6	34.0	
General	87.5	118.3	135.6	179.7	214.8	
Total "Other Income"	185.7	225.0	280.5	330.7	368.4	
Central Government Grants and Fees	—	49.2	72.1	87.1	100.8	
Local Government	—	90.1	96.6	101.6	120.7	
Local Government Grants	—	9.2	6.6	5.8	7.0	
Total Central and Local Government Grants and Fees	128.0	148.5	175.3	194.5	228.5	
Total Income	705.8	819.5	956.7	1223.0	1318.2	
Total Voluntary Income at 1985/86 Prices[2]	493.1	516.0	579.9	733.8	721.4	46.3
Total Other Income at 1985/86 Prices	233.5	260.3	280.5	347.8	368.4	57.8
Total Central/Local Government Grants and Fees at 1985/86 Prices	161.0	171.8	193.1	204.6	228.5	41.9
Total Income at 1984/85 Prices	887.6	948.1	1053.5	1286.2	1318.2	48.5
Central/Local Government Grants and Fees as Proportion of Total Income (%)	18.14	18.12	18.32	15.90	17.30	

Source: Charities Aid Foundation (1986).
Notes:
[1] CAF statistics prior to 1982/83 do not include income from central or local government. Earlier data are therefore not included in this table.
[2] Consumers' expenditure implied deflator, Central Statistical Office (1986).

Martin Knapp, Eileen Robertson, and Corinne Thomason

Table 6: Central Governments Grants to Voluntary Organizations 1976–77, 1979–80 to 1985–86[1]

Department	1976–77 £000	1979–80 £000	1980–81 £000	1981–82 £000	1982–83 £000	1983–84 £000	1984–85 £000	1985–86 £000
Agriculture, Fisheries, and Food	—	50	69	93	91	99	103	118
Defence	—	1,361	2,004	2,637	2,361	2,644	3,285	3,544
Education and Science	7,200	12,400	11,454	12,381	11,175	14,318	16,583	18,089
Employment[2]	8,600	18,147	21,391	23,207	26,380	27,720	29,180	30,316
Energy[3]	—	—	—	91	134	91	344	865
Environment – direct grants	2,500	679	683	763	976	1,220	2,178	2,566
Environment – Urban Programme	1,900	13,500	22,000	27,000	37,500	46,500	54,000	76,300
Foreign and Commonwealth Office (including ODA from 1982/83)	—	449	524	584	9,031	11,520	24,840	32,256
Health and Social Security	2,800	10,090	12,247	13,775	13,462	23,123	30,068	32,046
Home Office	6,300	10,875	14,466	15,396	15,559	16,890	17,088	18,300
Industry	—	627	501	479	660	604	669	691
Lord Chancellor's Department	—	400	469	529	583			
Northern Ireland Department	4,600	11,564	16,885	20,398	9,481	12,091	13,711	16,801
Overseas Development Administration	—	4,797	5,709	6,393	—	—	—	—
Scottish Office – direct grants	1,700	3,531	4,741	5,515	6,500	6,823	7,413	8,247
Scottish Office – Urban Programme	—	544	1,007	3,189	4,897	6,750	10,200	11,700
Trade and Industry	1,200	1,887	4,063	4,965	5,600	6,221	7,370	8,063
Transport	—	370	423	451	440	509	564	605
Welsh Office – direct grants	200	1,679	1,929	2,448	3,280	3,821	4,615	5,094
Welsh Office – Urban Programme	—	170	244	690	862	1,325	2,200	2,375

Other Departments	200	—	—	—	—	—	—	—
Total	37,300	93,123	120,809	140,984	150,970	182,270	224,411	267,977
Total at 1985 Prices[4]	93,250	166,702	175,173	180,909	182,422	201,749	237,515	267,977
Real % Increase or Decrease Over Previous Period	—	+78.77	+5.08	+3.27	+0.84	+10.59	+17.73	+12.83
Total as a Proportion of Total Central Government Expenditures (%)[5]	0.21	0.37	0.38	0.40	0.38	0.42	0.49	0.54

Sources: 1976–77, Hatch (1983) – 1979–80 – 1984/85, Charities Aid Foundation (1986) – 1985–86, Hansard, 2nd March 1987, p. 464.

Notes:
1 The figures in this table exclude grants made for religious activities, to educational bodies which form part of the established educational system (e.g. adult education research institutes, independent schools), and to the arts.
2 These monies are administered through the Manpower Services Commission and relate to sheltered employment and Community Industry schemes. The 1982–83, 1983–84, and 1984–85 figures do not include MSC payments, for which see Table 7 below.
3 Figures relate to a new energy conservative programme introduced in 1981–82.
4 Implied index of general government final consumption used as deflator. Source: Central Statistical Office (1986).
5 Total central government expenditure on goods and services. Source: Central Statistical Office (1986).

Table 7: Non-Departmental Public Bodies' Grants 1982–83 to 1985–86[1]

NDPB	1982–83 £000	1983–84 £000	1984–85 £000	1985–86 £000
Manpower Services Commission:				
Voluntary Projects Programme	980	4,300	7,300	7,830
Youth Training Scheme (and YOP)	86,700	81,000	132,300	132,400
Community Programme	51,130	200,000	275,000	366,000
Housing Corporation:				
HAG England	489,000	907,300	776,982	768,579
Wales	34,800	33,000	45,014	
Scotland	92,200	108,300	111,500	105,734
Department of the Environment for Northern Ireland. Grants to Housing Associations and Societies	—	—		39,648
Arts Council: England[2]	85,730	90,485	95,124	99,673
Arts Council: Scotland	9,907	11,012	11,122	12,114
Arts Council: Wales	5,757	5,703	6,148	6,304
Sports Council	—	9,070	11,473	12,415
Sports Council for Wales	—	—	891	1,061
Development Commission	1,639	1,692	1,864	2,359
Countryside Commission	—	—	1,688	2,405
Countryside Commission of Scotland	—	—	394	287
Commission for Racial Equality	—	—	1,416	3,828
Nature Conservancy Council	—	—	1,227	1,552
Highlands and Islands Development Board	—	—	557	650
British Council	—	—	98	—
Equal Opportunities Commission	—	—	79	61
Health Education Council	—	—	—	864

Health Education Council – Northern Ireland	—	—	—	278
Other NDPBs[3]	—	—	—	10,000
Total	857,843	1,451,861	1,480,177	1,574,042
Central Government Grants Plus NDPB Grants	1,008,813	1,634,131	1,704,717	1,842,019
Central Government and NDPB Grants at 1985 Prices[4]	1,198,999	1,808,771	1,804,262	1,842,019
Central Government and NDPB Grants as a Percentage of Central Government Expenditure[5]	2.56	3.75	3.71	3.70

Sources: Charities Aid Foundation (1987) and Hansard, 2nd March 1987, p. 465.

Notes:

[1] Figures are not available for all NDPBs. The figures presented in this table are those provided by the Home Office and represent the largest and, financially, the most significant NDPBs. However, not all figures for each year were available, and these figures should therefore be treated with due caution. See also note 3.

[2] These figures are the total amount which the Arts Council distributes. Not all grants are made to voluntary bodies.

[3] Estimate based on a postal collection of financial information from a large sample of NDPBs, *not* including those itemized in this table.

[4] Implied index of general government final consumption used as deflator. Source: Central Statistical Office (1986).

[5] Total central government expenditure in goods and services. Source: Central Statistical Office (1986).

complex and changing links between them, the hidden nature of many forms of support, such as tax exemptions, the payment of capital grants spread over a number of years, and the fact that voluntary bodies still pay *some* taxes back to local and central government. The other difficulty is that we have to use the accounting heads employed in published statistics for the voluntary sector as there defined, and can do so for only a few years. Public sector support — now viewed from the public sector spending perspective rather than voluntary sector receipts — has grown. This is true for central government departments (Table 6), NDPBs (Table 7), local authorities, and the National Health Service (Table 8). The figures are summed in Table 9, where we also include the most realistic estimate of hidden forms of support, based on the work of Ashworth (1985) and Leat, Tester, and Unell (1986). Hidden aid to voluntary organizations can be substantial. It includes "low rent/rent free premises, rate reduction, free/reduced telephone, travel and transport, unclaimed expenses, stationery, photocopying and printing, various free or reduced professional services ..., the use of central purchasing arrangements, free or reduces heating, lighting and cleaning, and so on" (Leat et al. 1986: 43). Leat and her colleagues estimated that this could amount to as much as 50 % of total grant aid from a local authority. The most recent estimates (Charities Aid Foundation 1987) put the level of rate relief (from local property taxes) at £ 129 million for 1985 − 86. This suggests that the "hidden" support estimate for local authorities (see Table 9 below) is of the correct order. In addition, there are tax exemptions worth an estimated £ 7 million (Ashworth 1985). This estimate lends some support to Martin's (1987) view that "the 1984 − 85 quoted figure of £ 500 million in tax concessions could be considerably higher." Overall, public sector support to the voluntary sector is some £ 3.1 billion each year, which represents around 7 % of total central government expenditure on goods and services.

Some general comments can be made about government funding. The level of support is far from uniform. The proportion of a government agency's budget devoted to the support of the voluntary sector varies many-fold across agencies. For example, the statistics on local authority and health authority support reveal huge variations. The importance of government funding to voluntary bodies is equally variable. In purely quantitative terms, public support varies from 0 to 100 % of total income, but organizations receiving identical proportions from public sector sources will be vulnerable to quite different degrees to a cut in support.

Some forms of government support work through the demand side of voluntary organizations' transactions. They tend to be non-selective or non-specific, not distinguishing public, voluntary, or private producers as recipients of trade, and they are difficult to measure. They are *not* included in the figures given in any of the tables. Examples of demand-side support are

Table 8: Local Authority and Health Authority Support of the Voluntary Sector, 1983–84 to 1985–86[1]

(a) Local Authorities

	1983–84 (£ m)			1984–85 (£ m)			1985–86 (£ m)		
	Grants	Fees	Total	Grants	Fees	Total	Grants	Fees	Total
Education and Arts[2]	40,8	31,1	71,9	33,4	52,8	86,2	32,0	58,6	90,6
Housing	12,9	0,1	13,0	13,8	0,9	14,7	10,7	0,2	10,9
Personal Social Services	52,2	108,6	160,8	61,3	107,9	169,2	53,2	67,9	121,1
Leisure and Recreation	20,8	0,1	20,9	48,2	0,6	48,8	39,4	0,2	39,6
Police and Protection[3]	0,9	–	0,9			–	0,5	0,1	0,6
Other	83,2	0,3	83,5	110,0	0,4	110,4	54,9	0,3	55,2
Total	210,8	140,2	351,0	266,7	162,6	429,3	190,8	127,2	318,0
Total at 1985–86 Prices[4]	235,1	156,4	391,5	282,3	172,1	454,4	190,8	127,2	318,0

(b) Health Authorities Grants and Donations

	Total (£) and sample size (no. of DHA)	Average per District Health Authority (£)	Scaled up total (£)
1984–85	10,425,357 (198)	52,653	11,583,729
1985–86	18,293,707 (163)	112,231	24,578,661
1984–85 (at 1985 prices)	11,034,136	55,728	12,260,150

Source: Charities Aid Foundation (1987).

Notes:

[1] Information obtained from surveys by the Charities Aid Foundation of local and health authorities other than parish councils in the UK. The survey of health authorities has been carried out only for the year 1984–85.

[2] In 1984–85, the "Arts" were included in the "Leisure and Recreation" category.

[3] "Police and Protection" was not treated as a separate category in the 1984–85 survey.

[4] Central Government final consumption implied deflator, Central Statistical Office (1986).

Table 9: Total Public Sector Support of the Voluntary Sector, 1984–85 and 1985–86

	1984–85 (£m)	1985–86 (£m)
Central Government Departments	224.4	268.0
Quangos	1,480.3	1,574.0
Local Authorities	429.3	318.0
Health Authorities	11.6	24.6
Total direct support	2,144.5	2,184.6
Total at 1985 prices	2,269.7	2,184.6
"Hidden" Support estimates		
Tax exemptions[1]		795
"In kind" support[2]		
Local Authorities		159
Health Authorities		12
Total		966
Total Support		3,150.6

For sources see individual tables 6, 7, 8.
Notes:
[1] Based on Ashworth's (1985) estimates for 1983–84 inflated to 1985–86 prices and excludes rate relief.
[2] Calculated as 50% of direct grant aid (Leat et al. 1986).

third-party reimbursements such as board and lodging allowances and other social security payments, vouchers, and service credits.

A further point to make is that public sector support is not "route neutral." Different routes are associated with different conditions and carry different public sector expectations. They are open to very different influences — from local and central political interests (which often conflict), from non-elected bodies, and so on. Increasingly, voluntary bodies are receiving funding and other support from more than one public agency. Multiple sources of income require multiple negotiations and impose multiple sets of regulations. This multiplicity can itself quickly constrain and divert.

Some organizations are *so* dependent upon public support that by some criteria they barely qualify as voluntary bodies at all. The Women's Royal Voluntary Service receives 100% funding from central government and its director is a government appointee. Some small voluntary child care organizations *only* accommodate local authority children under contracts which cover almost all of their costs, and will alter their care programmes in response to local authority suggestions. What is called a "partnership" between public and voluntary sectors is often simply a euphemism for the kind of domination that follows readily from the scale, anonymity, and monopsony power of a large public bureaucracy. Voluntarism and "vendorism" are not perhaps natural bedfellows (Kramer 1979: 7–12).

The general trend in the UK, then, has been of a gradual increase in resources flowing to the voluntary sector, including those from government. This has been the case despite the slowing down and cutback in overall public expenditure. In the USA, by contrast, the public expenditure trend reversal was accompanied by quite severe cutbacks in funding for the voluntary sector. Both US and UK governments have aimed to slow down public expenditure growth and increase the role of the voluntary sector (Salamon 1985, 1987); the UK appears to have been more successful in the latter aim.

4. Rationales for Government Support

There is no shortage of suggestions as to the contributory role of voluntary organizations within British society. Virtually every article and book written on the voluntary sector — and certainly every policy document or commentary — contains a listing of the advantages enjoyed by voluntary bodies. They are heralded as innovative, flexible, participative, cost-effective, exemplary, and (simply) different. Many listings start with the classic work of Sydney and Beatrice Webb (1912) who rejected the *"parallel bars"* view of voluntary bodies, in which they were seen as providing services alongside the state but for a different clientele, in favour of the *"extension ladder."* Voluntary bodies were superior to the government sector "in invention and initiative, in their ability to lavish unstinted care on particular cases, and in the intensity and variety of the religious influences that they can bring to bear on personal character" (ibid.: 240). They were, the Webbs argued, better at complementing the state sector than substituting for it: "carrying onward the work of the Public Authorities to far finer shades of physical, moral and spiritual perfection" (252).

Many subsequent enquiries have reinforced or restated the Webb's views of voluntary bodies. Gradually a comprehensive, not to say imaginative, compendium of attributes has developed. Most such statements of these attributes are based on conjecture. It is rarely the case that one can detect either an empirical or a conceptual basis for the listings of the desirable features of voluntary organizations vis-à-vis other agencies and sectors.

4.1 Links with Economic Theory

When assessing why voluntary organizations are founded or formed in the first place, and why it is that they survive in mixed capitalist economies, we have found it useful to refer to a small set of effectively "economic" theories of voluntary or nonprofit agencies. These theoretical perspectives also cast light on some of the rationales for government funding.

Weisbrod's theories (1977) concentrate on the demand side. The existence of "supra-median" or heterogeneous demand — the government is seen either as not providing enough of certain quasi-public goods, or not offering the right quality of output — creates a demand for services produced by nonprofit agencies. Individuals have an incentive to join together to produce more or different outputs, and free-riding and high transaction costs make it more likely that voluntary rather than private (for-profit) firms will be established. Government financial support for these agencies does not necessarily contradict the basis from which this theory is developed, for there are multi-tiered governments, public agencies may wish to (covertly) ignore the wishes of the median voter, and anyway the preferences of the median voter are rarely known and governments respond to the intensity of pressure. From Weisbrod's theoretical perspective, we therefore have a number of possible rationales for government support of voluntary activities, particularly the promotion of consumer choice, specialization of production, and cost-effectiveness in production. There are some similar strands in Hochman and Rodgers' (1977) discussion of preferential tax treatment for voluntary bodies. They argued that choice was one of two efficiency justifications for such treatment.

Douglas (1980, 1983) developed Weisbrod's demand model and suggested five constraints on government provision that might let in the voluntary sector. The *time horizon constraint* on government contrasts with the ability of some voluntary bodies to specialize in activities which confer benefits only over many years. Recognizing the value of these benefits, government support could be forthcoming. The *categorical constraint* limits a government's capacity to innovate and experiment, and the *bureaucratic constraint* will make it unresponsive, insensitive, and inflexible when faced with changes in need and demand. The *knowledge constraint* immediately suggests an advocate's role for the voluntary sector — government cannot have a monopoly on knowledge and good practice. Citizen and policy advocacy are relevant voluntary sector responsibilities, and consumer or patron control often leads to the establishment of an organization that may attract government support. The *size constraint* also suggests a need for citizen and policy advocacy, for participative structures and for flexible approaches to satisfying needs and wants.

Supply-side theories offer hypotheses about the characteristics of voluntary organizations, their founders, and their supporters (James 1987; James and Rose-Ackerman 1986). *Inter alia*, these supply theories suggest that voluntary organizations may enjoy a cost advantage (committed supporters of an organization's ideology will offer their services or make donations to further the cause) and have a captive audience (eventually this is a differentiated demand consideration). Over time, the large and well-established organizations may extract a premium from government agencies.

The *contract failure* perspective of Hansmann (1980, 1987) and the *transaction cost* perspective of Krashinsky (1986) supplement and to some extent link these demand and supply theories. They describe the circumstances under which a government agency, having already decided to subsidize but not produce a service, chooses to support voluntary rather than private sector agencies. They may also offer a selective subsidy to the voluntary sector because of the relative difficulties it faces in raising venture capital.

Of course, the reasons for government support for the voluntary sector are not all positive. Salamon (1987), for example, has described the effects on government action of what he calls "voluntary failure." One can see clear reasons for government subsidies or payments in the event of *philanthropic insufficiency* (not enough non-public money to survive, provided that the service is worth subsidizing in the first place), *philanthropic particularism* (choice), and *philanthropic paternalism* (government money can counterbalance wealthy philanthropists and their excessive influence).

These theories suggest, then, a number of rationales for government funding including consumer choice, specialization, cost-effectiveness, flexibility, innovation, advocacy, and participation. We discuss each in turn. We should first note that many voluntary sector activities attract support "because they are there" (Judge and Smith 1983; Leat 1985). The transaction costs of doing otherwise, such as moving all production to the public sector, may just be too great. Salamon's approach obviously stresses tradition — "historical accident" — as an explanation for government involvement, but not a reasoned exposition for large areas of continued funding. "Where existing institutions are already performing a function, government can frequently carry out its purposes more simply and with less cost by enlisting them in the government programme, thereby avoiding the need to create wholly new organisational structures or specialised staffs" (Salamon 1987: 110). Another reason for public support is the power wielded by large and long-established voluntary bodies which may perhaps be used to increase or extend public support. Traditional supply may thus offer an "irrational" explanation for government funding. It is not itself a rationale; "traditional" suppliers may continue to be supported by governments for other reasons — specialization, choice, and cost-effectiveness are obvious examples — and we shall therefore not separately examine tradition as a rationale. As Ferris and Graddy (1986) argue, tradition is often just a shorthand term for the historical importance of differentiated demand in shaping the balance of provision between the sectors. It is misleading to elevate it to a position of equivalence with the rationales listed above. The original reasons for the existence of these voluntary suppliers may have long since disappeared into the mists of time, but we still need to search for present day rationalizations for public funding.

4.2 Consumer Choice

The voluntary sector has the opportunity to produce slightly different services in response to slightly different consumer tastes, fashioned perhaps by religious, cultural, ethnic, political, or linguistic differences. Evidence supports the hypothesized link between population heterogeneity and voluntary sector provision (James 1987). It is also likely that centralization will encourage voluntary provision. The smaller the unit of government, the greater the likelihood of citizens' diverse demands being met by public provision, because of the geographical concentration of religious, ethnic, cultural, and other groupings which may express different demands for quasi-public goods. Wide differences between the levels and quantities of services provided by British local authorities, reflecting differences in citizens' preferences, will help to explain the unequal incidence of voluntary organizations and services across the country.

The theoretical rationales for, or explanations of, output heterogeneity suggest two slightly different reasons for government funding. Governments can encourage pluralism via demand-side or supply-side subsidies in the belief that choice confers benefits on service users. In addition, the government may promote a specialist role for the voluntary sector when it is itself the purchaser of the good or service. We use the term *choice* to refer to situations in which citizens purchase services (perhaps heavily subsidized on the demand side by government, but nevertheless at least semi-autonomous), and *specialization* to refer to purchases by public agencies, on behalf of citizens.

If consumer choice is valued in its own right, but the market cannot be left to its own devices, governments must seek to regulate non-public providers. Even if the quasi-public nature of the service or other factors rule out private, for-profit production, government intervention may be justified. Consumers may benefit from a choice between a publicly provided and voluntary sector service, or from the opportunity to choose from a number of suppliers *within* the voluntary sector. Because voluntary sector provision will not be even across the country, or not sufficient for certain groups, or because it is subject to particularly marked economies of scale, governments may subsidize it in an effort to preserve choice. Even the most vociferous supporters of pluralism concede a major role for government (Gladstone 1979, Hadley and Hatch 1980). Governments may fund consumer choice through grant aid, tax exemptions, and production subsidies on the supply side, and through consumer subsidies (vouchers and the like) on the demand side.

Often, however, government funding will be contingent upon satisfaction of certain standards and conformity with government policies. "Coercive isomorphism," in DiMaggio and Powell's (1983) terminology, may follow from the public subsidy. Isomorphism obviously narrows the choice that is available to either public sector or individual patrons, and is therefore to be guarded against if choice is the primary rationale for fiscal support. However, many forms of subsidy are not primarily concerned with preserving choices, and may even demand for their realisation a greater degree of similarity rather than variety.

4.3 Specialization

Closely allied to consumer choice is specialization. We distinguish them here by separating purchases by citizens (for their own or an associate's consumption) and purchases by public agencies. Specialization, the latter of these, will be supported partly by tax exemptions, but mainly via purchase of service contracting. Specialized voluntary sector provision will be publicly supported not only because it satisfies differentiated demands or needs, but also because it is more cost-effective. Responsibility for many services rests with local authorities which are often too small to provide an economical service to meet unusual or rare needs. It is more cost-effective for these authorities to contract out. Activities with effects only in the very long term are among the specialized outputs of the voluntary sector, as are innovative provision and advocacy.

There is no shortage of examples of the specialist role of the voluntary sector. Kramer reports how "English voluntary agencies extend the range of some rationed statutory services for constituencies that may have low visibility or low priority within the broad scope of the local authority, such as paraplegics, the deaf, alcoholics, autistic children, or persons with multiple sclerosis, muscular dystrophy, or cerebral palsy" (1981: 242–243). Hatch, in his study of voluntary agencies in three English towns, found voluntary provision of residential accommodation for "vagrants or those requiring short-stay accommodation in an emergency; others like alcoholics, drug addicts, ex-mental patients, and ex-offenders need a supportive environment over a long period. A further category are homeless families, including battered wives and their children." In his three areas, "voluntary agencies were both pioneers and sole providers" (Hatch 1980: 102). Later he cites other supplementary activities – the Red Cross, Hospital Friends, the National Childbirth Trust – which, if they receive public money, must be competitors for funds (substitutes) though they are complements in service terms. The ability to organize and deliver services on a national basis, drawing clients from the whole country, is an obvious form of specialization falling naturally to the voluntary sector when public sector responsibilities fall to *local* authorities.

As with the choice rationale, public funding has its drawbacks. When the purchase of voluntary services is the responsibility of public authorities, the contracting arrangement may engender dependency in both agent and principal, again generating input, process, or output isomorphism.

4.4 Cost-Effectiveness

The cost-effectiveness rationale needs to be distinguished from specialization. It is often claimed that services are produced more cost-effectively in the voluntary sector because of the style of governance, a less bureaucratic administration, a ready supply of volunteer labour, or fewer constraints from trade unions. It is also hypothesized to be easier for voluntary organizations to charge for quasi-public goods, and a cost-effectiveness advantage may arise from a variety of "multiplier effects": public purchases subsidized from charitable donations.

These claims do not always stand up to close scrutiny. A number of empirical investigations have been undertaken. The most sensible generalization to make about the evidence is that it is impossible to generalize about the presence or direction of any cost-effectiveness difference between the sectors (Knapp 1988). Conclusions reached for one industry or country are not transportable to other industries or countries, and often cost-effectiveness or efficiency differences are markedly greater *within* sectors than between them.

When a cost-effectiveness advantage is found for the voluntary sector (or merely assumed), government funding — particularly through specific grant aid and purchase of service contracting — is likely to increase. Knapp, Baines, and Fenyo (1988) found that the contracting-out of residential child care by local authorities was responsive to differences in the ratio of voluntary sector fees to public sector costs. But the very process of contracting-out, or public funding more generally, can reduce or even remove the cost-effectiveness differential. Public subsidies have been found to inflate voluntary sector costs through a number of channels. The administrative burden of "grantsmanship" and contracting raises overhead costs. Higher wages are paid to staff, sometimes as a condition of contracting, in some cases, because government subsidies erect protective barriers around agencies, increasing the influence of organized labour in the voluntary sector, and, in some cases, because management now has the facility to pay more to retain high quality employees. Further, because the cost-effectiveness difference encourages a substitutability relationship between the sectors, governments have an incentive to continue to contract-out until the difference disappears, other things being equal. The relative positions of the sectors may change if the balance of provision shifts, and public subsidies based on the assumption that efficiency is greater in the voluntary sector must respond flexibly to changing circumstances.

4.5 Flexibility

Small, local voluntary organizations are often argued to be less bureaucratized. There may be other reasons for assuming a flexibility advantage stemming from Douglas' (1983) various "government constraints." Flexibility offers an improved service, responding to differences and changes in need in a way that bureaucracies cannot or will not do. Flexibility, then, allows the voluntary sector to match services to the expressed wants and perceived needs of citizens; bureaucratic public agencies can only squeeze citizens into the rigidly structured services of the public sector. For these reasons, it is rationalized, public sector departments should contract with, or otherwise subsidize, the voluntary sector in order to offer an improved service, more efficiently produced and more efficiently targeted on the needs of the population.

It is very difficult to find *evidence* of the relative rigidities or inflexibilities of the two sectors. Kramer (1987: 241) argues that beliefs about the sectors are based on "invidious organisational stereotypes whereby government is perceived as intrinsically rigid, riddled with bureaupathology, and offering mass standardised services that are dehumanising." These beliefs, according to Brodkin and Young (1986: 50), may not be "untestable empirically," but may well be "empirically irrefutable ... that is ... not readily vulnerable to data." The beliefs are not invalid, merely hard to validate except by recourse to the experiences of public and voluntary sector managers themselves, whose views are, of course, caught up in the beliefs they inherited in the first place. Generally, it would be perverse to maintain that voluntary agencies with unelected management committees must *necessarily* be more responsive to the views of users and citizens than are elected public sector policy makers.

There are two broad limitations that must be placed on the flexibility rationale for public support of the voluntary sector. First, flexibility often carries unacceptable associated characteristics, such as inconsistency and lack of accountability. Second, public funding may itself impair the flexibility of voluntary agencies, and this may occur even if the public sector chooses to ignore these associated characteristics. Leat et al. (1986) found some evidence of a positive relationship between the level of grant aid and expressed feelings of a loss of independence. Furthermore, government funding, whether through purchase of service arrangements, grant aid, or tax advantages, will have the effect of raising "entry barriers" into the industry, deterring other voluntary organizations (with fewer production subsidies) and private (for-profit) producers (with fewer still). This protection will not encourage existing agencies to respond to changes in demand. Thus, even *without* added administrative burdens, public support can reduce the sector's flexibility.

At the end of the day, we are left with limited evidence of the inherent flexibility of voluntary organizations. If they remain small or federated, if they can withstand or efficiently accommodate the public sector's demands for accountability and conformity, if they can suitably balance responsiveness against fadishness, and if they can gather the necessary information to be responsive in the first place, then flexibility should certainly offer a supportable rationale for public funding.

4.6 Innovation

An obvious corollary to flexibility is innovative potential. This hypothesized attribute will also follow from the categorical constraint and from the argument that an innovative organization might develop in response to differentiated demands. If it is the case that the voluntary sector is more flexibly organized than the public, then the potential is there for greater innovative development and experimentation. The pioneering characteristic of voluntary organizations has been cited so frequently as to become legendary. But, like all the best legends, the truth has sometimes been colourfully embellished to make a better story.

There is, in fact, no real shortage of evidence to suggest that the voluntary sector has been innovative in the past, is still innovative today, and is likely to continue to be innovative well into the future. More pertinent, however, are questions about the differences in innovative potential between public and voluntary sectors, and the willingness and ability of public sector providers to build on the experimental evidence offered by the voluntary agencies they are supporting. In fact, it could be argued that a multiplicity of agencies and energetic managers maximizes the potential for innovation. Thus even if the voluntary sector was no more innovative than the public, the continued existence of voluntary producers alongside statutory agencies would enhance innovative activity. Provided those innovations could be built upon in subsequent delivery systems, public subsidies would be worthwhile.

A number of researchers have argued that the public sector is at least as innovative as the voluntary (Beck 1970; Brenton 1985; Kramer 1981; Moore and Green 1985; Morgan 1984; Rodgers 1976). Of course, any such comparison must bear in mind the very different scales of enterprise to be found in the two sectors and the ticklish problem of how to measure innovative activity in the first place. Schorr went a little further, arguing that "most significant attempts at pioneering in the social services during the 1960s ... were largely inspired and set in motion by government. Thus the decade's major examples of pioneering have marginal connections with voluntary (or proprietary) social services or owe it nothing" (1970: 431). Schorr's point has relevance today, though it is also the case that some "innovatory forces within the statutory sector" are more easily channelled through voluntary agencies (Brenton 1985). The voluntary sector becomes the "creative arm" of the public sector. Many of the innovative practices of voluntary agencies uncovered by Kramer (1981) in his four-country study were initiated from within the public sector. If a public agency "wishes to avoid being locked into long-term delivery" (Judge and Smith 1983: 218), arms-length innovation or experimentation may be ideal.

Unfortunately, evidence from one British study suggests that short-term government funding may incline voluntary agencies "to pursue more traditional and reliable projects than to risk scarce resources on new and ambitious projects" (Jackson 1983: 53). With long-term funding, on the other hand, the security of income may remove the necessity and impetus to innovate. Funding, that is, may encourage complacency and lassitude.

4.7 Advocacy

Fundamental to almost all discussions of the role of the voluntary sector today is advocacy. Kramer (1981) writes of "the quintessential function" of the sector, and that advocacy and service provision — "case and cause" — is a good description of a large proportion of voluntary sector activity. Advocacy is particularly relevant at a personal level: giving advice to individuals, setting up self-help groups, offering counselling and befriending services and, at a public level, campaigning for and speaking on behalf of clients or communities. These are the *citizen advocacy* and *policy advocacy* roles of the voluntary sector.

Citizen advocacy is offered by organizations such as Citizen's Advice Bureaux, Law Centres, Legal Advice Centres, specialist bodies such as Shelter, the Disability Alliance, the Unemployment Alliance, Youthaid, the Ramblers Association, the National Council for One-Parent Families, and the Child Poverty Action Group. Johnson (1981: 96—105) offers an account of their activities, policies, and problems in Britain. Citizen advocacy will receive public sector funding, although recent history would suggest that advocacy programmes are often the first to disappear when public budgets are cut. One reason for public support is that advocacy is often directly complementary to the work of public agencies, particularly when organizations are advocating higher quality services. A second explanation for public support is the multi-layered nature of government. Many local authorities either employ staff, or fund voluntary agencies to employ staff, whose principal task is to (legally) exploit the services offered by central government.

Policy (or public or social) advocacy is the campaigning role of voluntary bodies. The success of policy advocacy is well documented in a number of areas, "success" being defined variously but usually with a degree of validity.

Thus, for example, Mellor (1985) reports successful pressure group activities in the social services area, as did Johnson (1981, ch. 4) and Kramer (1981, ch. 11) before him, and Forsythe (1980) describes human rights advocacy and its effects on US foreign policy. Policy advocacy groups have been criticized for being "far more effective in raising issues and shaping the political agenda than in developing solutions and forcing compromises" (Jenkins 1987: 312), but then many would claim that they are in no position to do any more than this. In this activity, it is obviously only an agency independent of government which can unrestrictedly criticize it. So why might public funding be offered?

Pressure on the public sector to mend its ways will often attract public sector funding again because of multi-tiered government and because the public sector recognizes its own constraints. It is the *knowledge* and *size constraints* facing governments which lead them to offer inadequate quality services, poorly targeted on needy populations and unresponsive to the wishes of users (Douglas 1983). With the best will in the world, no government agency can be omniscient, nor sufficiently accessible and hospitable to the enquiries or complaints of citizens. They may have few incentives to actively solicit those enquiries or complaints, and anyway they are unlikely to have much success with some rightly suspicious users. The voluntary sector can add to the government's stock of knowledge, can bring a different perspective to bear on policy issues, can represent the reluctant critic, and can campaign for change. In each of these activities, independence from government is a desirable attribute. In addition, public support, direct or indirect, overt or covert, may be necessary to make a cause financially viable, "and if some groups are wealthier, more vociferous or more politically skilful than the majority, then they may succeed in attracting more than a fair share of resources to their cause or to the client group they represent" (Johnson 1981: 63). These are examples, to use Salamon's terminology, of philanthropic insufficiency and particularism.

The greatest danger of public funding is that policy advocacy groups cease to be independent of government. Kramer (1979, 1981) could find no evidence a few years ago to suggest that governments pull the rug out from underneath embarrassing or irritating policy advocacy groups in the voluntary sector. Nor did his study bear out the familiar concern that the administrative burdens generated by the requirements of fund-raising and accountability to government divert voluntary bodies from what they do best. Johnson (1981) and Brenton (1985) reached the opposite conclusion.

4.8 Participation

Few accounts of the role of the voluntary sector will fail to mention the benefits of participation. Voluntary agencies, it is argued, offer opportunities for citizens to voluntarily contribute their money, time, and skills to promote certain services and activities. They allow citizens a part in decision-making processes and thus, perhaps, "democratize" and "de-concentrate" resource allocation procedures. They improve the target efficiency and local accountability of service provision, tailoring resources to local needs and wants. Participation, then, is the promotion of volunteerism, self-help or mutual aid, democracy, efficiency and effectiveness, and communication. It counters the dirigisme of the state. As Douglas (1983) has described, governments face a host of constraints which can leave them impervious to the needs and preferences of citizens and unable to offer opportunities for reciprocation. Participation as a local, democratic, consumerist vehicle for allocating resources and changing patterns of provision can enhance social stability, reduce alienation, strengthen consensus and social control, generate greater equality, and offer opportunities for self-realization.

Participative organizations, which foster consumer or patron control and citizen involvement, may attract the approval and money of governments. In particular, volunteerism becomes a rationale for funding. Even though the public sector makes extensive use of volunteers (for example, see Holme and Maizels 1978; Kramer 1981), voluntary organizations are the *primary* conduits for volunteerism (Hadley et al. 1975; Steinberg 1986; Weisbrod 1982; Wolfenden 1978). Volunteers can increase the total amount of a service offered; they supplement that statutory, private, and voluntary sector provision which is only made possible by the employment of paid staff. Services produced in part or in total by volunteers will thus often be cheaper than their alternatives, although politicians take great pains to emphasize that volunteerism is not promoted to save money. Volunteering confers benefits on the volunteers from altruism, self-interest, and sociability (Aves 1969). There are also "negative rationales" that can be just as powerful in explaining public sector support. Public money may be injected into the sector to expand provision or to open up volunteerism to groups presently under-represented. Again, Salamon's four dimensions of philanthropic failure are relevant to the British context.

Self-help or mutual aid groups also promote participation. Members have rights and responsibilities which help to blur the distinction between the "helper" and the "helped," between service provider and service consumer. This is consumerism in its purest form (Ben-Ner 1986, 1987; Ellman 1982; Katz and Bender 1976). It complements statutory provision; it does not substitute for or duplicate it. Public sector funding can subsidize the administrative costs of these organizations, offer respite and complementary support, and facilitate the purchase of expertise and advice. Public funding can therefore be justified on the grounds of *cost-effectiveness* (greater service outputs and enhanced community benefits from the same or smaller funding bases), *empowerment*, and *consumerism*.

But, the reality of self-help is not always so rosy. Informal, mutual, or neighbourhood provision can be very costly to the providers. It is not uncommon for self-help and mutual aid groups to become dominated by a small elite. Finch (1984), for example, catalogues the difficulties encountered in trying to impose the middle-class concept of a pre-school play group on working-class mothers in economically deprived areas. The groups were tainted with the patronage of the middle-class volunteer, or dominated by a small group with expertise or professional competence in the service area of the organization.

Mutual aid organizations may grow as a direct consequence of government funding, and will need to be increasingly alert to the onset of undemocratic procedures. Large size brings with it the need for formalized systems of governance, and many of the original participative benefits may quickly evaporate (Brenton 1978; Mellor 1985; Rowe 1978). Indeed, public agencies may require a hierarchical governance structure as a condition for funding, for a "participative regime ... loosens administrative control ... and makes it more difficult for the executive to translate its intents into action" (Young 1987: 172). The very existence of public support, therefore, may immediately introduce a centrifugal force which pulls "helper" and "helped" apart, thus changing, marginally or fundamentally, the nature of the organization.

5. Whose Welfare?

Public funding is warranted insofar as the voluntary sector contributes (in any number of ways) to the mixed economy, but funding alone is not enough to *guarantee* such a contribution. Funding will usually be accompanied by regulatory practices and accountability requirements, and, as we have seen in the discussion of the rationales, regulation can have a number of undesired by-products which threaten the independence of the sector. In most cases, the dampening of the contribution of the voluntary organization is not an *inevitable* consequence of public funding, but danger lurks in the wings. This danger takes four inter-linked forms: bureaucratization, inappropriate regulation, a threat to autonomy and to the "mission" of the organization, and financial insecurity.

5.1 Bureaucratization

We noted earlier that voluntary organizations will find it hard to sell themselves to donors and to government agencies as alternatives to an over-bureaucratized, unresponsive public sector if they themselves are administratively cumbersome. With regard to the participation rationale, for example, public funding may encourage the bureaucratization and professionalization of organizations, yet these are anathema to the concepts of volunteerism and mutual aid. Similarly with the cost-effectiveness rationale, public subsidies and contract fees have been found to inflate voluntary sector costs. Generally, it is the costs of obtaining, receiving, and accounting for public support which can become so burdensome (Leat et al. 1986). The burden tends to be greater when an organization receives funding from more than one public sector agency (Hartogs and Weber 1978), although, at the same time, a multiplicity of funding sources is usually less threatening to an organization's autonomy (see below).

The recording and reporting requirements of public agencies impose both time and skill costs. Numerous studies have documented the administrative burden of public funding on both sides of the Atlantic (Kahn 1977; Lanning 1981; Leat et al. 1986; Rosenbaum 1981, 1982; Terrell and Kramer 1984; Young and Finch 1977). Judge (1982) and Kramer (1979) tend to disagree. However, Salamon noticed a tendency among voluntary agency managers to exaggerate the bureaucratization effects of government funding, since "the pressures for improved agency management, tighter financial control, and use of professionals in service delivery do not, after all, come solely from government" (1987: 115). Nevertheless, public support does have an administrative impact, yet voluntary agencies are rarely able to negotiate an additional funding component to cover these additional costs. This diverts an organization's revenue away from direct service provision to the detriment of present and potential users, the diversion being proportionately greater in smaller organizations. Voluntary organization consortia might ease the burden, but it is unlikely that public sector accountability demands will ease: in most cases, in Britain, the accountability requirements imposed on voluntary bodies already lag some way behind those employed within public authorities.

5.2 Inappropriate Regulations

Some of the administrative practices developed to attract (and cope with) public support may actually be conditions of the funding process. Public agencies will want to audit income and expenditure, given that most of the revenue comes from individual patrons or from tax revenues and that the nondistribution constraint may encourage organizations to allocate any surpluses to staff via higher salaries and hidden benefits. The public sector may also wish to maintain the standard of the product, since voluntary organizations can develop into bureaucracies with their own organizational slack and unresponsiveness, or they may pursue prestige to the neglect of the individual consumer. Such checks are needed because the governance structure of most organizations does not render them representative of consumers or citizens at large — the familiar philanthropic paternalism issue.

Regulations can be established at almost any point within the "production process." They may govern input ratios, input prices, outputs and their prices, access to and distribution of the product, financial probity, and governance. These various forms of regulation have attracted criticism both from government and the voluntary sector. Some see the regulations as little more than minimal (Home Office Statement in Hatch 1980; Judge 1982; Kramer 1981; Wolfenden 1978). This marginal influence is explained by Brenton (1985: 93) by "the diminutive nature of the amounts involved from the government's point of view", the wish by public agencies not to counter the autonomy and flexibility of recipient bodies, and because close monitoring of all recipients is simply impracticable. Others are concerned about the disincentives that regulations may create. The Wisconsin nursing homes study of Weisbrod and Schlesinger (1986) found greater compliance with input and "intermediate output" regulations by for-profit homes when compared with nonprofit, but a greater frequency of resident complaints in the former sector. If those complaints reflect final outputs, albeit imperfectly, we have a good illustration of the need for sensitive output monitoring. The difficulty is to make it feasible and manageable. And if this is achieved, it has to be remembered that the management structures within voluntary agencies will often militate against performance-based incentives (Young 1987: 174). All of these difficulties will be compounded when voluntary bodies are regulated by more than one public agency.

5.3 Threats to Autonomy

As we have seen with regard to participation, accountability may threaten the informal democracy of small agencies, and may drive a wedge between the "helper" and the "helped" when many agencies are trying hard not to make the distinction. Public funding may narrow the choice available to individual purchasers when government funding is contingent upon satisfaction of certain standards and conformity with government policies. When we consider the advocacy rationale, it is clearly important that financial assistance for programmes directed at criticism of either government or private sector producers must not interfere with the independence of voluntary organizations.

As James (1987: 409) argues, from a *normative* standpoint, society has a right and a duty to exercise some control over how public funds are spent, whilst from a *positive* perspective, politicians "have the power to demand a *quid pro quo*." There are some well-publicized examples of interference — in some instances, out-and-out withdrawal of all public funding — but they are isolated cases. They do not tell us whether "Manser's Law" — "an agency's freedom and effectiveness in social action or advocacy are in inverse proportion to the amount of public money it receives" — is generally applicable (Manser 1974). Indeed, Kramer's (1981) argument is that there are at least four reasons why autonomy may *not* be breached when government funding is received: a multiplicity of funding sources, the predominance of POSC arrangements, countervailing oligopsony power in the voluntary sector, and an awareness among government agents that voluntary autonomy must be preserved.

5.4 Financial Insecurity

The last of the four potential dangers associated with public sector funding is, paradoxically perhaps, the financial insecurity that it can engender. Public subsidies may cover only a portion of the total cost of production, may be delayed, may never arrive, may be pegged at inappropriate levels, and may encourage over-investment. Vladeck looks at the last of these tendencies. Rampant over-investment in expensive-to-maintain capital facilities is a "product of direct or indirect federal largesse" in bygone years (Vladeck 1976: 96). Voluntary agencies can over-extend themselves, having to direct hard-won revenues into maintaining their capital stock. Some may not survive.

5.5 The Impact on the Citizen

For the individual citizen, the voluntary sector has much to commend it. It can offer an opportunity to participate, to give something back to the community, to improve human capital, and to share in decision making. It can offer variety in the choice of services, a haven for specialist and idiosyncratic provision, a stimulus for change, a venue for experimentation, a forum for dissent and lobbying, and generally a countervailing force to oppose a government monopoly. Public subsidies can bolster each of these welcome attributes. But, as we have argued, public subsidies are not without their drawbacks. They have consequences for voluntary agencies themselves and they may hinder the public sector in its pursuit of an efficient and equitable allocation of the nation's resources. They may, in the eyes of some critics, undermine the very foundations of the "welfare state" itself.

By encouraging voluntary action, the public sector may be relinquishing some control over some of its resources. The result can be fragmentation, discontinuity, complexity, low-quality outputs, poorly targeted services, productive inefficiencies, horizontal and vertical inequities, wasteful duplication and inappropriate replication, sectarianism, and paternalism. Pumping more public resources into the voluntary sector may be a long way form "giving government back to the people." But maintaining sufficient control can quickly become administratively burdensome for governments.

For the two sectors to work together to the benefit of citizens, there is therefore a need for each to recognize the potentialities and failings of the other. Salamon's view of the relations between public and voluntary sectors in the US are directly relevant to the UK, and we endorse his views:

"To the extent that cooperation between government and the nonprofit sector reflects a fit between the respective strengths and weaknesses of the two, ... the appropriate standard is one that acknowledges the need to correct the shortcomings of the two sectors without doing unnecessary damage to their respective strengths. In practice, this means that government's need for economy, efficiency and accountability must be tempered by the nonprofit sector's need for a degree of self-determination and independence of governmental control; but that the sector's desire for independence must in turn be tempered by government's need to achieve equity and to make sure that public resources are used to advance the purposes intended" (1987: 113).

References

Ashworth, M. (1985): "Tax and Charities," Mimeograph, London: Charities Aid Foundation.

Austin, M. and J. Posnett (1979): "The Charity Sector in England and Wales: Characteristics and Public Accountability," *National Westminster Bank Quarterly Review* 40–51.

Aves, G. (1969): *The Voluntary Worker in the Social Services*, London: Bedford Square Press.

Beck, B. M. (1970): "The Voluntary Social Welfare Agency: A Reassessment," *Social Service Review* 44, 147–154.

Ben-Ner, A. (1986): "Nonprofit Organisations: Why Do They Exist in Market Economies?" in *The Economics of Nonprofit Institutions*, S. Rose-Ackerman (Ed.), New York: Oxford University Press, 94–113.

Ben-Ner, A. (1987): "Nonprofit Collectivist Organizations," in *The Nonprofit Sector: A Research Handbook*, W. W. Powell (Ed.), New Haven: Yale University Press, 434–446.

Brenton, M. (1978): "Worker Participation and the Social Service Agency," *British Journal of Social Work* 8, 289–300.

Brenton, M. (1985): *The Voluntary Sector in British Social Services*, London: Longman.

Brodkin, E. and D. Young (1986): "Political Economy of Privatization," Mimeograph, SUNY, Stony Brook.

Central Statistical Office (1977): *Social Trends No. 8*, London: HMSO.

Central Statistical Office (1986): *National Income Accounts 1986 Edition*, London: HMSO.

Charities Aid Foundation (1979): *Charity Statistics 1978/79*, Tonbridge: CAF.
Charities Aid Foundation (1980): *Charity Statistics 1979/80*, Tonbridge: CAF.
Charities Aid Foundation (1981): *Charity Statistics 1980/81*, Tonbridge: CAF.
Charities Aid Foundation (1985): *Charity Statistics 1984/85*, Tonbridge: CAF.
Charities Aid Foundation (1986): *Charity Statistics 1985/86*, Tonbridge: CAF.
Charities Aid Foundation (1987): *Charity Trends 1986/87*, Tonbridge: CAF.
DiMaggio, P. and W. Powell (1983): "Institutional Isomorphism," *American Sociological Review* 48, 147−160.
Douglas, J. (1980): "Towards a Rationale for Private Nonprofit Organizations," PONPO Working Paper 7, Yale University.
Douglas, J. (1983): *Why Charity? The Case for a Third Sector*, Beverly Hills: Sage.
Ellman, M. (1982): "Another Theory of Nonprofit Corporations," *Michigan Law Review* 80, 999−1050.
Falush, P. (1977): "Trends in the Finance of British Charities," *National Westminster Bank Quarterly Review* 32−44.
Ferris, J. and E. Graddy (1986): "Contracting-Out: For What? With Whom?" *Public Administration Review* 46, 332−344.
Finch, J. (1984): "The Deceit of Self-Help: Preschool Playgroups and Working Class Mothers," *Journal of Social Policy* 13, 1−20.
Forsythe, D. P. (1980): "Humanizing American Foreign Policy: Nonprofit Lobbying and Human Rights," PONPO Working Paper 12, Yale University.
Gladstone, F. (1979): *Voluntary Action in a Changing World*, London: Bedford Square Press.
Hadley, R. and S. Hatch (1980): *Social Welfare and the Failure of the State*, London: Allen and Unwin.
Hadley, R., A. Webb and C. Farrell (1975): *Across the Generations*, London: Allen and Unwin.
Hansmann, H. (1980): "The Role of Nonprofit Enterprise," *Yale Law Journal* 89, 835−901.
Hansmann, H. (1987): "Economic Theories of Nonprofit Organization," in *The Nonprofit Sector: A Research Handbook*, W. W. Powell (Ed.), New Haven: Yale University Press, 27−41.
Hartogs, N. and J. Weber (1978): *Impact of Government Funding on the Management of Voluntary Agencies*, New York: Greater New York Fund/United Way.
Hatch, S. (1980): *Outside the State*, London: Croom Helm.
Hatch, S. (1983): "Grants to Voluntary Organisations by Central Government 1976−77 to 1981−82," in *Charity Statistics 1982/83*, Tonbridge: Charities Aid Foundation, 13−19.
Hochman, H. M. and J. D. Rodgers (1977): "The Optimal Tax Treatment of Charitable Contributions," *National Tax Journal* 30, 1−19.
Holme, N. and J. Maizels (1978): *Social Workers and Volunteers*, London: Allen and Unwin.
House of Commons Public Accounts Committee (1988): *Sixteenth Report: Monitoring and Control of Charities in England and Wales*, HCP 116, Session 1987−88, London: HMSO.
Jackson, H. (1983): "Developing Local Voluntary Action: Four Experimental Small Grants Schemes," *Home Office Research Bulletin* 16, 51−53.

216 Martin Knapp, Eileen Robertson, and Corinne Thomason

James, E. (1987): "The Nonprofit Sector in Comparative Perspective," in *The Nonprofit Sector: A Research Handbook*, W. W. Powell (Ed.), New Haven: Yale University Press, 397–413.

James, E. and S. Rose-Ackerman (1986): *The Nonprofit Enterprise in Market Economies*, London: Harwood Academic Publishers.

Jenkins, J. C. (1987): "Nonprofit Organisations and Policy Advocacy," in *The Nonprofit Sector: A Research Handbook*, W. W. Powell (Ed.), New Haven: Yale University Press, 296–314.

Johnson, N. (1981): *Voluntary Social Services*, Oxford: Martin Robertson.

Judge, K. (1982): "The Public Purchase of Social Care: British Confirmation of the American Experience," *Policy and Politics* 10, 397–416.

Judge, K. and J. Smith (1983): "Purchase of Services in England," *Social Services Review* 57, 209–233.

Kahn, A. J. (1977): "A Framework for Public-Voluntary Collaboration in the Social Services," in *The Social Welfare Forum 1976*, New York: Columbia University Press.

Katz, A. H. and E. I. Bender (1976): *The Strength in Us: Self-Help Groups in the Modern World*, New York: New Viewpoints Books.

Knapp, M. R. J. (1988): "Inter-Sectoral Differences in Cost-Effectiveness: Residential Child Care in England and Wales," in *The Nonprofit Sector in International Perspective*, E. James (Ed.), Oxford: Oxford University Press, 193–216.

Knapp, M. R. J., B. Baines and A. J. Fenyo (1988): "The Price Elasticity of Demand for Contracted-Out Residential Child Care," Discussion Paper 539, Personal Social Services Research Unit, University of Kent at Canterbury.

Knapp, M. R. J., E. Robertson, and C. Thomason (1987): "Public Money; Voluntary Action: An Economic Examination of Public Sector Support of the Voluntary Sector", Discussion Paper 500, PSSRU, University of Kent at Canterbury.

Kramer, R. (1979): "Voluntary Agencies in the Welfare State: An Analysis of the Vanguard Role," *Journal of Social Policy* 8, 473–488.

Kramer, R. (1981): *Voluntary Agencies in the Welfare State*, Berkeley: University of California Press.

Kramer, R. M. (1987): "Voluntary Agencies and the Personal Social Services," in *The Nonprofit Sector: A Research Handbook*, W. W. Powell (Ed.), New Haven: Yale University Press, 240–257.

Krashinsky, M. (1986): "Transaction Costs and a Theory of the Nonprofit Organisation," in *The Economics of Nonprofit Institutions*, S. Rose-Ackerman (Ed.), New York: Oxford University Press, 114–129.

Lanning, H. (1981): *Government and Voluntary Sector in the USA*, London: NCVO.

Leat, D. (1985): "Making Sense of Grant Aid," in *Charity Statistics 1985–85*, Judith McQuillan (Ed.), Tonbridge: Charities Aid Foundation, 45–49.

Leat, D., S. Tester and J. Unell (1986): *A Price Worth Paying? A Study of the Effects of Government Grant Aid to Voluntary Organisations*, London: Policy Studies Institute.

Manser, G. (1974): "Further Thoughts on Purchase of Service," *Social Casework* 55, 421–474.

Martin, M. J. (1987): "Recent Tax Concessions for Charities," in *Charity Trends 1986/87*, J. McQuillan (Ed.), Tonbridge: Charities Aid Foundation, 38–39.

Mellor, H. (1985): *The Role of Voluntary Organisations in Social Welfare*, London: Croom Helm.

Moore, J. and J. M. Green (1985): "The Contribution of Voluntary Organizations to the Support of Caring Relatives," *Quarterly Journal of Social Affairs* 1, 93–130.

Morgan, J. (1984): "The Voluntary Sector and the National Health Service," *Yearbook of Social Policy* 12, 107–121.

Moyle, J. and D. J. Reid (1975): "Private Non-profit Making Bodies Serving Persons," *Economic Trends*, 78–86.

Posnett, J. (1984): "A Profile of the Charity Sector," in *Charity Statistics 1983/84*, J. McQuillan (Ed.), Tonbridge: Charities Aid Foundation, 56–61.

Posnett, J. (1987): "Trends in the Income of Registered Charities, 1980–1985," in *Charity Trends 1986/87*, J. McQuillan (Ed.), Tonbridge: Charities Aid Foundation, 6–8.

Rodgers, B. N. (1976): *Cross-National Studies of Social Service Systems*, New York: School of Social Work, Columbia University.

Rosenbaum, N. (1981): "Government Funding and the Voluntary Sector: Impacts and Options," *Journal of Voluntary Action Research* 10, 82–89.

Rosenbaum, N. (1982): "Government Funding and the Voluntary Sector: Impacts and Options," in *Volunteerism in the Eighties: Fundamental Issues in Voluntary Action*, J. Harman (Ed.), Washington: University Press of America, 82–89.

Rowe, A. (1978): "Participation in the Voluntary Sector: The Independent Contribution," *Journal of Social Policy* 7, 41–56.

Salamon, L. M. (1985): "Government and the Voluntary Sector in an Era of Retrenchment: The American Experience," Paper presented at the *Interphil II Conference*, Venice, 1985.

Salamon, L. M. (1987): "Partners in Public Service: Toward a Theory of Government – Nonprofit Relations," in *The Nonprofit Sector: A Research Handbook*, W. W. Powell (Ed.), New Haven: Yale University Press, 99–116.

Schorr, A. L. (1970): "The Tasks for Volunteerism in the Next Decade," *Child Welfare* 49, 425–434.

Steinberg, R. (1986): "Labour Economics and the Nonprofit Sector: A Literature Review," Virginia Polytechnic Institute and State University, Blacksburg, Va.

Terrell, P. and R. M. Kramer (1984): "Contracting with Nonprofits," *Public Welfare* 31–37.

Vladeck, B. C. (1976): "Why Nonprofits Go Broke," *The Public Interest* 42, 86–101.

Webb, S. and B. Webb (1912): *The Prevention of Destitution*, London: Longmans.

Weisbrod, B. A. (1977): "Toward a Theory of the Voluntary Nonprofit Sector in a Three-Sector Economy," in *The Voluntary Nonprofit Sector*, B. A. Weisbrod (Ed.), Lexington: D. C. Heath, 51–74.

Weisbrod, B. A. (1982): "Assets and Employment in the Nonprofit Sector," *Public Finance Quarterly* 10, 403–426.

Weisbrod, B. A. and M. Schlesinger (1986): "Public, Private, Nonprofit Ownership and the Response to Asymmetric Information: The Case of Nursing Homes," in *The Economics of Nonprofit Institutions*, S. Rose-Ackerman (Ed.), Oxford: Oxford University Press, 133–150.

Wolfenden, Lord (1978): *The Future of Voluntary Organisations*, London: Croom Helm.

Young, D. R. (1987): "Executive Leadership in Nonprofit Organisations," in *The Nonprofit Sector: A Research Handbook*, W. W. Powell (Ed.), New Haven: Yale University Press, 167–177.

Young, D. and S. Finch (1977): *Foster Care and Nonprofit Agencies*, Lexington: Lexington Books.

3.4
The Nonprofit Sector and Government: The American Experience in Theory and Practice[1]

Lester M. Salamon

A curious paradox dominates the recent history of the voluntary sector in the United States. For almost fifty years prior to 1980, the nonprofit or voluntary sector effectively disappeared from American political discourse and debate, as public attention focused instead on the role of government in responding to national needs. Yet, during this period, the private, nonprofit sector expanded as never before, growing in both scale and scope. By contrast, during the five years since 1980, attention to the voluntary sector has soared. Yet, during this period, the sector has experienced extraordinary economic strains.

It is the purpose of this essay to unravel this paradox and to explore the implications of the "crisis of the welfare state" for voluntary organizations in America. To do so, however, it is necessary to examine some of the basic characteristics of the American voluntary sector and its relationships with government. This is so because much of the paradoxical character of recent American policy toward the voluntary sector results from a misunderstanding of how this sector operates and how it fits into the American version of the welfare state. Indeed, few aspects of American society have been more consistently overlooked or more poorly understood. This is unfortunate not only because it leads to poor policy, but also because it obscures a model for the provision of welfare-state services that may have great relevance for other nations, particularly those interested in exploring alternatives to exclusive reliance on the state.

The purpose of this paper, therefore, is to address the following questions: What role does the voluntary sector play in the American welfare state? What is the relationship between the voluntary sector and government and what implications does this have for our theories of the nonprofit sector? How has this relationship been affected by recent national policy changes? And what implications flow from this for the future evolution of the voluntary sector, in the United States as well as elsewhere in the world?

---

[1] This chapter draws heavily on two previously published articles: Salamon (1986a) and Salamon (1987). The views expressed here are those of the author only and do not necessarily represent the views of The Johns Hopkins University or any other organization.

1. Nine Observations

Fortunately, several new bodies of research, including a major inquiry into the scope of the nonprofit sector and its relationships with government that the present author directed during the early 1980s, make it possible to answer these questions concretely for the first time (Salamon and Abramson 1982a, 1982b; Salamon 1984). For our purposes here, the results of this research can be conveniently summarized under nine major observations:

(1) *The evolution of the voluntary sector in the United States defies conventional theories, particularly conventional conservative theories, about the relationship between voluntary organizations and the state.*

According to conventional accounts, a fundamental conflict exists between voluntary organizations and the state. Government social welfare activities, according to this view, crowd out private, voluntary ones and leave voluntary organizations functionally obsolete. As government grows, therefore, this theory would lead us to expect private, nonprofit activity to shrink, at least in the fields where the two are both involved.[2]

In fact, however, little of this sort has occurred in the United States. Although the growth of public institutions has put serious pressures on many private, nonprofit ones in the field of higher education, in most fields the private, nonprofit sector remains a major presence despite the very rapid growth of government. As of 1980, for example, the public-benefit, service portion of the American nonprofit sector alone had expenditures of approximately $116 billion, as shown in Table 1.[3] This represented about 5 % of the

---

[2] This theory was articulated most forcefully in late eighteenth and early nineteenth century conservative political philosophy, but it has been given modern form in the writings of sociologist Robert Nisbet (1982: 109), who identified the conflict "between State and social group" as "the real conflict in modern political history." For a fuller discussion of this theory, see Salamon and Abramson (1982a: 223 – 224).

[3] Throughout this discussion, I will be using the terms "nonprofit," "voluntary," and "charitable" interchangeably to refer to a broad range of organizations that share four crucial features: (1) they are privately controlled but are not profit-seeking businesses and are therefore exempt from federal income taxation; (2) they are eligible to receive tax-exempt charitable gifts from individuals and corporations; (3) they provide services; and (4) they are primarily dedicated to assisting a broad public and not just the immediate members of the organization. This definition includes hospitals, universities, museums, arts groups, day care centers, nursing homes, foster care agencies, family counselling centers, neighborhood development groups, advocacy organizations, and many more. It does not include three other sets of organizations that are also exempt from federal income taxation in the United States and are therefore formally part of the "nonprofit sector": first,

Table 1: Expenditures of Nonprofit Public-Benefit Service Organizations in the United
States, 1980 ($ billions)

Type of Organization	Expenditures	
	Amount	As % of Total
Health Care	70.0	60
Education/Research	25.2	22
Social Services	13.2	11
Community Devel./Civic	5.4	5
Arts, Culture	2.6	2
	116.4	100

Source: Salamon and Abramson (1982a).

gross domestic product and a slightly larger share of national employment.
In fact, nonprofit organizations account for about one in every five service
industry workers. And in many fields its dominance is even greater. Thus
nonprofits represent 54 % of all general hospitals, 53 % of all museums,
70 % of all four-year colleges, and over 50 % of all social service agency
employees. In many localities, the expenditures of the nonprofit sector
outdistance those of city and county government, despite the American
tradition of substantial local self-government. Quite clearly, the American
nonprofit sector has hardly withered away with the growth of the modern
welfare state.

Not only is the American nonprofit sector large, but also much of its
growth has occurred in recent years. In fact, a survey we conducted of
nonprofit organizations other than hospitals and higher education institutions revealed that two-thirds of the organizations in existence as of 1982
had been created since 1960, which was a period of very rapid growth in
governmental welfare activities (Salamon 1984: 17). This growth significantly
extended the structure of the American voluntary sector, adding to the
traditional sectarian organizations numerous organizations with roots in the
anti-poverty, civil rights, consumer, environmental, and related movements
of the 1960s and 1970s. In short, the expansion of the American welfare

professional associations, labor unions, social clubs, and other organizations that
exist primarily to serve the immediate members of the organization; second,
churches, synagogues, mosques, and other sacramental religious congregations; and
third, funding intermediaries such as private foundations and fundraising groups,
whose expenditures show up in the activities of the public-benefit service organizations that are covered. For more detail on the basis of the sector size estimates
reported here, see Salamon and Abramson (1982a: 13 – 15).

state has hardly displaced the voluntary sector. To the contrary, the sector has experienced some of its most impressive growth during precisely the era of most rapid governmental expansion.

(2) *The continued expansion of the nonprofit sector in the face of governmental growth is in substantial part a consequence of the peculiar form the welfare state has taken in the American context.*

One of the major problems with the conventional image of the relationship between government and the voluntary sector is its failure to take account of how government operates in the American setting. In the domestic sphere, at least, government — particularly the federal government — does very little itself. What it does, it does through other institutions — state governments, city governments, county governments, banks, manufacturing firms, hospitals, higher education institutions, research institutes, and many more. The result is an elaborate pattern of "third-party government" in which government provides the funds and sets the directions but other institutions deliver the services, often with a fair degree of discretion about who is served and how (Salamon 1981, 1988).

This pattern of government action is a product of the conflict that has long existed in American political thinking between the desire for public services and hostility to the governmental apparatus that provides them. "Third-party government" has emerged as a way to reconcile these competing perspectives, to increase the role of government in promoting the general welfare without unduly enlarging the administrative apparatus of the state. Where existing institutions are available to carry out a function — whether it be extending loans, providing health care, or delivering social services —, they therefore have a presumptive claim on a meaningful role in whatever government program might be established. Indeed, government has often created such institutions where none existed in order to carry out a public purpose without extending the governmental bureaucracy.

This pattern of government action has also resulted from America's pluralistic political structure. To secure political support for a program of government action, it is frequently necessary to win at least the tacit approval, if not the whole-hearted support, of the key interests with a stake in the area. One way to do this is to cut them into a "piece of the action" by building them into the operation of the government program. Thus, private banks are involved in running the government's loan guarantee programs, private health insurers and hospitals in the operation of its health programs, states and private social service agencies in the provision of federally funded human services.

By virtue of their "public" or charitable objectives, and their presence on the scene in many of the fields where government involvement has occurred, private, nonprofit organizations have been natural candidates to take part in this "third-party" system. What is more, government support has stimulated the creation of nonprofit organizations in a number of fields, elaborating the basic structure of the sector and encouraging its expansion into new areas. In the process, an extensive government — nonprofit partnership has taken shape, extending the reach of the voluntary sector and underwriting its operations in important part.

This elaborate partnership takes a variety of different forms — outright grants from the federal government to nonprofits, federal grants to state and local governments which then enter into "purchase-of-service" contracts with nonprofits, payments to nonprofits to reimburse them for services provided to individuals, and many more. Perhaps because of this complexity, this system was not charted until very recently. Yet it turns out to be immense. According to estimates my colleagues and I developed, for example, the federal government alone provided approximately $40 billion in aid to the private, nonprofit sector in 1980 (Salamon and Abramson 1982a: 42−43). As reflected in Table 2, this represented over one-third of the funds that the federal government spent in the service fields where nonprofit organizations are active. And in some fields, such as social services, research, arts and humanities, and health, half or more of all federal spending went to support services provided by private, nonprofit groups!

Table 2: Estimated Federal Support of Nonprofit Organizations, FY 1980 ($ billions)

Field	Federal Support to Nonprofits		
	Total Federal Spending	Amount	As % of Federal Spending
Research	4.7	2.5	54
Social Services	7.7	4.0*	52
Arts, Humanities	0.6	0.3	50
Health	53.0	24.8	47
Employment and Training	10.3	3.3	32
Elementary/Secondary Education	7.0	0.2	2
Higher Education	10.3	2.6	25
Community Development	11.5	1.8	16
Foreign Aid	6.9	0.8	11
Total	111.6	40.4	36

Source: Salamon and Abramson (1982a), 42−43.
* Includes a limited amount of income assistance aid not covered in column 1.

An even clearer picture of the extent of government reliance on nonprofits to deliver publicly financed services emerges from Table 3, which draws on work we have done at the local level in sixteen localities of different sizes throughout the United States, and which covers state and local as well as federal spending. What these data show is that, on average, about 40 % of the money government spends on services in five key human agencies service fields goes to private nonprofit providers. By comparison, public organizations absorb only about 39 % of the funds, with the balance delivered by for-profit firms. This means other nonprofits actually deliver a larger share of the services government funds than do government agencies themselves. And in some fields, such as social services, nonprofits absorb over half of the funds government spends.

Table 3: Share of Government-Funded Human Services Delivered by Nonprofit, For-Profit, and Government Agencies in Sixteen Communities, 1982 (Weighted Average)[a]

Field	Proportion of Services Delivered by			
	Nonprofits	For-Profits	Gov't.	Total
Social Services	56 %	4	40	100 %
Employment/Training	48	8	43	100
Housing/Comm. Devel.	5	7	88	100
Health	44	23	33	100
Arts/Culture	51	*	49	100
Total	42%	19%	39%	100%

Source: The Urban Institute Nonprofit Sector Project, Salamon (1984).

* Less than 0.5 %.

[a] Figures are weighted by the scale of government spending in the sites. Percentages shown are computed by dividing the total amount of government support received by each type of provider in each field in all sites by the total amount of government spending in that field in all sites.

In short, one of the major reasons the expansion of the welfare state has not displaced nonprofit organizations in the United States is that government has turned extensively to nonprofit organizations to deliver publicly financed services. Indeed, in the fields where the two sectors are involved, nonprofits are the principal service providers, handling more of the public funds than government agencies themselves. Contrary to widespread beliefs, it is this government — nonprofit partnership that thus forms the core of the human service delivery system in the United States.

(3) *Government is the principal source of nonprofit-sector income.*

Given the extent of government reliance on nonprofit organizations to deliver publicly funded services, it should come as no surprise to learn that government, not private charity, is the principal source of private, nonprofit organization income in the United States. Compared to the $ 40 billion they received from the federal government in 1980, for example, nonprofit service organizations received only $ 25.5 billion from all sources of private giving combined, including corporations, foundations, United Way, religious federations, direct individual giving, and bequests. This point emerges even more forcefully from a survey we conducted of some 3,400 nonprofit organizations exclusive of hospitals and higher education institutions. As reflected in Table 4, this survey showed that government accounted for 41 % of the revenues of these organizations as of 1981. The second largest source of support, accounting for 28 % of total revenues, was fees and service charges. Private giving accounted for only 20 % of the revenues. In short, the government – nonprofit partnership has not only become a dominant feature of the American version of the welfare state, but also the central financial fact of life of the nation's substantial voluntary sector.

Table 4: Sources of Support of Nonprofit Human Service Agencies, Exclusive of Hospitals and Universities, 1981

Source	Percent of Nonprofit Income
United Way	5
Other Federations	3
Direct Individual	6
Corporate	3
Foundation	3
Subtotal, Private Giving	20
Government	41
Fees, Service Charges	28
Endowment	5
Other	6
Total	100

Source: Salamon (1986)[a].

[a] Figures are weighted by the scale of government spending in the sites. Percentages shown are computed by dividing the total amount of government support received by each type of provider in each field in all sites by the total amount of government spending in that field in all sites.

(4) *Government—nonprofit collaboration is in no sense a new development in the United States; rather, it has roots deep in American history.*

Within some portions of the voluntary sector, the expansion of government support has been viewed as a violation of the nonprofit sector's historic pattern of independence. But such cooperation is in no sense a new development in the United States. Rather, it is rooted deep in American history. In fact, some of the nation's premier private, nonprofit institutions — such as Harvard University, Columbia University, Dartmouth College, and the Metropolitan Museum of Art — owe their origins and early sustenance to government support. As early as 1890, 57% of all public expenditures on aid to the poor in New York City went to support services provided through nonprofit organizations. So widespread was the practice of government support for private hospitals in the late nineteenth and early twentieth centuries that an American Hospital Association report referred to it in 1909 as "the distinctively American practice." Until late in the nineteenth century, in fact, nonprofit organizations were viewed in America as part of the public sector, not the private sector, because they served "public purposes" (Nielsen 1980: 25—48; Salamon 1986b).

While this pattern of government—nonprofit cooperation has roots deep in American history, however, it has expanded in scope and scale in the period since the New Deal of the 1930s, and particularly during the 1950s and 1960s, as the scope of government activity grew. Thus, the Medicare program established in 1965 made ample provision for government reimbursement of private hospitals as the cornerstone of the nation's system of health care for the aged. The Social Security Act Amendments of 1967 opened the door for state and local contracting with nonprofit providers under the federal government's new social service program. The Economic Opportunity Act of 1964 led to the creation of a network of federally funded nonprofit organizations to orchestrate local anti-poverty efforts. Through these and other actions, the existing pattern of government—nonprofit cooperation mushroomed in scale and complexity. But the basic contours of the relationship had been set decades — indeed centuries — before.

(5) *Despite its considerable scale and historical roots, the widespread pattern of government—nonprofit relations in the United States has been overlooked until recently. That this is so is due not simply to a lack of research, but more fundamentally to a failure of theory.*

Although the nonprofit, public-benefit service sector in the United States receives more of its support from government than from any other source, and government agencies rely more heavily on nonprofit organizations than on their own instrumentalities to deliver government-funded human services, the reality of government—nonprofit interaction went largely unnoticed in the United States until relatively recently. No empirical data on the scope of government reliance on nonprofit organizations, or on nonprofit reliance on government, were assembled until the early 1980s, except for a preliminary estimate developed for the Commission on Private Philanthropy and Public Needs in 1974. Nor did this partnership figure prominently in the debates over social welfare policy until the early 1980s. Even students of the voluntary sector sometimes downplayed or overlooked the phenomenon. A major project on public policy toward the nonprofit sector completed by the conservative-oriented American Enterprise Institute in the late 1970s, for example, strongly recommended that government make use of the nonprofit sector to deliver public services, but largely ignored the massive extent to which this recommendation was already embodied in existing government programs (Berger and Neuhaus 1977). Even where government support of the voluntary sector was recognized, it was largely bewailed as an unfortunate departure from a golden era of nonprofit sector "independence." That such cooperation could have practical and theoretical advantages as a preferred mode of operation for both government and the nonprofit sector hardly surfaced as a possibility.

Why is this so? Why has so central a part of the fiscal base of the nonprofit sector and so major a feature of the American welfare state gone so unnoticed for so long? The answer to this question, I believe, lies not so much in a lack of research as in some basic shortcomings in the theories available to guide research. Both the theory of the welfare state and the theory of the voluntary sector, moreover, seem flawed.

The Prevailing Conception of the Welfare State. Perhaps the major conceptual problem impeding clear understanding of the extent of government – nonprofit cooperation in the United States has been the prevailing conception of the modern "welfare state." Focusing on the dramatic expansion of Federal government expenditures since the New Deal of the 1930s, observers of the American scene have jumped easily to the conclusion that what has been underway in the United States has been a gigantic enlargement in the apparatus of government at the expense of other social institutions. This view essentially carries over uncritically into the American context an image of the state that is essentially European in origin. The central image is that of a rigid bureaucratic apparatus, hierarchic in structure and monolithic in form. Not accidentally, such a view serves some useful political purposes, both for those on the right and for those on the left. Conservatives, for example, find it useful to exaggerate the power of the modern American state in order to emphasize the threat that the expansion of governmental social programs poses to liberty. But liberals, too, have had reason to emphasize the role of the state in order to cast doubt on the capacity of private institutions in the social welfare field and thus buttress the case for greater governmental involvement.

Whatever the motivation, however, the result has been to portray an ever-expanding, bureaucratic state that is increasingly monopolizing social problem-solving and leaving little room, either conceptually or practically, for private, nonprofit groups. Indeed, most accounts of the American welfare state up through the late 1970s made it seem as if the voluntary sector had ceased to exist, or at least had ceased to perform a significant social function.

The Prevailing Theories of the Voluntary Sector. If the prevailing conception of the modern welfare state provides one part of the explanation for the failure to recognize the existence of a vibrant pattern of government — nonprofit cooperation, the prevailing theories of the voluntary sector provide the other part. They have done so by over-emphasizing the distinctions between the sectors and thus casting doubt on the theoretical justification for cooperation between them. This is certainly true of the two major theories of the voluntary sector extant in the economics literature.

The first of these, associated with the work of Burton Weisbrod (1978), attributes the existence of the private, voluntary sector to a combination of what economists term "market failure" and "government failure," i.e. of certain inherent limitations of both the private market and government in supplying certain kinds of goods, in particular "collective goods."

"Collective goods" are products or services like national defense or clean air that, once produced, are enjoyed by everyone whether or not they have paid for them. Providing such goods exclusively through the market will virtually ensure that they are in short supply, since few consumers will volunteer to pay for products they could enjoy without having to pay. With market demand low, producers will produce less of these goods or services than the public really needs and wants. This phenomenon is commonly referred to as the "free rider" problem, and it serves in traditional economic theory as the major rationale for government. Since government can tax people to produce "collective goods," it can overcome this "market failure."

But government, too, has certain inherent limitations as a producer of collective goods. Most importantly, in a democratic society, it will produce only that range and quantity of collective goods that can command majority support. Inevitably, this will leave some unsatisfied demand on the part of segments of the political community that feel a need for a range of collective goods, but cannot convince a majority of the community to go along.

It is to meet such "unsatisfied demand" for collective goods, the argument goes, that a private, voluntary sector is needed. Private, nonprofit organizations thus exist, according to the "market failure"/"government failure" theory, to supply a range of "collective goods" desired by one segment of a community, but not by a majority. From this it follows that the more diverse the community, the more extensive the nonprofit sector it is likely to have. Because the nonprofit sector is viewed as a substitute for government, providing goods and services that the full political community has not endorsed, however, government support to nonprofit organizations has little theoretical rationale. To the contrary, under this theory, to the extent that nonprofits deliver services that government underwrites, they violate their theoretical *raison d'être*, which is to supply the goods government is not providing. The "market failure"/"government failure" theory would thus predict that little government — nonprofit cooperation would occur, and that what little of it exists cannot be easily justified.[4]

The second broad theory of the voluntary sector attributes the existence of voluntary organizations to a different kind of market failure, what one theorist terms "contract failure" (Hansmann 1980). The central notion here is that for some goods and services, such as care for the aged, the purchaser is not the same as the consumer. In these circumstances, the normal mechanisms of the market, which involve consumer choice on the basis of adequate information, do not obtain. Consequently, some proxy has to be created to offer the purchaser a degree of assurance that the goods or services being purchased meet adequate standards of quality and quantity. The nonprofit form, in this theory, provides that proxy. Unlike for-profit businesses, which are motivated by profit and therefore might be tempted to betray the trust of a purchaser who is not the recipient of what he buys, nonprofit firms are in business for more charitable purposes and may therefore be more worthy of trust.

Since most government programs involve a substantial amount of regulation, however, this theory provides little rationale for government reliance on nonprofits, or for government regulation of nonprofits. In fact, since government agencies might be expected to have even less reason to betray trust than nonprofit ones, this theory might lead one to expect more reliance on government agencies than nonprofit ones.

Toward a New Formulation: Third-Party Government and Voluntary Failure. To come to terms with the reality of government-nonprofit relationships, therefore, it is necessary to alter the conceptual lenses through which this reality is being viewed. In particular, two conceptual changes are needed. In the first place, we must replace the prevailing theory of the welfare state with the concept of "third-party government," which corresponds much more accurately with the long-standing reality of government operations in the United States (Salamon 1981). The central precept of the "third-party government" concept is that a distinction must be drawn between govern-

---

[4] Burton Weisbrod, the principal architect of this theory, does acknowledge the possibility of government subsidization of voluntary organizations, but this is treated as an exception, not as the core of our human-service system (Weisbrod 1978: 66).

ment's role as a financier or arranger of services, and government's role as an actual provider of services. In the United States at least, the growth of government in recent decades has largely been in the first of these capacities — as financier and arranger. For a variety of political, ideological, historical, and practical reasons, at least the national government has turned extensively to third parties — cities, counties, universities, hospitals, banks, private businesses, and others — for the actual delivery of the services it is financing. By virtue of their "public-regarding" missions and their prior involvement in many of the fields government was newly entering, private nonprofit organizations have been prime candidates to take part in this widespread system of third-party government. Far from an aberration, in short, the widespread pattern of government—nonprofit cooperation emerges, when viewed from this theoretical perspective, as just one manifestation of a much broader pattern of government operations characteristic of this country.

In addition to replacing the prevailing theories of the welfare state with the concept of "third-party government," a clear appreciation of the realities of government—nonprofit relations will also require replacing the existing "market failure"/"contract failure" theories of the voluntary sector with what might be termed the "voluntary failure" theory instead. Three key precepts underlie this alternative theory. In the first place, instead of viewing the voluntary sector as a residual line of defense for the provision of collective goods that government will not supply, as existing theories do, the "voluntary failure" theory views the nonprofit sector as the first line of defense instead. This makes sense, given the "transaction costs" involved in mobilizing government to act on social problems, regardless of the degree of homogeneity in a community. In the second place, however, the "voluntary failure" theory acknowledges that voluntary organizations have certain inherent limitations in responding to social needs. One of these limitations is *philanthropic insufficiency*, the fact that it is difficult to secure contributions from all of those who will benefit from the good works that charities do, and that the voluntary resources to meet social needs are often not available where the needs are greatest. Another is *philanthropic particularism*, the fact that private charities tend to focus on particular problems or groups of individuals, creating gaps in coverage and the potential for considerable duplication. A third is *philanthropic paternalism*, the fact that private charity can at best establish aid as a privilege, but not as a right, thus creating a residue of dependence. A fourth is *philanthropic amateurism*, the reality that voluntary aid is frequently too uneven and volatile to establish the professional forms of care that are often needed.

Interestingly, however, these areas of voluntary failure correspond very nicely with the areas of governmental strength. As a general rule, government is in a position to generate a more reliable stream of resources than is private philanthropy, to set priorities on the basis of a democratic political process instead of the wishes of the wealthy, to offset part of the paternalism of the charitable system by making access to care a right instead of a privilege, and to improve the quality of care by instituting quality-control standards and ensuring a stable source of support. On the other hand, however, voluntary organizations are in a position to overcome some of the inherent limitations of government service provision, such as over-bureaucratization, excessive rigidity, inadequate competition, and impersonality. In short, far from diverting attention from government — nonprofit cooperation, the theoretical notions outlined above explain why such cooperation might be both likely and desirable. To the extent that a theory that does a better job of accounting for the facts is the one that deserves our adherence, there is thus a strong case for taking these alternative notions very seriously.

(6) *Despite its strong theoretical rationale and great promise, however, the extensive pattern of government — nonprofit cooperation in the United States has also had its problems, and these problems became increasingly evident during the 1970s.*

Based on the discussion above, it thus appears that the extensive pattern of government — nonprofit cooperation that has evolved in the United States has much to recommend it. Potentially at least, it makes it possible to set priorities and raise funds through a democratic political process while still delivering services through smaller-scale voluntary organizations. Properly managed, it can also reduce costs by inducing a degree of competition in the service-delivery system. Finally, it helps to sustain a network of institutions that engage private citizens in the solution of community problems, and thus promotes an important national value stressing pluralism and private action. In all likelihood, had this system of service provision not been invented long ago in this country, Americans would be busily inventing it now.

For all its potential strengths and advantages, however, this system of government — nonprofit partnership has also had its problems. For one thing, despite its scale and importance, this system has evolved in *ad hoc* fashion, with little systematic understanding of the roles and responsibilities of the respective partners and little public awareness that the partnership even exists. As the scale of the interactions has increased, therefore, tensions and confusions have resulted. Nonprofit organizations, for example, have sometimes been distressed by the accountability and paperwork requirements imposed by government and by the impact of government regulations on their operations. There has also been concern about the potential dilution of board control of agencies, as government contract officers have come to play a larger role in agency operations, and about the tendency of government to encourage professionalization and bureaucratization of nonprofit organizations. The sheer fragmentation of government program structures has also caused problems, making it difficult for nonprofits to fashion integrated approaches to human problems. For their part as well, government officials have frequently found it difficult to exercise adequate control over the spending of public funds, and often find it necessary to support the range of services the existing network of agencies can provide, even when it is not fully consistent with what the legislation or community needs may require.

As these strains intensified in the 1970s, moreover, they were joined by concerns about the apparent erosion of the private philanthropic base of the voluntary sector. Between 1969 and 1979, for example, private giving as a share of gross national product declined from 2.1 % to 1.8 % in the United States. In part, this was a result of the impact of inflation. But in part also it was the byproduct of a series of changes in the tax system that liberalized the so-called "standard deduction," causing fewer people to "itemize" their deductions and thus reducing the value of the special tax deduction that is provided for charitable contributions.[5] At the same time, there was mounting evidence that a change in the laws governing private foundations in 1969, coupled with adverse market conditions, was eating into the assets of private foundations, threatening this source of private charitable support as well. Under these circumstances, leaders of the voluntary sector became increasingly concerned about the future of this set of institutions that had played so vital a role in American life (Commission on Private Philanthropy and Public Needs 1975).

These concerns about the future of the voluntary sector surfaced, moreover, at a time when public confidence in government as a mechanism for solving social problems − never very strong in America − was again in ebb tide. The Vietnam events, escalating inflation rates, hostility to the social regulation of the 1960s and 1970s, and backlash against the social policies of the Great Society of the 1960s all contributed to a climate of reaction against the "welfare state." Since the public had little awareness of the

---

[5] Under American tax law, individual taxpayers can deduct their contributions to charitable or educational organizations from their income before computing their tax obligations. This has the effect of reducing the out-of-pocket "cost" of the contribution, since part of this cost is offset by tax savings. However, prior to 1981 only taxpayers who "itemized" their deductions were eligible for this treatment. Taxpayers who chose to take a flat "standard deduction" instead did not receive additional deductions for their charitable deductions. As the size of this "standard deduction" increased, fewer taxpayers had an incentive to "itemize." By the 1970s, in fact, over two-thirds of the taxpayers were taking the standard deduction. Because the availability of the tax deduction has been found to be an incentive for charitable giving, the fact that fewer taxpayers were in a position to claim this deduction meant that the incentives for charitable giving were reduced.

existing partnership between government and the voluntary sector, this hostility to governmental programs translated into support for greater reliance on the nonprofit sector instead.

(7) *In response to the pressures and concerns that surrounded the voluntary sector and the growing disenchantment with government, an interesting consensus took shape during the 1970s behind a program of reforms that would strengthen the nonprofit sector and rationalize its relationships with government.*

Stimulated by the problems identified above, important efforts were made during the 1970s to examine the status of the voluntary sector and to rethink its role in national life. These efforts took place on both the political right and the political left and created an interesting opportunity to upgrade the status of the voluntary sector and improve the existing *ad hoc* pattern of government – nonprofit ties.

Among the most important of these efforts, four deserve special mention here: first, the formation in 1973 of a blue-ribbon Commission on Private Philanthropy and Public Needs (the Filer Commission), composed of key business, government, and philanthropic leaders, which amassed a substantial body of new information on the voluntary sector and formulated a voluntary-sector agenda that endorsed continued governmental support to the voluntary sector but also called for changes in the tax laws to increase the incentives for private charitable giving (Commission on Private Philanthropy and Public Needs 1975); second, the publication in the mid-1970s by the business-oriented American Enterprise Institute of a series of reports calling for a more explicit and active policy of governmental utilization of "mediating structures" such as voluntary organizations to carry out public objectives (Berger and Neuhaus 1977; Woodson 1981); third, the formation in 1979 of Independent Sector, a new national association representing all the components of the Third Sector and devoted to strengthening its role in national life; and fourth, the publication by the conservative Heritage Foundation of a report on private philanthropy that reached many of the same conclusions as the Filer Commission and that added a strong conservative voice to the defense of a set of institutions that during the 1960s and early 1970s had acquired a decided liberal following as well (Butler 1980).

By the time the Reagan administration took office in 1981, therefore, an unusual consensus had formed among leaders on both the political left and the political right in favor of strengthening nonprofit and voluntary groups and broadening and rationalizing existing relationships between such groups and government. To be sure, the strands of analysis and insight had yet to be drawn together into an integrated program of action. What is more, voluntarism still engendered considerable skepticism on the political left, while conservatives sometimes found it hard to reconcile their theoretical enthusiasm for the concept of voluntary organization with the reality of many of the radical, neighborhood, and public-interest groups that had formed in the 1960s. Nevertheless, the degree of consensus was still quite surprising, especially in view of the wide divergence of political perspectives it embraced. Coupled with the growing disaffection with traditional welfare-state policies, the pieces were therefore in place – both politically and analytically – for a significant policy initiative featuring an expansion of the role of voluntary groups and a more explicit policy of government – nonprofit cooperation. Here was a unique opportunity indeed for an administration committed, as the 1980 Republican Party platform put it, to the restoration of "the American spirit of voluntary service and cooperation, of private and community initiative."

(8) *Rather than seizing this opportunity, the Reagan administration adopted policies that threatened to dismantle, or at least significantly reduce, the prevailing pattern of government – nonprofit cooperation.*

Although strongly committed conceptually to encouraging the voluntary sector, the Reagan administration did precious little to build on the consensus that had developed during the 1970s in support of a positive program of cooperation between government and nonprofit groups. To the contrary, the administration subsumed its policy toward the voluntary sector under its overall economic program, which called for substantial cuts in government spending and in tax rates in order to stimulate economic growth (Salamon and Abramson 1982b). In a sense, the administration retreated to the traditional theories that viewed government and the nonprofit sector as competitors. By cutting back on government, therefore, the administration could argue that it was creating new opportunities for the nonprofit sector. To help encourage the private sector to "pick up the slack" and "fill the gap" left by governmental withdrawal, moreover, the administration established a White House Office on Private Sector Initiatives and organized a Task Force on Private Sector Initiatives composed of prominent business and philanthropic leaders (Berger 1985).

What this approach largely overlooked, however, was the fundamental fact detailed above: that government and the nonprofit sector were not inherently in conflict in the American setting, and that an extensive partnership linked the two. By cutting back on government spending, therefore, the administration also cut into the revenues of many private, nonprofit groups. In fact, the administration's initial budget proposals would have reduced the support that private, nonprofit organizations received from the federal government by some $ 33 billion – about 20 % – during the period 1982–1985. For some types of organizations, moreover, the projected loss of federal support would have been considerably more severe. Thus, under the administration's initial proposals, federal support to nonprofit social service organizations would have been 64 % lower in FY 1985 than it had been in FY 1980, after adjusting for inflation. Community development organizations would have lost 65 % of their federal support, and education and research organizations 35 % (Salamon and Abramson 1982a: 32, 51). Because government represents a large source of income for these organizations, moreover, these reductions posed a significant challenge to existing agency operations.

Although Congress ultimately refused to go along with the administration's proposals completely, significant cuts did occur. In particular, outside of the health field, where spending continued to increase, overall federal spending in fields where nonprofit organizations are active declined by almost $50 billion below pre-Reagan levels over the four years between 1982 and 1985. As reflected in Table 5, this in turn translated into significant reductions in government support of nonprofit organizations. According to our estimates, after adjusting for inflation, nonprofit organizations outside of the health field lost $17 billion in government support during this period compared to what would have been available had 1980 spending levels been maintained. For some types of agencies, moreover, the reductions in federal support were particularly severe: 36 % in the case of social service organizations, 35 % in the case of housing and community development organizations, 20 % in the case of higher education institutions (Salamon and Abramson 1985: 49 – 50). In short, while encouraging voluntary organizations to do more, the Reagan administration, through its budget proposals, was forcing them to do less.

While the administration's budget proposals affected nonprofit receipts from government, moreover, the other prong of its economic strategy — tax cuts — threatened to reduce nonprofit receipts from private charitable

Table 5: Changes in Federal Support of Nonprofits, FY 1982 – 1985, in Constant FY 1980 Dollars ($ Billions)

Type of Organization	FY 1980 Federal Support	Enacted Changes FY 1982 – 85	% Change FY 1985 vs. FY 1980
Social Services	6.5	− 9.3	−36
Community Development	2.3	− 2.8	−35
Higher Education	2.6	− 1.9	−20
Other Education/Research	2.9	− 0.5	−
Health	24.9	+16.7	+26
Foreign Aid	0.8	− 0.4	+11
Arts, Culture	0.4	− 0.6	−41
Total	40.3	+ 1.3	+ 7
Total without Medicare, Medicaid	16.7	−17.1	−25

Source: Salamon and Abramson 1985.

sources. By reducing tax rates and changing the tax treatment of bequests, the tax bill that passed in 1981 limited the financial incentives for private charitable contributions (Clotfelter and Salamon 1982). Furthermore, although the 1981 tax bill as ultimately passed incorporated a new provision favored by the philanthropic community to permit taxpayers who take the so-called "standard deduction" to claim a deduction for charitable contributions anyway, this pro-charities provision was opposed by the administration.

In addition to pursuing an economic program that threatened to reduce the revenues of the voluntary groups it claimed to want to help, the administration also took a number of administrative actions that were also widely perceived to be hostile to the voluntary sector. These included: (1) the elimination of the federal government's principal vehicle for promoting community-based voluntary organization (the Community Services Administration, formerly the Office of Economic Opportunity); (2) the reduction in the postal subsidy for nonprofit groups, which is important in direct-mail charitable fund-raising; (3) an effort to restrict access by less established groups to the federal government's annual work-place charitable drive, the Combined Federal Campaign; and (4) the promulgation of a new regulation that would require nonprofit organizations receiving more than 5 % of their funds from federal program sources to maintain separate books and facilities for their service and "advocacy" functions to avoid having federal resources used in support of advocacy.

In short, committed to a budget strategy designed to reduce government spending, but wedded to a political theory that obscured the existing pattern of government – nonprofit cooperation, the Reagan administration found itself in the curious position of encouraging the voluntary sector at the rhetorical level while undermining it at the programmatic level, and not really appreciating the conflict between the two. In the process, the administration alienated substantial segments of the voluntary community, undermined emerging liberal support for a voluntary agenda by tying this agenda to a retreat from public responsibilities, and thus squandered an important opportunity to develop a positive program of change that would strengthen the nonprofit sector and improve the prevailing pattern of government – nonprofit cooperation.

(9) *As a result of the budget reductions proposed by the Reagan administration and partially enacted by Congress, nonprofit organizations have been forced to seek alternative sources of funding or to reduce their operations. Generally speaking, the sector has been far more successful in boosting its commercial income than its charitable income.*

As reflected in Table 6 below, the budget cuts enacted at the federal level in the early 1980s did show up in the balance sheets of the nation's private,

Table 6: Changes in Nonprofit Support from Government, by Type of Agency, 1981—82, in Inflation-Adjusted Dollars

Type of Agency	% Change in Government Support
All Agencies	− 6.3
Legal Services/Advocacy	−28.8
Housing/Community Development	−15.6
Employment/Training	−12.7
Social Services	− 8.8
Mixed	− 8.1
Education/Research	− 7.3
Culture/Arts	− 1.3
Health Services	− 1.3
Mental Health	− 0.1
Institutional/Residential	+ 4.1

Source: The Urban Institute Nonprofit Sector Project Survey, Salamon (1984).

nonprofit organizations. Based on a survey we conducted of all such organizations except for hospitals and universities, government support for nonprofit service providers declined by 6% overall between 1981 and 1982 after adjusting for inflation. However, in some fields the reductions were quite a bit more severe than this. Thus legal services and advocacy organizations lost 29% of their federal support, housing and community development organizations 16%, employment and training organizations 13%, and social service organizations 9% (Salamon 1984).

Despite these losses in government revenue, however, the nonprofit sector as a whole registered real growth in total income over this period. Taken as a group, the agencies we surveyed grew by 0.5% between 1981 and 1982, after adjusting for inflation.

The principal reason for this recovery from government cutbacks was not, however, growth in private charitable support, as the Reagan administration had hoped. Although private charitable income grew, it offset no more than a quarter of the government losses. The major source of replacement income — accounting for 70% of the total — came, rather, from service charges and fees. In other words, the nonprofit sector managed to recover from government cuts chiefly by charging their clients more for their services or by instituting fees where none formerly existed (Salamon 1984).

While this shift from public to commercial income has much to recommend it, it raises important questions about the future of this set of institutions and about their role in the American welfare state. Conceivably, the more agencies must rely on service fees to survive, the more they will be forced to tailor their services to clientele who can pay for them, and the less they will focus on those in greatest need. This is particularly troubling in view of two important facts that emerge from our surveys. In the first place, far fewer of these agencies focus on the poor and needy than might have been expected. Of the human service agencies we surveyed, less than 30 % reported that poor people comprise the majority of their clients, and about half reported that poor people comprise less than 10 % of their clients. In the second place, the agencies overwhelmingly agreed that government support has played an important role in inducing agencies to achieve the degree of attention to the poor that they have. The clear implication is that as government support declines, agencies will find it even harder to continue to serve the poor. Some evidence of this is apparent in the variations in agency ability to bounce back from government budget cuts. In particular, while on average the agencies we surveyed registered an 0.5 % gain in income between 1981 and 1982, agencies serving the poor ended up with a significant overall decline. Generally speaking, the agencies with the best access to paying clients did best in response to the recent budget cuts while those with the least access did worst. As the nonprofit sector shifts from governmental to commercial sources of income, therefore, the structure of the sector could change as well.

Beyond the questions of what the nonprofit sector does and whom it serves, the shift to greater reliance on fee income also raises questions about the basic rationale for the nonprofit form of organization. This is particularly problematic in view of a challenge that has been posed to the nonprofit sector in the United States by the small business community, which is jealous of the tax advantages enjoyed by nonprofit organizations. As nonprofits move more actively into commercial activities, and as they come to rely more heavily on fees for services to finance their operations, the more serious this challenge is likely to become.

2. Conclusion

The American voluntary sector stands at an important crossroads in its development. More than its counterparts in most other countries, this set of organizations has maintained a substantial role despite the growth of the welfare state. It has done so, however, not so much in opposition to government as in cooperation with it. The resulting pattern of government–nonprofit partnership in the provision of welfare-state services stands in stark contrast to the direct governmental provision of services that is the central feature of the welfare state in many other western nations.

As a system of service provision, this pattern of government — nonprofit partnership has much to recommend it, combining the capacity to generate resources and set priorities through a democratic political process and the ability to deliver services through smaller, locally oriented, private nonprofit groups. It thus makes welfare-state benefits available as a matter of right while still preserving a useful degree of competition and pluralism in the service-delivery structure.

Despite its scale and importance, however, this pattern of government — nonprofit partnership is surprisingly poorly understood, both in the United States and elsewhere in the world. Government — nonprofit cooperation took shape not as a matter of conscious policy but as an adaptation to powerful political realities — the political strength of the voluntary sector, the widespread hostility to governmental bureaucracy, and the general tepidness of public support for welfare services. In part because of this, this partnership — for all its strengths — has serious operational and theoretical problems.

Although serious efforts were made during the 1970s to face up to these problems and come to terms with them, these efforts were shortcircuited by the budget and tax program of the Reagan administration, which, in the name of strengthening the voluntary sector, subjected this sector to serious economic strains and made voluntarism and the voluntary sector a front for cutbacks in government spending. Ironically enough, while other countries are contemplating a partnership between government and voluntary organizations of the sort that have long existed in the United States, American policy, however unwittingly, seems to be taking this partnership apart.

Whether the political support that was developing for a conscious policy to strengthen the voluntary sector and rationalize government — nonprofit cooperation can be revived in the United States remains to be seen. But the opportunity is certainly there. What is more, the importance of this government — nonprofit partnership to the functioning of the American welfare state, and its role as a model for other countries interested in new approaches to the delivery of welfare-state services, makes it imperative that this opportunity be seized.

References

Berger, Peter and J. Neuhaus (1977): *To Empower People*, Washington: American Enterprise Institute.

Berger, Renee A. (1985): "Private Sector Initiatives in the Reagan Era: New Actors Rework an Old Theme," in *The Reagan Presidency and the Governing of America*, L. M. Salamon and M. S. Lund (Eds.), Washington: The Urban Institute Press, 181 – 211.

Butler, Stuart (1980): *Philanthropy in America: The Need for Action*, Washington: The Heritage Foundation and the Institute for Research on the Economics of Taxation.

Clotfelter, Charles and Lester M. Salamon (1982): "The Impact of the 1981 Tax Act on Individual Charitable Giving," *National Tax Journal* 35, 2 (June), 171–187.

Commission on Private Philanthropy and Public Needs (1975): *Giving in America: Toward a Stronger Voluntary Sector*, np: Commission on Philanthropy and Public Needs.

Hansmann, Henry (1980): "The Role of Nonprofit Enterprise," *Yale Law Journal* 89, 5, 835–901.

Nielsen, Waldemar (1980): *The Endangered Sector*, New York: Columbia University Press.

Nisbet, Robert (1982): *Community and Power*, 2d edition, New York: Oxford University Press.

Salamon, Lester M. (1981): "Rethinking Public Management: Third-Party Government and the Changing Forms of Government Action," *Public Policy* 29, 255–275.

Salamon, Lester M. (1984): "The Results Are Coming in," *Foundation News* 25, 4 (July/August), 16–23.

Salamon, Lester M. (1986a): "Government and the Voluntary Sector in an Era of Retrenchment: The American Experience," *Journal of Public Policy* 6, 1, 1–20.

Salamon, Lester M. (1986b): "Partners in Public Service: The Theory and Practice of Government–Nonprofit Relations," in *Nonprofit Sector Handbook*, W. Powell (Ed.), New Haven: Yale University Press, 99–117.

Salamon, Lester M. (1987): "Of Market Failure, Voluntary Failure, and Third-Party Government: Toward a Theory of Government–Nonprofit Relations," *Journal of Voluntary Action Research* 16, 1, 29–49.

Salamon, Lester M. (1989): *Beyond Privatization: The Tools of Government Action*, Washington: The Urban Institute Press.

Salamon, Lester M. and A. J. Abramson (1982a): *The Federal Budget and the Nonprofit Sector*, Washington: The Urban Institute Press.

Salamon, Lester M. and A. J. Abramson (1982b): "The Nonprofit Sector," in *The Reagan Experiment*, J. L. Palmer and I. Sawhill (Eds.), Washington: The Urban Institute Press, 219–243.

Salamon, Lester M. and A. J. Abramson (1985): "Nonprofits and the Federal Budget: Deeper Cuts Ahead," *Foundation News* 26, 2 (March/April), 48–52.

Weisbrod, Burton (1978): *The Voluntary Nonprofit Sector*, Lexington: Lexington Books.

Woodson, Robert (1981): *A Summons to Life*, Washington: American Enterprise Institute for Public Policy Research.

3.5
The Relationship Between Voluntary Associations and State Agencies in the Provision of Social Services at the Local Level

Peter C. Lloyd

As the demands made of the modern welfare state continue to escalate, two contrasting discourses grow in intensity. One, which we might call the "liberal" discourse, calls for more popular control of the welfare state; the other, the "conservative" discourse, calls for its reduction in scale. Richardson (1983) has described how an interest in popular participation developed during the 1960s as, increasingly, people became unwilling "to sit idly by while decisions were made on their behalf... [they] proceeded to demand a right to participate in the policy making process." She attributed this to a growing tendency to question authority in both public and private spheres; people are becoming more assertive, more involved (pp. 102 – 103).

The counter view is expressed by Bolger et al. (1981). The current conservative ideology of welfare sees the "over coddling" and excessive dependence on state welfare as contributing to the decline of society. It sees as wrong those institutions which have been founded on the belief that the state ought to take responsibility for people's lives — wrong indeed for those who receive the services, for they destroy the morality of the individuals involved as well as sapping the political will of the nation (p. 5). From this flow continual conservative references to the sanctity of the family, the virtues of self help.

Both of these discourses, when translated into policy recommendations, extol the virtues both of the informal sector — the networks of friends and neighbours — and of the voluntary sector — the myriad of small local associations — in constituting a link between the family and the state and in providing supplementary and complementary services. "Community" has become a buzz word; but the contribution expected from community action differs between the two discourses.

To give one example: "community care" for the dependent elderly has been a widely proclaimed policy for many years; yet the term is ambiguously used. To some, it suggests removing people from the large geriatric hospital wards to small nursing homes located within the neighbourhood but involving little or no ongoing relationship with the neighbourhood; to others, it means sending the elderly back to their families where close kin (usually daughters) can fulfil their "proper" roles. Sometimes community care is interpreted as meaning the intensive provision of personal services by staff of state welfare agencies within the home of the elderly person; more often it is posited that friends and neighbours — "the community" — can and should provide these services. In the ideal world, there would be an "interweaving" of services provided by family, neighbours and friends, voluntary agencies, and stated institutions which would provide far more personalized care, greater client control, and, hopefully, lower financial costs to the state.

Two sets of questions arise from such a vision: firstly, can the "community" carry out the tasks expected of it; do informal networks and voluntary agencies have the necessary skills (in nursing for example), resources (sufficient volunteers), or management abilities? Secondly, what is seen as the appropriate relationship between these associations operating within the neighbourhood and the state agencies? How far should voluntary associations act as junior partners in a state enterprise; can they sustain a role as critic and innovator?

The purpose of this paper is to explore this latter issue. It is an issue which arises, I believe, in all countries and in a similar form; idioms of partnership and consensus tend to deny its existence as a problem, idioms of conflict emphasize it. I write, however, within the British context, indicating the manner to which the issue has been expressed and indicating an approach which would clarify it.

1. Community

Community is a most ambiguous term. In many contexts, it implies nothing more than locality. But to the sociologist, "the two fundamental *communal* elements of any social system are a sense of solidarity and a sense of significance" (Clark 1973). Such solidarity and significance are seen as virtues in current ideology. Yet, as Abrams (1980) argued, the traditional neighbourhood type of social network is a relic of the past — of a past, moreover, that one would not wish to see reproduced today. Collective attachment, reciprocity, and trust, the internal features of such networks were the survival strategies developed as a response to specific social conditions marked by constraint, isolation, and insecurity (p. 14).

Modern neighbourhoodism, according to Abrams, is of a very different character. It is an attempt by newcomers in an area to create a local social world politically mobilizing old and new residents to protect amenities, enhance resources, and vest control in local hands rather than outside authorities (p. 18).

Academics are thus highly sceptical of the role which the "community" can play in service provision. They range from those who would argue that the "community" as conceived does not exist, through those who believe that the activities of informal networks and voluntary associations whilst undeniably extensive, cannot be developed further, to those who, optimistically, believe that a potential for expansion does exist but that it must be purposively fostered — it will not come of its own accord (for example, Bulmer 1987: 70). Academic radicals argue, furthermore, that the concept of community is stressed in conservative discourse to counter class-based analysis of the crisis of capitalism. As Bolger et al. argue, "community work represents a new method whereby the state can structure its relationship with the working class, at home and in the locality" (1981: 118).

Academic scepticism notwithstanding, government policies increasingly stress the contribution expected from the community. As noted above, community care of the elderly, in relying more heavily upon family, informal social networks, and voluntary agencies, is expected to cut the financial costs to the state — the costs of family, friends, volunteers go unrecorded.

Another mode of cost cutting is the reduction of government grants to many local authorities, by rate capping, and the abolition of metropolitan authorities, a direct consequence of which has been their inability to support a wide range of voluntary associations. At the same time, government affirms its support for these associations. However, they have been assisted by a number of schemes organized by the Manpower Service Commission, Urban Aid programmes, and the like whereby unemployed youths are employed on "community projects." These are thus removed from the register of unemployed, given some training (though voluntary association workers complain that they have too little time to give to training and that few jobs exist commensurate with the skills imparted); contracts are usually brief — for a year or two — with the consequence that a service once organized and appreciated may subsequently be withdrawn.

A further factor affecting the role of voluntary associations is the introduction of the "patch" system of social service delivery. Instead of specialist social workers operating out of a central borough office, local offices servicing neighbourhoods of c. 20,000 people and staffed by generic social workers have been set up by many local authorities. As Hadley et al. (1984) describe it, this alternative mode of service delivery focusses on communities rather than client groups or cases, recognizing the primary of informal care and seeking to involve individual citizens, community, and voluntary associations in the planning and provision of services (p. 5).

This approach demands from social service workers a very detailed knowledge of their "patch," its characteristics and potentialities, and a policy of developing local voluntary associations. The involvement of volunteers and the greater popular participation are heralded as virtues (though it will not escape notice that the greater involvement of underpaid, volunteer workers is yet another cost-cutting ploy). The success of this operation is, however, constrained by the reluctance of specialist social workers to embrace a community orientation and by continuing financial cuts which propel service workers into direct care of the most seriously disadvantaged rather than preventative measures within the locality; workers in the patch office still, in many cases, see themselves as working with individual clients. In many areas, the specific community workers have been withdrawn; the patch team leader, saddled with increased managerial tasks, has less time to develop a community orientation among his staff.

These policies all presage a close relationship between voluntary associations and the state agencies. On the one hand, there is an assumed consensus in their goals — to provide efficient and caring personal services. On the other, it remains a fact that a high proportion of the incomes of the voluntary associations continues to derive from grants from central and local government. In the conservative discourse, partnership is stressed; and the financial links enforce acceptance of this idiom. Yet conflicts of interest between state and voluntary association obviously exist. In some ways, this dichotomy parallels the distinction made between community development and community action — the stimulus for the former coming from above (Bryant 1972).

2. The Aims of Voluntary Associations

The voluntary associations, however, have their own conception of their proper role. As Mellor (1985) notes, the voluntary association, because of its independence and small scale, can better experiment and bear risks than can the large bureaucratic state agency. Concentrating more singlemindedly on specific issues, it can both act as a watchdog and promote creative suggestions for statutory policy (p. 11).

People join voluntary associations because they wish to change something for the better. As Mellor states, in their early days, their strengths usually lay in the personal enthusiasm of their members. These people have, furthermore, ideas about how change might be achieved; indeed Jameson (in Scott and Wilding 1986: 15) believes that the exploration of new ideas should take precedence over the provision of services; innovation is the key task of the voluntary association. Sills (1975) would go even further in arguing that community groups in particular aim to bring about a redistribution of power in society; in attempting to provide or sustain services, they have to reckon with the exercise of power in their locality, and they seek to influence decision-making processes.

Initiative, innovation, independence, participation are all concepts stressed in the voluntary association's own discourse. They exist to articulate demands — demands which might be met either by a statutory body or by self help, by others or by themselves.

But they are heavily reliant upon state funding. Nevertheless, the National Council for Voluntary Organisations issued in 1984 "A Code for Voluntary Organisations" urging upon them caution and prudence in seeking and accepting statutory funding:

(1) Each voluntary body must regard its freely-chosen aims and objectives as paramount under the law in determining its policy and conduct.

(4) In all financial dealings with government, voluntary bodies should make a distinction between "arms-length" support for voluntary activity as such (albeit in a particular sector) and contractual payments on a customer/supplier basis for specific services rendered or functions fulfilled.

(9) ... voluntary bodies should judge all offers of government financial support, whether "arms-length" or "customer/supplier," by reference to that body's aims and objectives and without primary regard to the possibly different, but overlapping, aims of government policy in offering that funding.

Most voluntary associations perceive no incompatibility in acting as a pressure group and providing a local service; and most are engaged in both. But whilst the liberal discourse speaks of participation, protest, and control, the conservative discourse stresses partnership.

3. The State Response

The response of the state is ambivalent. Many nationally recognized "protest organizations" are in fact state funded, their repeated articulation of grievances is seen as functional in defusing tensions. Senior local government officials will often welcome a local pressure group as a means of keeping junior staff alert, on their toes. This issue was taken up in the Wolfenden Report (1977: 98): the critic, whether the Old Testament prophet or the modern protester, has never been popular; whilst some critics do enjoy widespread support, others are self-appointed and not representative; there is a danger that those who shout loudest will claim greatest attention.

The fear with which some extremists view the threat of more vocal voluntary associations is encapsulated in the comments of Sir Alfred Sleeman, Director of the Centre for Policy Studies — a government think-tank: as central and local governments have made funds available to voluntary associations, so have they become dominated by unelected professional politicians — as an open jam pot attracts flies and wasps; left-wing groups which fare badly in elections operate freely in "this undercover world of the Shamateur circuit" (cited in *Community Care*, July 21, 1983).

A recent government ruling prohibits voluntary associations from using their statutory funds in making any criticism of government policies. The state thus seeks to interpret partnership in such a way as to stifle criticism and probably to inhibit innovation. The role assigned, *in extremis*, to the voluntary associations is thus to provide, at the behest of the state, those services which it cannot or is unwilling to deliver — to provide them at lower cost, through unpaid or underpaid workers, though perhaps with a greater element of personal attention. What is apparently envisaged is a two-tiered system of service delivery with the voluntary agency in the position of the subordinate partner. Such a role conflicts, of course, with that perceived by the voluntary associations.

The external observer has the task of showing how one form of relationship between state and voluntary association may be more politically or financially expedient; for the actors in the situation the importance of seeing through the obscurantism of the rival discourses is paramount. For both observer and actors the key concepts are those of power and control.

4. Modes of Relationship

The concept of incorporation, used to denote the relationship between voluntary associations and the state, is not new, but it is ill-defined. As Thomas (1985) says, one must "recognise different degrees and forms of incorporation, and other consequences for workers, residents and agencies." Some forms of interpretation might provide opportunities for productive work which increases the relevance of state services to dependent families and households. We should be more concerned with the "exploitation and colonization of community work" by those agents which seek to impose their own agendas without reference to the needs of the communities.

The Wolfenden Comittee (1978) cites two attempts to classify the types of relationship.

"In his booklet, *Bargain or Barricade*, Giles Darvill summarises the attitudes of social service departments towards the volunteer programmes and this has some relevance also to voluntary organisations. In light-hearted terms he classifies the categories as: 'the abstention attitude', where professional and voluntary services function separately; 'the call-girl attitude' which looks upon voluntary organisations as a shameful but necessary convenience; the most common of all, 'the suburban attitude', in which the department requires polite, obedient, cheap and respectful service from voluntary workers; the 'King Henry VIII attitude', by which volunteers are encouraged to experiment and lose their heads if their experiments are not successful; and finally, 'the intimate enemy attitude' in which there is conflict but it is brought out into the open and regarded as healthy. Dr Cousins, in his study on voluntary organisations and local government in South London, discusses the relationship of voluntary organisations with official council committees and sub-comittees and distinguishes five broad categories:

a) those groups which worked closely with the council departments and which were in contact with officers frequently, although they also furnished many coopted members for council committees; b) those groups which were in receipt of council aid (financial or otherwise), and which in general did not oppose the council publicly. Officers, and less often, councillors were contacted by these groups, the relations being good; c) those groups which commonly found themselves in conflict with the council, but which confined themselves to using orthodox means of influence when contacting the council; d) those groups which often found themselves in conflict with the council and which pursued this opposition, in general by using more extreme methods — petitions and demonstrations for example; e) those many groups which only contacted the council infrequently, and then purely as a matter of routine — booking halls or hiring equipment, for example. Any contacts were with junior staff" (1978: 89 – 89).

In a study of voluntary associations in York, Sills (1975) described them as the good, the bad, and the ugly, in terms of perceptions held by official-dom. The same modes of relationship were encompassed by Abrams (1980) in the terms colonization, coexistence, and conflict. Writing about modern neighbourhood associations (see the definition above), Abrams shows a preference for coexistence as appropriate to the concept of neighbourliness, whilst recognizing that colonization may produce *more efficient service delivery*. This creates an acute moral dilemma for those responsible for the formulation of policy. Abrams defines coexistence as a position which the informal or voluntary sector is strengthened so that it may deal on equal terms with agencies in the formal state system. Whereas with incorporation, the norms and relationships of the informal sector are remade to suit the administrative purposes of the formal system, in coexistence, notwithstanding the degree to which formal and informal care are meshed together, they are sustained as a basis for social policy in their own right.

Conflict he rejects — for "unless it leads somewhere, it is in the end a sterile and demoralizing prospect" (similarly Sills' "bad" associations were those which protested in such a way that they alienated the statutory bodies and achieved nothing).

Colonization may take several forms, though all involve dependency. Abrams distinguishes domination, appropriation, and incorporation. Of these, domination occurs where statutory bodies impose their own hierarchies of control, setting the boundaries defining distinct spheres of action. Appro-priation is a more encompassing relationship in which boundaries are re-drawn so that activities of the informal sector are included within an ex-panded formal sector. Abrams then uses the term "incorporation" to describe a position in which the more powerful formal agencies do not simply respect the "untidy integrity" of the informal sector but build some measure of informality into their own procedures. Incorporation is thus seem as a more extreme form of appropriation or a strategy moving towards coexistence.

Abrams' terms direct us much more towards the essence of the relationship than do the previously cited classifications; but equally they are difficult to employ empirically — which is perhaps why such a seminal idea from a noted British sociologist seems to have lain dormant. Nevertheless, it is an analysis of this type which is needed today.

5. The Relationship Studied

I would not wish to imply that little or nothing has been written in the past decade about the relationship of voluntary associations to the statutory sector. The literature has in fact been quite extensive. Studies seem to fall into two categories.

In the first, the principle of participation set forth by successive government committees — Plowden, Wolfenden, Barclay — is accepted. With consensus (as opposed to conflict) assumed, the problems arising from the relationship are seen as technical issues, to be resolved by the goodwill of those concerned. The focus is on those associations which do collaborate with statutory agencies; those which do not have no place in the discussion.

Two excellent studies of this type are those of Diana Leat and her colleagues. The first, *Voluntary and Statutory Collaboration: Rhetoric or Reality* (1981) deals with the roles of Councils of Voluntary Service and Rural Community Councils and is not directly pertinent to this paper. The second is highly relevant; in *A Price Worth Paying? A study of the effects of government grant aid to voluntary organisation (1986)* the authors (funded by the Home Office) surveyed four areas to establish whether statutory grant aid drove away contributions from the general public; their conclusion was that the more successful a voluntary association was in attracting such grant aid, the greater its success overall in expanding its activities. However, their data provided "no clear conclusion on the effects of statutory funding on perceived loss of independence."

Loss of independence takes two forms — a loss of freedom to make public and critical statements, and constraints observed within the organization, the type of activity undertaken, the purposes for which funding is sought. Leat et al. describe how mutual trust is developed between grantor and grantee; the concept of power tends to be ignored. They compare the relationship to that between husband and wife — complementary but un-equal, and argue that, like wives, voluntary associations should be more assertive. In three of the four local authority areas surveyed, a quarter of the voluntary associations recognized a loss of independence in receiving aid; if participant observation of the associations' activities rather than the formal interview of officers had been the mode of enquiry, the apparent concensus between the parties might have been dispelled further.

A very different type of study is emplified by that of Butcher and his colleagues, *Community Groups in Action: Case Studies and Analysis* (1980). This provides a detailed examination of five associations made through intensive study and participant observation. The focus is on the mobilization of these associations, and in a comparative study, the authors identify the factors which led to the success or failure of each. But, as they admit, they paid little attention to the statutory agencies with which their associations were in a situation of confrontation.

Valuable though both of these studies undoubtedly are, each has a serious deficiency: Leat et al. underplay the conflict of interest implicit in the voluntary – statutory relationship; Butcher and his colleagues, in describing the mobilization of their associations, give insufficient attention to the relationship with statutory agencies. To meet these deficiencies, one must define an arena in which voluntary associations and statutory agencies meet to pursue their respective and conflicting interests; one must describe how each perceives the situation in which they are involved, how they formulate their goals, mobilize support, and pursue their strategies and tactics.

For purposes of simplicity, the relationship between voluntary association and statutory agencies has been presented as a dyadic one; a triad would better define the parties involved – the voluntary association, the statutory agency (or some service department), the elected local government councillors. The agency and association may collaborate in service provision; but it is the councillors who vote for the association's funding – and who also may wish to use the association as a political platform or support, or who may fear the association's threat to their position as the properly elected representative of their localities. Indeed, the arena is extraordinarily crowded with rival associations, rival statutory agencies, rival politicians all competing for power and status, forming multiplex alliances and introducing diversionary themes to detract from major issues.

But what is power, and how is it exercised? In their respective books, Leat at al. and Butcher et al. give many examples.

Leat et al. are specifically concerned with government grant aid and its effects. Thus they distinguish between aid in money, and in services; between aid given for a defined purposed and that given "without strings" (noting that the former seems to be on the increase; between control exercised over use of money or activities of a worker in making the anward, in overseeing its management, or in ultimate audit. It is also clear how power is exercised by local government councillors or officials in the exercise of their roles in voting for or approving such grants. In practice, many awards seem to be given with few constraints on their use, with the mildest forms of accountability; only rarely are voluntary associations blackmailed into unwelcome action. But then, it is agreed, they are rarely likely to ask for something that would have little chance of being given.

Butcher et al. focus, on the other hand, on the power exercised by mobilized voluntary associations in making their demands. They classify strategies as *collaborative* − where there is agreement about the existence of a problem and the need to tackle it; *campaign* − where it is felt that the debate must move beyond technical considerations to the legitimacy of the problem, and *coercive* − where the existence of a problem is disputed. As they indicate for each strategy, there are appropriate tactics. A collaborative strategy would embrace the collection of data and information and presenting it in public enquiries, in letters to politicians or the media, in petitions; this implies a broad consensus over the definition of the issue and the implication that the debate is over technical matters, for the right of the targeted body to make decisions is acknowledged. With campaigning strategies, this right is still acknowledged, but there may be conflict over the definition of particular issues, and tactics are extended to include rallies, marches, and picketing. A coercive strategy results when the right of the targeted body to make resource allocation decisions is disputed; strikes and other forms of direct action are the appropriate tactic here (p. 148).

Valuable as this model is, we need, I believe, a more conceptually oriented analysis of power; and this is provided by Lukes (1974) in his discussion of the three dimensions of power.

6. The Analysis of Power

For Lukes (1974), the one-dimensional view of power involves a focus on behaviour in the making of decisions where there is an observable conflict of subjective interests, seen as express policy preferences. A two-dimensional view extends this to embrace behaviour designed to prevent the taking of decisions on potential issues in which conflicts of interest are apparent; in other words, the setting of the agenda is thus a form of power.

Lukes is critical of this two-dimensional view inasmuch as it implies that interests, grievances, and the like must be articulated for a power relationship to develop. But as he argues, the most insidious form of power lies in preventing people from articulating their interests; they are led to accept their place in the existing order, they see no alternative to it, for it is natural and unchangeable or divinely ordered and beneficial. To assume that an absence of grievance implies consensus is to rule cut the possibility of false consensus by definitional fiat. His three-dimensional view of power thus enables us to study how potential issues are kept out of the political arena, and a contradiction between the rival interests remains latent, those involved may not be conscious of their interests.

Lukes' model of three-dimensional power provides us with a useful tool by which to analyse the control exercised by the state and its agencies over the voluntary agencies.

As both the literature and the findings of my own students currently working in the Brighton area demonstrate, an increasing degree of direct control is being exercised. Statutory agencies are sub-contracting service provision to voluntary associations which are paying their staff lower wages but are perhaps providing a more personal service to their clients. As a consequence, the voluntary association workers are beginning to collectively organize in trades unions to demand the same pay scales as state employees. For their part, the professionally qualified state employees argue that their status is being undermined if unqualified people are encouraged to replace them; but if it is acceptable for an untrained daughter to nurse her aged mother, why not an untrained friend or neighbour?

The more subtle forms of control are equally pervasive. As Leat et al. and our Brighton data show, members of voluntary associations are, in the situation of financial stringency, increasingly likely to frame their requests for funding in terms believed to be acceptable to the donor bodies. And the role of agents of the latter, who sit on the voluntary associations' management committees, becomes more influential. One can, as an observer of these meetings, note how the definition of the problem enunciated by the state representatives comes to prevail over other formulations.

But perhaps the most important forms of control derives from the close personal relationships which frequently exist between the leaders of voluntary associations and officials of statutory agencies. As Kramer (1981) describes, he found in England, Israel, and the Netherlands a "cozy" network of informal relationships between leaders of voluntary associations and government officials, people sharing the same cultures, recognizing their interdependence and anxious not to disturb the relationship — a bureaucratic symbiosis (p. 164).

The same theme is embodied in Leat et al.'s discussion of trust. A point is reached when the leaders of voluntary associations cease to be aware of their *real interests*, interests embraced within the concepts of participation and control, innovation and protest as outlined in the voluntary associations' own charters. The probable reason why the classificatory systems of Abrams and others have not been used in empirical investigations is that members of voluntary associations have become so captivated by the discourse of partnership that issues of independence, participation, and control have been relegated as being of insufficient practical importance.

7. Conclusion

Voluntary associations are in a highly ambiguous position. By definition, they are independent of the state, and their role is to confront the state — by pointing out deficiences and inequalities in the statutory provision of services. Remedies lie in the persuasion of the statutory agencies to improve their services or in the provision, by self help, of additional alternative services.

The concepts underpinning the voluntary associations — popular participation, self help — are applauded by the state and its officials; even the critical role of the associations is welcomed as functional in providing an outlet for tension and stimulating bureaucratic efficiency. But the tendency exists for statutory agencies, in supporting the voluntary associations' role as service providers, to seek to incorporate them into their own structure, as partners in a subordinate position. When so much of the funding which enables the associations to function so successfully comes as government aid, it is inevitable that the independence of the voluntary associations is threatened. The range of possible relationships between voluntary associations and statutory agencies has been indicated by Abrams; the manner in which power may be exercised by Lukes; with examples of financial control provided by Leat et al. and of influence strategies by Butcher et al. At one extreme, one will thus find the association with a radical ideology, perhaps with a working class membership with few personal contacts or ties with senior state officials, which chooses a confrontational stance; demands and protests are vociferously made. But the ensuing opposition by the statutory agencies renders their success improbable. Far more typical are those voluntary associations which exploit the social networks of their members to lobby officialdom. But in the atmosphere of consensus and mutual trust so created, the voluntary associations are only too liable the lose sight of their original objectives, to fail to recognize how far they are being used by, or made subordinate to, the statutory agencies. Such colonization may, as Abrams suggests, be a more *efficient* way of providing social services; it is, however, a denial of the original objectives of the voluntary associations.

References

Abrams, Philip (1980): "Social Change, Social Networks and Neighbourhood Care," *Social Work Service*, 22 February, 12—23.
Bolger, Steve, Paul Corrigan, Jan Docking, and Nick Frost (1981): *Towards Socialist Welfare Work*, London: Macmillan.
Bryant, R. (1972): "Community Action," *British Journal of Social Work* 2, 2.

Bulmer, M. (1987): *The Social Basis of Community Care*, London: Allen and Unwin.

Butcher, Hugh, Patricia Collis, Andrew Glen, and Patrick Sills (1980): *Community Groups in Action*, London: Routledge and Kegan Paul.

Clark, D. B. (1973): "The Concept of Community: A Re-Examination," *Sociological Review* 21, 3.

Hadley, Roger, Peter Dale, and Patrick Sills (1984): *Decentralising Social Services*, London: Bedford Square Press.

Kramer, Ralph M. (1981): *Voluntary Agencies in the Welfare State*, Berkeley: University of California Press.

Leat, Diana, G. Smolka, and Judith Unell (1981): *Voluntary and Statutory Collaboration: Rhetoric or Reality*, London: Bedford Square Press.

Leat, Diana, Sue Tester, and Judith Unell (1986): *A Price Worth Paying? A study of the effects of Government Grant Aid to voluntary organizations*, London: Policy Studies Institute.

Lukes, Stephen (1974): *Power: A Radical View*, London: Macmillan.

Mellor, Hugh W. (1985): *The Role of Voluntary Organisations*, London: Croom Helm.

Richardson, Ann (1983): *Participation*, London: Routledge and Kegan Paul.

Scott, Duncan and Paul Wilding (Eds.) (1986): *Beyond Welfare Pluralism*, Manchester: Manchester CVS.

Sills, P. (1975): "Power and Community Groups," *Community Development Journal* 10, 1 (January), 24–28.

Thomas, David (1985): "The State and the Neighbourhood," *Community Care*, 31 January, 24–25.

Wolfenden Committee (1977): *The Future of Voluntary Organisations*, London: Croom Helm.

3.6
Nonprofit Social Service Agencies and the Welfare State: Some Research Considerations

Ralph M. Kramer

Despite the enormous expansion of governmental social services during the last 20 years, voluntary, nonprofit social service agencies have grown in number and importance.[1] Their number has increased substantially, and new types have emerged such as alternative agencies, many of which were started and supported with governmental funds. The expansion of the welfare state was accompanied by the pervasive mingling of public and private funds and functions based upon *the separation of financing from service delivery*. Governmental funds were transferred by means of subsidies, grants, and payments for service, often in the form of contracts, to nonprofit organizations to provide an ever-growing number of personal social services to a clientele for whom there was a public responsibility.

Welfare states vary considerably in the extent to which they utilize nongovernmental agencies. The Netherlands, where voluntary agencies constitute the primary social service delivery system, stands at one end of a continuum; Sweden, where practically no voluntary agencies are used, although some are subsidized for the purposes of advocacy, stands at the other. Closer to the Netherlands is West Germany, where about half of the social services are subsidized by the government but are provided by voluntary agencies. Other countries with similar patterns are Belgium, Switzerland, Austria, and Italy. The United States is about in the middle, preferring the voluntary agency as an agent and sometime partner to complement a governmental system that uses a variety of service providers. The United Kingdom stands closer to Sweden because of the dominance of its statutory agencies, while France, Israel, and Canada stand somewhere between it and the United States (Kramer 1985b: 133 – 134).

In each country, the particular division of responsibility between governmental and voluntary agencies is not formalized, but reflects a distinctive

---

[1] The nonprofit organizations which are the subject of this chapter are responsible for the delivery of the *personal social services* which refers to the care and support provided to the needy elderly, the mentally ill or retarded, physically handicapped persons, deprived or neglected children and youth, i. e. all disadvantaged persons with serious psycho-social problems.

history and socio-political context. While welfare states differ in the extent of their reliance on non-governmental organizations for the provision of social services, they all share a basic perception of voluntary agencies: these organizations are expected to be innovative and flexible, to protect particularistic interests, to promote volunteer citizen participation, and to meet needs not met by government. Together with government and profit-making organizations, voluntary agencies may relieve, replace, or reinforce the primary social systems of family, neighbors, and friends. In relation to the public sector, voluntary agencies may substitute for, influence, extend, and improve the work of government, or they may supplement, offer complementary services different in kind, or function as a vendor or public agent. Voluntary services may also compete with profit-making organizations in many fields of social service (Kramer 1987: 241).

Voluntary agencies are used by government because, as in the United Kingdom, the Local Authority Social Service Departments may not have appropriate, specialized, or sufficient resources; or because, as in Holland, they are, for historical and religio-political reasons, the providers of first choice; or, for more pragmatic reasons, in the United States and Israel, they may provide an economical, flexible service which is often a means of avoiding bureaucratic or budgetary constraints. These public fiscal policies enabled voluntary agencies greatly to enlarge the scope of their services and more than compensated them for any decline in contributions. As they became increasingly dependent on governmental funds, voluntary agencies became, in effect, public agents, raising worrisome questions about their autonomy and their accountability. The future fate of voluntary agencies became inexorably linked to that of the welfare state, and they have become highly vulnerable to recent reductions in public spending (Demone and Gibelman 1984; Salamon 1986).

In addition, the organizational differences between them and other providers of personal social services — in government and in the market — have diminished considerably, because they all draw their funds from the same governmental sources, are subject to the same regulations, and utilize the same types of professionals and other staff members. Over the years, many voluntary agencies, like other social service providers, have become more bureaucratic and professionalized and, in the United States, more entrepreneurial and political (Gronjberg 1982).

1. The Mixed Economy

In general, the welfare state has encouraged an inter-organizational environment in which the traditional dichotomy between public and private has become artificial and obsolete. The blurring of sectoral differences is reflected in labels such as the "new political economy" (Smith 1975), "the contract state," the "mixed economy of welfare" (Kamerman 1983), or "welfare pluralism" (Brenton 1985: 154—174). They all refer to the interpenetration of five institutional systems through which the personal social services are provided: government, voluntary agencies, the market, employers, and informal social systems such as the family (Morris 1982). Governmental funds are the most important element and account for the existence of the same types of personal social services under different auspices, although not necessarily for the same population. What is evident is that *we have not yet developed the appropriate concepts, models, paradigms, and theories to reflect this new reality of the mixed economy of welfare.*

On the international level, there is great similarity in the types and patterns of personal social services in welfare states, despite the differences in their dependence on voluntary agencies. Welfare states have also encountered similar difficulties in the operation of their greatly expanded delivery systems for the personal social services, including over- and under-utilization and other problems of access, spiralling costs, and lack of accountability. Personal social services in most welfare states are usually described as fragmented, lacking coherence and coordination, and riddled with "bureau-pathologies" (Kahn and Kamerman 1981).

2. The Significance of Auspices

This experience suggests that auspices (legal ownership), i.e. whether the governmental or nonprofit sector is used for service delivery, may be less significant than is generally believed. In fact, little is known what difference it makes if personal social services are provided by government, a voluntary agency, a profit-making organization, an employer, or a neighborhood association.

A concern with the significance of voluntary or governmental sponsorship is particularly relevant now in considering the future of the welfare state in a period of retrenchment or at least slowed growth. In the face of retrenchments and other efforts to halt the expansion of the welfare state, there has been a revival of interest and renewed political pressure to rely more extensively on the voluntary sector, particularly in the United States and United Kingdom. Other countries have also experienced, in varying degree, a backlash against public spending and considerable distrust and disillusionment with government administration, as well as growing support for privatization and the "empowerment" of voluntary organizations to carry out public purposes (Berger and Neuhaus 1977). Ideological backing for the voluntary sector comes both from the Left and the Right, and stems from its perception as a bulwark against further governmental intervention, or at least as an alternative if not a substitute for it, while some even see voluntarism as a way of recovering a lost sense of community (Hadley and Hatch 1981; Janowitz 1976). However, in this attempt to reverse the process of *Gemeinschaft* to *Gesellschaft*, it may be unwise to assume too soon that we have reached the limits of state welfare. A facile acceptance of "the end of the welfare state" can become a premature, self-fulfilling prophecy, too easily tolerating governmental failure to continue providing benefits that only the state can ensure. Voluntarism is not a substitute for services that can best be delivered by government, particularly if coverage, equity, and entitlements are valued. Nor does the voluntary sector have the capacity to compensate for drastic cuts in governmental allocations for the personal social services (Brenton 1985: 211 – 223; Salamon 1986).

3. Critique of Empowerment

Enthusiastic supporters of the nonprofit sector tend to lump together indiscriminately all forms of volunteerism and "mediating structures" and to regard them as equally desirable and effective in combatting excessive governmental size and intrusion. There are, however, considerable differences between the use of volunteers as unpaid staff and peer self-help; between mutual aid, neighborhood, and community-based service organizations; between the various forms of citizen participation, as well as vast differences in the institutional structures of family and religion. They are no substitute for necessary services best delivered by professionals and other types of paid staff (Graycar 1983; Pinker 1985).

Sufficient attention has not been given to the great variation in the effectiveness of voluntary organizations as service providers and in nurturing citizen participation. Proponents of the voluntary sector often fail to appreciate that its strengths are at the same time the source of its limitations. Whether based on locality, ethnicity, religion, or other sectarian interests, voluntary organizations as service providers are usually narrow and exclusionary in their scope. Because the individuals are dependent for social services on the initiative, resources, and capabilities of a particular group with which they are administratively identified, the substitution of voluntary for governmental agencies can result in even more inconsistent and inequitable services. Although evidence of their service delivery capability is rather sparse, experience with various forms of neighborhood organizations suggests that they can become just as institutionalized, rigid, inaccessible, unresponsive, and undemocratic as professionalized bureaucracies (Gilbert and Specht 1986: 199−201; O'Brien 1974; Rich 1979).

There is also a romantic myth of a Golden Age of voluntarism in local communities in which neighbors helped each other. This popular belief underlies proposals such as those embodied in the 1982 Barclay Report in the United Kingdom advocating the provision of resources to informal networks of social relations to deal with the community care of the mentally ill, the infirm aged, physically and mentally handicapped persons, etc. Substitutions of voluntary for governmental effort are, however, subject to three sets of constraints: (1) the social networks may be non-existent, or unacceptable to the person in need of care, or vice versa; (2) the available resources may be inadequate, or the informal relationships cannot be sustained with the required intensity, duration, and competence; (3) accountability for public funds and the performance of a public function are especially difficult for such social systems. It is often forgotten that the present, more formalized modes of care and support developed because of the failure of the local community, the informal and more voluntaristic institutional systems to perform these functions (Pinker 1985; Segal 1979).

4. The Nonprofit Sector as an Object of Research

Until recently there was a paucity of policy-oriented research on nonprofit organizations, and most of the discussion about voluntarism, empowerment, or privatization in the personal social services was usually impressionistic and heavily ideological. Although organization theory has generally neglected the serious analysis of nonprofit organizations, during the last decade, a beginning has been made at theory-building by a small number of economists and political scientists who have tried to answer the question, why do nonprofit organizations exist (James and Rose-Ackerman 1986; Salamon 1987)? Most of these theories are based on some version of institutional "failure," e. g., government in the case of Weisbrod (1977) and Douglas (1983); the market for Hansmann (1980), or the voluntary system itself for Salamon (1987a). There are also untested and not always explicit assumptions made about the nature of the state and the intrinsic character of organizations under governmental, nonprofit, or profit-making auspices.

Two sets of theories have been proposed to account for the existence of a third sector in addition to government and the market: (1) In comparing nonprofit organizations with government in the production of quasi-public or merit goods, the existence of non-governmental agencies has been explained as a form of "government failure" due to the existence of excess demand and heterogeneous tastes in situations where economies of scale are small and which government is unable or unwilling to meet. (2) In comparing nonprofits with profit-making organizations, where there is inadequate or "asymmetric" information regarding outputs, "contract failure" is invoked whereby nonprofits are regarded as more trustworthy because of the non-distribution constraint, i. e. board members do not derive any direct financial gain from their participation.

These attempts to develop a single, macro-economic model of nonprofit roles and behavior have not been very successful. Their explanatory power is weak even when applied to particular sub-sectors such as the arts, the social services, or health (DiMaggio 1987: 204–205; Steinberg 1987: 126–134). They lack a comparative dimension in not being able to account for cross-national variations in the size and character of the nonprofit sector (James 1989). In addition, they are insufficiently grounded in empirical research and neglect crucial historical and sociological dimensions (Anheier 1988).

So far, no consistent set of factors has been idenfified which can explain the presence of nonprofit organizations in widely different countries — democratic and totalitarian, highly centralized or decentralized regimes, religiously heterogeneous or homogeneous, etc.; or the particular mix between government, the market, and nonprofit organizations in different fields of service. Nor have any theories been proposed to account for the origin, development, and change over time of the sector or its components in relation to government. Consequently, it has been suggested that governmental utilization of nonprofit organizations is better understood as a mixed product of historic, political, and pragmatic fiscal factors rather than a function of market behavior by consumers (James 1986).

Two conclusions for the future development of theory can be drawn:

(1) research may be more productive if directed toward the development of middle-range theories which consider historical, political, sociological, and economic factors in particular fields on a cross-national basis; or which compare the same sub-sectors in countries varying along political-legal dimensions (Anheier 1988).

(2) A more radical approach is to question the basic validity of the mega-concept of the nonprofit sector as the unit of analysis. It is significant that there is still no consensus on the definition and classification of nonprofit organizations (Douglas 1987: 44, 53, 87). Whether referred to as the voluntary, the non-governmental, the independent, the third, or nonprofit sector, the term generally has the character of a residual category by including any organization that is not strictly governmental or profit-seeking. As a result, the use of the sector metaphor tends to obscure both the extraordinary internal diversity and the external convergence of the organizational charac-

ter of all social service providers in the mixed economy of welfare, whether governmental, profit-making, or nonprofit. Hence, it is at least doubtful whether the "non-distribution constraint" or tax exemption (Independent Sector 1987) are suitable and valid grounds for distinguishing a class of organizations about which empirical generalizations can be made, i. e. the "nonprofit sector" may lack sufficient univocality as a research concept.

The separation of governmental funding from service delivery — called "third party government" in the U. S. (Salamon 1981) or "indirect administration" in West Germany — seems to have produced an analogue of a marble cake rather than a demarcated segment of a circle. Consequently, future theory-building must somehow take into account the blurring of sectoral boundaries, their overlapping and interpenetration, as well as the existence of hybrid organizations such as quangos (Langton 1987: 142 – 145).

5. Distinctive Character of Voluntary Nonprofit Organizations

Yet even if the sectoral metaphor may be obsolete and of questionable validity, social policy decisions must still be made regarding who will be served by *whom* and with what service. It would, therefore, be important to have a more rational basis for policy decisions based on what might be expected from nonprofit organizations in their interaction with government. For example, although the following characteristics are more likely to be found among voluntary nonprofit social service agencies than governmental or profit-making organizations, their implications for service delivery — for access, accountability, efficiency, or effectiveness — have yet to be identified:

(1) Market behavior does not influence their decision making; their income is derived typically from multiple sources and is not related to performance, but rather to their fund-raising capacity and a budget (Drucker 1973).

(2) Values, ideologies, and public policy have great influence on the governance and management of nonprofit organizations (Hasenfeld 1983; Kramer 1987: 244 – 248).

(3) Their authority structure is an ambiguous hybrid of bureaucracy, voluntary association, and informal social systems, dependent on a staffing mix of professionals, para-professionals, and volunteers (Billis 1987).

(4) Their unpaid governing boards and executive leadership system have much more influence on policy than their clientele, and board members have a high potential for a power struggle with staff (Kramer 1985a; Middleton 1987).

(5) They are dependent for virtually all of their resources on the external environment (Pfeffer and Salancik 1978).

(6) Their four major roles are: specialization, advocacy, consumerism, and service delivery; their principal vulnerabilities are institutionalization, goal-deflection, minority rule, and ineffectuality (Kramer 1981: 257– 267; Salamon 1987).

6. Three Examples of Interorganizational Research

In view of the likelihood in most countries of continuance of the policy of separating funding from provision, greater attention should be given to *inter-organizational research* in order to learn more about the consequences of governmental delegation of its direct service function to non-governmental organizations. Three recent studies illustrate different approaches and their possibilities:

(1) In investigating the "sources of intersectoral cost differences in the production of welfare," Judge and Knapp (1985) found that *intra*-sectoral differences may be more significant. In the course of their work, these researchers at the Personal Social Services Research Unit at Kent developed a theoretical framework that has been used to determine the cost-effectiveness of nursing homes for the elderly, day and residential care for children under governmental, proprietary, and nonprofit auspices. While they recognize that valid and reliable measures of outcome have yet to be developed, they do not share the scepticism of those, such as Gilbert (1983), who doubt the feasibility of determining which service functions best under which auspice. They stress the importance of comparing equivalent units and taking into account the size of the organization, the nature of the clientele, the staff, and mode of treatment – elements that seem to account for the differences in cost-effectiveness.

These and other relevant organizational variables whose influence on cost-effectiveness or access would be worth studying can be grouped into four classes:

– *Structural* (size of budget, staff, caseload; degree of formalization, decentralization, professionalization)
– *Fiscal system* (percentage of income from different sources)
– *Governance* (board member composition; turnover, participation)
– *Service technology* (routine, complex, and discretionary; care, treatment)

Some hypotheses which might be tested are: controlling for organizational size, type of staff, and clientele, what is the effect of degree of bureaucratization on decentralization, and service technology on cost-effectiveness? Of income and program diversity and degree of professionalization?

A note of caution should be added, because cost comparison studies are exceedingly complex, difficult to replicate, and they have generally produced equivocal results.

Two different approaches in the U.S. to the study of inter-organizational relations are represented in studies of purchase of service contracting in the State of Massachusetts and the San Francisco Bay Area.

(2) Among the most extensive studies of its type, a team of researchers surveyed the results of the Massachusetts experience in contracting-out virtually all of its community mental health programs through 2,000 contracts valued at $175 million with over 500 non-governmental organizations (Schlesinger, Dorwart, and Pulice 1986). Their findings do not support the belief that competitive bidding and contracting-out results in more efficient and effective community mental health services. Three alternative strategies are examined, each with its respective strengths and weaknesses: increasing competition among small organizations; institutionalizing oligopolistic competition among a small number of private providers; and returning services partially or completely to government. The deficiencies identified in this system and the reforms proposed are also relevant for other types of social services.

Similar studies of purchase of service contracting are needed, because they can help answer policy questions such as the following: When is competition undesirable? Should low bids always be accepted? How can government avoid driving out smaller agencies that may be unable to compete in the bidding process? Should nonprofit agencies always be preferred over profit-making organizations? How can fair costs be determined? And finally, what difference does all this make to clients?

(3) Another type of research focussed on the use of governmental funds in seven different programs in nine countries, including an exploratory study of five child abuse prevention agencies, and an in-progress, longitudinal survey of change and continuity over a five-year period among 25 nonprofit social service agencies — all in the San Francisco Bay Area (Kramer and Grossman 1987; Kramer and Terrell 1984). The research identified the conflict between the different interests of government and its service providers as they moved through the five stages of the contracting process. The picture that emerged revealed a *quasi-market system* shaped by supply and demand, the type of service purchased, political influence, and other contextual factors such as the history of governmental — voluntary relations in the community and informal social networks. This view is at variance with the more conventional one of a "partnership" in which power considerations are minimized. Within a political economy framework, a market model drawing on the concepts of power/dependency and exchange in the inter-organizational "task

environment" (Milofsky 1987) is a more useful research tool in reflecting
more accurately the realities of the mixed economy (Baldwin 1978; Kimberly
1975; Provan 1980). For example, in the operational and monitoring phase,
among the external factors which limited both public accountability of the
voluntary agency and any infringements upon its autonomy were the following: the payment-for-service form of most transactions, which involves less
control than grants or subsidies; the diversity of voluntary agency income
sources, which lessens dependency on anyone; the countervailing power of
a voluntary agency oligopsony (few sellers) of a service required by a
governmental agency for its clients; political influence of the voluntary
agency; and the lack of capacity and incentives for stricter accountability by
government. Other conditions limiting governmental control over its vendors
are the fragmented structure of the social services which makes close supervision exceedingly costly, and the inherent methodological difficulties of
evaluating the outcomes of the social services.

In addition to the ways in which nonprofit organizations cope with
the strain between autonomy and accountability, one study (Kramer and
Grossman 1987: 43 – 48) also identified the major strategies used to manage
fiscal resource dependencies. There were recurrent problems associated with
underfunding because of: reimbursement rates frozen below actual costs;
grants that were less than requested or expected due to unforeseen budget
restrictions, cut-backs or cancellations; budget errors regarding costs, such
as underpricing or failure to include overhead; unforeseen, non-reimbursable
contingencies such as an unexpected demand for service, costly accidents, or
emergencies; cash-flow delays due to the actions of legislative or funding
bodies.

To deal with these contingencies, agencies utilized the following *strategies*:

(1) Greater emphasis on *advocacy* either alone or as part of provider
coalitions pressing for more equitable, higher, and stable rates of reimbursement. In addition, contracting agencies mobilized their clientele to influence
legislative bodies.

(2) *Resource development* through securing supplemental funds from corporations, foundations, or fund-raising events made up the difference between governmental payments and the actual costs of services. Other strategies involved increasing fees, establishing a profit-making enterprise, utiliz-
ing more volunteers, and obtaining in-kind contributions.

(3) Another strategy was *inter-organizational collaboration* to achieve economies in operation which compensated for the competitive disadvantage of
small, single-program agencies.

(4) *Service delivery modifications* were adopted in which the more promising
or least expensive cases were selected as a means of showing positive, cost-
efficient outcomes. Other measures included increasing the work load and
occasionally reducing the quality of service.

(5) The fundamental source of most economies in the use of non-governmental social agencies came from the *use of unpaid and/or lower-paid staff*. This included employing indigenous volunteers, low-paid para-professionals, pre-professional interns, unlicensed professionals, lower-paid part-time staff with flexible schedules, and contracting with consultant staff members to avoid paying various personnel benefits.

7. Conclusion

Assuming that non-governmental organizations will continue to be used to implement public policy, it is essential to learn more about how this process actually functions and how to make it work better. Future research agendas should therefore give much more attention to inter-organizational studies that could contribute to theory-building, policy development, and better organizational management.

References

Anheier, H. (1988): "The Public Sector and the Private: Organizational Choice and the Third Sector in Europe," Paper presented at the *Spring Research Forum of the Independent Sector*, March 17–18, 1988, San Francisco: Calif.

Baldwin, D. (1978): "Power and Social Exchange," *American Political Science Review* 72, 4, 1229–1242.

Berger, P. and R. Neuhaus (1977): *To Empower the People: The Role of Mediating Structures in Public Policy*, Washington, D.C.: American Enterprise Institute for Public Policy Research.

Billis, D. (1987): "Some Puzzles and Models of Voluntary Organization," Paper presented at the 1987 conference of the *Association of Voluntary Action Scholars*, Kansas City, Kansas.

Brenton, M. (1985): *The Voluntary Sector in British Social Services*, London: Longman.

Demone, H. and M. Gibelman (1984): "Reaganomics: Its Impact on the Voluntary Non-Profit Sector," *Social Work* 29, 421–427.

DiMaggio, P. (1987): "Non-Profit Organizations in the Production and Distribution of Culture," in *The Non-Profit Sector: A Research Handbook*, W. Powell (Ed.), New Haven and London: Yale University Press, 195–220.

Douglas, J. (1983): *Why Charity?*, Beverly Hills, Calif.: Sage Publications.

Douglas, J. (1987): "Political Theories of Non-Profit Organization," in *The Non-Profit Sector: A Research Handbook*, W. Powell (Ed.), New Haven and London: Yale University Press, 43–54, 87.

Drucker, P. (1973): "On Managing the Public Service Institution," *Public Interest* 33, 43–60.

Gilbert, N. (1983): *Capitalism and the Welfare State: Dilemmas of Social Benevolence*, New Haven, Conn.: Yale University Press.

Gilbert, N. and H. Specht (1986): *Dimensions of Social Welfare Policy*, 2nd ed., Englewood Cliffs, N. J.: Prentice-Hall.

Graycar, A. (1983): "The Interrelationships of Voluntary, Statutory and Informal Services," *British Journal of Social Work* 13, 4, 379–393.

Gronbjerg, K. (1982): "Private Welfare in the Welfare State: Recent U. S. Patterns," *Social Service Review* 56, 1, 1–26.

Hadley, R. and S. Hatch (1981): *Social Welfare and the State*, London: Allen and Unwin.

Hansmann, H. (1980): "The Role of Nonprofit Enterprise," *Yale Law Journal* 89, 835–901.

Hansmann, H. (1987): "Economic Theories of Non-Profit Organization," in *The Non-Profit Sector: A Research Handbook*, W. Powell (Ed.), New Haven and London: Yale University Press, 27–42.

Hasenfeld, Y. (1983): *Human Service Organizations*, Englewood Cliffs, N. J.: Prentice-Hall.

Independent Sector (1987): *National Taxonomy of Tax Exempt Entities*, Washington, D. C.: National Center for Charitable Statistics.

James, E. and S. Rose-Ackerman (1986): *The Non-Profit Enterprise in Market Economics*, New York: Harwood Academic Publishers.

James, E. (1989): "Introduction," *The Non-Profit Sector in International Perspective: Studies in Comparative Culture and Policy*, E. James (Ed.), London: Oxford University Press, 3–27.

Janowitz, M. (1976): *Social Control of the Welfare State*, New York: Elsevier.

Judge, K. and M. Knapp (1985): "Efficiency in the Production of Welfare: The Public and Private Sectors Compared," in *The Future of Welfare*, R. Klein and M. Higgins (Eds.), London: Basil Blackwell, 131–149.

Kahn, A. and S. Kamerman (1981): *Social Services in International Perspective*, New Brunswick: N. J. Transaction Books.

Kamerman, S. (1983): "The New Mixed Economy of Welfare: Public and Private," *Social Work* 28, 5–11.

Kimberly, J. (1975): "Environmental Constraints and Organizational Structure: A Comparative Analysis of Rehabilitation Organizations," *Administrative Science Quarterly* 20, 1, 1–9.

Kramer, R. (1981): *Voluntary Agencies in the Welfare State*, Berkeley, Calif.: University of California Press.

Kramer, R. (1985a): "Toward a Contingency Model of Board-Executive Relations," *Administration in Social Work* 9, 3, 15–33.

Kramer, R. (1985b): "The Welfare State and the Voluntary Sector: The Case of the Personal Social Services," in *The Welfare State and its Aftermath*, S. N. Eisenstadt and O. Ahimeir (Eds.), London: Croom Helm, 132–140.

Kramer, R. (1987): "Voluntary Agencies and the Personal Social Services," in *The Non-Profit Sector: A Research Handbook*. W. Powell (Ed.), New Haven and London: Yale University Press, 240–257.

Kramer, R. and B. Grossman (1987): "Contracting for Social Services: Process Management and Resource Dependencies," *Social Service Review* 61, 1, 32–55.

Kramer, R. and P. Terrell (1984): *Social Services Contracting in the Bay Area*, Berkeley, Calif.: University of California, Institute of Governmental Studies.

Langton, S. (1987): "Envoi: Developing Non-Profit Theory," *Journal of Voluntary Action Research* 16, 2, 134 – 148.

Middleton, M. (1987): "Non-Profit Boards of Directors: Beyond the Governance Function," in *The Non-Profit Sector: A Research Handbook*, W. Powell (Ed.), New Haven and London: Yale University Press, 141 – 153.

Milofsky, C. (1987): "Neighborhood-based Organizations: A Market Analogy," in *The Non-Profit Sector: A Research Handbook*, W. Powell (Ed.), New Haven and London: Yale University Press, 277 – 295.

Morris, R. (1982): "Government and Voluntary Agency Relationships," *Social Service Review* 56, 3, 333 – 345.

O'Brien, D. (1974): *Neighborhood Organization and Interest-Group Process*, Princeton, N. J.: Princeton University Press.

Pfeffer, J. and G. Salancik (1978): *The External Control of Organizations: A Resource Dependence Perspective*, New York: Harper and Row.

Pinker, R. (1985): "Social Policy and Social Care: Division of Responsibility," in *Support Networks in a Caring Community*, J. A. Yoder (Ed.), Dordrecht: Nijhoff, 103 – 110.

Provan, K. (1980): "Environmental Linkages and Power in Resource-Dependence Relations Between Organizations," *Administrative Science Quarterly* 25, 2, 200 – 225.

Rich, R. (1979): "Roles of Neighborhood Organization in Urban Service Delivery," *Urban Affairs Papers* 1, 81 – 93.

Salamon, L. (1981): "Rethinking Public Management: Third-Party Government and the Changing Forms of Public Action," *Public Policy* 29, 255 – 275.

Salamon, L. (1986): "Government and the Voluntary Sector in an Era of Retrenchment: The American Experience," *Journal of Public Policy* 6, 1, 1 – 20.

Salamon, L. (1987): "Of Market Failure, Voluntary Failure and Third-Party Government: Toward a Theory of Government-Non-Profit Relations in the Modern Welfare State," *Journal of Voluntary Action Research* 16, 1 and 2, 29 – 49.

Salamon, L. and A. Abramson (1982): *The Federal Budget and the Non-Profit Sector*, Washington, D. C.: The Urban Institute Press.

Schlesinger, M., R. Dorwart and R. Pulice (1986): "Competitive Bidding and States' Purchase of Services," *Journal of Policy Analysis and Management* 5, 2, 245 – 263.

Segal, S. (1979: "Community Care and Deinstitutionalization: A Review," *Social Work* 24, 521 – 527.

Smith, B. L. R. (1975): *The New Political Economy: The Public Use of the Private Sector*, New York: Wiley.

Steinberg, R. (1987): "Non-Profit Organization and the Market," in *The Non-Profit Sector: A Research Handbook*, W. Powell (Ed.), New Haven and London: Yale University Press, 118 – 138.

Weisbrod, B. (1977): *The Voluntary Non-Profit System*, Lexington, Mass.: D. C. Heath.

Part IV
The Third Sector: International Perspectives

4.1
Nonprofit Organizations in International Perspective

Rudolph Bauer

The survey in this part demonstrates the presence of nonprofit organizations in virtually all societies. It also shows the great variation in form, size, composition, and importance of the nonprofit sector in different countries, political systems, and cultures. In recent years, political and scholarly interest in the nonprofit sector has increased not only in countries with deeply rooted philanthropic traditions, like Switzerland, but also in countries, such as France, which, historically, have tended to discourage voluntary activities; not only in industrialized and technically advanced countries, like Japan and West Germany, but also in rapidly industralizing nations such as Spain. Furthermore, to some extent, the attention paid to the nonprofit sector seems independent of whether the economy is capitalist or socialist. For example, in previously socialist Hungary, Marschall argues in chapter 4.2, the financial restraints and public sector inefficiency led to the reemergence of voluntary nonprofit activities; particularly towards the reestablishment of private volunteer organizations and the "rehabilitation" of the third sector. In France, also, the government and the private nonprofit sector, which have had a long-standing conflictual relationship, now view their interests as complementary. As Archambault in chapter 4.3 emphasizes, the French "social economy" serves as an instrument for implementing the government's decentralization policy. Japan provides another example of public co-optation, where, as Thränhardt in chapter 4.7 reports, local authorities are required incorporate voluntary neighborhood associations into social service activities. In addition, in Switzerland, the encouragement of self-help schemes and the decentralization of service delivery units has both reduced costs and improved social service provision. As in Switzerland, current Spanish legislation seems to favor the nonprofit sector at the expense of the public sector, especially in the provision of private health insurance.

The advantages of small-scale nonprofits, as they themselves see them, in comparison the large-scale ones, center around the benefits of debureaucratization, decentralization, deprofessionalization, volunteerism, and privatization. Both the political left and the political right promote the advantages of small-scale nonprofits: the political left sees self-determination, basic democracy, mutual aid, and self-governance, which nonprofits exhibit, as fundamental ingredients of postindustrial society, while the political right sees nonprofits as instruments reducing state expansion through increasing client participation and responsibility in the welfare state.

1. Comparative Advantages of Nonprofit Organizations

We will discuss the comparative advantages of nonprofits following Archambault's study of the relationship between public authorities and "social economy" in France. Thus, we adopt, as she does, Musgrave's classification of functions — allocation, redistribution and regulation — in order to outline the comparative advantages of the nonprofit sector.

Nonprofits who use voluntary labor can allocate services with great flexibility. Volunteers who are often embedded in local social communities can cultivate close, personal relations with social service recipients. As a result, volunteers are not only less costly than professional workers, they also tend to be more effective.

Voluntary work, along with donations and gifts, is also part of the redistributive function of the nonprofit sector. Put simply, the nonprofits intervene in the precarious relations between "the have's" and the "have-not's"; they provide for a "soft" redistribution of resources from the former to the latter; thus they not only protect the rich from the poor's resentment, but can also convey the poor's gratitude; finally they can highlight "the have's" responsibility to be charitable to the "have-not's."

A further advantage of NPOs is that they smooth social frictions caused by conflicting or incompatible social policies that aim to the same group. For example, nonprofits fulfill their regulative functions through their participation in employment and policies. In France, for instance, employment in the nonprofit sector has increased, while it has fallen elsewhere.

In the Federal Republic of Germany, nonprofits have taken over many regularly functions from the state since the nineteenth century. They have acted as a form of social control over middle- and lower-class movements in order to neutralize the "dangers" of socialism and communism; they have exerted control over the working class, especially among youth and women; they have also organized programs to combat juvenile delinquency, alcoholism, prostitution, and homelessness.

Furthermore, the large-scale West German welfare associations who, in 1987, had 758,000 employees (in addition to an estimated 1.5 million volunteers), also help reduce the government's direct role in social policy. As a part of their allocation function, they provide services to new client groups like drug abusers, battered women, among others. A division of labor has evolved between the larger charity associations and small-scale nonprofits including self-help groups. While the large associations are mostly conservative, the smaller nonprofits are often the nuclei of social innovations and instruments of social changes. However, there is also a tendency for the large charity associations to incorporate small-scale initiatives and their potential for social change. In addition, state and local governments aim to integrate self-help groups. To this end, they introduced funds for self-help groups. This guarantees public regulation, on the one hand, and, on the other hand, allows for control over social service allocation and expansion.

2. Limits and constraints

The major limitations and constraints on nonprofits are financial. In most cases, public funds and philanthropic efforts fail to reach the grassroots, innovative nonprofit sector. Consequently, these nonprofits lack the necessary financial means to provide urgent services. In order to compensate for the lack of funds, they resort to using volunteers or contributions in kind, which often results in "self-exploitation" by volunteers and eventually "burnout." Try as they might, volunteers can not be more than a supplement to a system of compulsory redistribution such as the public Social Security system.

Burnout, however, is not the only risk when self-help groups and volunteers try to compensate for governmental cut-backs in the Social Security system. If risks and social problems, otherwise covered by Social Security, are transferred to nonprofits and private mutual-aid societies, the most likely result would be a strengthening of social inequalities; this would hurt the middle and lower classes most. Such seems to have been the case in the Spanish health system, where the rising costs of health care eroded the public compulsory insurance, enabling private insurance companies to expand at the expense of the coverage for low-income groups.

The consequence of inequality also effects the allocative function of nonprofit activities particularly on the ideological level. In Western countries, volunteers tend to be middle class and therefore share middle-class assumtion. There is the risk of paternalism. In addition, nonprofits tend to disregard labor laws and trade union agreements while, as in Spain, they also tend to lack professional management. Bureaucratization also poses obstacles for nonprofit activities. Archambault concludes that, in France, "Parkinson's law exists in the nonprofit sector." Powerful lobbies use their privileged status and take advantage of competition. Large-scale nonprofits have been able to obtain monopoly or quasi-monopolistic dominance in specific fields of social services provision. They then, like for-profit firms, sell their services, leaving unresolved the important issues of accountability.

Given the constraints on nonprofits, we cannot give wholehearted support to the nonprofit sector and the "myth of voluntarism." At best, we can conclude that nonprofits provide some social services in democratic societies that to some degree help to promote social equality: Their services are often sensitive to social needs, competent and effective, innovative and flexible, well funded and jointly controlled by the public and clients. At worst, we may decide that nonprofits meet common needs in a bureaucratic and routine way similar to public "monopolies"; that they are controlled neither by society nor their clients; that they lack funds and professional competence; and finally that they exhibit a paternalistic "middle-class" attitude towards their clients.

In other words, we have to pay more attention to the great variations in nonprofit characteristics like management, resources, competence, professional staff, effectiveness, accountability, and participation (see chapter 2.8 by Leat).

3. Concluding Remarks

The following studies demonstrate the variability, advantages, and constraints of mediating structures in different countries. Historically, the role of nonprofits has fluctuated; their importance has increased in times of economic and social crisis, and has decreased in times of economic expansion and growth of public budgets.

Other than this one similiarity of cyclical development, nonprofits in different countries manifest distinct histories and socio-political contexts (see Bauer 1987). First, they experience different regulation and distribution regimes — the conservative, the liberal, and the social democratic. The conservative type is rooted in a mixture of *étatist*, paternalistic reformism and the Catholic social doctrine of subsidiarity. By the order of subsidiarity, governments are responsible to fund welfare activities, but private voluntary associations enjoy the privilege to establish and carry out their own insitutions by government financing. Such is the case in West Germany, France, Italy, Belgium, Austria, and, to some extent, Japan und Turkey, where aspects of the conservative type were adopted in the early twentieth century. The nonprofits in these countries tend to be state-oriented associations which accentuate public utility.

The liberal tradition of "welfare capitalism" dates back to the Poor Law Act of 1601 in England, and exists today in countries such as the United

Kingdom, the United States, Canada, and Australia. In these cases, nonprofits are market-oriented and emphasize the principle of voluntarism. Finally, the "social democratic" tendency, which exists in the Scandinavian countries, emphasizes the state's social responsibility and therefore produces a relatively less developed and less important nonprofit sector.

Further sources of diversity in nonprofit sectors across different societies are found in different levels of economic development and the emergence of civil society. For example, Ireland combines the tradition of the Poor Law with Catholicism, where Catholic nonprofits dominate the welfare system. Turkey, a semi-industrialized country, has a nonprofit sector dominated by the state, yet influenced by Islamic tradition.

References

Bauer, R. (1987): "Intermediäre Hilfesysteme personenbezogener Dienstleistungen in zehn Ländern. Eine Einführung," in *Verbandliche Wohlfahrtspflege im internationalen Vergleich*. R. Bauer und A. M. Thränhardt (Eds.), Opladen: Westdeutscher Verlag, 9 – 30.

4.2
The Nonprofit Sector in a Centrally Planned Economy

Miklós Marschall

1. Introduction

Discussing the problems of the voluntary, nonprofit sector in a socialist country such as Hungary is both delicate and inspiring. It is delicate, because the mere existence of nonprofit organizations assumes their relative independence of the one-party state. It is inspiring, because their presence suggests that the omnipotence of the state is retreating, leaving space for voluntary initiatives. In the past few years, Hungary along with Poland, the Soviet Union, and East Germany have witnessed the emergence of voluntary activities independent of the state.

In this paper, I first discuss some problems of defining "nonprofit" in a one-sector economy. Moreover, the nonprofit sector in Hungary must be distinguished from the "third sector" in the United States; its services, activities, and relationship to public sector have a specific Eastern-European character. Finally, I discuss the recent "Renaissance" and future of the Hungarian nonprofit sector such as civic associations and foundations.

2. Nonprofit Sector in State-Socialism?

For three reasons, it is difficult to define the nonprofit sector in an Eastern-European "state-socialist" economy.

First, the model of the socialist economic systems was formed as a negation of market-oriented economies. Using the language of classical economics, we can say that in socialist economies production is for use rather than exchange. Hence, the whole of these economic systems may be considered as an altogether nonprofit economy, at least by virtue of the peripherial function of earning profits within these systems. State enterprises operating with public funds are the leading actors.

In socialist economies, companies must implement the tasks entrusted to them regardless of whether they earn profits or not: the state appropriates all profits and makes up all losses. Thus, there are many similarities in the behavior of formal "for-profit" socialist business enterprises and institutions providing public goods[1] such as hospitals, since all public enterprises, agencies, and institutions are heavily dependent on the state for funds and directives.[2]

Second, distinguishing the nonprofit sphere from business[3] is difficult for an economist in Eastern Europe, because neither a second nor a third sector

[1] The most common definition of public goods refers to those goods where the marginal cost of satisfying one more consumer is zero. These goods need to necessarily be publicly financed. However, especially in state-socialist countries, the term is often used simply to mark goods that are publicly financed, usually by the government.

[2] In Hungary, state-run firms have been given relative managerial freedom, at least when compared to those of other state-socialist countries. In theory, there are no centralized compulsory targets. Instead, decisions on input- and output-mix, financing, and pricing are made by the firm's management. However, central control still prevails but now is exerted increasingly through monetary and financial means. For instance, 80% of profits "earned" by companies go to the state budget. (In a non-market economy, "earning profit" does not necessarily mean the real net economic gain produced by the company because, in the absence of competition, profits at company level are often random products of state regulations.) In addition, government taxes, which change annually, preclude the possibility of precalculation by companies. Consequently, the managerial autonomy of state-run for-profit enterprises is restricted. On the other hand, about 30% of the state's annual budget is spent on subsidizing enterprises with deficit. Not surprisingly, then, Hungarian business do not pursue profits with much intensity, and several supposedly for-profit firms operate like public nonprofit institutions. In addition, some other firms exist which might be called limited-profit enterprises (cf. Hansmann 1987). For-profit and limited-profit enterprises pay profit tax (50% in 1988), social security contributions (40% payroll tax), "accumulation tax" (tax imposed on capital expenditure), and sales tax on their products, public institutions such as schools, libraries and museums pay less social security (10%) and are exempt from any other taxes, including sales taxes, on their service.

[3] Nonprofit entities are generally defined as "organizations that are legally prohibited from earning and distributing a monetary residual" (James 1987: 398). This definition, however, seems to be too broad. I will narrow the definition by including only those organizations which combine three important attributes: "1. they are legally and structurally nonprofit, as described above; 2. they provide socially useful services; and 3. they are philanthropics, deriving a large part of their revenues from (tax-deductible) contributions" (James 1987: 398). I prefer the term "third sector," which is more general and includes political, sociological, and philosophical aspects, while "nonprofit sector" refers to economic characteristics only. The term "third sector" covers, in my view, an autonomous sphere of activity which is protected from the omnipotence of both the state and the market. Hence, I consider the third sector to be part of the "civil society." Especially, the third sector might be

have developed there. Eastern-European societies are, in this respect, one-sector societes: the autonomous business or "second sector," which was always weak in Hungary, was destroyed after the communist takeover; and a third sector, or "civil society," has never emerged to counter the central government.

Third, Hungary's economic and political situation differs radically from that of the West, thus making Western-based terminology inappropriate. Until quite recently, except for churches, no Western-Type voluntary, i. e. non-governmental nonprofit, organizations were allowed to exist in Hungary. In Hungary, as in the other socialist countries, the organs of health care, education, culture, and social security are public institutions that operate with public fund subsidies, and whose leaders are appointed by the state authorities. In addition, both long-term goals and the details of everyday activities are governed by state regulations. The state took over practically all the functions of the third sector and, until quite recently, it deployed all the available legal and political means to assure exclusive monopolistic rights of its institutions. Consequently, apart from professional organizations, voluntary activity has been within the confines of public institutions.

3. State-Socialism Is not Welfare Socialism

Political and financial centralization has not resulted in more generous financing of the public sector. On the contrary, it has become evident that many central decisions are determined by short-term economic constraints. In the absence of voting pressure, the importance of maintaining infrastructure and providing public goods in the central bargaining process has declined over time. Moreover, industrial pressure groups, especially those of heavy industry, promote their interests behind the scenes of the state and party's public mission. Consequently, infrastructure and public services receive relatively less government financing and support.[4]

In analyzing the reasons for Hungary's counter-productive social policy, we must take into account the main characteristics of Eastern-European planned economies.

considered, using Kornai's (1983) term, the sphere of "ethical coordination," which is the sector's major organizing principle.

[4] According to the statistics, in the last 40 years, infrastructure (productive as well as human) has had an average share of less than 50% in the country's total investment, which is considerably less than those figures of industrialized western countries (*Magyar Statisztikai Evkonyv* 1987). Unless otherwise stated, all statistics are taken from The Hungarian Statistical Yearbooks (*Magyar Statisztikai Evkonyv*).

First, state ownership dominates the economy. This applies to both sharing profit and disposing capital.

Second, as a result of state ownership, most capital and investment decisions are controlled by the hierarchical system of centralized management of the state.

Third, there is an owerwhelming system of public transfers, where more than half of the GDP goes through the central budget.

Fourth, there are hidden means of redistributing income other than through taxation and budget policy, for instance, through state pricing. In planned economies, there are no real market prices. The "distribution" of prices, like that of investments, is mainly the outcome of "bargaining" between enterprises and state authorities. Therefore, enterprises need not be responsive to costs and prices or, to use Kornai's terminology, their budgetary limits are soft (Kornai 1980). Not only can they bargain for higher prices when they need them, they can also overspend at will, because the government usually subsidizes losses.

Fifth, the relative autonomy of firms in market economies is replaced by the concerted efforts of enterprise, ministries, planning offices, and government and party organs. The traditional functions of an enterprise are distributed across a hierarchical system of decision making.

Sixth, in the absence of market regulation and market prices, supply and demand cannot meet which, in turn, results in an economy frequently characterized by shortages.

Seventh, integration and information is taken over by planning. Yet planning, as practised in Hungary, is a slow and bureaucratic method for registering consumer and social needs. It has become a defensive rather than offensive instrument for elementary coordination of the economy, whose bargaining process regulates the economy the same way, *"ex post,"* as the market does. Though it was originally intended to be, planning is no longer a manifestation of social consciousness on a level higher than the market.

Eighth, the elimination has caused the substitution of impersonal market relations by personal relations. The planned economy often operates like a game with constantly changing rules, thereby increasing the significance of informal, personal relations between the enterprise managers (being the players) and government officials (making the rules). The planning process consists of a series of bargaining rounds intertwined with personal contacts and agreements, which are neither subject to permanent rules nor to public control.

Overall, the public sector has a weak position in that game and must constantly fight for financial resources and influence on the "hidden battlefields" of the centrally planned economy.

In state-socialist countries, the public sector, which includes health care, educational, cultural, and welfare institutions, as well as the whole public sector infrastructure, is called the "non-productive sphere" as distinct from the productive sectors like industry and agriculture. This term obviously shows the ideological devaluation of public services.

In the actual practice of planned economy, the public sector suffers from a double disadvantage: a long-term, strategic disadvantage at the macro-economic level, and a short-term, "technical" disadvantage at the enterprise level.

3.1 The Long-Term Disadvantages of the Public Sector

The circumstances in which socialist planned economies were born (e. g. the necessity of economic development, the impact of the war, Stalinism) led to an emphasis on industrial development and a lack of interest in public services. The Stalinist economic "philosophy" looked upon economy as a "machine" having more important and less important parts. In this approach, heavy industry and energy production took priority, while consumption, services, commerce, and the non-productive infrastructure became less important. Forced economic growth, radical structural change, and high rates of accumulation were aggressively promoted, while the consumption was curbed and the infrastructure neglected.

As a result, while in 1950, 82% of total capital resource were registered in infrastructure and only 18% in industrial sectors and agriculture, in 1980, the situation had radically changed with the infrastructure having 56% and the industrial and agricultural sectors 44% of total capital resources. The centrally planned economy experiences permanent shortages of investment resources. A peculiar mechanism for the allocation of capital expenditures has evolved, as described by Kornai (1980), which may be termed the mechanism of "delay — emergence — delay." Under these conditions, firms must attain a limit of tolerance, or in other terms, they must wait until they have arrived at a crisis before the state apportions some of the limited available resources. "Many are the demands and few are the investment resources. (...) And if in this situation an applicant says that his unit is in trouble, then the few free resources will have to go there. It is like firefighting: the beginning of an investment is to be concentrated where the differential costs, owing to delaying, hit the limit of tolerance" (Kornai 1980: 244). Where no crisis exists, decisions may be postponed, and investment may be further delayed. Yet delay has its limits: sooner or later, it leads to an emergency situation where the lack of investment would destroy the company or industry in question. Only when grave emergence arises will the government disburse the investment money. Thus, production in state-planned economies staggers from crisis to crisis (Kornai 1980).

Sectors with relatively low limits of tolerance, where the delay of investment becomes unbearable sooner than in other areas, have an advantage in this "competition." The lower the limit of tolerance, the greater the competitiveness for investments; the higher the limit, the lower the competitiveness becomes. Thus, the public sector will lag behind, because its limits of tolerance are higher than that of the other sectors. This is so for three reasons.

First, input – output relations are more complex here than in the industrial sector and demand long-term solutions and strategies. Furthermore, problems tend to develop more slowly and appear less evident. Finally, restrictions deriving from low investments are usually felt outside the public sector and occur with considerable delay.

Second, deterioration of quality in supplies remains hidden longer than in other sectors, because state-financed public services offer many opportunities to delay capital expenditure. In addition, declining performance can be concealed, because no independent quality control and guarantees exists. For instance, the output of education can simply be "enhanced" by increasing class size, and the performance of public health institutions may be augmented by increasing the number of beds. These strategies not only save capital expenditures (e. g. building new schools or hospitals), they also improve the sector's statistical records which is the main concern of the government officials. This characteristic of public service, the ability to increase output with unchanged input, puts them constantly at the bottom of the list of governmental investment priorities.[5]

Third, in general, outputs of public services are quantitatively less measurable than those of the industrial sectors. That produces a lack of reliable data, a "loss of cue" in the planning process which, in turn, tends to reduce the priorities assigned to the sector by bureaucrats in the planning office.

Since a centrally planned economy was introduced in Hungary in 1946 – 48, the inter-sectoral breakdown of capital expenditures has been determined by two principles (Kornai 1980): adaptation to economic cycles, and "regulation according to norms." These principles result in a fluctuating pattern of government investment, whereby a sector, which receives a low level of investment previously, will obtain more next time around, and vice versa. These small "pluses" and "minuses" are balanced out; thus, in the long run, a particular sector's share in total investment is stable.

The first of the two principles mentioned above applies to those sectors which receive a large share of total investment, because the top decision makers give them top priority. These sectors get everything the government can afford to give them. Consequently, the only restriction on what they receive is due to the overall performance of the economy. Consequently, the dynamics of their capital spending more or less follow the general cycles

---

[5] All these remind me of notions like market-failure, asymmetrical information, lack of consumer control and such which are widely discussed in western literature (cf. Hansmann 1987).

of the economy, which means, again, that the traditional preferences are reproduced in the investment cycles as well: if more resources are available than before, they will be allocated first to sectors such as heavy industry.

The public sector, whose capital spending is regulated by the second principle, is far less likely to enjoy the benefits of increased overall investments. The public sector's position is like that of the army's field-kitchen: left behind when marching forward and sent back first when withdrawing.[6] Decisions on the allocation of capital to the public sector have been made without any kind of economic consideration; the only "guidance" for the decisions has been the accepted practice of the past, or "the norm," to use Kornai's term. We may infer from this practice that the top decision makers, who are most often representatives of the industrial interests groups unexposed to public voting pressure, have little concern about public services.

3.2 The Short-Term Setbacks of the Public Sector

In planned economies, public institutions, financed partly or entirely from central funds, face vertical (i. e. in their relations to governing bodies) and horizontal (i. e. in their relations to business) disadvantages.

Vertical disadvantages: The rigid accountability requirements of public institutions, on the one hand, and the increased business autonomy which occurred after the 1968 reform, on the other, produced a regulation gap. Thus, while the "maneuvering capacity" of business companies has grown with respect to the authorities, an important factor during plan-bargaining, public institutions' dependence on authorities has not changed much.

The influence of organizations operating in a heavily hierarchized economy depends on their size (numbers of staff, levels of production). Because of their smaller size relative to business enterprises, public institutions are less competitive and have a weaker bargaining position vis-à-vis the state. Furthermore, government's wishes for certain kinds of restrictions can be more easily imposed on public institutions who lack the business enterprises' "means" for softening government requirements. Moreover, as they are less able to manipulate with their financial records, the authorities are aware of all the public institutions' resources. Consequently, they are much more vulnerable than business enterprises to government capriciousness. The relative autonomy of enterprises has produced certain automatic mechanisms, permitting them to constantly adjust to changing economic conditions. Public institutions, in contrast, need individual decisions made by the government auditing departments. These decisions coming from "above" always need

---

[6] I borrowed this phrase from a Hungarian politician, Imre Pozsgay, who argued — by saying this — for more government investment in public education.

negotiations and take time, and, as a result, public institutions' adjustments are usually delayed.

Horizontal disadvantages: The sellers' market of a shortage economy creates special "techniques" of protection, a kind of "vulpine law" in the behavior of the enterprises. Since they are not equal partners in doing business with such mammoth firms as exist, for instance, in the building industry, public institutions are forced to find a niche in order to survive in a disadvantageous environment.

Mutual favors between enterprises play an important role in a shortage economy, because constant overdemand often makes it difficult to reinforce contractual relations between enterprises. Thus, reciprocity is of great importance in day-to-day business. Companies that need not rely on contracts alone are in a better position to buy or sell favors, as they posses attractive products or important services. Public institutions, in contrast, are rarely in that position and therefore cannot engage in the informal reciprocal arrangements which smooth business interaction in a centrally planned economy. Moreover, a common strategy in a seller's market is stockpiling. Owing to shortages, and low levels of cooperation, all enterprises accumulate larger amounts of materials, products, and even labor than they would need in normal business. Public institutions, however, with their strict accounting systems, do not have access to the discretionary funds that are needed for large inventories.

Nevertheless, the fundamental reason why the public sector has been neglected by state-socialist economies lies in the unclarified and contradictory function of the state itself. The omnipotent state is directly responsible for the daily operation of the business sector causing them to be mired in the day-to-day details of a highly inefficient enterprise sector. As a result, in the 1980s, 16−18% of GDP and about 30% of total budgetary expenses in Hungary were spent on subsidizing money-losing state-owned enterprises. At the same time, however, the state is still expected to fulfill its "socialist welfare mission." In reality, the probability of meeting this dual challenge is small. Short-term economic pressures are always stronger than long-term welfare promises, thus welfare redistribution becomes subordinated to the more urgent economic redistribution. The two functions of the state have turned out to be incompatible.

3.3 The Quasi-Voluntary Sector: The Shadow Economy

In state-socialist societies, paradoxically, some of the third sector's role in welfare capitalism is taken over by the second or shadow economy.[7]

---

[7] I use a broad definition of second or shadow economy which contains everything outside the dominant "socialized" economy. In this interpretation, shadow economy

Table 1: Economy, Welfare Redistribution, and Social Inequalities in Capitalism and
State-Socialism

	Welfare Capitalism	State-Socialism
The dominant mechanism causing primary inequalities	Market	Economic redistribution; pseudo-welfare state
Secondary mechanisms correcting primary inequalities, but inducing secondary inequalities	Welfare redistribution by government	Market (shadow economy)
"Third mechanisms" reducing inequalities and preventing the accumulation of primary and secondary inequalities	Private philanthropy, self-assistance, the voluntary nonprofit or third sector	???

Source: Manchin and Szelenyi (1986).

According to Manchin and Szelenyi's (1986) model, primary social inequalities in capitalism, which derive from market mechanisms, are reduced by welfare redistribution, while in state-socialism, the same mechanism works the other way around: Inequalities induced by the state redistribution (which includes welfare redistribution as well) are counterbalanced by a special market known as the second economy.

One of the striking characteristics of state-socialist countries is that, in terms of wages, they have relatively egalitarian economies. Thus, social inequalities are chiefly an outcome of unequal access to public goods provided by the state. Empirical research in Hungary has revealed that privileged social groups, such as the party and managerial elites, have much better access to subsidized state-housing, higher education, and health service than the public at large (Manchin and Szelenyi 1986).

For the less privileged, the only means of compensating for their disadvantaged position is offered by the second economy. Getting rid of the crippling restraints of the state-run economy, people are ready to work hard to get back a portion of benefits they have been denied by the socialist "compassionate" state. Besides its obvious economic efficiency, the second economy has something in common with the western nonprofit voluntary sector: Because

includes traditional small businesses (private retail stores), household farming, and even the overtime-working teams formed within state-run plants and, of course, the illegal or black economy as well. Shadow economy overall, according to some estimates, produces about 15–20% of GDP in Hungary.

it encourages and benefits private entrepreneurship, the second economy represents a sort of limited − or even distorted − civil autonomy. It was the shadow economy which revitalized such values as individualism, autonomy, self-consciousness, and civic engagement, in contrast to the obedience required by the state-socialist society.

Nevertheless, these "second mechanisms" themselves − welfare bureaucracy in capitalism, and a quasi-market of the shadow economy in state-socialism in turn − create new inequalities. Thus a third layer of mechanisms is needed to reduce both primary and secondary inequalities. The model indicates that these third mechanisms are different from both the primary and secondary ones. While in capitalism, the voluntary nonprofit sector contains a large variety of third level mechanisms, in state-socialism, they have yet to be established − although some might already be present in distorted form in the shadow economy.

4. The Revival of Hungary's Private Voluntary Sector

In the 1980s, it has become evident that the state is neither able nor willing to pay the bill for its own omnipotence. As Table 2 shows, public institutions, which represent 19% of the GDP, and operate in fields like health care, education, arts, and research, have increasingly had to rely on earned income.

Table 2: Dynamics of the Main Financial Indices of Public Institutions (in %)

Year	Earned income	Government Support	Total
1978	100.0	100.0	100.0
1983	402.3	115.5	148.1

Source: Radnai (1985).

Facing less resistance in the public sector here than in the industrial sectors and also the pressures of the economic crisis, the government would now like to get rid of its responsibility. Its newly established "stand-on-your-own-feet" attitude towards public institutions has pushed the public sector in general, and health and educational institutions in particular, into severe trouble. Since 1983, the situation has worsened: State subsidies have dropped in real terms, and, in some cases, the daily operation of public institutions has become endangered.

Further exacerbating the situation is the increased demand for more freedom and pluralism as a result; it appears now that the rehabilitation of the once oppressed third sector is beginning in Hungary. Civil organizations — unthinkable 5–10 years ago — have been mushrooming in this state-socialist country. Recently, hundreds of private voluntary associations have been founded. By 1988, their actual number might have exceeded 6,000 (Harangi 1986; however, this is still less than half the number of civil associations registered in 1932, when the right-wing regime allowed limited pluralism). Most of these new associations, which range from historical societies to smallholders clubs are local ones, representing a rebirth of local civic responsibility. In general, they support themselves through membership and service fees.

To found an association is a constitutional right in Hungary. Ten members, a statutory meeting, and a written statute is all that is required for registration. However, the procedures to get an association started have serious shortcomings: When people intend to start organizing a private society or association, they must report this to the proper state authority, before they start the legal procedure. If the authorities refuse "permission," there is no way to appeal. Many consider this permission to exercise a constitutional right to be entirely unconstitutional.[8] Furthermore, rather than independent courts, government authorities register and supervise the associations in question, which, again, allows far-reaching government control and influence.

In the late 1980s, many private foundations were formed in Hungary. In 1988, estimates count over 600 private foundations with a total asset of 500–600 million Forint ($ 10 million).[9] Donations are given — as everywhere in the world — by individuals and corporations. In 1988, new legislation freed a number of the foundations' financial arrangements. Having regained their legal personalities, foundations are no longer required to keep their capital in closed accounts. Now they are allowed to invest their capital in shares, bonds, and real estate. Moreover, foundations receive preferential tax-treatment: Individuals can deduct donations from taxable income, while corporations enjoy a deduction from pre-tax profits.[10]

---

[8] If it is a nation-wide organization, previous permission is issued by the central government (usually by the ministry responsible for the field in question); if it is a local one, the permission is issued by the local municipality. By the end of 1988, a new law on associations is likely to come into effect that will abandon this sharply criticized practice of prior permissions.

[9] The 1988 estimate was published by the Ministry of Finance.

[10] The first insightful report ever published about Hungary's growing nonprofit sector in a Western magazine was written by Roger Williams and can be read in the U.S. Magazine of Philanthropy, the "Foundation News" with the title "Opening the Curtain" (Volume 28, No. 6).

5. Conclusion

Despite their promising nature, there is, of course, a deep uncertainty about the pace and durability of the changes I briefly described above. One thing, however, seems to be clear. Facing deep and painful social and economic changes which we might call *late modernization*, Hungary needs some corrective and compensating "third mechanisms" operating in the society. A question of vital importance which relates to "Ottomanization" or modernization — as T. G. Ash put it[11] — is whether these third mechanisms will remain distorted and pressed back into the half-legal shadow economy, or whether they will become a part of a broad modernization. Either way, they will be anticipated as a crucial component of civil liberties and freedom in modern society. There is a widely accepted myth that the state-socialist economies are now doing poorly because they have spent more on social welfare than they could really afford. This is simply not true. While state socialism has produced a basic comprehensive social security system, the most striking impression one might get in these countries is the poor quality of infrastructural services such as housing, schools, hospitals, roads, and telephone lines. In contrast with the highly acclaimed social welfare provisions, Hungary has, for instance, one of the highest rates of suicide and alcoholism, one of the lowest birthrates in Europe, and a declining life expectancy for males (*Magyar Statisztikai Evkonyv* 1987).[12]

Public money was consumed by ill-planned and mismanaged industrial giants, not by public hospitals and schools. There is little room in the welfare sector for government to pull out in order to let private nonprofits move in. Abolishing the state monopoly in the provision of public goods does not mean that the state should or could remove itself from the welfare sector. A rather realistic scenario would be to have social policy include more government funding in order to compensate for declining welfare investments and, at the same time, more freedom for private nonprofit organizations. An overall restructuring of the economy is also needed, because in the present price- and wage-system in Hungary, the nonprofit organizations can hardly be expected to rely on considerable private contributions; neither in money

---

[11] Ash (1988) refers to the long and slow decay of the Ottoman (Turkish) empire between the seventeenth and nineteenth century, which might represent an analogy to the possible decline of East-European state-socialist systems, unless they are able to reform their economies.

[12] Of course, low birthrate and declining life-expectancy have nothing directly to do with the neglected human infrastructure. But an indirect relationship may exist between them.

nor in time. (The private entrepreneurs in small business who are wealthy enough to make donations might represent the only exception.)[13]

Finally, it must be emphasized that the role played by the private nonprofit sector in providing public goods is still limited in Hungary; the emerging "third sector" represents a breakthrough in political rather than in welfare or economic terms. However, in an optimistic scenario, the third sector might become similar to the "Trojan horse" which creates pluralism in a politically non-pluralistic society.

Postscript*

This is one of the rare occasions where, prior to publication, a paper which focusses on long-term political and economic developments is suddenly taken over by current events. This is what happened to the present paper "The Nonprofit Sector in a Centrally Planned Economy", when the revolutionary developments in Eastern Europe radically altered the social, political and economic conditions for the third sector. When writing the paper between 1987 and 1988, the ideological erosion of the Communist Party's monopoly had already begun; however, its institutional monopoly, most visible in the form of the one party state, was still intact.

In Hungary, the transition from a one-party state to political pluralism was peaceful and remarkably smooth. One reason for the relatively calm transition has been the re-emergence of civil society, which preceded the rapid restructuring of the political landscape in 1989. Outside the direct influence of the Communist Party, numerous "non-political" civic association and clubs ("forums") had already been created. For Hungary's one-party system, they turned out to be a "political Trojan horse": when the Party retreated from its position of political monopoly, the newly founded third sector organizations were able to gain political ground rapidly. For example, the two leading opposition parties, the Hungarian Democratic Forum and the Alliance of Free Democrats, were originally founded as civic associations and debating societies. Similar examples may be found in other eastern European countries.

---

* February, 1990.

13 After some ideological obstacles were put aside recently, the size and scope of private business is expected to grow rapidly. Among others, the employment limitation for private enterprises has increased to 500, which allows middle-size private companies with considerable potential to operate. This emerging private sector may represent a growing source of private philanthropy.

The rapidly expanding third sector in Hungary consists largely of foundations, civic associations and mutual benefit societies. The are indications that this segment of the third sector has grown more rapidly than social service, welfare-oriented organizations. This reflects the need of civil society for self-governance, which at present seems to surpass social welfare needs. However, the re-emergence of religious welfare organizations is equally remarkable. During the refugee crises in the fall of 1989, they helped serve the needs of thousands of East German and Romanian refugees entering Hungary.

At present, the foundations in Hungary might be classified as follows:

- grantmaking foundations established and funded almost exclusively by the government;
- corporate grantmaking foundations created and operated by new banks, insurance companies and, to a lesser extent, by manufacturing firms. (However, the donor companies are still largely state-owned, which raises the question whether these foundations are private or public.)
- private grantmaking foundations established by individual donors, many of whom live outside Hungary.
- operating foundations which deliver direct services in the fields of education and social welfare.

New legislation facilitated the rapid expansion of the third sector. Laws on the right of assembly as well as laws on associations and foundations were introduced in 1988 and 1989. Registration procedures were greatly simplified and new tax regulations favor third sector activities.

It is certainly beyond the scope of this postscript to offer a full discussion of the new tax rules and a brief summary will have to suffice. Mutual benefit organizations and foundations are exempt from income tax. Moreover, they are allowed to operate for-profit businesses, provided the proceeds benefit the charitable purposes laid down in the statutes of the organization. Individuals and corporations can deduct their donations to foundations from taxable income in contrast to other countries, no ceiling for deductions is specified in the tax law. With some modifications, the same regulations apply to mutual benefit organizations.

At present, it is difficult to present a reliable picture of the third sector in Hungary. No reliable data are available on the sector's size and scope. Nor are there reliable estimates of private and corporate giving. This, however, is hardly surprising considering how fast civil society and the third sector have changed and expanded in less than two years.

Finally, it should be emphasized that political pluralism has not been accompanied by a full shift away from central planning and state control of the economy. Despite highly publicized reprivatization, state ownership is still the dominant form in the production and service sectors of the economy. Thus, as decribed in the paper, the weakness of the public sector remains.

References

Ash. T. G. (1988): "The Empire in Decay," *The New York Review of Books* 35, 14, 53 – 60.

Hansmann, Henry (1987): "Economic Theories of Nonprofit Organization," in *The Nonprofit Sector. A Research Handbook,* Walter Powell (Ed.), New Haven: University Press, 27 – 42.

Harangi, Laszlo (1986): "The Role of Voluntary Organizations in Hungary," Working paper. *Research Institute for Culture,* Budapest.

James, Estelle (1987): "The Nonprofit Sector in Comparative Perspective," in *The Nonprofit Sector. A Research Handbook,* Walter Powell (Ed.), New Haven: Yale University Press, 397 – 415.

Kornai, Janos (1980): *A hiany,* Budapest: KJK. (In English: *Economics of Shortage,* Amsterdam, New York: North-Holland.)

Kornai, Janos (1983): "Bureaucratic vs Market Coordination," in *Kozgazdasagi Szemle* 9, 1025 – 1037.

Magyar Statisztikai Evkonyv (1987), KSH: Budapest.

Manchin, R. and I. Szelenyi (1987): "Social Policy Under State Socialism: Market Redistribution and Social Inequalities in East-European Socialist Societies," in *Stagnation and Renewal in Social Policy: The Rise and Fall of Policy Regimes,* G. Esping-Andersen, et al. (Eds.), Armonk, N.Y.: M. E. Sharpe (Comparative Public Policy Analysis Series), 102 – 139.

Nove, Alec (1980): *The Soviet Economic System,* Second Edition, New York: Allen and Unwin.

Radnai, György (1985): "The Stepchildren of the Budget?" *Tervgazdasagi Forum* 2, Budapest, 35 – 45.

Szelenyi, Ivan (1983): *Urban Inequalities Under State Socialism,* Oxford, New York: Oxford University Press.

Weisbrod, Burton (1986): "Toward a Theory of the Voluntary Nonprofit Sector in a Three-Sector Economy," in *The Economics of Nonprofit Institutions: Studies in Structure and Policy,* Susan Rose-Ackerman (Ed.), Oxford: Oxford University Press, 21 – 44.

4.3
Public Authorities and the Nonprofit Sector in France

Edith Archambault

1. Introduction

In France, the term *social economy* has been used since 1982 to describe the nonprofit sector. It basically includes cooperatives, mutual benefit societies, and voluntary associations. Mutual benefit societies are nonprofit insurance companies. Voluntary associations refer to a diverse group of organizations such as charities, trade unions, cultural organizations, social movements, private schools, welfare organizations, and nonprofit hospitals.

For historical reasons, the relationship between authorities and social economy, has been ambivalent. During the French Revolution, the *Le Chapelier Act* (1791) suppressed guilds and any other kind of association: "no one is allowed to incite citizens to have an intermediate interest, to separate them from the Nation by spirit of cooperation." Successive centralized Jacobine governments, whether Republican or Bonapartist, were suspicious of both corporatism and the labor movement. They saw a revival of the Old Regime in corporatist tendencies, and feared the prospects of anarchism and workers' control in the labor movement, which reached its peak with the Paris Commune of 1871.

This long-term and deep-seated conflict between the state and the trend towards association has been resolved only gradually: the crime of coalition was abolished in 1864, trade unions were legalized in 1884, mutual benefit societies in 1898 and, finally, voluntary associations in 1901. Still, mutual mistrust remains and the limited legal capacity granted to voluntary associations in 1901 continues to be a root cause of their financial difficulties.

Peaceful coexistence between public authorities and the social economy was characteristic for most parts of the twentieth century. Many aspects of the social economy are complementary to those of the public authorities — a complementarity which was revealed during the crisis of the welfare state in France. When economic growth slowed down and unemployment began to rise, many public health and public welfare organizations experienced financial difficulties. As a result, they sought the cooperation of social economy organizations. At the political level, the revival of economic *laissez-*

faire ideologies in the United States and the United Kingdom increased, *inter alia*, the public awareness of the social economy in France. We are reminded of the eighteenth century writer Hawke, who wrote in 1775 that in America "voluntary associations have become the usual way of dealing with any civic problem which the government refuses to tackle" (quoted in Collard 1978). This theme was also taken up by the French philosopher Tocqueville who considered the ability of American citizens to take initiatives by establishing voluntary associations as one of the sources of democracy in America.

In France, however, governmental recognition of such initiatives came much later, around the 1960s. The relation between the centralized state and the social economy remained "top down" and imbalanced, until the *Decentralization Act* of 1983 reduced the direct influence of the state and introduced a more egalitarian dialogue between social economy and public authorities.

In this paper, I present an economic analysis of the relationship between the public authorities and the social economy. I employ Musgrave's functional approach to public economics (1959) which distinguishes three economic functions of modern public administration: the allocation of public goods and services, the redistribution of income, and the regulation of economic growth. The social economy contributes to all three functions, albeit to a lesser extent than the public sector. Finally, using examples, I illustrate the complementarity between the functional activities of the public sector and the social economy.

2. The Allocation Function

The allocation of resources to produce public goods and services is rarely the monopoly of public authorities, except in such areas as defense or the judiciary. In the other spheres, such as education, health, culture, or social work, production is generally shared between the state and the private sector. In the latter, the production of public goods is generally associated with private nonprofit organizations rather than for-profit businesses. Within the social economy, "management associations" and mutual benefit societies deliver services which complement those supplied by public administrations.

"Management associations" are relatively large associations, which offer market and non-market services, hire both wage earners and volunteers. Since they provide public goods and services, they receive partial financing by public authorities. Management associations are different from clubs, which produce services only for their members and function only with voluntary work. Mutual benefit societies provide insurance complementary to that supplied by the official social security scheme, as well as running health and welfare centers.

2.1 Collective Utility and Public Financing

In France, four areas constitute the arena of the social economy: health and social welfare, education and sport, professional training, recreation and tourism. Typically, goods and services produced in these fields are quasi-public goods: While they can be shared among individual users, as divisible goods, they also have an external effect on non-users. For example, treating patients prevents the risk of contagion, education of the population improves productivity, slum clearance helps decrease delinquency. Thus, the government maintains strong interest in monitoring the quantity and quality of quasi-public goods produced by organizations in the social economy (Benard 1986).

Direct government production is an alternative to the social economy. However, contractual agreements between government and nonprofits constitute a more efficient arrangement. A government statement, issued in January 1975, declared that "the state and the public local communities do not hold the monopoly of public welfare. In many instances, private initiative was first able to meet these needs. Besides, the state and local communities, together with the public institutions which come under their authorities, have been led to entrust associations governed by the 1901 act with tasks of general interest."

The degree of collective utility in a social economy institution is evaluated in a contractual agreement which determines both the extent of public financing and the degree of public control. There are three basic types and titles granted to social economy institutions: *"Public service mission"* can justify total public financing as in the case of some health and welfare organizations which act on behalf of the public authority; *"Socially useful mission of general interest,"* where public authorities supply a part of the funds and exercise less control, which is common in the spheres of sports, youth and the arts; and, finally, *"Socially useful mission geographically or thematically restricted,"* where the organizations experience the least public support and control.

The negotiation of contractual agreements between public authorities and nonprofit organizations are, if successful, necessarily accompanied by public financing with *a priori* and *a posteriori* public controls, together with various regulations concerning accountability and management. This procedure is usually applied to institutions or services which are subsidized on a permanent basis by the Social Security. It is automatic when public financing is higher than that 30% of the resources of the institutions.

2.2 Examples of Services Provided by the Social Economy

According to Jeantet (1984), in 1982 French mutual benefit societies operated 71 pharmacies, 186 optical centers, 191 dental surgeries, 174 nursing homes, day care and convalescent centers in the area of health. In the field of welfare, they ran 146 recreation centers, and 181 institutions for the elderly and the handicapped. Associations are more important in both fields: In the health field, they account for 16% of total financing. In 1982, they provided 82,000 jobs with a turnover of FF 16 billion. In the welfare area, they run 51% of all institutions, and accounted for 55% of their financing. Altogether associations provide 230,000 jobs in the social welfare area, with a budget of FF 30 billion (I. G. A. S. 1984).Three quarters of all health and welfare activities provided by the social economy are financed by mainly social security or other public funds. Preponderance of public financing emphasizes their classification as "public service mission" and their close control by the General Inspection of Social Services.

What are the consequences of public control? Are social economy organizations correctly managed? A recent governmental report (I. G. A. S. 1984) focussed on the quasi-monopoly of association mainly in the welfare field, which, according to the report, leads to inefficiencies and social inequities. For example, the associations run 80% of the places for disabled children and offer 90% of all services in this area. Often they systematically prefer recruitment to boarding schools, although alternative methods of care are available. Their logic is one of "filling places." Thus, the dominant method preferred by the associations has financial and psychological costs. Conversely, when there is competition between social economy and public organizations, social policy is more innovative and management improved, as in the case of drug prevention.

In the field of recreation, sport associations run 37,000 clubs which together provide jobs for more than 100,000 employees. The area of vocational training is served by 2,000 associations, representing 50% of the total turnover in this area. Finally, 12% of tourism activities are provided by associations, representing a turnover of FF 5 billion and providing 70,000 jobs (Jeantet 1984).

3. The Redistribution Function

Redistribution of income is a fundamental aspect of both, the social and public economies. Private redistribution predates public redistribution, as mutual benefit societies existed nearly a century before the creation of social security in France (1945). The introduction of public social security did not necessarily entail a decline of mutual benefit societies: they serve 25 million people today compared to 6 million in 1949 and 2,5 million in 1900 (Wagner 1984).

In France, the whole population is covered by social security, and half of the population by mutual benefit societies. Despite their growth in absolute numbers, the mutual benefit societies now represent but a small part of the vast social protection system: they finance only about 1% of total social protection system, whereas public social security finances 75%, employers 11%, grants in aid from the central administrations 8%, and local communities 5% (Wagner 1984).

What are the links between mutual benefit societies and public social security? Today, mutual benefit societies complement public social security in three ways: first, patient deductibles of compulsory protection are covered by mutual benefit societies; second, the mutual benefit system provides higher sickness, accident, or death benefits; thus they compete with insurance companies; finally, the extension of social security to the whole population was slower than planned, and some social security systems are wholly managed by mutual benefit societies: the civil servants system (3,000,000 members), students (400,000), the self-employed (650,000), and, above all, the Agricultural Mutual Benefit Society (5,600,000). The latter, under the supervision of the Ministry of Agriculture, constitutes a completely autonomous social security system and represents a special public service mission (Caire 1984).

The redistribution carried out by humanitarian and philanthropic associations seems to be very different from that implemented by the mutual benefit societies and public social security system. It constitutes a strictly vertical redistribution, encouraged by public authorities. The maximum deduction from taxable income increased from 1% to 5% in 1984. Similarly, corporate philanthropy may account for up to 1% of total turnover. *However, in 1985 the total tax-exempt donations were only FF 510 million, that is less than 1% of household disposable income.* In contrast, in Anglo-Saxon countries, private donations reached 2 to 3% of disposable income (Collard 1978). Voluntary work, which is a form of redistribution in kind, is also certainly less spread in France. However, no data are available on the extend and the characteristics of volunteering.

What are the advantages and disadvantages of redistribution in a social economy? When compared to public redistribution, private redistribution offers several advantages: through mutual benefit societies, it encourages self-help, mobilizes new financial and human resources through individual donations and corporate contributions (economic theory shows that in the case of short-term mutual aid, cheating behavior is less common than in the context of public goods), encourages the inclusion of more segments of the population in social policy, and private redistribution tends to reduce red tape and bureaucratic delays. It allows for fast intervention and support programs, such as *Catholic Help* and *Emmaüs* did in the winter of 1984–1985, or *"Restaurants of the Heart"* in the following years.

The advantages of redistribution through the social economy do not compensate for its obvious limitations in comparison with public redistribution. Short-term mutual aid may strengthen inequalities and primarily help elites.

Moreover, and this is the essential point, voluntary redistribution has clear financial limits and can only constitute an extra help in relation to a system of compulsory contributions. The limits of a "two-speed" social coverage, in which Social Security would only cover basic risks while mutual benefit societies, insurance, or assistance cover others, too, are therefore evident.

4. The Regulation Function

The regulatory function is the economic function most specific to government, and best characterizes an interventionist state. Its purpose is to steady, as much as possible, economic cycles, employment, price levels, and terms of trade. Geographically, its purpose is to harmonize economic growth and standard of living. The regulation function is thus at the very heart of governmental economic and social policy. Nevertheless, institutions of the social economy have recently increased their participation in the social and economic policies of employment and decentralization.

4.1 The Social Economy and Employment Policy

The SIRENE files list firms which employ at least one person, or which have paid taxes in the course of the five previous years. Table 1 shows that employment in the social economy represents 6% of total employment, which is equivalent to the employment provided by the consumer goods industry. Moreover, in contrast to manufacturing, employment has increased in social economy enterprises. In 1979, the social economy employed 603,282 wage earners, and employment increased by 33% up to 1985. During the same period, employment declined in the economy as a whole (Archambault 1984).

However, there is reason to assume that part of the increase in social economy employment represent jobs which are seasonal, part-time, and temporary (Kandel and Marchal 1984). Moreover, the growth of employment in associations is partly the result of improved accounting practices through the inclusion of some associations which had previously been excluded from official labor statistics. Nevertheless, local surveys seem to support the growth of employment in social economy institutions. The fact that social economy enterprises are still job-creating in spite of the present economic

Table 1: Firms and Employment in the Social Economy (1985)

Branch	Number of firms	Number of establishments	Number of employees	Average number of employees per establishment
Cooperatives	25,745	34,533	236,551	8,8
Mutual benefit societies	3,461	7,432	142,196	19,2
Associations	139,374	157,237	802,083	5,1
Foundations	24,563	26,253	179,431	6,8
Professional unions	5,141	5,620	16,892	3,0
Joint-production committes	1,560	1,934	10,277	5,3
Total	199,844	233,009	1,387,340	6,0

Source: Sirene File, INSEE.

situation can be explained, for the most part, by a long-term structural effect: jobs created by the social economy are mostly filled by women. In France, female employment increased throughout the last decade, while male employment has decreased in the same period. Furthermore, many new jobs, particularly in the associative sector, are part-time and temporary. Finally, the new jobs created are related to "up and coming" branches. They are tertiary jobs in the industries that have expanded most in recent years, such as health, leisure, and professional training.

Another reason for social economy employment expansion has been the successive youth employment schemes which were implemented to offset the highest youth unemployment rate of any OECD country except Italy. 60% or 25,000 of the *"Public service jobs,"* created in 1979 and financed by public authorities with FF 24,000 each, are located in cultural, health, and social welfare areas (Gaudin 1982). Since 1982, training programs for "young volunteers," between 18 to 26 years of age, provide jobs in both public service and educational associations. The government pays a monthly salary of FF 2,568 for a period of 6 to 12 months to each of the approximately 10,000 volunteers in this program.

The most important attempt to alleviate long-term youth unemployment is the *Collective Utility Works* (CUW), modelled after community work programs in Quebec. Since 1984, CUW have provided part-time work and complementary training for periods of 3 to 12 months. The monthly salary of FF 1,200 for participants is paid by the government. Only nonprofit organizations or public agencies can receive collective utility workers and associations represent 40% of the recipient organizations. In 1985, 350,000 people were employed in CUW programs.

These examples demonstrate that the social economy is the preferred partner for employment policies initiated by the government. But the very aim of social economy enterprises can be to create or preserve jobs, acting as an "incubator" for recently established firms or serving as a financial security for firms in difficult transition or consolidation period. For example, "fragile" social organizations like *worker's production cooperatives* have experienced an expansion in numbers, increasing from 600 in 1977 to 1,300 in 1985. And we can observe a sort of life cycle of the legal status of the emerging enterprise: projects are often tested as associations; if a project proves to be viable, the legal status of workers' cooperative is adopted; when it becomes more profitable, the form of limited liability or joint-stock company is adopted. It is partly due to this transition via the social economy that, for the first time since 1974, more companies were created than dissolved in 1985–1987. Since associations do not pay taxes and can deduct net profits occurring to wage earners from taxable profits, they experience a substantial fiscal advantage.

Another form of protected economic environment are the *"intermediate production" enterprises* which supply temporary jobs for disadvantaged segments of the population. These associations are a hybrid of firm and training institution which offer their clientele an intermediary position between employment, public assistance, and vocational training. Their efficiency is remarkable, since 80% of these people find jobs or additional training positions, as compared to 20% of those leaving traditional training programs (see also Forse 1984).

Having considered the direct and indirect quantitative contribution of the social economy to employment, we now shift to the qualitative aspect of employment in the nonprofit sector. In the social economy, we must differentiate between cooperatives and mutual benefit societies, on the one hand, and associations, on the other. Jobs in the former are essentially secure, full-time jobs, while those in the latter are mostly temporary and part-time, with low pay and little security. Moreover, recently created jobs tend to be more precarious than already existing ones.

Thus, in the fields of health and welfare, culture, and education, we can understand the propensity of public agencies to delegate some work to social economy as a means of retrenchment in public employment. Some manufacturing industries use service enterprises for tertiary tasks, which they used to perform in-house, such as cleaning, security, accounting, repairs, or computing. Similarly, using associations to perform tasks which are traditionally the responsibility of public administrations serves often as a way to avoid the granting of civil servant status to employees.

Because of the nature of the job it provides, as well as its role in employment policy, the social economy thus contributes to the increasingly blurred boundary between employment, inactivity, and unemployment. Furthermore, voluntary work is also considered as an intermediate activity between unemployment, inactivity, and employment (Archambault 1984; Chadeau and Willard 1985).

4.2 The Social Economy and Decentralization

The social economy organizations have become one of the essential vehicles of decentralization, especially in rural areas. Decentralization policy is recent in France (1983) and runs counter to a long tradition of centralization. The progressive transfer of state functions to local communities affects fields of the social economy: job training, welfare, education, and culture. Thus, most new regional organizations have adopted cooperative or associative rather than public agency forms.

Thanks to its cooperative banking network, the social economy contributes to the financing to local initiatives, the Crédit Agricole in particular. This network is also adapted to the raising of funds and to the collection of neighborhood savings (Greffe, Dupuis, and Pflieger 1983).

The social economy has also become a nursery for local elites. To have been president of an influential association or a mutual benefit society is often the first step in a local political career. Career moves between public organizations and social economy are common. However, tensions exist between volunteers and the local elite. Volunteer's legitimacy comes from co-optation and is estimated lower than the legitimacy coming from the ballot box. So, when a local authority subsidies an association, it means sometimes a political allegiance that the volunteers reject (Gremion 1976).

Because of their irreplaceable knowledge of the local environment, social economy partners participate in the various forms of dialogue which lead to local policy. 25% of the seats of regional economic and social councils are held by social economy representatives. Decentralization has brought social economy organizations closer to the administrations they depend upon, power relations are less unequal, and dialogue is easier. Social economy representatives take part in the formulation and implementation of regional plans. Thus incorporated into an elaborate network of increased interdependencies, the French nonprofit sector has become a flexible regulatory sphere located between the state and the for-profit world, and thus is an important vehicle of decentralization.

References

Archambault, E. (1984): "Les associations en chiffres," *Revue des études cooperatives* 1, 9–46.
Bénard, J. (1986): *Economie publique*, Paris: Economica.
Caire, G. (1984): "Syndicalisme, Sécurité Sociale et mutualité," *Revue de l'économie sociale* 15, 167–178.

Chadeau, A. and C. Willard (1985): "La mesure de l'emploi dans l'économie sociale," *Revue des études Coopératives* 15, 63 – 89.

Collard, D. (1978): *Altruism and Economy, a Study in Non-Selfish Economics*, Oxford: Martin Robertson.

Forsé, M. (1984): "Les créations d'associations: un indicateur de changement social," *Observations et diagnostics économiques* 6, 125 – 145.

Gaudin, J. (1982): *Initiative locale et création d'emploi*, Paris: La Documentation française.

Greffe, X., X. Dupuis, and S. Pflieger (1983): *Financer l'économie sociale*, Paris: Economica.

Gremion, P. (1976): *Le pouvoir périphérique*, Paris: Le Seuil.

Inspection Générale des Affaires Sociales (I. G. A. S.) (1984): *La politique sociale et les associations*, Paris: La Documentation Française.

Jeantet, T. (1984): "Rapport du groupe innovation-Recherche au Comité Consultatif de l'économie sociale," unpublished manuscript.

Kandel, I. and E. Marchal (1984): *L'emploi associatif en Seine-et-Marne*, Paris: Centre d'étude de l'Emploi, n°12.

Musgrave, R. (1959): *Theory of Public Finance*, New York, MacGraw-Hill.

Wagner, C. (1984): "La protection sociale," *Données Sociales*, INSEE.

4.4
The Nonprofit Sector in Switzerland: Taxonomy and Dimensions

Antonin Wagner

This paper assesses the place of philanthropy, nonprofit institutions, voluntary agencies, and self-help groups within Switzerland's human service delivery system. Size and growth of the nonprofit sector are quantified, with the help of the National Account Statistics. However, first it is useful to introduce the taxonomy of the System of National Accounts which is employed in our qualitative and quantitative analysis of the Swiss nonprofit sector.

1. The System of National Accounts (SNA)

The System of National Accounts (SNA)[1], first formulated in 1952 and revised by the Statistical Commission of the United Nations in its 15th session, provides a comprehensive framework for the systematic recording of transaction flows in an economy. The system categorizes into "sectors" institutional entities which perform similar or identical economic functions. These sectors are as follows:

The *government sector* (central, state, and local government) includes providers of government services (defense, regulation of the public order, and health, cultural, and social services), and government industries which supply goods and services to other units of government, such as printing plants and arsenals. This sector is sometimes called the "first sector."

Corporate and quasi-corporate enterprises form the "second sector," which is often referred to as the *business sector*. The SNA includes in this sector not only private, for-profit, or nonprofit enterprises, but also public enterprises which supply goods and services for the market.

The "third sector" includes private, nonprofit institutions serving households by providing educational, health, cultural, recreational, and other

---

[1] The present system is published in *A System of National Accounts*, Studies in Methods, Series F, No. 2, Rev. 3 (United Nations Publication, Sales No. E. 69. XVII. 3).

social and community services free of charge or below cost. Unlike those in the "first sector," these institutions are not mainly financed and controlled by central, state, or local government. As distinct from the "second sector," third sector goods and services being offered free or below cost are not produced for the market.

The "fourth sector" includes primarily households and is, therefore, referred to as *household sector*. But SNA also includes in this sector private, nonprofit institutions serving households, if they employ less than the equivalent of two full-time persons. The "rest of the world" constitutes the "fifth sector," in order to account for transactions in an open economy with foreign institutions.

According to the SNA classification, nonprofit institutions are to be found not only in the third sector, but also in the government sector, the business sector, and the household sector. It is therefore preferable to use – in analogy to "first" and "second sector" – the designation "third sector," rather than "nonprofit" or "not for-profit sector." First, second, and third sectors have in common that they provide the economy with goods and services, while they may differ with respect to structural elements (like ownership) and ways of distribution (market vs. non-market).

Although the SNA emphasizes that the different economic sectors are interconnected in many ways, it has become quite common – especially in U.S. literature – to refer to the third sector as the "independent" sector. However, far from being independent, the third sector in a modern welfare state depends heavily on the government sector, both directly and indirectly. For example, in a very direct manner in the modern welfare state, the government has a substantial degree of discretion over the spending of public funds through "third-party implementors" (Salamon 1981). Not only local and state governments, but also third sector institutions are used to carry out governmental functions. More indirectly, the government can influence individual and corporate contributions to nonprofit organizations through the tax system. Thus, these tax deductions constitute an indirect government subsidy to the so-called independent sector.

2. The Third Sector and the Modern Welfare State

In the last 25 years, advanced industrialized countries like Switzerland have experienced a dramatic growth in their public sectors. The average government disbursement/GDP ratio of the 24 OECD countries increased from 26.2% in 1961 to 37.6% in 1981 (OECD 1981). In Switzerland, the ratio has reached 40% and lies, therefore, above the OECD average.

Social policy related expenditures have contributed much to this expansion. Voters' growing resistance against paying increasingly higher taxes requires a shift in social policy, with more emphasis on service delivery rather than income transfers. As services achieve greater significance relative to income transfers, alternative delivery systems are needed to contain costs and inhibit program deterioration. Advanced industrialized countries are therefore forced to undertake various measures to improve productivity in their service delivery systems (Wagner 1984).

A common first strategy to improve productivity in delivering human services is the *decentralization* of service production. The delivery of human services entails two kinds of costs: costs related to service production and costs related to consumer motivation. Thus, one can differentiate two types of human services: (1) capital-intensive human services, such as health care, in which production costs are primary, and (2) labor-intensive services, such as counseling, in which motivation costs prevail. An example of the former would be the care for patients with kidney disease. The optimal production unit for this type of service requires a relatively large catchment area in which centralization of service delivery produces economies of scale and decreasing costs per person served. Although one might expect motivation costs per person to grow as the catchment area expands, due to better outreach and greater travel and time costs for patients, motivation costs are — in relation to production costs — irrelevant in the case of capital-intensive human services such as kidney dialysis.

However, if we examine a labor-intensive service, such as counseling, we see the reverse situation: motivation costs are primary, and production costs are relatively insignificant. Consequently, the per capita costs for service delivery increase rapidly with the number of potential clients and the size of the catchment area. Therefore, the optimal production unit size for this kind of service provision is relatively small. Decentralization and delegation of service delivery to local governments should therefore lead to decreasing costs per person served. However, the reduction in costs for the public sector as a whole may be minimal, because in some cases service delivery is merely reallocated from higher to lower levels of government, without being shifted to other sectors of the economy.

In order to reduce costs to the public sector, therefore, decentralization is often coupled with *(re)privatization* of public activities. Since the early 1970s, local governments in particular have tried to turn over certain functions to the business sector. The advantages of (re)privatizing social programs are limited, however. In many cases, for both technical and cost reasons, the so-called exclusion principle cannot be applied to the provision of social welfare, thereby making market-type delivery impossible. In those cases (like psychotherapy), where, from a technical or cost point of view, privatization of human services is advantageous, the government — from an allocative-efficiency standpoint — may still have to step in, by producing or subsidizing additional services. This is the case with so-called "meritorious goods," for which consumers do not reveal their true preferences and tend to conceal their willingness to pay.

Both types of market failure — the non-applicability of the exclusion principle and concealed preferences — prevent the allocation of social services solely through market mechanism and the full privatization of human services. Furthermore, full privatization would reduce both the legally guaranteed social benefits and collective security. Therefore, government continues to play an important role in the area of human and social services by providing funds, by giving directions, and setting the rules. In the actual delivery of services, however, government might turn extensively to other institutions, mainly to those of the third sector.

Consequently, in many advanced industrialized countries, government is neither the major, nor the sole provider of human services. In most of these countries, non-governmental human service organizations exist on a federal, regional, and local level with sectarian, political, trade union, or other interest group origin. They constitute, together with the public sector, the *primary level* of a two-tier system of human service provision. These organizations tend to be bureaucratic and traditional in approach. They carry out functions required by law, but are rarely involved in activities which are "preventive" in nature.

The *secondary level* of this two-tier system of human service provision offers innovative, informal, and perhaps more consumer-oriented services. This recent tendency of presenting a more participatory and localized service provision is often referred to as *debureaucratization*. Whereas decentralization and (re)privatization aim to improve the productivity and to increase the cost efficiency of the institutions offering services, debureaucratization is a demand-oriented productivity strategy directed at the consumers. Therefore, it not only constitutes a cost-saving strategy, but also improves the quality of human services by activating consumer motivation and strengthening the participatory aspect of social policy. Hence the various new forms of social organization — self-help groups, local initiatives such as neighborhood coalitions, and new social movements such as the women's or peace movement — supplement public and bureaucratic social welfare activities by providing a necessary back-up system to the primary level of service delivery.

The above description highlights the heterogeneity of the third sector: it consists of the bureaucratic, but non-governmental segment of the first tier and the non-bureaucratic institutions of the second tier, both of which perform many different activities. Despite this heterogeneity, the third sector is characterized by a specific set of service deliverers who prevail in the third sector. A typology of sectors should, therefore, be based upon the nature of the service deliverers or actors, rather than upon the institutional entities and their activities.

In general, the following types of service deliverers can be identified:

— Paid workers, mostly skilled labor and salaried professionals.
— Organizational members. Member status includes a fee and/or an enrollment of a sometimes symbolic character. Citizenship in this respect can be considered as a form of membership.
— Volunteers who are neither paid workers nor enrolled members.

In the first sector, one finds both types of service deliverers: paid workers, usually bureaucrats, as well as "members," who, by virtue of their citizenship, also play an important role in the public sector. Paid workers also predominate in the second sector, where shareholders may be considered as "members." In the third sector, all three types of service deliverers are to be found, but in the second tier of service provision, volunteers are dominant.[2] Nevertheless, it becomes evident that the third sector is often improperly called "voluntary sector" because, if "voluntary" refers to the use of volunteers, only a portion of the third sector is voluntary. It is that segment of the third sector which in French is called *"bénévolat"* (Fragnière 1987).

3. Size and Growth of the Third Sector Within Swiss Social Policy

Using the above taxonomy, we now quantify the involvement of each economic sector in the social welfare field in Switzerland, and then analyze the extent to which service strategies like (re)privatization, decentralization, and debureaucratization have influenced the provision of human services in this country.

This analysis uses data from Switzerland's National Account Statistics which are based on SNA. However, with respect to the social security system, SNA has been adapted to take into account the private character of various

---

[2] One of the most important items on a research agenda for the third sector and its significance for the future of a modern welfare state is the interrelationship among different categories of service deliverers. For example, the growing activation of non-professionals and the involvement of volunteers in the human service delivery system is perceived, by many, as a threat to the professional aspirations of social workers. However, new types of service deliverers have to be seen as supplementing professionals, rather than replacing them. What is needed therefore are clear and commonly accepted criteria for the assignment of tasks, particularly within the second tier of the third sector (Spiegel and Wagner 1986).

social security institutions in Switzerland. Since health insurance companies and pension funds in particular are largely organized privately — rather than through government —, social security institutions in the Swiss version of SNA have been clustered into a special "social security sector."

Table 1 gives an overview of social welfare expenditures in Switzerland (Wagner 1985). Column 1 lists the different types of social welfare expenditures and constitutes Switzerland's social policy account or social policy budget. The itemization of the budget corresponds to the two fundamental intervention strategies in social policy: provision of human services (including the administration of the system) and transfers of income to households. The two types of expenditures are attributed to either the "public sector" (government sector and public segment of the social security sector) or the "private sector" (third sector and private segment of the social security sector).

In column 2, the two types of expenditures are summarized in order to emphasize the basic paradigm underlying Switzerland's social policy. Expenditures for the provision of goods and services, including administrative costs, are shown as a percentage of GDP and labelled as the "service quota," which in this case is 2%. Income transfers, however, are related to total national income, where the corresponding relative figure is called the "distributional quota." This figure shows the extent to which income generated in the production process is channelled to those members of society who no longer actively contribute to production. The distributional quota has increased over the years, from about 10% in 1970 to almost twice that value in the mid-1980s. But, whereas income transfers have almost doubled in relative size, the service quota has grown only marginally, by about half a percentage point from 1.4 (1970) to 2%. Thus, Swiss social policy continues to emphasize income transfers rather than service delivery.

In column 3, social policy expenditures are subdivided by the purposes they serve in order to identify the main goals of social policy in Switzerland. National account statistics divide general government expenditures into three broad categories: general welfare, housing policy, and "other" expenditures. Social security expenditures, however, can more easily be attributed to specific social policy goals. For example, as in most advanced industrialized countries, Switzerland's social policy for the elderly constitutes the single most important element. But this categorization does not show the relative importance of expenditures related to health care, because the operating costs for hospitals are not considered as social policy expenditures, but as health policy expenditures.

For our purposes, column 4 represents the most important part of the social policy budget. It shows the extent to which service strategies like (re)privatization, decentralization, and debureaucratization have had an effect upon the service delivery system in Switzerland.

The relative importance of the private sector (third sector and private social security institutions) has to do with the specific structure of the social security system, in which health insurance is largely organized privately. Moreover, (re)privatization and debureaucratization seems not to have had a major impact on Swiss social policy yet: most of the private sector expenditures in Table 1 (7.2 billion Swiss francs) represent income transfers to households, while expenditures attributable to the third sector remain relatively small. However, the small size of third sector expenditures (250 million Swiss francs) underrepresents actual contributions, since only expenditures of the first tier are quantifiable. Still, the budget figure of the third sector includes the net expenditures of non-public voluntary welfare organizations at federal, cantonal, and local levels, after deduction of government subsidies, but excludes social service activities by the churches, which in Switzerland represent an important provider in the third sector. In addition, most private nonprofit institutions operate at the secondary tier of service provision, using voluntary labor, and are thus considered households. Their activities therefore do not appear in the production account of the national account statistics.

According to column 4 in Table 1, decentralization seems to be the only strategy which has an impact on human service provision in Switzerland. Given the importance of cantonal and local governments as service providers and Switzerland's long-standing tradition of federalism, it is not surprising that most social welfare expenditures of the service type (97%) are located at cantonal and local levels.

4. The Third Sector: Supplement Rather Than Substitute

Government cost containment strategies should result in a shift of services to the third sector, especially to the second, non-bureaucratic tier which therefore might be expected to expand. There are, however, statistical difficulties in identifying and assessing the size and growth of the non-bureaucratic portion of the third sector. On the other hand, little empirical evidence exists to support the assumption of an expanding third sector, because the structure and dynamics of Switzerland's third sector seem to differ significantly from those of other industrialized countries:

(1) The main role of the third sector, in general, is the provision of services. However, as highlighted in Table 1, Switzerland's social policy continues to emphasize income transfers rather than service delivery, and therefore offers relatively little opportunity for typical third sector activities.
(2) The size and growth of the third sector reflects two important characteristics of Switzerland's political configuration: its federal constitutional

Table 1: Switzerland's social policy account (million Swiss Francs, 1984)

Social policy account	Types of expenditures	Quota	Target of expenditures	Sector / Institutions

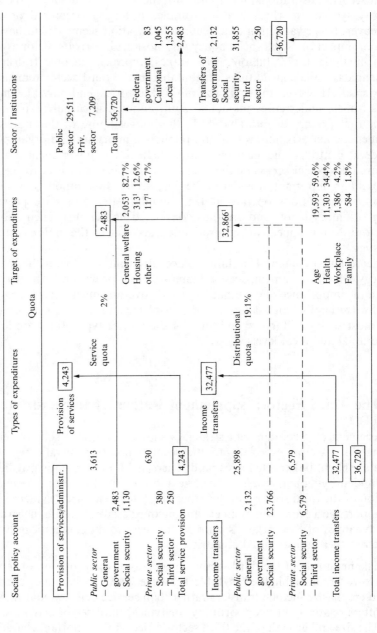

Provision of services/administr.

Public sector
- General government — 3,613
- Social security — 2,483 / 1,130

Private sector
- Social security — 380
- Third sector — 250
- Total service provision — 4,243

Income transfers

Public sector
- General government — 2,132
- Social security — 25,898 / 23,766

Private sector
- Social security — 6,579
- Third sector — 6,579
- Total income transfers — 32,477

36,720

Provision of services — 4,243 → Service quota — 2%

Income transfers — 32,477 → Distributional quota — 19.1%

General welfare — 2,053[1] — 82.7%
Housing — 313[1] — 12.6%
other — 117[1] — 4.7%
2,483

32,866[1]

Age — 19,593 — 59.6%
Health — 11,303 — 34.4%
Workplace — 1,386 — 4.2%
Family — 584 — 1.8%

Public sector — 29,511
Priv. sector — 7,209
Total — 36,720

Federal government — 83
Cantonal — 1,045
Local — 1,355
2,483

Transfers of government — 2,132
Social security — 31,855
Third sector — 250
36,720

Source: Figures are from National Account Statistics, with the exception of [1]: Data provided by the Social Security Administration.

structure, which distributes governmental functions between federal, cantonal, and local governments; and its grassroots democratic nature which emphasizes citizen participation. The federal arrangement encourages cantonal and local governments to become the primary service providers, and thus form a valuable alternative to "nonprofit federalism" (Salamon 1987: 43). At the same time, localized government tends to promote less tax resistance in its citizens and, therefore, less need to stimulate private philanthropy through such incentives as tax-deductible donations.

(3) Social security funds are, to a large extent, organized privately and exercise substantial autonomy in a decentralized environment. They partially replace the cash and in-kind benefits transferred through charitable agencies which exist in other countries.

Based on our analysis, we conclude that voluntary organizations in Switzerland are less a substitute for than a supplement to public programs, especially where the government does not offer the full range of services needed. In this way, rather than replacing public institutions, the third sector shares responsibility with the first sector. Yet, to the extent that a decentralized public sector along with private social security institutions are able to adjust social services to the needs of clients, voluntary organizations play a more limited role. They assume the function of secondary or "derivative" institutions (Salamon 1987: 39), filling in for inherent limitations of government. Nevertheless, this assessment should by no means diminish the importance of philanthropic and self-help activities for the future of the Swiss welfare state, especially where these new forms of service delivery complement rather than challenge the public sector.

References

Fragnière, J.-P. (1987): *Action sociale et bénévolat social*, Rapport à l'intention du Conseil suisse de la science sur les problèmes de recherche dans le domaine du travail social non-marchand et de l'action bénévole, Lausanne: EESP.

OECD (1981): *The Welfare State in Crisis*, Paris: Organization for Economic Cooperation and Development.

Salamon, L. M. (1981): "Rethinking Public Management: Third Party Government and the Changing Forms of Public Action," *Public Policy* 29, 255–275.

Salamon, L. M. (1987): "Of Market Failure, Voluntary Failure, and Third Party Government: Toward a Theory of Government-Nonprofit Relations in the Modern Welfare State," *Journal of Voluntary Action Research* 16, 29–49.

Spiegel, M. V. and Wagner, A. (1986): "Resocializing Social Policy: A Strategy for Survival of the Modern Welfare State and Its Impact on Social Work Education," *International Social Work* 29, 123–134.

Wagner, A. (1984): "Decentralization, Privatization, and Deprofessionalization: Is Small Always Beautiful?" in *Education for Social Work Practice: Selected International Models*, Charles Guzzetta, A. J. Katz, and R. A. English (Eds.), New York: Council on Social Work Education, 9–17.

Wagner, A. (1985): "L'évolution du budget social de la Suisse," *Revue Française des affaires sociales* 39, 41–57.

4.5
A Profile of the Third Sector in West Germany

Helmut K. Anheier

1. Introduction

This paper presents a brief survey of the size, scope, composition, and history of the third sector in West Germany. For comparative purposes, the German third sector is interesting for several reasons: First, more than any other sector, the third sector represents continuity in a country characterized by historical discontinuity; second, the third sector operates in a highly complex legal system which classifies organizations differently than other (common law) countries; third, large segments of the third sector are legally, politically, and economically defined within the special state – church relationship which exemplifies neither separation nor union; fourth, the third sector is the result of a tradition of political pragmatism in conflict management which, among other consequences, led to monopolistic tendencies among third sector organizations linked to the welfare state; sixth, as part of a political system with corporatist tendencies, business and status associations have historically been influential and continue to play politically powerful roles.

The paper also raises several theoretical issues. Presently, several promising developments exist at the theoretical level (Douglas 1983; Hansmann 1987; James 1987; Salamon 1987; Weisbrod 1988), and, to varying degrees, they all face difficulties in explaining size, scope, and importance of the West German third sector. The German third sector is neither primarily the result of market or governmental failures, nor primarily the result of societal heterogeneity, nor the direct reflection of other demand and supply factors. This is not to say that theories based on institutional failures, societal heterogeneity, excess demand, and supply of ideological entrepreneurship are necessarily false. To the contrary, the paper suggests that they "interact" in ways that are presently neither adequately conceptualized nor understood.

The German case is a good example for the complexity of this interaction. For lack of a better term, "contradictory" may well be the adjective that best describes the German third sector: It largely originated in the period of nineteenth century etatism, but flourishes under liberalism. Its development is related to religious heterogeneity of society, but owes many privileges from "homogenizing" political powers. It incorporates a great diversity of business and status interests, largely, however, because political/status interests could not translate into political parties. The characteristic federalism of organized local and regional interests rests itself on organizational principles carried over from the period of Prussian hegemony.

Some of the contradictory tendencies can be explained if we related previous societal conflict configurations to third sector outcomes. The present legal, political, and organizational profile of the third sector offers more information about the conflicts of German society as they existed at the beginning of the century than it does about present conflicts. To some extent, the third sector provides an organizational "repository" of previous conflicts. As conflict situations change, so do the interactions and organizational responses of institutional failures, heterogeneity, excess demand, and supply of ideological entrepreneurship. Thus, the third sector incorporates different social responses to previous social conflicts, which, *ex post*, appear as contradictory elements.

The paper is divided into several parts: First, I introduce major characteristics of West Germany which shape its third sector. Then, I present a general profile of the German third sector and focus on three of its major segments: foundations, business associations, and welfare associations.

2. Relevant Characteristics of West German Society

West Germany[1], a country of about 96,000 square miles (roughly the size of Oregon) and a population of 62 million, is the third largest economy in the Western world, with current GNP surpassing DM 2 trillion ($ 1,2 trillion). In 1986, agriculture contributed 1.7% to GDP; manufacture/industry accounted for 42.8%, and services for 55.5% of GDP. In 1986, state's total involvement in GDP (public quota) was 46.8%, with public consumption and statutory transfers as the two largest items accounting for about 75% of the state's GDP proportion. The "social budget," i. e. public and private provision of social services and statutory (usually welfare) transfers to individual and organizations, accounted for 31.1% of GNP.

Several general features of West German society are important in shaping the nature, scope, and importance of the country's third sector.

1. Federalism. West Germany is a federal republic in which the individual 11 states (*Länder*) enjoy a relatively high degree of political power. This is particularly so in the field of education and culture, the "traditional" domains of the third sector, which is almost exclusively a *Länder* matter. Moreover,

[1] Unless otherwise indicated, all data reported in this section are from the Statistisches Jahrbuch 1987.

at the federal level, the *Länder* are represented in the *Bundesrat* (Federal Council). In the *Bundesrat*, the *Länder* enjoy veto power: all legislation from parliament addressing *Länder* matters must pass the *Bundesrat*. As a result, the federal government, in particular the chancellor, is in a weaker position than the French President or the British Prime Minister.

There is no single, centralized locus of power, neither in a geographical, political, nor economic sense. Certainly, while Bonn has emerged as the central reference of political life, regional, economic, and cultural centers guard their status avidly. This is not to say, however, that the country presents a clear case of third sector decentralization; rather, a key aspect of the West German political and organizational structure seems to be the organization of decentralized constituencies into more central units which, in turn, jointly form (usually several) "peak" associations. For example, some 3,900 local and regional welfare associations form the *"Paritätischer Wohlfahrtsverband,"* which, together with other consortia, is organized into a "peak" association at the federal level. Likewise, the Federal Association of German Industry (BDI), itself a member of the *Gemeinschaftsausschuß der Deutschen Gewerblichen Wirtschaft* (Council of German Business and Commerce), consists of 39 consortia, which themselves divide into some 600 associations to represent about 100,000 member organizations. Peak associations, as the representatives of local, regional, and special (cross-cutting) interests, negotiate with political bodies at the state and the federal level.

Complex legal system. West Germany is a civil law country. The *Bürgerliches Gesetzbuch* or BGB (civil code) came into effect only in 1900. The BGB, a late legal product of the enlightenment, stands in the tradition of codification and legal abstraction. Codification assumes that a body of written law can, without contradiction, codify and regulate society. Legal abstraction (the principle of *lex specialis derogat legi generali*) implies that special laws (such as the stock corporation law, foundation law, the association code, and "lower level" ordinances and procedural rules) all derive from a general body of law such as the BGB. These two legal ideas lead to an self-generating expansion of the legal system, or in Max Weber's terms, become key agent of *Vergesellschaftung*. Several legal bodies and "layers" of law are devoted to third sector matters. For example, a special legal statute, the *Sammlungsgesetz* (collection law), regulates giving and donations to charities.

While civil law regulates the relations among individuals and legal personalities, public law regulates the relations among state and public entities, and between the public and the private. The distinction between civil law (*ius privatum*) and public law (*ius publicum*) is anything but clear-cut, and, combined with the ideology of codification and legal abstraction has generated a legal landscape of utmost complexity. Moreover, many civil code stipulations find public law equivalences. For example, the code of associations (*Vereinsrecht*) is public law and regulates legal personalities established under civil law in their relation to the state.

The BGB classifies legal personalities into two broad categories: associations — *Vereine* — (section 21, 55 ss BGB) and societies — *Gesellschaften* — (section 705 BGB). The two categories share a common feature in that they are all outside the realm of public law. All third sector organizations are BGB-associations, while all non-registered and informal groupings are classified as "societies."

The distinction between profit versus nonprofit is not fully represented in the BGB. Among associations, ideal associations (*Idealvereine*) are set apart from "economic" associations (*wirtschaftliche Vereine*). "Ideal associations" are associations with no business interest. "Economic associations" are business-oriented such as the stock corporation, the limited liability company, cooperatives, or a professional nonprofit theater company. (An amateur theater company would be an ideal association.) Thus, the law classifies associations according to their more abstract or general *raison d'être*, not according to the profit motive. The profit – nonprofit issue is the subject of "lower-order" ordinances and various tax laws (Bundesministerium der Finanzen 1988).

Ecclesiastical law is constitutionally equivalent to public administrative law. Churches are established not under civil but under public law, and they form *"Körperschaften des öffentlichen Rechts,"* corporations of public law. This legal privilege applies to the member churches of the *Rat der Evangelischen Kirchen Deutschlands* (Council of Protestant Churches in Germany, whose congregations comprise 41.5% of the population) and the Roman Catholic Church (43.3% of the population) only. Other religious communities, in particular the numerous "free religious associations" and the close to 2 million Moslems, form civil law organizations. The reasons for the special treatment of the two state churches are historically as complex as they are politically controversial. One important reason is the "church tax," a portion of income tax which is levied by the state for the churches' benefit, who, in turn, pay an administration fee for tax collection.

The principle of subsidiarity is important for understanding the development of the state – church relationship in the Federal Republic (see contributions in Bauer and Dießenbacher 1984). The principle originated in Jesuit thinking and was first formulated by Pope Pius XI in the 1931 encyclical *Quadragesimo anno*. In essence, subsidiarity means that the larger social unit should only assist the smaller social unit if the latter can no longer rely on its own resources. The principle served as the basis for the division of labor and between state and church in the field of social welfare, as it developed in the 1950s, when church – state relations were particularly cordial.

2.1 A Brief History

The present political system in West Germany contains many corporatist elements — a result of continuous conflict accommodation and discontinuous conflict resolution. It is beyond the scope of this paper to review all relevant major changes and discontinuities which have influenced the development of the third sector. However, the Napoleonic wars seem an appropriate starting point for a sketch of third sector history, since the dissolution of the Empire resulted in wide-ranging secularization. Consequently, the third sector, then almost exclusively church-oriented, diminished substantially.

Unlike England and France, no broad democratic and revolutionary tradition had taken root in Germany by mid-nineteenth century; what little had developed was reversed by the "restoration" that followed the revolution of 1848. Paradoxically, the underdevelopment of democracy turned out to be of advantage for parts of the third sector. Furthermore, unlike other countries (such as the French *Loi de Chapelier* of 1791 or the *General Combination Act* of 1799 in England), no legislation attacked the remains of late medieval society, in particular the status groups (estates, *Stände*) and business associations of commerce and crafts. With general political representation lacking, these associations (*Verbände*) became influential economic and political instruments in the period of rapid economic development between 1850 and 1900. The state, however, was not a passive recipient of associational interests. To the extent that the associations learned the ways of politics, the state intervened in associational affairs, supported the hierarchical arrangement into "peak" associations, and, when politically necessary, also created some associations, most notably in the field of social policy.

In other areas, however, the relationship between state and third sector was more conflictual. The increased emergence of Prussian hegemony, from the Vienna Congress to the proclamation of the Second Empire in 1871, culminated in the *"Kulturkampf."* This conflict between Bismarck and the Catholic regions of the *Reich* lasted from 1871 to 1891 and was, to a large extent, a political struggle between secular and religious powers over the division of labor as well as influence and responsibility in the areas of education, culture, and welfare. Major arenas of conflict were (a) the school governance law (*Schulaufsichtsgesetz*) which excluded ordained priests from teaching in public schools in Catholic parts of the Prussian Rhine Province and the Eastern provinces with large proportions of Polish inhabitants, (b) the ban on the Jesuit Order; and (c) the mandatory introduction of civil marriage.

Likewise, when Bismarck laid the foundation for a relatively comprehensive welfare system, he did so for political reasons and against the opposition of established religions. Social insurance and welfare was used as a tool of social and political control (Rimlinger 1971: 114; Sachse and Tennstedt 1986); social rights to welfare were granted, in part, to prevent the transfer of greater political rights. The decidedly political nature of the origin of the welfare state cannot be overstated. Increasingly, the traditional support system (family, church, charity) was proving inadequate to meet working-class demands.

The major lines of conflict in German society, already visible in the late nineteenth century, culminated in the tumultuous years between 1918 and 1923: Catholics versus Protestants; nationalist versus regional and separatist movements; working class associations and parties versus bourgeois groups; agrarian status groups versus the new urban-based industrialists; political opponents of the Republic versus monarchists and democrats; and communists versus fascists. None of these conflicts were fully settled in the brief democratic interlude which lasted until 1933.

The Weimar Republic witnessed a third sector expansion, in the areas of politically oriented associations, economic interest organizations, and the welfare system (see below). Industry, commerce, and the third sector succeeded in revitalizing and expanding a complex system of associations (*Verbände*) which became major proponents of corporatist tendencies in the early 1930s. The legal authorities assumed a more passive role, and laws which restricted the creation of voluntary associations were liberalized. For example, the Weimar Constitution of 1919 (section 124 II, 2) changed section 61 II BGB (1900) ("The administrative authority can reject registration if, according to the Code of Association [*Vereinsrecht*], the association is illegal, or may be declared illegal, *or follows political, socio-political or religious objectives.*"), and dropped the italicized part of the sentence. In a similar vein, the discrimination against religious, in particular Catholic, organizations, was replaced by more accomodationist policies initiated by the (largely Catholic) Zentrum, the perhaps most influential political party of the Weimar Republic.

The Third Reich from 1933 to 1945 was not only a period of third sector contraction but also a period of far-reaching levelling of the organizational landscape. For example, foundation matters were extremely restricted. The free welfare associations were first regrouped under a single (NS-controlled) umbrella organization, and soon, with the exception of the Red Cross, reorganized as the National-Socialist People's Welfare (NSV).

Paradoxically, the Federal Republic became unwanted beneficiary of the NS-policy of *"Gleichschaltung,"* the organizational levelling, streamlining, and incorporation of all major aspects into the political party machine. In 1945, many previous conflicts, while never resolved or settled, no longer "existed." Regional differences and separatist tendencies became much less manifest, and no regional party has been represented in parliament since 1957. The weakened agrarian groups were incorporated into the Christian Parties, which in turn made attempts to avoid confessional politics. Combined with the allied licensing system for associations and parties between 1945 and 1949, the overall result was a far-reaching leveling, "de-politization," and "de-ideologizing" of the organizational landscape. By 1950, Germany was a more homogeneous country than ever before in its history.

Since then, it has developed into a society of organizations and associations, where, according to the eminent political scientist von Beyme (1987), little "association-free" terrain remains. Particular business and political interests have all become organized, incoporated interests, represented in an estimated 5,000 major associations. Note that these associations are, in fact, associations of associations and not individual membership associations. Moreover, political movements such as the environmentalists organize their interests in the form of a political party, a nonprofit bank (*Öko-Bank*), and a foundation (in the case of the "Greens"), or as a "Federal Association of Citizen Initiatives – Environment" with 350 member organizations and about 1,000 local initiatives.

3. A Profile of the Third Sector in West Germany[2]

While some data describing the German third sector are available, no data base or research exists which would be comparable to the *Dimensions of the Third Sector* by Hodgkinson and Weitzman (1984), Rudney (1987), and Salamon (1987), or the pathbreaking comparative work by Kramer (1981). There are four major reasons for this. First, the recent interest in the third sector among social scientists in Germany is strongly policy-oriented and shows a conspicuous absence of broader empirical work. Second, data compiled by the Federal Statistical Office (*Statistisches Bundesamt*) is not readily available in trichotomous (proprietory – nonprofit – public) form.

Third, much useful information for third sector researchers is simply not available in aggregate form. Different registration procedures apply to different third sector organizations. For example, associations (*Vereine*) are registered in the association registry (*Vereinsregister*) at 551 different county courts (*Amtsgerichte*), with no central or regional reporting practice. By contrast, and depending on specific *Länder* foundation law and type of foundation, foundations register with a foundation registry (*Stiftungsverzeichnis*). Ecclesiastical law recognizes regions different from secular law, and, in some cases, church provinces do not coincide with the boundaries of the *Länder* and those of the Federal Republic.

---

[2] Unless otherwise indicated, data reported in this section is from the Statistisches Jahrbuch 1987. Trend data was compiled using the earlier issues of the Statistisches Jahrbuch. The 1987 census of all work places will be available in the spring 1989.

Finally, in terms of taxation, no central institution like the Internal Revenue Service exists, where all nonprofits have to apply for treatment under 501(c) (3) of the Internal Revenue Code. Financial and tax administration is typically carried out through local tax authorities, in application of numerous legal codes relating to tax matters. Moreover, there is no legislative equivalent to the Freedom of Information Act. Contrary to the American experience, all tax information, with some notable exceptions such as the stock corporations, is confidential and not accessible to the public.

Data on special industries and services. Table 1 shows that the total of 3,098 hospitals is divided evenly among the three sectors, with each accounting for about one third of all hospitals. In terms of the number of beds, however, we see that public and nonprofit hospitals provide the great majority of hospital beds.

Table 1: Hospitals and Hospital Beds by Sector (1985)

Sector	Hospitals	Beds
Public	1,104	343,044
NPO	1,049	237,565
For-profit	945	94,742
Total	3,098	675,351

In the educational system, 9.3% of all schools are private nonprofit (Table 2). These schools, predominantly Catholic, educate 6.6% of all students up to university level (*Abitur*). With very few exceptions (e. g. the Catholic University in Eichstätt or recently established private universities), universities are public institutions, although the churches maintain considerable influence in theological seminaries. Research organizations such as the 60

Table 2: Schools and Students by Sector (1985)

Sector	Schools	Students
Public	25,173	6,649,147
NPO	2,350	467,000
Of which:	Catholic	290,000
	Protestant	70,000
	Waldorf	45,000
Total	27,523	7,116,147

Max Planck Institutes or the *Fraunhofer Gesellschaft* are registered associations, although they rely almost completely on public funds. At the other end of the spectrum, there are 855 nonprofit open enrolment community colleges with 4.8 million students, and numerous Catholic and Protestant "academies" which organize seminars dealing with a wide range of topics.

Cooperative societies are traditionally well-developed, e. g. the Raiffeisen cooperative concern. There are 8,700 cooperatives, including 3,360 cooperative banks, with a total of 12 million members. Nonprofit building societies represent 8.1% of all house owners, including private homes. Large concerns such as *Neue Heimat* building society, before its partial liquidation among the largest construction contractors world-wide, originated as nonprofit housing societies in the 1950s to meet surging housing demand.

In other areas, the third sector is also represented: Of the 433 professional theaters, 67 are nonprofit resident, and 70 are nonprofit non-resident companies. Of the 19,614 libraries, more than half (8,086) are nonprofit organizations of which the great majority (7,522) belong to the churches. Similarly, about 52% (828) of the 1,586 (major) museums are nonprofit organizations.

Little and inconclusive data are available on volunteerism. The Red Cross (2.5 million members) has 398,053 volunteers, other, similar voluntary associations such as the *Malteser Hilfsdienst*, the *Arbeiter-Samariter-Bund*, and the *Johanniter-Hilfsdienst* gather between 30,000 and 20,000 volunteers each. 900,000 people volunteer in the local fire brigades, and the free welfare associations claim 1.5 to 2 million volunteers. Braun and Röhrig (1986) report that in the mid-1970s, 6% of the population volunteered once a week, and 27% less than once a month. A 1979 survey found that 42% of the adult population had volunteered at least once during the past two years (Institut für Demoskopie 1979). A survey in medium-sized cities by Braun and Röhrig (1986) reached similar conclusions for the mid-1980s.

3.1 Aggregate Measures

Table 3 shows that the nonprofit sector increased its proportion of GNP from about 1% in 1960 to somewhat less than 2% in the mid-1980s. In 1985, nonprofit GNP represented 16% of public GNP and 2.4% of production/industry GNP. It can also be seen that all sectors have expanded at about the same rate since 1960, with public GNP expansion slightly larger than NPO-GNP. As has been observed in other countries (Salamon 1987), the growth patterns of public sector and nonprofit sector are very similar to each other, and both differ from that of the for-profit sector.

However, the data presented in Table 3 should be interpreted with great caution: some services provided by nonprofit organizations are subsumed under different categories. We should recall that the law does not classify

Table 3: Gross Domestic Product by Sector (million DM)

(a) Sector	1960	1970	1980	1984
Public	21,610	62,560	172,390	200,030
NPO	3,170	8,920	25,770	32,780
Production/industry	268,290	551,810	1,115,692	1,366,700
NPO as % of GNP	(1.05%)	(1.32%)	(1.75%)	(1.88%)

in 1980 prices:

(b) Sector	1960	1970	1980	1984
Public	80,810	124,990	172,390	180,550
NPO	13,110	18,570	25,770	29,100
Production/industry	574,610	895,050	1,115,692	1,200,020

1960 = 100

(c) Sector	1960	1970	1980	1984
Public	100	155	213	223
NPO	100	142	196	221
Production/industry	100	156	194	209

Table 4: Investments by Sector (million DM)

Sector	1960	1970	1980	1984
Public	44,740	103,060	100,900	74,100
NPO	6,940	11,440	10,360	9,160
Production/industry	383,300	590,540	678,820	637,440

Table 5: Employment by Sector 1982−1985 (in 1,000 Jobs)

	1982	1983	1984	1985
Total employment	20,471	20,146	20,040	20,378
Of which:				
Churches	108	112	116	120
Other NPOs	224	232	247	265

organizations as profit or nonprofit, but primarily as "economic" or "non-economic" and "public" or "private." National accounts operate similarly: Services which are "non-business, nonprofit services" (*Idealvereine*) are classified as nonprofit (*nicht-erwerbswirtschaftlich*), while business, nonprofit activities (*Wirtschaftsvereine*) enter the "economic," largely for-profit part of GNP. Thus, the GNP contribution of the third sector is underrepresented in national accounts; and the data presented in Tables 3–5 and Figure 1 can be interpreted as most conservative approximations to "true" third sector GNP. Likewise, public GNP is undervalued. It includes the contribution of "core" public administration, legislature, the judiciary, while excluding the 1,139 "economic" associations established under public law (public enterprises) (Himmelmann 1985).

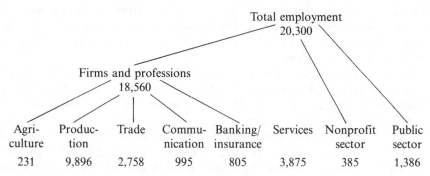

Figure 1: Employment by Sectors in 1985 (in 1,000 Jobs)

While investments have slowed down for all three sectors between 1980 and 1985, investments by the NPO and the public sector have been declining in relative and absolute terms since the 1970. We can assume that the decline in the NPO-sector investment is a result of cuts in public transfers and subventions.

The NPO-sector employment represents about 4% of total employment in industry and manufacture. While is employs more people than agriculture, it provides about half as many jobs as the banking and insurance industry. Note that in Figure 1 the service sector contains the employment provided by business nonprofits.

Since 1982, employment in the nonprofit sector has increased, while overall employment has somewhat declined. Thus, the nonprofit sector has increased its share of total employment from 1.62% in 1982 to 1.88% in 1985. Although a more detailed analysis is needed, we can assume that a considerable proportion of the job increases is the result of publicly subsidized (through the Federal Employment Agency) job provision programs. Hence, while the NPO sector was affected by the recession of the early 1980s and subsequent budget cuts in accordance with the budget balancing act (*Haushaltsstruktur-gesetz*), it also benefited from public sector policies to reduce unemployment. Therefore, some of the increase in third sector employment may well be disguised unemployment through labor subsidization.

3.2 Foundations

Because Germany is a country characterized by political and economic discontinuity over the last two centuries, few of its organizations are older than the foundations. Not surprisingly, the German foundation sector is the product of different historical conditions. Foundations exist in a complex legal environment. Legal and statistical profiles of German foundations are complicated by the absence of a binding legal definition of what constitutes a foundation (sections 80−88 BGB). Thus, the term "foundation" can mean either a foundation, or any of its many legal forms including *ersatz* versions, or even a for-profit firm.

Some of this complexity is introduced by the constitutional status of the churches (section 140 *Grundgesetz* [basic law]; section 41 constitution of Rhineland-Palatinate; sections 142−150 of the Bavarian Constitution). The constitution recognizes the "special status" of the churches and, while avoiding the granting of quasi-governmental rights, grants them far-reaching legal autonomy. As corporations under public law, the churches enjoy internal regulatory autonomy outside the realm the public law, and can act as creator of foundations under church law. By legal implication, church foundations are also foundations under public law. Thus, church foundations form a parallel legal and organizational universe next to "secular" foundations.

Data on German foundations usually refer to "secular" foundations[3]. In 1985, 5,000 "secular" foundations existed, including some 500 family foundations. In addition, there are 5,000 foundations which are not independent legal personalities, such as special collections in a museum (*Museumsstiftung*), corporate foundations (*Betriebsstiftungen*) or for-profit firms, and municipal foundations dependent on city hall. In 1985, the "secular" foundations spent DM 600 million in total grants (about 10−15% of the total grants by U.S. foundations). Not included are the about 40,000 Catholic and 15,000 Protestant church foundations in West Germany. Moreover, in Bavaria, the 1,500 Protestant church foundations form a federation organized under *public* law.

A special case are the political party foundations. With the exception of the Social Democratic Friedrich-Ebert-Foundation (created in 1925), they

---

[3] Data in this section are based on Neuhoff (1978) and Neuhoff, Schindler, and Zwingmann (1983).

are a product of the 1950s when the British and American powers tried to encourage the development of democratic parties and trade unions.

The German foundation sector has been subject to severe disruptions during the last century, in particular the political turmoil following World War I, the economic collapse of the early 1920s, and the Nazi-Period, when foundations faced a very restrictive policy environment.

Although the oldest German foundation dates back to the year 917 (the *Hospitals-Stiftung*), about 40% of all the foundations in the country were founded after 1960. 15% were created in the first post-World War II decade, between 1951 and 1959; and another 15% during the Weimar Republic in the 1920s. About 20% were created in the nineteenth century; 10% between the sixteenth and eighteenth century, with about 100 foundations predating the year 1500. During the 1970s, about 60 new foundations were created, while between 30 to 50 were dissolved each year. In the early 1980s, there has been an increase in the birthrate of foundations: 131 were established in 1983 and 120 in 1984, with only 36 terminations in the course of the two years. In general, since the nineteenth century, the church was replaced by the urban industrialist and individual philanthropists as principal founders, and the state itself has frequently created foundations established under public law and delegated specific functions to them.

Table 6 shows that the number of foundations has increased from about 4,000 to about 5,000. Again, we are reminded that the data base is incomplete and may contain definitional difficulties. This applies to public law foundations in particular, and the fluctuations in numbers may be due to incomplete reporting.

How do foundations compare to other organizational forms in terms of numbers? When compared to the sectoral behavior of stock corporations, foundations have expanded more (Table 6). However, it would be wrong to assume a "dynamic, expansionist" foundation sector. The actual organiza-

Table 6: Number of Foundations by Legal Form

Foundation under	1972	1976	1979	1985*
Civil law	3,751	4,028	4,243	4,500
Public law	551	744	639	500
Total	4,302	4,772	4,882	5,000
number of stock corporations	2,271	2,177	2,139	2,141
limited liability companies	100,690	147,233	225,209	339,541

* 1985 data are estimates.

tional "explosion" occurred neither in the foundation sector, nor among stock corporations, nor in the public sector as such, but among limited liability companies. Between 1972 and 1985, limited liability companies (GmbH, an "economic association") more than tripled in number.

3.3 Associations of Commerce and Business

The creation of economic "interest association" among members/firms in the same trade or industry has a long history in Germany. The guild-like craft associations go back to medieval times, and are better preserved in Germany than in the UK or France. Together, economic associations (*Wirtschaftsverbände*) are perhaps the proto-typical example of liberal corporatism. Compared to other groups, they enjoy privileged treatment in the legislative process. The *Verbände* are represented at parliamentary committees (usually linked to a department or ministry). In the course of the legislative process, committees must schedule hearings at which the *Verbände* can present their case.

Table 7 presents an overview of *Verbände*. In the strength of their political influence, they surpass all other institutions of the third sector, including

Table 7: Associations of Commerce, Industry, Professions, Employers, and Unions

Sector/Type	Number of peak associations	Number of regional associations	Number of other member associations	Number of firms/member associations
Crafts sector	1	41	6,202	492,000 small firms
Crafts branches	66	331	6,176	—
Agriculture	1	56	305	750,000 farms
Industry	2	35	144/355	100,000 larger firms
Professions	1	74	408	?
Trade	1/10	31	336	570,000 firms
Import/export	1	12	42	100,000 firms
Employers	1	12	46/751	?
Unions (DGB)	1	9	17	7,300,000 members

All data reported in Tables 1−7 and Figure 1 are compiled from the Statistisches Jahrbuch (1987).

foundations and the welfare associations. The "business — state" orientation constitutes one of the major characteristics of the German third sector, where the for-profit sector organizes common interests as nonprofit organizations in the third sector. The for-profit sector utilized the third sector to further its political, public sector interests. As von Beyme (1987) remarked, the economic emphasis coexists with a relative paucity of political third sector organizations.

To some degree, the importance of the *"Verbände"* derives from their high participation rate. Weber (1977) reports that 90% of all industrial establishment are members of the Federal Association of German Industry (BDI). The membership of the BDI overlaps with the BDA (The Federal Council of Employers Associations), itself a consortium of 44 "peak" associations, representing a total of 751 member associations. It is estimated that 80% of all (eligible) employers are members of the BDA.

3.4 The Free Welfare Associations

The "free welfare associations" (*freie Wohlfahrtsverbände*) in West Germany are a prime example of the close relationship between corporatist arrangements of the welfare state and the value rationality (*Weltanschaulichkeit*) of the third sector. The five free welfare associations were founded in the nineteenth and early twentieth century, and in the 1920s even the communist party ran its own charity organization, the *Rote Hilfe* (Red Help).

Organized in a "peak" association as the Federal Consortium of Free Welfare (*Bundes-AG der Freien Wohlfahrtspflege*), they run 60,517 institutions in the area of health care, youth and family services, as well as services for the handicapped, elderly, and the poor[4]. They provide 70% of all family services, 60% of all services for the elderly, 40% of all hospital beds, and 90% of all employment for the handicapped. The free welfare associations employ nearly 500,000 full-time and about 175,000 part-time staff. The number of volunteers is estimated to range between 1.5 and 2 million. Operating independently but organizationally linked to its 60,517 institutions are 22,120 self-help groups, clubs, and local voluntary associations. *Caritas* alone employs more people than the industrial conglomerate Siemens, one of the largest employers in the Federal Republic. In 1985, the total reinvestment value of the free welfare associations amounted to 141.2 billion marks; taking provisions for appreciation this amounts to a total net worth of 70 billion marks.

---

[4] Unless otherwise indicated, data in this section is from Bundesarbeitsgemeinschaft der Freien Wohlfahrtspflege (1985).

Each of the free welfare associations represents an institutional response to basic dilemmas (Bauer 1978; Bauer and Dießenbacher 1984; Heinze and Olk 1981): The *Diakonisches Werk* (Protestant), founded as the *"Innere Mission"* (Inner Mission) in 1848/9, developed outside the official Protestant church structures. It began as a welfare-oriented evangelical movement, often in conflict with the secular political world. In contrast, *Caritas*, ideologically grounded in Catholic social ethics and the principle of subsidiarity, developed within the Catholic church and is integrated into the religious hierarchy. *Arbeiterwohlfahrt* (Workers' welfare, secular), founded in 1919, has historically been linked to the Social Democratic Party. For the Social Democrats, who advocated public rather than private welfare provision, the creation of the *Arbeiterwohlfahrt* was a result of a "reconciliation of workers and the capitalist state" (Bauer 1978). The *Zentralwohlfahrtsstelle der Juden in Deutschland* (Jewish) was created in 1917. The *Deutscher Paritätischer Wohlfahrtsverband*, founded in 1920, is a consortium of non-denominational, non-partisan private welfare organizations. Like Jewish welfare associations, the *Deutscher Paritätischer Wohlfahrtsverband* was in part an organizational response to the expansion of denominational and partisan welfare. Finally, the Red Cross, international and humanistic in orientation, is perhaps the most autonomous of the welfare organizations.

The relationship between the free welfare associations and the state is complex and goes well beyond monetary transfers. In the immediate post-World War II era, the allies favored and supported the rapid re-establishment of free welfare associations who they regarded as politically less "suspect" than public welfare organizations. During the Christian Democratic administrations of the 1950s and 1960s, the free welfare associations were able to gain much ground vis-à-vis the state. The Christian Democrats institutionalized the principle of subsidiarity. Today, the free welfare associations occupy a quasi-monopolistic position: For example, since 1961, municipalities or other potential suppliers are barred from establishing child care and youth institutions if the free welfare associations are planning to do so. Alternative suppliers need the consent of the free welfare associations.

While the welfare associations may develop and protect local monopolies, they have also established a cartel at the federal level. For example, foreign workers are "assigned" to different associations which, while leaving the individual little choice, are then exclusively responsible for their well-being. Workers from the predominantly Catholic countries of Italy, Spain, and Portugal are assigned to the Catholic *Caritas*, as are Catholic Croatians from predominantly non-Catholic Yugoslavia. Non-Croatian Yugoslavs, Turks, Moroccans, Tunisians, i. e. those from predominantly Islamic countries, are domain of the secular *Arbeiterwohlfahrt* (workers' welfare). The Protestant *Diakonisches Hilfswerk* serves all the Greeks living in the Federal Republic.

In terms of services and finances, the state and the free welfare associations are closely interrelated. The *Arbeiterwohlfahrt* (workers' welfare) had a total operating budget of about DM 100 million in 1984. According to the (balanced) budget, it spent 40% on "participation in public task of the Federal Government" and received about 45% in public subsidies. Similarly, 25 – 30% of *Diakonisches Hilfswerk* funds come from public subsidies, while the figures for *Caritas* are 25 – 40%.

While acknowledging the immense importance of the free welfare organizations, critics such as Thränhardt (1983) argue that their historical development, which today leaves hardly any aspect of the average citizen's life cycle untouched, is not the result of purposive collective decisions to provide welfare and to cater for the public good. Most of these peak associations originated primarily for political reasons; the legal and social policy rationales of the system were introduced afterwards. They did not develop in a coherent fashion, but are largely unintended consequences of sometimes accidental policy decisions (Bauer and Dießenbacher 1984; Sachse and Tennstedt 1981).

4. Concluding Remarks

The West German third sector is part of a society in which a weakened tradition of political etatism coexists with a strengthened tradition of economic liberalism. Both traditions have impressed their mark on the third sector and shaped its present form. The German case presents a prime example of a third sector which is heavily utilized by both the state (public sector) and the for-profit sector. The German case suggests that political rather than economic motivations lead to the utilization of the nonprofit sector by the state. Economic (usually in the form of joint interests among potential competitors in the same market) rather than political reasons result in the utilization of the nonprofit form by for-profit firms. In this case, the nonprofit sector facilitates the profit-seeking of the for-profit sector.

The third sector does not primarily present the organizational response to both market and state failure only; sometimes, the third sector seems to act as a preventive organizational device to avoid such failures. In segments of the third sector, private and public spheres have become so intertwined that their analytic separation becomes little more than a convenient metaphor.

Organized religion, almost exclusively the Catholic and the Protestant Churches, maintain the largest and politically most protected presence in the third sector and are, historically, its most important part. To some extent, the third sector is both the terrain and result of the conflict between organized religion, political opposition, and the state over the division of labor and spheres of influence.

References

Bauer, R. (1978): *Wohlfahrtsverbände in der Bundesrepublik*, Weinheim, Basel: Beltz.

Bauer, R. and H. Dießenbacher (Eds.) (1984): *Organisierte Nächstenliebe: Wohlfahrtsverbände und Selbsthilfe in der Krise des Sozialstaats*, Opladen: Westdeutscher Verlag.

von Beyme, K. (1987): *Das Politische System der Bundesrepublik Deutschland*, München: Piper.

Braun, J. and P. Röhrig (1986): "Umfang und Unterstützung ehrenamtlicher Mitarbeit und Selbsthilfe im kommunalen Sozial- und Gesundheitsbereich," in *Freiwilliges soziales Engagement und Weiterbildung*, Bundesminister für Bildung und Wissenschaft (Ed.), Bonn: Bundesminister für Bildung und Wissenschaft, 1 – 167.

Bundesarbeitsgemeinschaft der Freien Wohlfahrtspflege (1985): *Gesamtstatistik 1984*, Freiburg: Lambertus.

Bundesministerium der Finanzen (1988): *Gutachten der unabhängigen Sachverständigenkommission zur Prüfung des Gemeinnützigkeits- und Spendenrechtes*, Schriftenreihe Heft 40. Bonn: Bundesministerium der Finanzen.

Douglas, J. (1983): *Why Charity? The Case for a Third Sector*, Beverly Hills: Sage.

Hansmann, H. (1987): "Economic Theories of Nonprofit Organizations," in *The Non-Profit Sector: A Research Handbook*, Walter Powell (Ed.), New Haven: Yale University Press, 27 – 42.

Heinze, R. G. and T. Olk (1981): "Die Wohlfahrtsverbände im System sozialer Dienstleistungsproduktion: Zur Entstehung und Struktur der bundesrepublikanischen Verbändewohlfahrt," *Kölner Zeitschrift für Soziologie und Sozialpsychologie* 1, 94 – 114.

Himmelmann, G. (1985): "Public Enterprises in the Federal Republic of Germany," *Annalen der Gemeinwirtschaft* 3: 365 – 391.

Hodgkinson, V. and M. Weitzman (1984): *Dimensions of the Independent Sector*, Washington, D.C.: Independent Sector.

Institut für Demoskopie (1979): *Die Stellung der freien Wohlfahrtsverbände*, Allensbach: Institut für Demoskopie.

James, E. (1987): "The Non-Profit Sector in Comparative Perspective," in *The Non-Profit Sector: A Research Handbook*, Walter Powell (Ed.), New Haven: Yale University Press, 397 – 415.

Kramer, R. M. (1981): *Voluntary Agencies in the Welfare State*, Berkeley: University of California Press.

Neuhoff, K. (1978): *Stiftungen, §§ 80 – 88 BGB*, Materialien aus dem Stiftungszentrum, 10, Essen: Stiftungszentrum im Stifterverband für die Deutsche Wissenschaft.

Neuhoff, K., A. Schindler, and H. J. Zwingmann (1983): *Stiftungshandbuch*, Baden-Baden: Nomos.

Rimlinger, G. (1971): *Welfare Policy and Industrialization in Europe, America and Russia*, New York: Wiley.

Rudney, G. (1987): "The Scope and Dimensions of Nonprofit Activity," in *The Non-Profit Sector: A Research Handbook*, Walter Powell (Ed.), New Haven: Yale University Press, 55 – 66.

Sachse, Ch. and F. Tennstedt (Eds.) (1981): *Jahrbuch der Sozialarbeit 4*, Reinbek: Rowohlt.

Sachse, Ch. and F. Tennstedt (Eds.) (1986): *Soziale Sicherheit und soziale Disziplinierung*, Frankfurt: Suhrkamp.

Salamon, L. (1987): "Of Market Failure, Voluntary Failure, and Third Party Government: Toward a Theory of Government-Nonprofit Relations in the Modern Welfare State," *Journal of Voluntary Action Research* 16: 29–49.

Statistisches Bundesamt (1987): *Statistisches Jahrbuch 1987*, Mainz: Kohlhammer.

Thränhardt, D. (1984): "Im Dickicht der Verbände. Korporatistische Politikformulierung und verbandsgerechte Verwaltung am Beispiel der Arbeitsmigranten in der Bundesrepublik," in *Organisierte Nächstenliebe: Wohlfahrtsverbände und Selbsthilfe in der Krise des Sozialstaates*, R. Bauer und H. Dießenbacher (Eds.), Opladen: Westdeutscher Verlag.

Weber, J. (1977): *Die Interessengruppen im politischen System der Bundesrepublik Deutschland*, Stuttgart: Kohlhammer.

Weisbrod, B. (1988): *The Nonprofit Economy*, Cambridge, Mass.: Harvard University Press.

4.6
The Role of Nonprofit Organizations in the Spanish Health Care Market

Juan Rovira Forns

1. Introduction

In Spain, as in many other countries, nonprofit organizations (NPOs) have been operating in the health care field for several centuries, especially in the hospital sector, where they continue to have a significant role. In 1985, NPOs owned 27,000 hospital beds (14% of the Spanish total), of which the Catholic church owned 14,400. However, most of the hospital services provided by NPO hospitals are financed by the social security system, which devoted 20% of its health care expenditure in 1985 to the purchase of health care services from external providers.

This paper deals primarily with NPOs providing health care insurance, and more specifically, with organizations which provide a given set of health care services in-kind in exchange for the prepayment of a fixed premium. This latter method prevails in Spain where it comprises 97.7% of health care insurance. In contrast, the monetary reimbursement modality constitutes only 2.3% of the total volume of premiums in the field of Spanish health care insurance (Rovira and Vidal 1987: 34).

Health care organizations can also be classified as "for-profit" or "nonprofit" according to their legal status. Present legislation allows the following kinds of private entities to undertake health care insurance:

(1) Limited Liability Companies

These are profit-oriented organizations where ownership and labor are clearly differentiated. However, not all limited liability corporations make a clear labor/owner distinction. There are, for instance, the *"igualatorios"* which were set up by physicians associations or physicians working in group practices: the *"iguala"* was a lump sum payed by individuals to a physician to cover their medical care needs. This arrangement, widespread in Spain in the past, especially in rural areas, was a *"sui generis"* form of insurance which later evolved into today's group practices.

(2) Mutual Benefit Societies (*Mutuas de Previsión Social*)

MBSs are nonprofit organizations which provide not only health care but also a wide range of social benefits to their members, who usually belong to a given professional group or sector of activity, e. g. lawyers or textile workers. MBSs have a long-standing tradition in the field of social aid, which dates back to the medieval guilds.

(3) Cooperatives

Cooperatives were barred from entering the insurance market until 1985. However, since 1976, the strong cooperative movement has indirectly made its way into the health insurance market through the purchase of commercial insurance companies.

2. Basic Features and Recent Trends in the Spanish Health Insurance Market

Leaving aside some specific features, NPOs are subject to the same kind of regulations and constraints, and face similar problems to those of for-profit organizations. Therefore, in order to understand the role and performance of NPOs, we need to examine the recent evolution and the present situation of the health care insurance industry (Rovira 1986).

The largest system of health care insurance in Spain is the compulsory public insurance scheme run by the social security, which has been growing steadily since it was established in 1942 and which now covers 95% of the Spanish population. The social security system not only finances but also produces most of the health care services provided for its beneficiaries[1]. The services purchased from the private sector by the social security system — mainly hospital and specialized services — amount to only 15% of its global budget.

Since the mid-1960s, private insurers have experienced a period of steady growth which arose partly as a result of the increasing tendency of some special social security regimes to subcontract health care provision to the private health care insurance industry. MUFACE, the social security system for civil servants, established in 1976, and ISFAS, its equivalent for the armed forces, chose to contract-out the health care provision for its members instead of setting up their own facilities. To that end, these special regimes signed agreements with several private insurers as well as with INSALUD. But this factor alone cannot explain the high rate of growth of the health care insurance industry: in 1984, only 7% of the volume of premiums paid belonged to this modality, and the remaining 93% corresponded to voluntary

---

[1] INSALUD is the public agency in charge of the provision of in- and out-patient services to the beneficiaries of the social security.

insurance, the growth of which resulted from the rising purchasing power of the population and to the high priority attached by individuals to the satisfaction of their health needs. The bulk of the insured population were people who had public coverage and voluntarily paid for additional private insurance. A recent survey of the insurance market in Catalonia showed that nearly 20% of the population were covered by voluntary insurance, but only 13% of them had exclusively voluntary insurance: the remaining 87% were covered by compulsory insurance as well.

In other words, 18% of those covered by a compulsory scheme chose to pay for a second insurance in the private market. Tables 1 and 2 show that the relative importance of both voluntary and double coverage is greater for the higher social strata, and for higher income groups.

The willingness of individuals to pay for a second insurance, giving up (partly or wholly) their rights to use the public system, may be explained by reference to the characteristics of the provision of services in the public and private sectors.

Private insurance is probably preferred, because it can provide more individualized treatment than the public system: ease of access, personal treatment, comfortable accommodation.

Tables 3 and 4 show that people with double coverage simultaneously use both systems and sometimes even pay directly for in-patient and out-patient care. The higher use of the social security for out-patient relative to in-patient care results from the unwillingness of private insurance companies to pay for drug treatment; hence, the only way to get subsidized drugs is to obtain a prescription from a social security doctor.

Finally, voluntary insurance has been positively affected by the surplus of doctors, which has kept fees down at a low level and has, hence, allowed insurers to charge moderate premiums; in the fee-for-service modality, physicians receive a fee of around 300 pesetas for an office visit[2]. Thus most of the physicians working for insurance organizations have their main job elsewhere — generally in the public system — and view their collaboration with private insurers as a complementary source of income and a source of future direct payment clients.

Consumer relationship to health insurance is by no means uniform. If we assume a certain degree of correspondence between the monetary value of the risks covered for the consumers and the premiums charged, we can see that the average premium varies from 2,000 to 20,000 pesetas per year depending on the insurer (Male and Dalmau 1986), which highlights the heterogeneous nature of the good "health care insurance."

---

[2] As a point of reference for comparison, the cost of a liter of milk is about 100 pesetas, and a haircut ranges between 500 and 1,000 pesetas.

Table 1: Type of coverage by social status (%)

	Social Status				
	High	Med/High	Med	Med/Low	Low
1. Social security	88	86	95	94	92
2. Social security and private insurance	33	32	20	11	6
3. Private insurance alone	3	6	2	2	2
4. Percentage of individuals covered by social security that buy also private insurance (2/1%)	37.5 (2,199)	37.2 (5,916)	21.0 (25,571)	11.7 (18,127)	6.5 (8,982)

Source: Instituto DYM, S.A. (1984).

Table 2: Type of Coverage by Family Income Level (%)

	Income (10^3 Ptas.)					
	More than 120	100−120	80−100	60−80	40−60	less than 40
% Private insurance	40	23	26	16	14	15
% Special s.s. regimes	7	1	4	4	2	1
% Social security	87	97	92	95	95	89
% Private insurance alone	5	2	2	1	2	3
% Special s.s. regime alone	58	75	71	82	84	88
% Double coverage	35	22	24	15	12	11
% Double coverage/public coverage	37.6 (3,601)	22.5 (3,113)	25.2 (4,829)	15.3 (9,602)	12.8 (12,810)	12.5 (10,100)

Source: Instituto DYM, S.A. (1984).

The bimodal distribution centering at the 6−8,000 and at the 14−16,000 intervals suggests that there might be at least two clearly differentiated segments in the health care insurance market: those consumers with partial coverage of a limited set of health risks, and those with comprehensive coverage. The former are probably either users from low-income groups who have no compulsory coverage, or people under compulsory coverage who use voluntary insurance as a complementary option only when they need some specific type of service. The latter seem more likely to be people who

Table 3: Utilization of In-patient Services by Type of Coverage

	Private insurance	Special s.s. regime	Social security	Social security + private insurance
% of respondents admitted to an in-patient service in the last three months	3	3	2	2
	(1,528)	(1,125)	(45,897)	(10,224)
Type of financing %				
Out of pocket	—	—	7	23
Private insurance	100	36	2	40
Social security	—	48	88	32
Other	—	15	3	5
	(39)	(36)	(1,120)	(247)

Source: Instituto DYM, S.A. (1984).

Table 4: Utilization of Out-patient Services by Type of Coverage

	Private insurance	Special s.s. regime	Social security	Social security + private insurance
% of respondents that visited a doctor in last two weeks	12	25	21	19
	(1,528)	(1,123)	(45,897)	(10,224)
Type of service in the last visit (%)				
Direct out of pocket payment	37	8	8	17
Private insurance	38	45	1	20
Social security	16	25	90	61
Other	10	22	1	2
	(188)	(278)	(9,765)	(1,946)

Source: Instituto DYM, S.A. (1984).

do not make use of the social security insurance, to which they may indeed be entitled in most cases.

There are two types of insurance modalities according to the mode of payment to the doctors, namely, capitation and fee-for-service. Most insurers sell only one type of insurance, but in recent years, an increasing number of insurers have been switching from the capitation mode of payment to the fee-for-service modality. The fee-for-service modality usually implies a larger group of physicians and, hence, a wider range of options for the insured to choose from and therefore a higher perceived quality. The premiums for fee-for-service are significantly higher than for the capitation modality, and, in general, there seems to be a strong association between level of premium, modality of payment, and the (perceived) quality of the services insured.

Before 1984, the health insurance market worked under a high degree of state regulation. Prices and products were strictly controlled by the government; the insurers were compelled to offer policies covering a minimum set of services which were supposed to protect the insurant against basic health risks. However, supplementary policies for specific services could be offered without restriction, although the state fixed the premiums both for the "minimum packages" and for the supplementary services. The stated objective of this interventionism was the protection of the consumers, but the consequences were negative for both consumers and insurers. As the rising cost of medical care could not always be translated into premium increases, the quantity and/or quality of the services diminished, and some insurers who did not increase their premiums experienced financial difficulties. Other insurers were able to bypass the price controls by inducing their subscribers to contract an increasing number of supplementary services which usually produced a higher financial surplus than the compulsory "minimum packages." Moreover, the establishment of "minimum packages" forced some consumers to pay for services they did not really want.

A new insurance law deregulated the sector in 1984, which removed most restrictions on the content of policies and the level of premiums. However, no major changes seem to have taken place up to now in the types of policies offered by the insurers or in the distribution of the existing types of policies sold. The long period of state interventionism has probably lowered the level of entrepreneurial dynamism and innovative capacity in the sector, and insurers tend to stick to traditional operating patterns. Moreover, they fear that the promotion of specific policies, tailored to the needs of some segments of the market, may induce subscribers to exchange their present comprehensive policies for more specific and cheaper ones, thus reducing their global revenues.

3. NPOs in the Health Care Insurance Market

The first paragraphs of this section describe the evolution and basic features of the two types of NPOs operating in the health care insurance market. The third paragraph analyses their performance in comparison with for-profit companies.

3.1 Cooperatives in Health Care Insurance

Cooperativism in the field of health insurance began in 1976, when LAVI-NIA, a doctors' cooperative, was set up. In 1977, LAVINIA became the sole owner of ASISA, an existing health care insurance company, as the law did not allow cooperatives to operate in the insurance business. A similar strategy was adopted by *Autogestión Sanitaria*, another doctors' cooperative which acquired the health insurance company ASCSA. By 1985, LAVINIA had 18,000 medical doctors as members and provided comprehensive health care to about 700,000 subscribers, while *Autogestión Sanitaria* had 3,500 members and 200,000 subscribers, that is a joint membership of 977,000 persons, 2.7% of the Spanish population; their market share rose between 1977 and 1985 from 13.6 to 20.0% (Camarasa, Oso, and Diez 1986).

Insurance cooperatives — like most health care insurers — do not own health care facilities, but contract-out medical and hospital services with private and sometimes public providers whom they pay on a fee-for-service basis. However, in 1974, the ASCSA group set up a consumers' cooperative, whose membership is practically coincident with that of the group, which started the construction of hospitals to serve the hospitalization needs of the ASCSA members.

The basic principles of the cooperative movement are fee-for-service mode of payment to the doctors and the freedom of the consumers to choose their physicians; these, they argue, are necessary requisites for a confident relationship between doctor and patient. Their strategy, up to now, has been to present themselves as a global alternative to public provision, which they deem to be bureaucratic, inefficient, and insensitive to the patients' expectations and needs. The cooperatives already compete directly with INSALUD for the provision of health care for civil servants and the armed forces. They are now lobbying to expand the competition to provide health care to all social security beneficiaries. They claim that nine out of ten social security beneficiaries in the army and the civil service choose private provision, which should be the proof of the superiority of private over public arrangements (Espriu 1986).

3.2 Mutual Benefit Societies (MBS)

In 1984, the population subscribing to MBSs accounted for 1,024,000 people, or 2.7% of the Spanish population. However, MBSs market share diminished from 20 to 15% of the global health care insurance market between 1977 and 1984. The reasons for this decline are probably twofold: demographics and conservative management. On the one hand, structural changes in the economy have resulted in a decline of certain occupations and a progressive ageing of others, consequently causing reduced incomes and increased expenditures, sometimes substantial financial losses, and even bankruptcy. On the other hand, many, though not all, MBS managements have not adapted to changing environments and users' needs. One prominent exception is the *"Quinta de Salud La Alianza,"* which collects more than half of the volume of premiums of the MBS subsector.

Another indication of MBSs' decline is the increasing dependence of MBS hospitals and other facilities on external sources of finance. For instance, 75% of the hospitalizations that took place in 1984 in the MBS hospitals in Catalonia were financed by the social security and 50% of their funds came from the social security budget.

3.3 The Performance of NPOs

What is the role of the NPOs in the Spanish health insurance market? What is the rationale for their existence?

Both types of NPOs — MBSs and cooperatives — in the Spanish health care market are of the entrepreneurial-commercial kind, as defined in Hansmann's classification (Young 1983: 12). Weisbrod suggested that the failure of the state to provide public goods encourages the existence of NPOs (1975, 1977). This hypothesis may explain the origin of MBSs, whose establishment preceded the large-scale governmental provision of health care insurance in Spain. But with the growth of public (social security) provision and coverage, MBSs have moved towards a more "private" kind of health care provision, characterized by shorter waiting times, more personal treatment, and private rooms. MBSs share this market niche, left by the public system, with the cooperatives and the for-profit organizations.

However, Weisbrod's hypothesis seems unable to explain the existence of cooperatives which began operation when social security was already in existence. These cooperatives were promoted by the providers, such as physicians, unlike the MBSs which were encouraged by the consumers. From the start, they presented themselves as a more "human" approach to health care when compared to the "bureaucratic" social security.

Nevertheless, their origin and stated goals — especially the fee-for-service principle — leads one to believe that they may be "profit maximizers in disguise" (Weisbrod 1975: 173). While this may seem paradoxical in view of the low fees that the cooperatives pay to their members, it becomes more understandable when one takes into account the excess supply and unemployment in the Spanish medical services market. Moreover, the physicians working in cooperatives may be receiving important intangible benefits in the form of a preferred mode of practice (fee-for-service) which is more akin to the prevailing ideology of the physicians, who in spite of progressive salarization, prefer to see themselves as liberal professionals.

However, given the profit maximization, albeit hidden, of MBSs and cooperatives, how can we explain their insistence on promoting their image as nonprofit providers? Perhaps they assume, as Young argues, that consumers prefer nonprofit organizations in areas of activity where the consumers are disadvantaged in their ability to discern or evaluate the quality of service (Young 1983: 14), i. e. because the higher trustworthiness of nonprofit organizations in relation to their proprietary (and perhaps also public-sector) counterparts. Nevertheless, empirical evidence does not show that the performance of NPOs meets this hypothesized trustworthiness. Moreover, the behavior of physicians is already assumed to be controlled by professionalism through ethical codes and professional standards. Finally, it is by no means evident that consumers associate nonprofit status with a higher degree of honesty and trustworthiness, that they distrust the profit motive, or that they are even aware of the profit or nonprofit status of the competing health care insurers.

It has also been argued that NPOs tend to produce outputs of higher quality, because in the absence of a direct incentive to maintain low costs, professionals prefer high standards. However, and aside from the difficulties of unambiguously defining quality in health insurance, it is more likely that the specific traits of private insurance reflect the aspects of the demand which the consumers cannot satisfy free of charge in the public sector.

To sum up, the main function of NPOs in the Spanish health care insurance market seems to be the satisfaction, in competition with their for-profit counterparts, of the demand for "private" health care insurance, which is not satisfied by the public system.

4. The Future of the Private Insurance Sector

By 1981, the expansion of the private insurance market seemed to have levelled off, and some signs of recession appeared. In 1984, compulsory public coverage was extended to self-employed workers (about 1.5 million people) who had previously been free to join the public insurance on a voluntary basis. (About two thirds of them had chosen private or self-insurance.) As a result of their compulsory incorporation into the public system, most of them gave up their private insurance, causing the number of subscribers in the private sector to decline for the first time in many years. The decreasing trend continued in the years that followed.

The future development of the private sector depends essentially on a set of factors whose evolution is not easy to predict: (a) the development of family income; (b) the quality of and access to the public system; (c) the response of the private sector to the new options opened by recent legislative changes; and (d) the development of health policy directly related to the private insurance sector.

The evolution of family income will have a great impact on the behavior of consumers. The public coverage of about 95% of the population, which, moreover, is expected to become universal in the near future, makes voluntary insurance a luxury good, and therefore, highly sensitive to family income.

The quality of and access to public health care depends on the willingness of the government to increase the resources devoted to the public system and on the ability of the latter to manage their resources in an efficient way.

Managerial skills are rather unevenly distributed across the insurance sector. In the last few years, a large number of organizations have disappeared or have been absorbed. This concentration is likely to continue, because many entities are too small to afford the best professional management. Others, however, will adapt to new challenges and will develop new marketing and pricing strategies to take advantage of the opportunities offered by the changing environment.

However, health policy developments may be the most significant factor for the future of private insurance. The recent liberalization of insurance activities has removed some of the obstacles that prevented its growth. But if private insurance has to be paid − as it is now − by consumers, its future expansion is likely to be very limited. On the other hand, given present financial restraints on the public budget and political priorities directed at equity and cost containment, changes in the policy of the social security regarding the contracting-out of health insurance is unlikely to occur.

If those covered by the social security had the option of choosing between private and public providers − even if the former option meant some direct co-payment by the consumers −, most likely the first to take advantage of the option would be those who already have voluntary insurance and are giving up their right to use the public services to which they are entitled. This would increase social security expenditure, as it should compensate private insurers for those beneficiaries opting out of public provision in favor of private provision, with no significant decrease in the utilization of its resources. In other words, the main impact of such a policy would be a net transfer of income from the social security budget to those individuals who now have a double coverage, most of whom belong to the higher income groups; this would, of course, mean a negative redistribution of income.

It may be argued that negative redistribution is the unavoidable cost of a greater freedom of choice and − at least in the long run − increased efficiency. The freedom-of-choice argument is to a great extent an ideological issue which cannot be discussed on empirical grounds; but the revealed preference of the members of MUFACE − 90% of the MUFACE population choose private provision − cannot be taken as conclusive evidence of its superiority, since the product offered by each sector is not the same, and adverse selection may be present. Furthermore, since little is know about costs, especially in the public sector, we can draw no conclusions about the relative efficiency of the two sectors.

The popular saying "more research is needed before something reliable can be said about it" again fits perfectly to this issue. However, there is one remarkable fact which seems to be well supported by the empirical evidence: real per capita health expenditure decreased between 1977 and 1985 in the MUFACE system, while it was experiencing an increasing trend both in the voluntary insurance sector and in the compulsory insurance systems with public provision (Rovira 1987). This can hardly be attributed to any other factors but the practice by MUFACE of contracting-out health insurance to the private sector. Unfortunately, it is not possible to determine whether this decrease has meant a reduction in the quantity or quality of the services provided.

5. The Future Role of NPOs in the Spanish Health Care System

What are the specific features of NPOs in this sector? Present legislation seems to favor NPOs over for-profit organizations: The Spanish Constitution established in 1978 recognizes, as well as the right of health professionals to free practice, the principle of free enterprise in the health care sector; moreover, the Health Care Law (*Ley General de Sanidad*), approved by Parliament in 1986, stipulates guidelines for the establishment of a universal and publically financed National Health System, and sets up the basic criteria for collaboration between the Public Health Administration and the private health care sector. This collaboration may take the form of contracting-out agreements, among others. In the contracting-out of health services, priority will be given to nonprofit organizations, when similar conditions of efficacy, quality, and costs to those of "for-profit" prevail. The Health Care Law also commits the Health Administration to fostering the activities of health care consumers' associations, NPOs, and health care cooperatives.

In April 1987, the Spanish Parliament passed a Cooperative Act which allows cooperatives to operate directly in the health insurance market, thus opening new opportunities for their future development. However, no further steps have yet been taken to develop and implement collaboration between cooperatives and Public Health Administrations. The Government has a high degree of discretionary power to shape this collaboration within the guidelines laid down in the present legislation.

It is not clear — leaving aside purely ideological preferences — why NPOs are, or should be, privileged by health care legislation. Mutual benefit societies charge, on average, lower premiums than commercial insurers, but this should not necessarily be attributed to more efficient management. It might also be the effect of selection biases, lower quantity or quality of the services provided, or of their generalized use of the capitation modality, which is cheaper than the fee-for-service one.

One possible advantage of NPOs, as opposed to for-profit organizations, is their reduced incentive to adopt undesirable behavior aimed at maximizing profits; for example, they may be less inolined to discriminate against high-cost patients or more willing to provide all the care that might be needed from a clinical point of view, regardless of the cost. On the other hand, lack of profit objectives could also mean a reduced commitment to efficiency. Moreover, working for NPOs can increase professional satisfaction if the providers feel that financial considerations are less likely to conflict with the independence of their clinic. Finally, providers' cooperatives can create an adequate financial structure for group practicioners, which apparently leads to a higher cost-consciousness and efficiency. In these settings, providers have a financial incentive and framework for peer-review and other forms of group control and incentives for efficiency.

References

Camarasa, J., A. Oso, and T. Diez (1986): *Efectos económicos y asistenciales del cooperativismo sanitario como combinación del sector público y privado*, Communication presented at the VI Jornadas de Economía de la Salud, Valencia, May 1986.

Direcció General D'Assistència Sanitària de la Generalitat de Catalunya (1981): "Encuesta a las Entidades de asistencia médico-farmacéutica," Barcelona, unpublished manuscript.

Espriu, J. (1986): *Cooperativisme sanitari,* Barcelona.

Guerrero de Castro, M. (1986): "El seguro de asistencia sanitaria y sus principales problemas," *Hacienda Publica Española* 98 (abril), 207 − 232.

Instituto DYM, S. A. (1984): *Informe Estudi La Salut a Catalunya*, unpublished report, Barcelona.

Male, A. and J. S. Dalmau (1986): "Assistència sanitària en règim d'assegurança lliure a Catalunya," *Gaseta Sanitària de Barcelona* 27, may − june, 97 − 104.

Ministerio de Hacienda (1985): *Estadística del Seguro Privado*, Madrid: Ministerio de Hacienda.

Rovira, J. (1986): "El seguro voluntario de asistencia sanitaria en España: apuntes para un debate," Communication presented at VI Jornadas de Economía de la Salud, Valencia, May.

Rovira, J. (1987): "Estudi sobre l'assistència sanitària en règim d'assegurança lliure a Catalunya," Barcelona, unpublished report.

Rovira, J. and I. Vidal (1987): *Posibilidades de desarrollo del cooperativismo sanitario español*, Madrid: Gabinete de Estudios y Promoción del Cooperativismo Sanitario.

Weisbrod, B. A. (1975): "Toward a Theory of the Voluntary Nonprofit Sector in a Three-Sector Economy," in *Altruism, Morality and Economic Theory*, E. S. Phelps (Ed.), New York: Russell Sage Foundation, 171–195.

Weisbrod, B. A. (1977): *The Voluntary Nonprofit Sector,* Lexington, Mass., Toronto: Lexington Books.

Young, D. R. (1983): *If Not for Profit, for what?* Lexington, Mass., Toronto: Lexington Books.

4.7
Traditional Neighborhood Associations in Industrial Society: The Case of Japan

Anna Maria Thränhardt

1. Introduction

In his best-seller, *Japan as Number One — Lessons for America*, Ezra F. Vogel (1980: 203) summarized the success of Japanese welfare:

"The Japanese have been able to provide for the well-being of their population without requiring many except the very old and infirm to become economically dependent on the state, and they have done it in such a way as to reinforce their communitarian ideals."

Some of the central institutional expressions of this "communitarian ideal" are the organized neighborhood associations (*chōnaikai/jichikai*)[1], which can be found all over rural and urban Japan. For mainly historical reasons, which will be discussed below, the *jichikai* have no legal base. The following sections describe the neighborhood associations themselves, their history, structure, functions, and socio-cultural background. The final section discusses new models of cooperation between municipalities and traditional neighborhood associations, and evaluates the integration of traditional institutions such as the *jichikai* into the Japanese public welfare system.

2. Neighborhood Associations and the Welfare System

As a result of various historical and political factors, neighborhood associations are not included in the basic structure of Japanese welfare institutions.

---

[1] Neighborhood associations exist under very different names, the most popular of which are *chonaikai* (urban ward associations) for associations founded before World War II, and *jichikai* (self-governing associations) for groups organized after the War. Some of the older organizations changed their names after the War to *jichikai* because of the more democratic connotations of this expression. I shall use this term throughout my paper, even if the actual name of the neighborhood association I refer to is different.

In order to understand the relationship between the *jichikai* and the welfare state, we have to consider the cultural background which shaped the origins of the Japanese welfare system: the reforms connected with the "Meiji-Restoration" of 1868. It was a time of far-reaching, even revolutionary, changes in Japan's political, economic, and administrative system, all of which aimed at the modernization of Japan. The predominant political-cultural orientation of that period was to the West, and the area of social policy was no exception. In the proclamation of the first social law of 1871, the "Relief Regulations", the Meiji central government copied Bismarck's social welfare system: both, Germany and Japan, at that time, had to cope with the pauperization of the rural population which resulted from early industrial development. Furthermore, while it developed, the whole structure of social law continued to reflect the German influence, as it centered around the people's economic role rather than their political role.

At the institutional level, the most striking import was that of the *"Elberfelder System"* of communal welfare commissioners (*minsei-iin*) in 1918. This model, created in the second half of the nineteenth century in the textile city of Elberfeld (now Wuppertal) in Germany, was Germany's first systematic attempt to control poverty on the local level. The system divided urban areas into welfare wards, each of which was supervised by appointed honorary welfare commissioners (*ehrenamtliche Bezirkswohlfahrtspfleger*). The commissioners, mostly local notables, decided whether to provide money in cases of emergency such as the sickness or unemployment of the breadwinner. However, they mainly emphasized counseling and helping people to return to a "decent life."

This system, once it was introduced nationwide, expanded to become one of the main pillars of Japan's non-governmental sector (Thränhardt 1987). While it is firmly based in the associational structures of *"jichikai,"* this German influence system did not formally include the institution of *jichikai* in the Japanese welfare system.

The next important steps towards the modern Japanese welfare state occurred after World War II. This, again, was an era of intense Western influence, this time by the United States, who, as an occupying power after Japan's defeat in the Pacific War, shaped the welfare system according to its own ideas and concepts. Article 25 of the new Japanese Constitution, which was imposed by the United States, guarantees: "All people shall have the right to maintain minimum standards of wholesome and cultured living" ... and "The State must take effort to promote and expand social welfare, social security and public health services to cover every aspect of the life of the people." The assumption of state responsibility led to the six basic social welfare laws, which were introduced in the following years:

1946/50   Public Assistance Law
1947   Child Welfare Law
1949   Law for the Welfare of Physically Handicapped Persons
1960   Law for the Welfare of Mentally Retarded Persons
1963   Law for the Welfare of the Aged
1964   Law for Maternal and Child Welfare.

Supplementing these laws were the Social Welfare Service Law of 1951 and the Community Welfare Volunteer Law (*minsei-iin hō*) of 1946, which was revised in 1948. However, it is important to note that no legal provisions were made to regulate *jichikai* within the welfare system.

Since the mid-1970s, however, paradigmatic shifts occured within Japan's welfare policy: shocked by the economic consequences of the 1973 oil crisis and disillusioned by the apparent problems of the Western model of the welfare state, the Japanese, burdened with huge budget deficits rediscovered their own traditions in order to confront the problems and mouting costs of the welfare state.

Table 1: Government Expenditure and National Burden, 1970–1981 (Ratio to National Income, %)

Year	Government expenditure	Fiscal burden rate	Social security transfers	Public bond interest cost	Final consumption	Public investment	Others
1970	24.0	24.8	5.8	0.7	9.3	5.7	2.5
1973	26.9	27.6	6.5	1.1	10.1	6.4	2.8
1976	34.1	27.5	10.6	2.0	12.2	6.4	2.9
1979	39.5	31.4	12.4	2.4	12.3	7.9	4.5
1980	40.9	32.8	12.9	4.1	12.5	7.7	3.7
1981	42.7	34.3	13.7	4.7	12.8	7.7	3.8

Note: Fiscal burden rate is tax rate and social security contribution.
Source: Economic Planning Agency, *Keizai hakusho* (1983: 359).

In their search for a "Japanese Model of a Welfare Society" (*Nihongata fukushi shakai*), they stressed the necessity of less state intervention and urged taking advantage of Japanese self-help traditions. As happened in other OECD countries at that time, attention shifted to the communal level. In contrast to the rest of the OECD, Japan could rely on a rich local associational tradition, which had not been destroyed by modernization and urbanization. But Japan's emphasis on *jichikai* as a means of providing social services at low costs is not without controversy.[2] While there is a general reluctance to go back to "feudal" or pre-industrial forms of social organization, it is primarily the recent history of *jichikai* in the 1930s and 1940s that produces ideological barriers.

3. The Ideological Legacy of Japanese Neighborhood Associations

In the literature, Japanese neighborhood associations have often been linked to pre-industrial forms of hamlet organizations in rural Japan or to traditional merchant associations. Nakamura (1979: 19), however, shows that almost three quarters of the neighborhood associations in Tokyo have been established since 1923, and that only 2% existed before industrialization at the turn of the nineteenth century. The establishment of many neighborhood associations in the 1920s and 1930s is linked to the problems connected with rapid urbanization and unprecedented economic growth. Although most local groups were created independently by local initiative (Bestor 1985: 125), the government supported their emergence in order to mobilize traditional values in the increasingly urban society.

In 1938, neighborhood associations finally received legal recognition (Steiner 1965: 219) and were soon incorporated into the emerging centralized, militaristic, and authoriarian system of the "Greater East Asian Prosperity Sphere." In 1940, all communities were compelled to form neighborhood associations with compulsory membership. During the war, the totalitarian government used them as instruments of propaganda and control, but they also served as agencies to distribute food and staple goods.

In 1947, the neighborhood associations were proscribed by the American Military Government because of their wartime role, although a minority within the American Advisory Committee had suggested preserving them as instruments for the democratization of new Japan (Braibanti 1948). In reality, the neighborhood associations continued to exist in a *subrosa* form under various different names, such as "crime prevention league" or "fire protection league." In the 1950s, they re-surfaced as *"jichikai"* (self-governing associations) legally independent of the government. In 1981, a nationwide survey counted 270,000 neighborhood associations and showed that more than half of the neighborhood groups were founded after World War II (*Shinseikatsu undō kyōkai 1982*, 85/1).

---

[2] For an illustrative description of the use the conservative ruling party LDP makes of *jichikai* structures in rural parts of Japan, see Curtis (1983: passim).

4. *jichikai* (Neighborhood Associations)

jichikai consist of the inhabitants of a locally defined area, ranging between 180 and 400 households. Their average size of about 200 households (ca. 800 individuals) allows the establishment of good face-to-face connections. In densely inhabited Tokyo, the defined area may be quite small, since eight hundred people may live in an area of about 200 m × 400 m.

Because membership is automatic, all households are usually members, although the level of active participation varies. The leaders and other functional offices are democratically elected, generally every two years, although, since there are few restrictions on reelection, long terms of incumbency often occur. In many cases, leadership posts are held by local notables which, according to some critics, makes the neighborhood association merely a stronghold of conservative thinking. However, as Allinson (1980: 122) shows, in a progressive environment, *jichikai* can also be mobilized by progressive politicians.

At the local level, the *jichikai* are a dynamic factor in daily life: "The presence of formally constituted groups provides a focus within which informal ties multiply, and local institutions reinforce the neighborhood's density of networks by providing convenient, generally recognized social boundaries" (Bestor 1985: 128). The *jichikai*, however, are not the only organized neighborhood groups: a range of sub-groups, as well as nominally independent groups, interlink with one another, thus forming the fabric of social life in the ward: Traditionally, the most important functional sub-groups are the merchants' associations (*shotenkai*) in urban areas and the farmers' associations (*nōsei rengokai*) in rural districts. The former represent the common interests of local merchants and would, for instance, oppose the construction of a new supermarket in a local area. Or they arrange the floral decorations in shopping districts to attract customers, or install common signboards in the main street to publicize their shops. The farmers' associations in villages and small rural towns play a central role in the organization of communal agrarian life; for example, by regulating the water distribution in rice-paddy cultivation. But with the reduced importance of rural society in Japan, and the changed production patterns (of all farm households in 1986, only 14.8% were exclusively engaged in agricultural work), the *social* importance of farmers' associations has declined. In contrast, the *political* role of *jichikai* in rural regions still seems strong and tends to serve as an organizational basis for the conservative Liberal Democratic Party.[3]

---

[3] This fact reduced acceptance of *jichikai* among Japanese social scientists. For this problem, compare Nakamura (1968: 188) and Thränhardt (forthcoming).

Women's groups (*fujimbu*) are a third sub-group, which have recently become more important. Women's role in the public sphere is gradually becoming accepted. In addition, the *jichikai* are central to women's lives, especially when childrearing reduces their mobility. *Fujimbu* arrange most social activities and hobby groups (see below) and organize services such as special-garbage collections, cooperative consumers' groups (which play a great part in controlling the quality of products in Japan), and fundraising for the Community Chest.

The seniors' groups (*rōjinkai*) and youth club (*seinenkai*) reflect traditional Japanese preference for cohort-specific associations. They engage in activities similar to the one offered by Christian parishes for old people in the West or the traditional sports clubs (*Sportvereine*) in Germany, mainly addressing young people. Since World War II, a separate, centralized movement for old people, the Seniors' Clubs (*rōjin kurabu*), have emerged. They were initiated by the Council of Social Welfare of the City of Osaka in 1951, and have been influenced by Britain's "old people's clubs"[4]. This movement, subsidized by the central government since 1963, expanded greatly in the following years. But having given financial support, the central government then sought to define the aims and content of the work of these seniors' clubs, in which they mostly were successful (Linhart 1983: 29).

For special activities, there are special committees: festival committees (*sairei-iin*) organize the annual local shrine festival (see 5.1), the health and sanitary committees (*eisei rengokai*) work together with municipal health-authorities to carry out desinfection and other hygienic campaigns, while the social welfare committees (*shakai fukushi-iin*), in charge of. fundraising for welfare purposes, plan the yearly "old people's" day and maintain connection to the officially appointed *minseiiin*.

Contacts also exist with other groups represented in the neighborhood itself or in the region, such as: the Parent-Teacher Associations (*PTA*), the local alumni clubs (*d-ōsokai*), voluntary fire brigades (*shobodan*), and politicians' support groups (*kōenkai*).

5. Functions of *jichikai*

The neighborhood associations have several social-economic, political, and administrative functions:

---

[4] In 1952, a Japanese translation of the official handbook *"Old People's Clubs"* by the British Committee for the Welfare of the Aged was published (Linhart 1983: 26).

5.1 Social-Economic Functions

Central to *jichikai*, social-economic activities is helping neighbors and people in the ward who are financially in need or struck by the accident, illness, or death of a family member. Or, as in the often related case, the *jichikai* organizes cooperative help for rebuilding a neighbor's house which has burnt down. In addition, most *jichikai* own a meeting place and might give short-term shelter to homeless families. The meeting place is usually the center for various hobby-groups, such as flower-arrangement circles, choral singing, folk dance, and similar activities, that involve local people, particularly women. (These activities are comparable to the social activities offered by Christian parishes in Western countries.) Once a year, a trip is arranged to a sightseeing spot or to one of the popular hot springs with its relaxed, sociable atmosphere. Or they may conduct excursions to playgrounds for children or check-ups of all the bicycles. In more traditional neighborhood associations, the festival of the local Shinto shrine is a high point of communal activity, and virtually all members are involved in its preparation and performance. On this occasion, a portable shrine is carried through the neighborhood, the borders of which are to be regarded carefully. Trespassing into the territory of an adjacent *jichikai* must be negotiated beforehand, and any members' unplanned detours into "foreign" territory during the festival are usually followed by an apology from the festival committee. This shows the highly symbolic value of this parade as an occasion for local identification and territorial demarcation (Bestor 1985: 131).

5.2 Lobby-Group Functions

Neighborhood associations provide an organizational vehicle for political lobbying and social mobilization. They might unite to support the construction of a new underground station, or to oppose the establishment of a "love-hotel," as occurred in a neighborhood association near Kyoto. In the latter case, members of the *jichikai*, upon noticing that their base of only one neighborhood association was too small, combined with the more influential local parent-teacher association (which encompassed three neighborhood associations) to negotiate with the local administration.[5]

The lobby-group function is of special importance for tenants in large appartment buildings, where the *jichikai* act mainly as a tenants' association against the big housing corporations (Kiefer 1976).

Environmental protection groups, especially in rural regions, have usually been successful once they secured the support of local neighborhood associations. In this case, it is the social acceptance and the identification of the

[5] Personal interview with the leader of the PTA in Otsu, Prof. Arifuku.

individual with the group that enables usually conservative people to oppose the accepted authorities (McKean 1976).

To understand this, we have to call to mind the different value structure of Japanese society, which — in contrast to Western individualistic thinking — esteems highly the aims and welfare of a group and tends to sanction individual solutions as "egoistic" and detrimental to group harmony. In section 7, I shall discuss the cultural background of this different social value system in more detail.

5.3 Administrative Functions

The third major function addresses the relationship between local administration and the *jichikai*. The neighborhood associations usually carry out quasi-official activities on behalf of the local administration. First, the association passes on information to the inhabitants, either by leaflets distributed to every household, or, in important cases, by a circulation system called *"kairamban"* in which every family, having read the document, has to put its seal on the bottom of the information sheet. The latter system has a long tradition in Japan and is designed to make sure (and prove, of course) that everybody has "officially" taken notice.

In many cases, the *jichikai* is in charge of the family registry, a duty fulfilled by registration offices in other countries.

jichikai also help to carry out public opinion polls on behalf of the communal administration, and once a month the *jichikai* obliges everyone to help clean the open sewage canals. Further activities common in most neighborhood associations are hygienic compaigns, earthquake drills, and the fire-watch walk (often together with the local police officer) every night. Special garbage campaigns or campaigns for more politeness in the ward can also be implemented on this level.

6. Financing of *jichikai*

The legal "non-existence" of the *jichikai* has financial consequences: They receive no funding from the central government. According to a nation-wide survey (*Shinseikatsu undō kyōkai* 1982, 95, 96), the annual income of the *jichikai* ranges from less than 10,000 Yen to more than 5 million Yen, the average income ranging between 500,000 Yen and 1 million Yen ($ 3,200 – $ 6,500). While many older neighborhood associations own property, such as woodlands, lakes, or real estate, generally the income stems from monthly membership fees ranging from less than 200 Yen to more than

1,000 Yen in a few cases (i. e. about US $ 2 – 10). On average, monthly fees amount to 200 – 300 Yen and are normally paid by all members. In many cases, *jichikai* receive financial support from the municipal administration, either as allowance for their meeting place or as pay for assuming local government functions. There are no exact data to permit an overall evaluation of these contributions, but roughly they constitute less than 10% of the budget. Thus the financial dependency of neighborhood associations on local governments is minimal.

7. The Cultural Background: Confucianism

Participation in neighborhood associations demands a comparatively large commitment, not only financially but also in terms of time and labor. To the Western observer, the degree to which the Japanese are *expected* to engage, and *actually do* engage in neighborhood activities is a matter of great astonishment. This can be explained by the different cultural background of Japan. Confucianism, unlike Christianity, urges socialization towards the group, not the individual. While in Western culture, self-realization is a central value, in Japanese society, the most important social assets are cooperation and willingness to adjust to the group.

The model for social relations is the family system (*ieseido*) which, with its strong Confucian elements, demands life-long dedication to prescribed roles in social intercourse. Of central importance are the ideals of harmony (*wa*) (which should not be destroyed by open opposition or individual deviation), and duty or indebtedness (*giri*) to other persons. Ruth Benedict (1946) is the first to have described this pattern of Japanese culture in her famous study *The Chrysanthemum and the Sword*. Ronald Dore in his classical work *City Life in Japan* (1958) has shown how Confucian ideals motivate neighborhood relations in a Tokyo "urban ward association," as he calls *jichikai*, during the 1950s.

More recent research confirms, that the wish for consensual decision making and harmonious relations still is prevalent both within *jichikai* interaction (Allinson 1979: 95 ff.) and, more generally, in Japanese society and economy.

Another legacy of Confucian traditions is the importance attached to hierarchical relationships, which Chie Nakane (1970) has analysed as the central structural principle of the Japanese "vertical" society. Sakuta (1978: 220 ff.), however, has pointed out the existence of important egalitarian horizontal elements as well, which counterbalance the vertical power structure. The high value placed on harmonious relations within the group as a whole helps to restrict the misuse of power of the leadership. For example, in decision making, the leader of a *jichikai* would usually adopt a decision, as soon as about two thirds of the group agree, even if he/she personally preferred an alternative (Allinson 1979: 95 ff.).

One might describe these social values as rather conservative and, according to one's ideological standpoint, deplore them — as indeed most of today's Japanese sociologists do[6] — or extol them. However, in contrast to general expectations of decline of the *jichikai* in a Western-style democracy, they have not only survived, but have developed new perspectives and agendas: They have served as a base for the environmental movement or have acted as lobby-groups within large housing complexes (chapter 5.2). Summarizing his results of research on *jichikai*, Bestor (1985: 133) has convincingly pointed out the problematic use of the term "traditional" in this context. He argues that the elements of traditionalism, which are used within neighborhood associations, are consciously or unconsciously manipulated metaphors to invoke the "symbolic creation and maintenance" of the neighborhood as a community, but that they are not an evidence of, and should not be mistaken for, "cultural stagnation of the individuals and social groups involved" (Bestor 1985: 133).

8. The Relationship Between *jichikai* and Community

Since the mid-1970s, local governments — backed by the Ministry of Home Affairs — have increasingly adopted their own "community building" policies (*machi-zukuri* or *komyuniti-zukuri*). In doing this, they have shown different grades of sensibility, developing participatory models for the inclusion of *jichikai* in the formal system, by which social life on the local level is determinded.

Falconeri (1976) analyzes one of the early examples of "community building" in Kanazawa, and reports the substitution of *jichikai* volunteers by a system of liaison-officers, who are public employees. While the administration speaks of more efficiency and equity, as well as superior knowledge in the new system, the *jichikai* volunteers resent the growing disinterest and passivity of the ward inhabitants, which has resulted from reduced functions. Falconeri's case study, however, was carried out in a district where the *jichikai* had been already weakened before the new policy was put into effect.

---

[6] About the background and reasons for this, see the interesting introduction to Nakamura's paper on "Urban Ward Associations" by Dore (1968). Also compare Thränhardt (forthcoming).

Bestor (1985: 130) reports a different situation. When the Tokyo administration planned to combine several neighborhood associations for greater administrative effectiveness, the *jichikai* leaders resisted, maintaining that they were "independent voluntary bodies organized by and for local residents." They were successfull in withstanding the takeover, and authorities had to give in.

In another case, the city of Mitaka, at the Western outskirts of Tokyo, seems to have found a more cooperative model of inclusion of local *jichikai*. Progressive leadership developed a model in which *jichikai* are formally included into the political body, and put in charge of the local "community center," where a wide range of social activities occurs. According to evidence from both sides, the model works well.[7]

9. Conclusion

The structural entity of *jichikai* encompasses a wide range of variations, which have developed differently according to local conditions. Furthermore, it is difficult to give an overall evaluation of the role *jichikai* play within the social system because of the lack of formal inclusion into the social system and the ensuing scarcity of official data. Moreover, in Japan, the strong political reservations which some have towards the *jichikai* have hindered scientific discussion.

While Japanese sources have tended to emphasize *jichikai's* recent decline (Fukutake 1981, Japanese National Committee 1986a), international observers, such as Bestor (1985: 133), argue that the neighborhood associations have retained their local influence.

The bulk of scientific research on neighborhood associations after World War II has centered on political functions, while their social role has been neglected. But with the shifting interest within social policy towards the communal level, a new evaluation of the social functions of *jichikai* is necessary. Some of the major advantages of the *jichikai* are:

Japanese neighborhood associations provide essential social needs at low costs. In contrast to the Western experience, Japanese voluntarism is neither middle-class nor selective, but includes all inhabitants of a given district. Furthermore, they can serve as a necessary restraint against the tendency to compartmentalize social problems, which occurs within vocationally trained and oriented welfare bureaucracies. Based on socially accepted cultural

---

[7] See Mitaka-shi (1986: 28) and interviews, which I carried out with representatives of this gremium and an official of the municipal administration.

values, they can reach — and, in cases of perceived danger, mobilize — a comparatively high ratio of the population. This seldom occurs in Western voluntarism, as it is based on individual activity. The *jichikai* capabilities as grassroots participatory institutions make them valuable instruments for constructing and implementing people-oriented social welfare policies at the local level.

References

Allinson, Gary D. (1979): *Suburban Tokyo. A Comparative Study in Politics and Social Change*, Berkeley/Los Angeles/London: University of California Press.

Allinson, Gary D. (1980): "Opposition in the Suburbs," in *Political Opposition and Local Politics in Japan*, Kurt Steiner/Ellis S. Krauss/Scott C. Flanagan (Eds.), Princeton, N.J.: Princeton University Press, 95 – 130.

Bauer, Rudolph and Anna M. Thränhardt (Eds.) (1987): *Verbandliche Wohlfahrtspflege im internationalen Vergleich*, Opladen: Westdeutscher Verlag.

Benedict, Ruth (1946, [12]1964): *The Chrysanthemum and the Sword — Patterns of Japanese Culture*, Tokyo: Charles E. Tuttle.

Bestor, Theodore C. (1983): "Miyamoto-chō: The Social Organization of a Tokyo Neighborhood," Ph. D. Dissertation, Stanford University.

Bestor, Theodore C. (1985): "Tradition and Japanese Social Organization: Institutional Development in a Tokyo Neighborhood," *Ethnology* 24, 2 (April), 121 – 134.

Braibanti, Ralph J. D. (1948): "Neighborhood Associations in Japan and Their Democratic Potentialities," *Far Eastern Quarterly* 7, 136 – 164.

Chiiki-shakai-kenkyūsho (Ed.) (1987): *Chōnaikai*, vol. 79, series: komyuniti, Tokyo: Dainippon-insatsu-kabushiki-kaisha.

Curtis, Gerald L. (1983): *Election Campaigning Japanese Style*, Tokyo: Kodansha.

Dore, Ronald P. (1958): *City Life in Japan*, Berkeley: University of California Press.

Dore, Ronald P. (1968): "Introduction to Nakamura's 'Urban Ward Associations in Japan'", in *Readings in Urban Sociology*, Richard E. Pahl (Ed.), Oxford/New York: Pergamon Press, 186 – 190.

Falconeri, G. Ralph (1976): "The Impact of Rapid Urban Change on Neighborhood Solidarity," in *Social Change and Community Politics in Urban Japan*, James W. White/Frank Munger (Eds.), Chapel Hill: University of North Carolina, 31 – 59.

Fukutake, Tadashi ([2]1981): *Japanese Society Today*, Tokyo: University of Tokyo Press.

Japanese National Committee of Social Welfare/Japanese National Community and Child Welfare Volunteers (Ed.) (1979): *Minsei-iin. The System of Community Volunteers in Japan*, Tokyo: Zenkoku-minsei-iin-jido-iin kyogikai.

Japanese National Committee (Ed.) (1982): "Public-Voluntary Social Welfare Interaction and Relationship in Japan Today," Report of the Japanese National Committee ICSW to 21st International Conference. Tokyo: Japanese National Committee, ICSW.

Japanese National Committee, ICSW (Ed.) (1986a): *Family and Community in Japan*, National Report of the Japanese National Committee to the 23rd Conference on Social Welfare, Tokyo: Japanese National Committee, ICSW.

Japanese National Committee/International Council on Social Welfare-Organizing Committee. Tokyo Conference on Social Welfare 1986 (Eds.) (1986b): *Social Welfare Services in Japan*, Tokyo: Japanese National Committee, ICSW.

Japanese National Council of Minsei-iin. Community/Child Welfare Volunteers (Ed.) (August 1986): *Minsei-iin: A System of Community Volunteers in Japan*, Tokyo: The Japanese National Council of Social Welfare.

Kevenhörster, Paul and Herbert Uppendahl (1987): *Gemeindedemokratie in Gefahr? − Zentralisierung und Dezentralisierung als Herausforderung lokaler Demokratie in Japan und der Bundesrepublik Deutschland*, Baden-Baden: Nomos.

Kiefer, Christie W. (1976): "Leadership, Sociability, and Social Change in a White-Collar Oanchi," in *Social Change and Community Politics in Urban Japan*, James W. White and Frank Munger (Eds.), 15 − 30.

Koyano, Shigeo et al. (1974): *Gendai Nihon no komyuniti*, Tokyo: Kawashima shoten.

Kreitz, Susanne (1987): "Nachbarschaftsvereinigungen als Formen lokaler Sozialpolitik am Beispiel der japanischen *'chōnaikai'* und *'jichikai'*", unpublished manuscript, University of Bielefeld.

Linhart, Sepp (1983): *Organisationsformen alter Menschen in Japan*, Beiträge zur Japanologie, vol. 19, Wien: Universitätsverlag.

Lörcher, Siegfried (1986): "Sozialpolitik in Japan," in *Japan − Geographie − Geschichte − Kultur − Religion − Staat − Gesellschaft usw.*, Manfred Pohl (Ed.), Stuttgart/Wien: Thienemann's, 189 − 197.

McKean, Margaret A. (1976): "Citizens' Movements in Urban and Rural Japan," in *Social Change and Community in Urban Japan*, James W. White/Frank Munger (Eds.), Chapel Hill: University of North Carolina, 61 − 99.

McKean, Margaret A. (1981): *Environmental Protest and Citizen Politics in Japan*, Berkeley/Los Angeles/London: Univ. of California Press.

Masland, John W. (1946): "Neighborhood Associations in Japan," *Far Eastern Survey* 15 (November), 355 − 358.

Mitaka-shi shiminbu komyunitika (Ed.) (1986): *Minna de kizuko komyuniti*, Mitaka: Koroni-insatsu.

Nakagawa, Go (1979): *Senzen no Tokyo ni okeru chōnaikai*, Tokyo: kokuren daigaku (Ningen to shakai no kaihatsu puroguramu kenkyū hōkoku HSDRJE-3 J/UNUP-23): United Nations University.

Nakagawa, Go (1980): *Chōnaikai*, Tokyo: Chuokoronsha.

Nakagawa, Go (1983): "Bōsai soshiki to shite no chōnaikai − Tokyo daishinsai wo chūshin to shite," *Toshi-mondai* 74, 11. Tokyo: Nukiziri.

Nakamura, Hachirō (1963): "Some Types of Chōnaikai in the Process of Urban Development," in *Local Community and Urbanization*, Social Science Research Institute (Ed.), International Christian University Publication II. A, Social Science Studies 9. Mitaka: International Christian University.

Nakamura, Hachirō (1968): "Urban Ward Associations in Japan," in *Readings in Urban Sociology*, Richard E. Pahl (Ed.) Oxford/New York: Pergamon Press, 190 − 208.

Nakamura, Hachirō (1979): *Senzen no Tokyo ni okeru chōnaikai*, Tokyo, kokuren daigaku (Ningen to shakai no kaihatsu puroguramu kenkyū hōkoku HSDRJE-3 J/UNUP-23).

Nakane, Chie (1970): *Japanese Society*, Berkeley: Univ. of California Press.

Norbeck, Edward (1972): "Japanese Common-Interest Associations in Cross-Cultural Perspective," *Journal of Voluntary Action Scholars* 1, 38–41.

Sakuta, Keiichi (1978): "The Controversy over Community and Autonomy," in *Authority and the Individual in Japan*, Koschmann (Ed.), Tokyo: University of Tokyo Press, 220 sq.

Shibata, Tokue (Ed.): *Public Finance in Japan*, Tokyo: University of Tokyo Press.

Shinseikatsu undō kyōkai (Ed.) (1982): *Jichikai, chōnakainado no genjō to tembo*, Tokyo: Yugengaisha.

Steiner, Kurt (1965): *Local Government in Japan*, Stanford: Stanford University Press.

Steiner, Kurt, Ellis S. Krauss, and Scott C. Flanagan (Eds.) (1980): *Political Opposition and Local Politics in Japan*, Princeton: Princeton University Press.

Thränhardt, Anna Maria (1987): "Organisierte Freiwilligkeit – Ehrenamtlichkeit als tragende Struktur des japanischen Sozialwesens," in *Verbandliche Wohlfahrtspflege im internationalen Vergleich*, R. Bauer/A. M. Thränhardt (Eds.), Opladen: Westdeutscher Verlag, 204–225.

Thränhardt, Anna Maria (forthcoming): "Nachbarschaftsvereinigungen nach dem Zweiten Weltkrieg," in *Festschrift für Bruno Lewin*, Hijiya-Kirschnereit and Stalph (Eds.), Bochum: Studienverlag Dr. Norbert Brockmeyer.

Vogel, Ezra F. (1963): *Japan's New Middle Class*, Berkeley/Los Angeles/London: University of California Press.

Vogel, Ezra F. (1980): *Japan as Number One – Lessons for America*, Cambridge, Mass.: Harvard University Press.

Ward, Robert (1965): "The Far Eastern Scene: The Socio-Political Role of the *Buraku* (Hamlet) in Japan," *The American Political Science Review* 45, 1025–1040.

4.8
Private Voluntary Organizations and the Third World: The Case of Africa

Helmut K. Anheier

1. Introduction

The overall performance of all but a few African countries in social, political, and economic terms has been disappointing during the last decade (see Berg and Whitaker 1986; OECD 1986; Rose 1985; Wheeler 1984; World Bank 1981). West Africa is facing a serious economic crisis, caused, to a considerable degree, by two decades of rising rates in population growth and stagnating, even declining agricultural production. In the 1980s, deteriorating international terms of trade for major export commodities, inefficient bureaucracies, and public corporations, together with widespread misallocations of state subsidies, continued to move more and more countries of this region into deeper debt. At the same time, international finance and capital markets have become increasingly tight, resulting in the attachment of multiple conditions and constraints to external finances. Often at considerable social and economic costs to debtor nations, international financing agencies and OECD governments demand greater efficiency, reinforcement of austerity measures, and economically more feasible investment patterns.

It is a truism that widespread and persistent poverty leads to a weak state; but within the African context, it is equally evident that weak states are responsible for poverty. On a continent characterized by one-party systems, military regimes, and short-lived democracies, the state has remained weak (Bienen 1983; Decalo 1976). In the early 1980s authors from across the political spectrum (Bauer 1981; Elsenhans 1981; Krauss 1983; Nohlen and Nuscheler 1982) began to argue that the West African state has caused much of Africa's malaise — a theme eagerly picked up by bilateral and multilateral donor agencies. Although subsequent studies revealed large differences in public sector performance across African countries (e. g. Rose 1985; Wheeler 1984), the "weak and inefficient" African state remains a central criticism of previous development approaches[1].

---

[1] As will be shown further below, in the African context, the comparative advantages of PVOs are usually derived with a "weak and inefficient" state in mind. It is

Within the present developmental situation, and regardless of political ideologies, governments in Africa find a narrower range of economic and political options available to them. While a detailed analysis of various development approaches is beyond the scope of this paper, it is nevertheless necessary to delineate several factors and tendencies in present and past policies in order to understand the recent focus on Private Voluntary Organizations (PVOs).

First, macro-policies aimed at African development overestimated the capacity of the state to initiate, implement, and monitor development policies and projects. Such approaches not only expected too much from the state, they also overlooked, to varying degrees, other organizational actors in the process of development such as private for-profit organizations and PVOs. In their origin and intent, modernization approaches, characteristic of development efforts in the 1960s, were certainly a policy of a for-profit world; its practice, however, was often one of large-scale state interventions and planned development in the form of five-year plans. The entrepreneur, central to modernization theory, was replaced by the state bureaucrat and became target rather than initiator of economic development.

Second, previous development approaches and policies allocated virtually no role to the third sector. Despite the past and present importance of nonprofit organizations in OECD countries — and indeed in the development of the West as such — governmental attitudes toward the third sector were characterized by neglect. Only in several economically most distressed African countries has the "state monopoly of development" (Hyden 1983: 123) been partially replaced by greater PVO involvement.

Third, as a result of the overall poor performance of most African countries and ideological shifts in the West, the postwar confidence in large-scale, often centralized, planning as well as massive technology transfers and capital-intensive projects gave way to an emphasis on decentralization, privatization, and intermediate technologies (Hyden 1983; Roninelli and Nellis 1986; Schumacher 1973).

2. Comparative Advantages of PVOs

The above factors provide the context which lead to the "pragmatic consideration" (Masoni 1985) of PVOs by official donor agencies. Their disap-

---

important to note that as long as causes of government failure in Africa are far from clear, PVO rationales based on the "inefficient state assumption" alone remain on weak grounds.

pointment in public sector performance increased the importance of PVOs in development efforts. While public sector activities continue to be heavily criticized for having contributed much to the present problematic situation in many third world countries (Ayres 1983; Griffin 1977; Jackson 1982; Lappe, Collins and Kinley 1980; Payer 1982; among others), PVOs are receiving much credit and gaining a greater status in development financing. Whereas disappointment in official government programs and projects is growing, PVOs have gained such prominence that "development transfers through PVOs have become 'big business'" (Rice 1983: 7). Annual net resource transfers to developing countries in the form of PVO grants increased from $ 2.31 billion in 1982, and $ 3.6 billion in 1983 (OECD 1983), to $ 4.8 billion in 1986 (OECD 1986). Based on data reported in OECD (1987), PVO transfers account for 4.1% of all transfers between Western countries and the Third World. They constituted 10% of the official OECD bilateral aid and 94% of all aid flows from OPEC nations; they are equal to the total of aid transfers from Eastern Bloc countries, and equivalent to 7.4% of private sector flows between the developed and the developing world. According to the OECD (1986), PVOs have become a "growth sector."

In contrast to official development agencies, PVOs are believed to have fewer overhead costs, to rely less on bureaucratic procedures, and to be less subject to political constraints (e. g. Hyden 1983; Sommer 1979). They tend to carry out small-scale projects, exhibit a greater degree of flexibility, aim at self-reliance and self-sufficiency, and generate new, innovative projects (e. g. Betts 1978; Bolling and Smith 1982). In addition, PVOs, as advocates of the marginalized and poor strata of Third World societies, try to stimulate participation of the poor (Ayres 1983; Korten 1987; Lappe, Collins, and Kinley 1980; Schneider 1985; Streeten et al. 1981). In general PVOs are being compared to the state rather than for-profit organizations. The comparative advantages of PVOs put forth in the literature can be summarized by four major arguments:

The social argument states that PVOs try to stimulate the participation of the poor and are able to reach those strata of African societies which are bypassed by public service delivery systems. In essence, this argument attaches greater social equity to private voluntary efforts than to the public sector. Because of shortages of public funds combined with cultural and social access problems, parts of Africa's population are difficult to reach by conventional service systems — a problem which is amplified by elite influences of governmental decision making. Thus, PVOs are in a better position to reach the poor and disadvantaged.

Yet research has shown that many PVOs are not necessarily participatory and do not necessarily reach the poor (see Smith 1987). Tendler (1982) analyzed evaluation reports of 72 PVO projects of different types from various parts of the Third World. She found that the commonly held assumption that PVOs are participatory did not hold up. On the contrary, many projects revealed top-down decision making by PVO staff or control of decisions by local elites, and the introduction of known techniques into new areas rather than innovation. Furthermore, target groups did not necessarily include the poorest 40% of the population[2].

In a study of 30 PVO projects aimed at income-generation in Senegal and Burkina-Faso, Gueneau and Morrisson (1985) found that PVOs themselves and not the local population acted as project instigators. Project organizations were hierarchical, and villagers were only marginally included in the project design phase. Innovation did not take place at the organizational level, but in most instances, it included the introduction of new equipments and technologies. Moreover, Gueneau and Morrisson found that PVOs represented sizeable importers of foreign, mostly Western-made, equipment. In Mali, Twose (1987: 8—9) reports that local PVOs and their projects are often initiated by laid-off government employees and recent university graduates with little prospect of employment in either public and private for-profit sector. These examples show that PVOs can be the result of local entrepreneurship that, for one reason or another, cannot be realized in other sectors of the economy.

The economic argument implies that PVOs carry out services more economically than governments, and that PVOs aim at self-reliance and self-sufficiency. Just as the social argument referred to equity, the economic argument addresses the greater efficiency of PVOs.

While no input—output ratios are available which would allow us to compare public sector and PVO efficiency, there is evidence to suggest that the economic argument needs modification: only 4 of the 15 PVOs surveyed in Togo, 11 of the 29 surveyed in Senegal, and only 1 in 5 (22%) of surveyed Nigerian PVOs enjoyed stable funding[3]. Funding instability, in turn, impairs the ability of PVOs to provide services continually, and therefore, more efficiently.

To some extent, the discontinuity of PVO operations is a direct result of chronic "under-funding." The ratio between the current budget and the additional funds needed is .36 to 1 in Senegal. In other words, Senegalese PVOs have to raise close to three times the amount of their annual budget to secure continued operations, in contrast to 50% for the average Nigerian PVO. In Togo, only two PVOs had a budget greater than the average amount of additional finances needed. While budget dependencies and shortages are

[2] Moreover, Tendler argues that advocates of the development "from below" approach neglected the importance of local elites. She introduces the factor of local elite control as an intervening variable determining the outcome of PVO projects.

[3] Unless otherwise indicated, reported data are based on a survey of all member organizations of national consortia in Nigeria, Senegal, and Togo. The survey was carried out in 1983 and 1984 by the present authors (see Anheier 1986, 1989).

more pronounced in Togo and Senegal than in Nigeria, where PVOs remain marginal actors in development, factors such as donor withdrawal, local political influences, and administrative delays in grant-processing, personnel shortages, and lack of planning contributed much to severe project discontinuities in all three countries[4].

Gueneau and Morrisson (1985) estimate that only about 25% of the projects surveyed in their study will eventually become self-sufficient and be able to operate without external financial and technical assistance. Moreover, they found that 40% of the projects showed a negative balance when taking provision for depreciation. The majority of economic benefits seemed to derive from the NGO-presence in the village as such (e. g. employment, construction), and only secondarily because of project results. In terms of economic multiplication and project diffusion, they estimate that about 50% of the projects are likely to generate such effects. Thus, PVO projects contain considerable redistribution components in disguise of projects aiming at self-reliance and self-help, which nevertheless benefit the local population as "quasi-welfare" payments.

Smith (1987) found evidence in support of greater PVO efficiency when compared to public projects, yet could not substantiate the claim that PVOs are more innovate. Greater efficiency of PVOs seems largely based on a major cost advantage, which is related to both lower labor costs and incomplete pricing. Examples of incomplete pricing are: not taking provisions for depreciation; relying on voluntary local inputs; not including transaction costs (project site selection, information, grant-seeking); and excluding long-range recurrent costs which occur at project sites or to target groups.

The political argument states that PVOs are relatively immune from changing political tides, while government policies and agencies are subject to unexpected change. An extension of the political argument refers to the "hidden agenda" and ultimately political motivation of official development assist-

---

[4] For the rural population, however, the question is more often than not having services provided at all (either by the government or by PVOs), and not so much by whom and how cost-effective. It should also be kept in mind that PVO projects tend to be of modest scale when compared to governmental projects. This implies that failure of governmental projects will be more costly than failure of PVO projects. For example, when the government had to admit the failure of a large-scale river basin irrigation project in mid-western Nigeria, several billion dollars, years of development efforts, and hundreds of jobs were lost. When a nearby irrigation project run by a church-related PVO failed, very little capital was lost, and no workers were laid off. "Governments can do things on a large scale, but when it makes a mistake, it makes it one a large scale too," we are reminded by Douglas (1983: 117). PVO failures, in turn, have much less impact on the economy as a whole.

ance[5]. PVOs are believed to be more "honest" and less guided by political considerations. PVOs often provide the only effective feed-back mechanism in the course of development projects. For example, PVOs, not government agencies, first reported on the increasingly problematic food situation in the Sahel during the 1983 – 85 drought[6].

Yet PVOs are certainly neither immune to politics nor "outside" the political arena. They are part of a political spectrum ranging from organizations in the political tradition of African socialism to European PVOs promoting liberal, social democratic, or conservative political values, from fundamentalist Protestant churches and Catholic operations advocating the theology of liberation to Islamic missionary societies[7].

The institutional history of several Nigerian PVOs suggests that their creation was closely linked to the emergence of political parties in the independence movement of the 1950s. In fact, the party which came to rule Western Nigeria in the 1960s started as a voluntary association, the Nigerian Youth Movement. Likewise, the political party in power from 1979 until the military coup of December 1983 originated as a social club in the mid-1970s. Moreover, during the colonial period, Islamic PVOs in the field of education were created to combat the increased Christian influence on political affairs through the introduction of missionary schools. Similarly, the 1987 religious riots in Northern Nigeria are linked to the influence of Islamic PVOs, supported by either Saudi Arabia or Iran, competing with each other and Christian missionary societies.

[5] Examples are the increased intertwining of strategic interests with official development flows, and the use of aid as a political tool. As the OECD diplomatically put it: "There is still a lack of precision in the formulation of objectives, and as in the industrial countries some confusion between ends and means" (OECD 1983: 26).

[6] Another dramatic example of early warning function fulfilled by PVOs occurred during the Ethiopian famine of 1984 – 5 when the government of Ethiopia, for political reasons, would initially not admit the growing food shortages.

[7] Again, much of the difference on how political factors influence PVO operations as opposed to governments is related to the scale of operations. For example, in 1983, just prior to federal elections, a rinderpest outbreak threatened livestock in Northern Nigeria (and thereby the livelihood of thousands of Islamic Fulani herders). The local state government, apparently unable to react to the growing problem in time, tried to downplay the threat and asked the federal government for help, which resulted in a political debate over state versus federal responsibilities. A small Protestant PVO ordered vaccine from the U.S., only to find that the import licence for the particular vaccine had suddenly been suspended by the state government. When the PVO, through personal channels, managed to get hold of vaccine produced in Israel, and began vaccinating cattle throughout the predominantly Moslem state, PVO personnel was arrested by the authorities and the vaccine confiscated.

The cultural argument stipulates that PVOs, embedded in the local culture, are more sensitive to local needs and their articulation. Rather than replacing indigenous social structures by large-scale organizations, PVOs try to nurture local organizations within their own cultural context.

However, evidence seems to suggest that PVOs tend to initiate projects rather than to enhance already existing ones initiated by the local population (Gueneau and Morrisson 1985). Among the 125 PVOs surveyed in Senegal, Togo, and Nigeria, the project initiated, designed, and implemented by indigenous groupings such as village associations without impetus from outside organizations remains the exception rather than the rule (Anheier 1986, 1987). Twose (1987) argues that indigenous Malian PVOs are not popular groupings at the grassroots level; rather, they are the organizational expression of a new "private sector alternative" (Twose 1987: 9).

Moreover, many PVOs are religious organizations which are to varying degrees integrated into the indigenous African culture (see Anheier 1986, 1987). Ultimately, however, Christian churches are rooted in the Judeo-Christian tradition, and not in an African one. Christian PVOs, many of which originated from missionary societies, did not originally come to Africa to preserve its cultures and belief systems. The issue of church indigenization, which, in particular, continues to be debated in the Roman Catholic church, has occupied missionary societies since they first started operating in Africa. This debate involves two opposed positions. The first one claims that a viable Catholic church in Africa has to be built on the social and religious values and customs of the indigenous population. The second position argues that "the indigenous culture, which is repugnant to Western Christianity and Rome, the fountain-head of Catholic orthodoxy, must be suppressed and replaced by the Western expression of Christianity" (Catholic Church of Nigeria 1982: 2).

In summary, there are four major shortcomings in the PVO literature. First, many studies fail to differentiate between different types of PVOs, e. g. self-help groups, grant-giving and operating foundations, indigenous and foreign, and secular and religious PVOs[8]. The fact that the Ford Foundation and the Progressive Young Farmers' Association are both nonprofit, does

---

[8] Because we are dealing with two quite different types of organizations, it is necessary to distinguish PVOs that more or less follow the Western organizational model, and self-help groups that originate, and are rooted in, the indigenous African society. The basic reason for this is the economic objective of PVOs and self-help groups. PVOs aim primarily at increasing the welfare of clients and external groups or organizations, while self-help groups, like cooperatives, try to maximize their own welfare. Self-help groups and related organizations (cooperatives, mutual aid societies, credit associations, chambers of commerce and craft, village associations) would require a separate analysis (see Anheier 1987).

not imply that they necessarily reveal comparable organizational behavior or face similar dilemmas.

The second problem of the PVO literature is its narrow, ahistorical focus. As an organizational species, PVOs, the organizational innovators in the Africa of the 1980s, are by no means recent arrivals on this continent. Many, in particular religious, PVOs predate the African states considerably. Indeed, church-related organizations are closely related to both colonialism and independence movements. Many PVOs are part of the last 50, sometimes even 100, years of African history, and they are not a recent response to a discouraging social and economic situation.

Third, internal and external changes in the organizational environment of PVOs have been neglected. This applies in particular to "bureaucracy" and "coordination." PVOs are often described as fearful of "bureaucracy" and as guarding their organizational autonomy most jealously. The irony is that some PVO projects are successful because they are bureaucratic, while others are unsuccessful despite their non-bureaucratic approach. Other PVO projects are successful because the organization, *de facto* or *de jure*, gave up autonomy, while others are unsuccessful, because autonomy resulted in organizational isolation (Paul 1982).

Finally, all too often, PVOs are seen in isolation from the surrounding larger political economy of other organizational actors in Africa and abroad. Like all organizations, PVOs exist in an environment of organizations. Therefore, in order to understand the potentials and constraints, as well as the behavior and impact of PVOs in Africa, the organizational field of their operation is one crucial area to examine.

3. PVOs and the Organizational Field of Development

Development efforts in Africa take place in an environment of organizations. The concept of "organizational fields" helps describe the aggregate of organizations which are responsible for a definable area of institutional life (DiMaggio and Powell 1983), in this case development. Organizational fields encompass a system of organizations, such as donor agencies, PVOs, government agencies, official development organizations, target groups, and for-profit corporations. The importance of an organizational field approach is demonstrated by the following example:

The Mauritanian city of Rosso, situated at the banks of the Senegal river, suffered from a massive influx of migrants, major flooding, pollution, and disease. In 1974, the government set up a public organization to meet the need of low-cost housing in Rosso and other parts of the country. With official French support, the public organization was responsible for the construction, renting, and maintenance of low-cost housing units. The public organization, however, failed to meet any project objectives. After the French donor withdrew further funding, and OPEC agency stepped in and allowed the public organization to survive for a few more years. *West Africa* reports, that the public organization "allowed certain local politicians to widen their clientele by placing relatives in salaried positions, granting housing units to tribal and ethnic allies, and provide construction contracts for their friends in the business community" (1985: 1043). It is estimated that only 3.5% of the population could have afforded to rent a three-room housing in the few ones actually constructed.

In the areas of finance and goal attainment, this public organization shared the fate of many other public corporations in Third World countries (Shirley 1983). What is unusual however, it that the public organization signed an agreement with a Pan-African PVO to carry out the low-cost housing project in Rosso. The public organization gave 30% of the total project costs to the PVO which promised to raise the remaining funds from private overseas donor agencies. Unlike the public organizations, which subcontracted to companies using Western techniques and imported building material, the PVO used the funds to finance research and experiments using local raw materials and building techniques. After successfully demonstrating the financial and other advantages of such a building construction to local residents, some 500 housing units were built between 1979 and 1982. The PVO encouraged residents to build a 3.5 kilometer long dike to prevent flooding, to construct sewage canals, and to improve sanitation. As a result, health indicators improved dramatically.

The PVO chose Rosso as a project site for one important reason. Rosso was sufficiently distant from the capital to discourage "the speculative appetite of established business and bureaucratic forces" (*West Africa* 1985: 1044). Yet the success of the low-cost housing project attracted other PVOs searching for recipient organizations and suitable target groups. Some PVOs tried to sell their particular version of intermediary technology to local residents. Other PVOs tried to move into Rosso to carry out similar projects. By the end of 1982, the project had lost much of its popular support among residents, and real estate speculation began to flourish.

The PVO itself was torn between the state bureaucracy (which by then had discovered a new interest in the project), outside donor agencies eager to support expansion and replication of the project operations, other PVOs, and its actual target group, the local residents. Unwillingly, the PVO found itself in the increasingly difficult role of a mediator between government, businesses, outside agencies, and the local residents. Internal conflict and dissent began to take root; both had grown to such proportions by 1983 that the PVO became defunct.

An analysis of the organizational field in which government agencies, donors, PVOs, and target groups operate helps understand why the Rosso project was first successful and then unsuccessful. As long as the PVO was able to keep its Rosso operations in relative isolation from outside organizations, the project was successful. Once Rosso shifted to a more central position and aroused the interest of other organizations (donors, government, for-profit businesses, other PVOs), the potentials for conflict and contradictions became prominent.

This case study does not necessarily imply that relative isolation is a prerequisite for project success. In other instances, we might find that relative isolation and, related to this, local PVO monopolies are the cause of discontinuities and failures. However, underlying an organizational field approach is the assumption that the objectives of individual organizations involved in a project do not necessarily add up to, and coincide with, those of the project or the target group. Development efforts, like most organizational fields, tends to create their own inter-organizational dynamics.

James (1987) has shown that nonprofits flourish under basically two demand-side conditions: excess demand not met by limited government production, and heterogeneous demand in religious, ethnic, and quality terms. Supply-side considerations, in particular nonprofit (often religious) entrepreneurship, are equally important. In the case of Rosso, we see that excess demand for low-cost housing and improved environmental quality existed. However, other organizations and donor agencies moving in tried to meet differentiated demand not met by the PVO, or attempted to create their own demand by suggesting new approaches and technologies to the local population. Moreover, while excess demand for PVO services seems characteristic of all African countries, there exists, at the same time, excess demand by PVOs for "high-quality" target and recipient groups. International PVOs search for reliable, promising, accountable, and trustworthy recipients. For this reason, as James (1987) noted, indigenous counterparts are sometimes created to receive funds from international PVOs. Sometimes governments set up PVOs, for either political or financial reasons.

Several aspects of relations within the organizational field need special attention. First, the often complex informal networks among PVOs and between PVOs and other organizations must be examined to understand information and resource flows. Likewise, formal sponsorship and counterpart relations between foreign and African PVOs have to be considered in order to understand both the organizational behavior and strategy of PVOs. Examples are relationships between the mother church and its African chapter or between church and laity organization. However, not all churches in Africa are linked to the Vatican or Protestant mother churches overseas. Many of the more than 5,000 African churches, which combine elements of

African religion with Christianity or Islam, are located outside the arena of counterpart relations, and are rare recipients of foreign aid.

Second, in order to understand sectoral and behavioral organizational shifts, we need to have more information on the organizational birth- and deathrates of PVOs (foundations, operating PVOs, local and self-help groups) in OECD and African countries. A recent survey by *Interaction* (1985) showed that about one third of all American PVOs active in Africa were established before 1939. Significant growth in the birthrate occurred in the 1960s and 1970s in response to the emergence of new African nations, while growth rates slowed down since then.

Third, while the PVO sector in OECD countries is usually described as diverse and made up of many small organizations, there are clear concentrations in terms of organizational size and financial magnitude of operations. The eight largest American PVOs (Catholic Relief Service, CARE, World Vision, American ORT, African-American Institute, Lutheran World Relief, ADRA International, and the Mennonite Central Committee) account for approximately 80% of all U.S. aid to Africa. Even if we exclude government contributions to PVOs, those eight organizations still constitute a 70% share of all private U.S. aid to Africa, with Catholic Relief Service and World Vision accounting for 45% alone. Similar tendencies can be shown in Europe, where a few PVOs are responsible for a disproportionate share of private aid to Africa, such as OXFAM in the UK, Misereor and EZE in West Germany, or similar organizations in the Netherlands, Austria, and Scandinavia. Do PVO sectors in OECD countries, in fact, represent the organizational analogue to a potentially oligopolistic market, with few dominant PVOs and many marginal organizations? Do African PVO sectors also show oligarchical tendencies?

Fourth, members of the organizational field of development operate in different legal and policy environments. Recently, several authors (see, for example, Glagow and Evers 1986) began to stress the corporatist development policy in a number of European countries, where PVOs carry out governmental functions on behalf of the state. Smith (1987) argues that PVOs are increasingly taking on developmental function in Africa that are delegated to them by governments in Europe or America. This arrangement shares several elements with forms of third party government in OECD countries (Salamon 1987). The increased recognition and incorporation of PVOs by governmental and international organizations (UN system; World Bank) in the course of development projects potentially points in a similar direction.

African PVOs face policy dilemmas different from corporatism and third party government. The political and policy problem of African PVOs has been called the "relevance trap" (Glagow and Evers 1986): in particular under authoritarian regimes, successful and politically "visible" African PVOs are likely to be taken over and controlled by the state. However, when PVOs manage to remain "irrelevant," they are tolerated by the authorities. Available evidence on the "relevance trap" thesis is far from clear. It seems to apply more to PVOs with explicit than with implicit political agendas. Moreover, in one of Africa's most authoritarian country, Togo, PVOs flourish, and were, indeed, almost an equal partner alongside the state during recent negotiations of a World Bank sponsored project (Baldwin 1986). On the other hand, in Senegal, a democratic country in a formal sense, PVOs face more political difficulties combined with occasional threats of governmental takeover (Anheier 1989).

4. Financial Flows

The field of development financing has become extremely complex. The tendency of progressive intertwining of private and official flows (OECD 1983: 49) combined with the growing importance of PVOs as financial intermediaries between official donors and private recipient groups, has made it increasingly difficult to classify aid flows and locate donors. For example, in 1985, the West German government transferred 7% of its official development assistance through PVOs; church-related PVOs such as Misereor received about 25% of their total non-administrative budget in state subsidies (BMZ 1985; Dams 1986). If we assume, that Misereor supports African PVOs, which, in turn, assist local self-help groups, the funding involves a chain of four organizations: the official West German donor organizations, Misereor, the African PVO, and the actual target group. At each step in the funding chain, the money meets different legal and accounting environments, and different organizational interests, but also funding flows from other private or official sources.

In 1982 dollars, indirect financing in the form of government matching grants has increased from $ 331.9 million in 1973 to $ 1.1 billion in 1985 (Smith 1987: 89). Similar conclusions in support of both the increasing complexity of development financing and the growing dependency of PVOs on public funds are reached by OECD (1986) and van der Heijden (1987).

What is the sectoral distribution of PVO finances in terms of education, rural development, relief, children, family planning, or health? Unfortunately, little data is available. As a proxy measure, the sectoral distribution of projects shows that four sectors (rural development [23%]; community development [23%]; health services [12%]; welfare and relief [17%]) account for 75% of all projects by U.S. PVOs in Africa (*Interaction* 1985). Similar data have been shown for Senegal, where the four sectors account for 60% of all projects, Nigeria (55%), and Togo (61%) (Anheier 1989).

What factors help explain sectoral differences and similarities between U.S. PVO projects and inputs on the one hand, and the activities of African PVOs on the other? Are similarities due to the shared perception of project priorities or the influence of donor organizations? Do international PVOs act as agenda-setting organizations for African PVOs? Are differences due to the divergent perception of project priorities between African and international PVOs, or are such differences an expression of the division of labor? Little information is available on the donor and recipient country distribution of PVO contributions. For three African countries, Anheier (1986) shows that the donor country representation of PVO, official, and private investment flows overlap almost completely. In the case of Senegal, Nigeria, and Togo, the major donor countries of official and private aid are, with few exceptions, identical to those providing the largest share of private investments.

What is the relationship between basic socio-economic indicators and the number of foreign PVO projects in African countries? Do PVOs from OECD countries work primarily in the most disadvantaged and poorest countries? A preliminary analysis based on data collected by *Interaction* (1985) and World Bank data (1984), shows a moderate correlation of $-.211$ between the number of U.S. PVO projects and per capita GNP, implying that there is a slight tendency of U.S. PVOs to have more projects in countries with lower per capita GNP. Similarly, there is only a weak correlation between rates of infant mortality and the number of U.S. PVO projects in a country: U.S. PVOs tend to work in countries with higher infant mortality. Relating back to the previous paragraph, U.S. PVOs tend to operate in countries with lower official per capita aid ($r = -.209$). Again, the modest correlation points to the influence of other factors. In a regression analysis, high per capita GNP and high per capita official aid had both a negative and significant influence on the number of U.S. PVO projects as the dependent variable, while accounting for only 11% of the variance. Clearly, further research is needed to clarify these issues.

5. Concluding Remarks

This paper examined several aspects of the "rise" of PVOs during the last decade, from their prominence as prime actors in emergency operations to their increased importance in developmental efforts. PVOs have become intermediary organizations located between the state and the market on the one hand, and between the local domestic and the international level on the other. The role of PVOs as linkage and broker organizations between the local and the "outside" world is demonstrated by their importance in the transfer of development financing. The notion of PVOs as intermediaries may lead to a discussion of central organizational dilemmas such as short-term versus long-term activities, volunteering versus professionalism, and the problem of resource dependencies and governance.

The often conflicting evidence on PVO performance implies a need for systematic analysis. It is suggested that the vantage point of organizational theory, and the conceptualization of development as an organizational prob-lem, may prove useful in this respect. The previous discussion has also demonstrated the weak link between work on PVOs in Africa as represented in the development literature, and the body of theories and approaches which help explain the role of PVOs in Western countries. Our understanding of PVOs in Africa can benefit from comparative analysis by incorporating knowledge of the historical and present role of PVOs in other countries and parts of the world. In the African case, the economic and political rationales for PVOs need further clarification, as do their comparative advantages when compared to the state agency or the for-profit enterprise: the role of PVOs in political mobilization, social movements, and policy formulation; and their economic importance in terms of resource mobilization, "gap-filling" activities, and the provision of public and semi-public goods.

References

Anheier, H. K. (1986): "Private Voluntary Organizations, Networks and Development in Africa: A Comparative Study of Organizational Fields in Nigeria, Senegal and Togo," Ph. D. Dissertation, Department of Sociology, Yale University.

Anheier, H. K. (1987): "Indigenous Voluntary Associations, Non-Profits, and Develop-ment in Africa," in *The Non-Profit Sector: A Research Handbook*, W. Powell (Ed.), New Haven: Yale University Press, 416–433.

Anheier, H. K. (1989): "Private Voluntary Organizations and Development in West Africa: Comparative Perspectives," in *The Non-Profit Sector in Comparative Perspective*, E. James (Ed.), New York: Oxford University Press. 339–357.

Ayres, R. L. (1983): *Banking on the Poor: The World Bank and World Poverty*, Cambridge, Mass.: MIT Press.

Baldwin, G. G. (1986): "World Bank/NGO Cooperation in Agricultural and Rural Development in Sub-Saharan Africa," DAC Seminar on the Role of NGOs in Rural Development in Sub-saharan Africa, June 3–4, 1986, OECD, Paris.

Bauer, P. T. (1981): *Equality, the Third World and Economic Delusion*, Cambridge, Mass.: Harvard University Press.

Berg, R. J. and J. S. Whitaker (Eds.) (1986): *Strategies for African Development*, Berkeley: University of California Press.

Betts, T. F. (1978): "Development Aid From Voluntary Agencies to the Least Devel-oped Countries," *Africa Today* 25, 48–68.

Bienen, H. (1983): "Income Distribution and Politics in Nigeria," in *The Political Economy of Nigeria*, W. I. Zartman (Ed.), New York: Praeger, 85–104.

BMZ (Bundesministerium für wirtschaftliche Zusammenarbeit) (1985): *Sechster Bericht zur Entwicklungspolitik der Bundesregierung*, Bonn: BMZ.

Bolling, L. R. and C. Smith (1982): *Private Foreign Aid: U.S. Philanthropy for Relief and Development*, Boulder, Co.: Westview Press.

Catholic Church of Nigeria (1982): *The History of the Catholic Church in Nigeria*, Lagos: Academic Press/Macmillan Nigeria.

Dams, Th. (1986): "Entwicklung, Entwicklungspolitik," in *Staatslexikon*, Vol. 2, Freiburg: Herder, 294–330.

Decalo, S. (1976): *Coups and Army Rule in Africa. Studies in Military Style*, New Haven: Yale University Press.

DiMaggio, P. and W. Powell (1983): "Institutional Isomorphism," *American Sociological Review* 48, 147–160.

Douglas, J. (1983): *Why Charity? The Case for a Third Sector*, Beverly Hills: Sage.

Elsenhans, H. (1981): *Abhängiger Kapitalismus oder bürokratische Entwicklungsgesellschaft: Versuch über den Staat in der Dritten Welt*, Frankfurt: Campus.

Glagow, M. and H. D. Evers (Eds.) (1986): "Unbürokratische Entwicklungshilfe?" Universität Bielefeld, Fakultät für Soziologie/Entwicklungssoziologie, Materialien 20.

Griffin, K. (1977): "Increasing Poverty and Changing Ideas About Development Strategies," *Development and Change* 8, 491–508.

Gueneau, M. C. and C. Morrisson (1985): "Economic Survey of a Sample of Small Development Projects," DAC Meeting on Aid Agency Cooperation with Non-Governmental Organizations, OECD, Paris (working document).

Hyden, G. (1983): *No Shortcuts to Progress: African Development Management in Perspective*, Berkeley: University of California Press.

Interaction (1985): *Diversity in Development. U.S. Voluntary Assistance to Africa. Summary of Findings*, New York: Interaction.

Jackson, T. (1982): *Against the Grain: The Dilemma of Project Food Aid*, Oxford: Oxfam UK.

James, E. (1987): "The Non-Profit Sector in Comparative Perspective," in *The Non-Profit Sector: A Research Handbook*, W. Powell (Ed.), New Haven: Yale University Press, 397–432.

Korten, D. C. (1987): "Third Generation NGO Strategies: A Key to People-centered Development," *World Development* 15, Supplement, 145–161.

Krauss, M. B. (1983): *Development Without Aid: Growth, Poverty and Government*, New York: New Press (McGraw-Hill).

Lappe, F. M., J. C. Collins, and D. Kinley (1980): *Aid as Obstacle: Twenty Questions About Food Aid and Hunger*, San Francisco: Institute for Food and Development Policy.

Masoni, V. (1985): "Nongovernmental Organizations and Development," *Finance and Development* 22, 38–41.

Nohlen, D. and F. Nuscheler (Eds.) (1982): *Handbuch der Dritten Welt, Band 4, Westafrika and Zentralafrika: Unterentwicklung und Entwicklung*, Hamburg: Hoffmann und Campe.

OECD (1983): *Development Co-Operation. 1983 Review*, Paris: OECD.

OECD (1985): *Twenty-Five Years of Development Cooperation. A Review*, Paris: OECD.

OECD (1986): *Development Co-Operation. 1986 Review*, Paris: OECD.

OECD (1987): *Development Co-Operation. 1987 Review*, Paris: OECD.

Paul, S. (1982): *Managing Development Programs: The Lessons of Success*, Boulder: Westview Press.

Payer, C. (1982): *The World Bank: A Critical Analysis*, New York: Monthly Review Press.

Rice, A. E. (1983): *The Role of NGOs in Development Cooperation*, Paris: OECD.

Roninelli, D. A. and Nellis, J. R. (1986): "Assessing Decentralization Policies in Developing Countries: The Case for Cautious Optimism," *Development Policy Review* 4, 3–23.

Rose, T. (1985) (Ed.): *Crisis and Recovery in Sub-Saharan Africa*. Paris: Development Centre, OECD.

Salamon, L. (1987): "Of Market Failure, Voluntary Failure, and Third Party Government: Toward a Theory of Government–Nonprofit Relations in the Modern Welfare State," *Journal of Voluntary Action Research* 16, 29–49.

Schneider, B. (1985): *La Révolution au pied nus* (Rapport au Club de Rome), Paris: Fayard.

Schumacher, E. F. (1973): *Small is Beautiful: Economics as if People Mattered*, New York: Harper and Row.

Shirley, M. M. (1983): "Managing State-Owned Enterprises," World Bank Staff Working Paper, No. 577, *Management and Development Series*, No. 4.

Smith, B. (1987): "An Agenda of Future Tasks for International and Indigenous NGOs: Views from the North," *World Development* 15, Supplement, 87–93.

Sommer, J. C. (1979): *Beyond Charity: U.S. Voluntary Aid for a Changing Third World*, Washington, D.C.: Overseas Development Council.

Streeten, P. et al. (1981): *First Things First: Meeting Basic Human Needs in Developing Countries*, New York: Oxford University Press.

Tendler, J. (1982): "Turning Private Voluntary Organizations into Developmental Agencies. Questions for Evaluation," *A.I.D. Program Evaluation Discussion Paper*, No. 12, Washington, D.C.

Twose, N. (1987): "European NGOs: Growth or Partnership?" *World Development* 15, Supplement, 7–10.

van der Heijden, H. (1987): "The Reconciliation of NGO Autonomy, Program Integrity, and Operational Effectiveness with Accountability to Donors," *World Development* 15, Supplement, 103–113.

Wheeler, D. (1984): "Sources of Stagnation in Sub-Saharan Africa," *World Development* 12, 1–23.

West Africa (1985): "Autopsy on a Housing Project," No. 3434: 1034–1045.

World Bank (1981): *Toward Sustained Development in Sub-Saharan Africa. A Joint Program for Action*, Washington, D.C.: The World Bank.

World Bank (1984): *World Bank Development Report 1984*, Oxford: Oxford University Press.

World Bank (1985): *World Development Report 1985*, Oxford: Oxford University Press.

Part V
Conclusion

5
The Third Sector in Comparative Perspective: Four Propositions

Helmut K. Anheier and Wolfgang Seibel

Research on the third sector has overcome many of the normative statements which often characterized discussions on "the welfare state in crisis" during the last decade. Professionals in or close to nonprofit institutions tend to see the third sector as an alternative, which combines, as Etzioni (1973: 315) once put it, "efficiency and expertise from the business world with public interest, accountability, and broader planning from government." Research has revealed several inherent deficiencies of third sector organizations such as goal diversion, lack of accountability, rent seeking, or philanthropic amateurism. Together, these failures and deficiencies account for a more realistic view of organizational behavior in the third sector. In this volume, such a view is exemplified by the contributions of Anheier, Kramer, Leat, and Seibel.

Ideological aims and political hopes continue to have an influence on thinking on the third sector. We argue that this tendency is a direct result of the sector's history. Voluntary agencies, foundations, and non-governmental organizations served, and continue to serve, both as tools of social and economic policy, and as symbols of political ideologies. The prominent role which third sector organizations occupy across the political spectrum in party platforms and actual policies alike is a good example in this respect.

Moreover, we should recall that the ideological relationship between the state and the third sector is neither a one-way street nor necessarily free of conflict. We are reminded of the way in which governments rely increasingly on third sector organizations in the formulation of policies. Often, governments are not in a position to develop viable, new policies and programs. Nonprofit "think tanks" meet the demand for policy innovation. The growth in both the sheer number and the influence of policy institutes and "think tanks" around Washington and London in the 1980s show clearly the third sector's role in politics.

There seem to be two principal reasons for the complex political and ideological relationship between the state and the third sector. First, the third sector appears historically as a repository of institutional responses to social and political conflicts (see chapter 4.5 on Germany by Anheier). The third sector not only accomodates heterogeneity, but it also seems to preserve differences in tastes and ideologies, which sometimes surface as de-modernized institutional niches in the fabric of modern society (see chapter 2.6 by

Seibel). Religious and ideological traditions may cause resistance against institutional modernization as advocated by government policies or economic competition. This is particularly the case for religious organizations, social movements, and grassroots associations. Here, the contributions by Hansmann (2.3), Lloyd (3.5), Pestoff (2.4), and Thränhardt (4.7) offer insight into the relationship between third sector organizations and the state under changing circumstances.

The state's utilization of the third sector presents the second reason for the complexity of the relationship between the two sectors. The crisis of the welfare state in most industrialized countries was basically a crisis of the public sector, not only in the West but also in eastern European countries, according to Marschall's contribution (chapter 4.2). However, there is no easily discernable common pattern in state—third sector relations. In France, for instance, the state fosters, even nurtures, third sector activities both by increased subsidies and by providing a favorable administrative environment (see Archambault's chapter 4.3). In the United States, in contrast, political rhetoric rather than fiscal policies supports the third sector as an "alternative to big government" (see contribution by Salamon [chapter 3.4]).

If national contingencies and national dispositions towards organizing (see chapter 2.5 by Hood and Schuppert) seem almost overwhelmingly important in shaping the third sector, to what extent can we assume cross-national, general, and "culture-free" reasons for its existence? Economists are inclined to explain the third sector by pointing to its competitive advantage vis-à-vis for-profit firms and public bureaucracies under specific characteristics of supply and demand (see chapter 2.2 by Badelt and chapter 1.2 James). The micro-economic approach assumes great flexibility in institutional choice and tends either to ignore the role of tradition, ideology, and culture, or to treat these factors as unspecified, exogenous variables.

Clearly, the challenge is to include factors outside the micro-economic model. In doing so, we should investigate the long-term effects of competitive advantages not only in terms of economic efficiency but also in the light of political stability, social integration, and maintenance of value patterns. By considering intangible goods provided by third sector organizations, Seibel (see chapter 2.6) is able to explain the survival of nonprofits despite low degrees of responsiveness and efficiency.

1. Four Propositions

It is beyond the scope of this paper to attempt a summary which would do justice to the major issues raised by the various contributions in this volume. Instead, we try to present a selective summary by concentrating on four general propositions.

Thesis 1: "Public" and "Private" are neither dichotomous nor does more "Private" necessarily imply less "Public," and vice versa.

Sociologists have long argued that public and private are neither constant concepts nor zero-sum combinations. The third sector seems to support this assumption. Research has shown that the expansion of the public sector does not necessarily lead to a contraction of private nonprofit activities (see Salamon's chapter 3.4). Even "core" third sector organizations receive often strikingly different legal and political treatment cross-nationally. Rosas (1984) has shown that the classification of national Red Cross societies ranges from "public associations" and "non-commercial membership organizations" under private law, to "mass voluntary public organizations" governed by public law.

The division of responsibility between private and public sectors is neither stable nor fully formalized (see chapter 3.6 by Kramer and chapter 3.4 Salamon). Divisions into sections are the result of institutional differentiation and legal codification. It could be argued that the more one increases differentiation and complexity, the less useful the whole concept of sectors becomes. We could argue that the designation of organizations into sectors may ultimately rest on research conventions rather than on strict empirical grounds. At present, two theoretical perspectives may help explain the blurring of institutional differentiation in modern society.

First, economic approaches such as institutional choice (see Badelt's contribution 2.2) try to "atomize" the formation and survival of institutional forms. From this point of view, designation to either the for-profit, third, or public sector is determined not by distinct boundaries but by the aggregation of individual choices over different combinations of transaction costs and informational asymmetries.

Second, economic and sociological approaches to coordination among individual actors (cf. Kaufmann et al. 1986; Williamson 1975) may provide a way to abandon the strict sector-centered view of institutional differentiation. As economists have argued, formal organizational boundaries are less important for collective action than horizontal and vertical mechanisms of coordination, namely markets and hierarchies. Sociologists have extended this perspective by adding other mechanisms of coordination such as solidarity, ethical principles, and political preferences and alliances. Accordingly, sectors may constitute different mixes of coordinating mechanisms. Both the public and the private for-profit sectors primarily represent mixes of markets and hierarchy, whereas the third sector may be formed by a mix of markets, hierarchies, solidarity, and ethical as well as political elements.

Thesis 2: Third sector organizations are both interest-mediating and service-providing institutions.

To a large extent, third sector research is characterized by two sets of assumptions. The first set of assumptions refers to the competitive advantages of third sector organizations relative to public agencies and for-profit firms (see chapters by Badelt [2.2], Hansmann [2.3], James [1.2] and Rose-Ackerman [3.1] in this volume). The second set of assumptions deals with micro-analytical issues of government – third sector relations (see contributions by Kramer [3.6], Leat [2.8], Lloyd [3.5], and Knapp et al. [3.3]).

Moreover, the intermediary zone between the market and the state has been analyzed by political scientists in great detail with respect to interest-mediation (Berger 1981; Lehmbruch and Schmitter 1982; Schmitter and Lehmbruch 1979). However, while political scientists have given their full attention to the political economy of interest mediation, they have tended to neglect organizational sociology. Vice versa, whereas much third sector research has focussed on organizational processes and variables at the micro-level, it has tended to lose sight of the larger context in terms of a political economy. In particular, little attention has been paid to the political functions of service-providing organizations like private welfare associations.

Service-providing organizations within the third sector have a socio-political twin function. They tend to combine aspects of social and political integration with economic objectives. Bauer (1978) and Kramer (1981) have shown that the rise of voluntary agencies providing public goods is connected with the emergence of social movements; charitable foundations have served as ideological shelters for business interests (Karl and Katz 1987), or as a tool for foreign policy (Arnove 1980). Thus, we are looking at only one side of the coin if we try to explain the existence of third sector organizations by greater efficiency. Third sector organizations may survive while being x-efficient (Leibenstein 1966, 1976). This is the case if economic efficiency as a performance criterion is partially replaced by social and political considerations (even pay-offs), loyalty (Hirschman 1970), or organizational myths and ceremonial rituals (Meyer and Rowan 1978).

Furthermore, analysis of third sector – government relationships must go beyond the description of financial transactions. The American third sector offers a good example in this respect. In the 1980s, the sector faced the paradoxical situation of receiving vivid rhetorical support from the government, while at the same time public subsidies were being cut (see Salamon and Abramson 1982; and Salamon's chapter 3.4 in this volume). This demonstrates clearly how institutions, or entire segments and sectors, are used as symbols for political ends (cf. Seibel 1989).

Thesis 3: National patterns of third sector arrangements are shaped more by functions of socio-political integration than by criteria of economic efficiency.

Observed national patterns of institutional arrangements in the third sector seem to suggest a lower flexibility than economic theories of institutional choice would lead one to assume. Generally, we observe in most countries a relatively stable division of tasks and responsibilities between the private, the public, and the third sector — a stability which seems to contain strong elements of institutional and structural inertia (Wilensky 1981). In any case, in the delivery of public and semi-public goods, there appears to be little flexibility of choice between institutional options, as demand and resource dependencies change.

Furthermore, it has been argued that the pressures created by the need to show economic efficiency are likely to cause organizations to become identical in structure and functioning, in turn leading to a predominance of formal bureaucratic organizations (cf. DiMaggio and Powell 1983). However, many of the contributions in this volume suggest that heterogeneity and pluralism rather than homogeneity and isomorphism are central characteristics of the third sector. The third sector does not seem to fit easily into theories which predict a more or less uniform and homogeneous development of the welfare state in modern societies (cf. Rokkan 1974). Third sector organizations apparently resist pressures of isomorphism. Recalling the twin function of third sector organizations, we may assume that national patterns of third sector arrangements are not due to the isomorphic pressures of economic efficiency but to the diverse needs and conditions of social and political integration.

In this respect, it is well worth comparing the three distinct national patterns as represented by West Germany, France, and the United States. In German history, the necessity to integrate powerful socialist movements, plus the fear of political extremism after World War II, has created a situation in which the government readily transfers public funds and delegates authority to non-governmental organizations in the field of social welfare. For the sake of political stability, the state surrenders sovereignty (as exemplified by the principle of subsidiarity). The creation of non-governmental, yet centralized organizational structures was favored by two factors: first, the development of a decentralized and fragmented institutional environment of the German state; and, second, the social homogeneity of the aristocratic elites in public bureaucracies.

In contrast, in France, the French Jacobinian tradition, centralized public administration, and republican government favored welfare étatisme. This was accompanied by the ideological "ambiguity of the Left" (Ashford 1986: 189) and challenged by influential opponents like the Catholic church and the lay movement, which together held large shares in the educational and health system.

In American history, as exhaustively described by historians, the experience of the successful struggle against colonial power, individualistic religions, and rapid geographical expansion decreased the importance of socialist movements and increased skepticism of government. As a result, collective protection against individual risks is generally less developed than in other

Western countries, whereas individual and corporate philanthropy remain relatively more important.

In most countries, the third sector depends substantially on public subsidies, and the relation between third sector and government is relatively well developed in all industrial countries (James 1989). However, great variations remain, and public subsidies may greatly reduce the sector's independence, or lead to relatively independent "private governments."

Thesis 4: The type of regulatory regime influences the orientation of the third sector.

Civil law countries, exemplified by France, Germany, Austria, and Italy, are rooted in a mixture of etatist (later often corporatist) reformism and Catholicism. With the exception of France, they are countries where the church played a dominant role in social reforms following the industrial revolution, and where absolutism was comparatively slowly or incompletely abolished. Although to some degree dependent on the degree of centralization, civil law countries developed a *state-oriented third sector*. Organizations in the third sector tend to resemble state agencies more closely than for-profit firms. Public service provision is emphasized over voluntarism.

In common law countries, the third sector is more *market-oriented*. It puts more emphasis on voluntarism than on public service, and nonprofit firms tend to be more like for-profit firms than like state agencies. The liberal third sector originated with the English Poor Law of 1601 and is today found in such countries as the United Kingdom, the U.S., Canada, and Australia. While in most common law countries the state, for political reasons, tried to incorporate social welfare into state affairs, the liberal state of civil law countries tried to restrict involvement in welfare activities.

Since civil law and common law each correspond to distinct political cultures and traditions, we may analyze the political context of the third sector along three dimensions. First, we distinguish between three regulatory regimes: the liberal and the conservative regulatory regime both of which reach back to the nineteenth century; and the social democratic regime, which is essentially a twentieth century phenomenon. The second dimension, that of religious homogeneity/heterogeneity, refers to whether a Catholic or Protestant hegemony exists or whether the population is religiously heterogeneous. The final dimension is the degree of centralization – decentralization of public welfare state activities. Equipped with these three dimensions, we can (a) identify and examine groups of countries with comparable attributes, and (b) investigate distinct third sector forms (such as foundations) across different groups.

For example, with the first two variables at hand, we can construct a simple typology of "pure" types, such as the Protestant – liberal combination with the United Kingdom as the prime example, or the Catholic – conservative combination in the case of Austria and Italy. We can also point to deviations such as the Netherlands (mixed – liberal), Germany (mixed – conservative), or the Irish case.

For other countries, the centralization – decentralization dimension may be more important. For example, in France, the absence of both state church and aristocracy after the revolution, combined with a strong republican or centralized state tradition, produced a weak third sector in the past. France has traditionally had a relatively centralized state, where "private" initiatives in "public" domains were regarded with great suspicion by the central state. Consequently, the new association movement during the last decade is closely related to the decentralization of political power and administration, and has led to a renegotiation of power at local levels.

2. Concluding Remarks

Comparative research on the third sector has just begun. As has become apparent on the previous pages, many research questions remain. We will briefly outline four major aspects. First, we must link third sector research to neighboring fields where a tradition of comparative research has already developed; for example, studies on the welfare state (Flora and Heidenheimer 1981; Heidenheimer, Heclo, and Adams 1983) or corporatism (Berger 1981; Lehmbruch and Schmitter 1982; Schmitter and Lehmbruch 1979).

Second, there remains a lack of comparative data on the size, scope, and composition of the third sector. Cross-national surveys confront formidable measurement problems in terms of validity and comparability.

Third, research is needed which combines micro- and macro-analytical perspectives. In particular, micro-economic hypotheses on the creation and maintenance of nonprofit organizations must be examined at the level of organizational fields, and combined with longitudinal analyses of their life cycles and organizational behavior. Finally, there is a need for historical research on the origins, emergence, and development of the third sector. Despite several historical studies on the sector in the United States, England, and Germany, comparative historical analyses remain all too rare.

References

Arnove, R. F. (1980): *Philanthropy and Cultural Imperialism. The Foundations at Home and Abroad*, Boston: G. K. Hall & Co.
Ashford, D. E. (1986): *The Emergence of the Welfare State*, Oxford and London: Basil & Blackwell.

Bauer, R. (1978): *Wohlfahrtsverbände in der Bundesrepublik*, Weinheim und Basel: Beltz.

Berger, S. (Ed.) (1981): *Organizing Interests in Western Europe. Pluralism, Corporatism, and the Transformation of Politics*, Cambridge and London: Cambridge University Press.

DiMaggio, P. J. and W. W. Powell (1983): "The Iron Cage Revisited: Institutional Isomorphism and Collective Rationality in Organizational Fields," *American Sociological Review* 48, 147–160.

Etzioni, A. (1973): "The Third Sector and Domestic Missions," *Public Administration Review* 3, 314–323.

Flora, P. and A. J. Heidenheimer (Eds.) (1981): *The Development of Welfare States in Europe and America*, New Brunswick and London: Transaction Books.

Heidenheimer, A. J., H. Heclo, and C. T. Adams (Eds.) (1983): *Comparative Public Policy. The Politics of Social Choice in Europe and America*, 2nd ed., New York: St. Martin's Press.

Hirschman, A. O. (1970): *Exit, Voice, and Loyalty. Responses to Decline in Firms, Organizations, and States*, Cambridge, Mass.: Harvard University Press.

James, E. (1989): *The Nonprofit Sector in International Perspective. Studies in Comparative Culture and Policy*, New York and Oxford: Oxford University Press.

Karl, B. D. and S. N. Katz (1987): "Foundations and Ruling Class Elites," *Daedalus* 116, 1–40.

Kaufmann, F.-X., G. Majone, and V. Ostrom (Eds.) (1986): *Guidance, Control and Evaluation in the Public Sector*, Berlin and New York: de Gruyter.

Kramer, R. M. (1981): *Voluntary Agencies in the Welfare State*, Berkeley (etc.): University of California Press.

Lehmbruch, G. and Ph. C. Schmitter (Eds.) (1982): *Patterns of Corporatist Policy-Making*, London and Beverly Hills: Sage.

Leibenstein, H. (1966): "Allocative Efficiency versus 'X-Efficiency'," *American Economic Review* 56, 392–415.

Leibenstein, H. (1976): *Beyond Economic Man. A New Foundation for Microeconomics*, Cambridge, Mass. and London: Harvard University Press.

Meyer, J. W. and B. Rowan (1978): "Institutionalized Organizations: Formal Structure as Myth and Ceremony," *American Journal of Sociology* 83, 340–363.

Rokkan, S. (1974): "Cities, States, and Nations," in *Building States and Nations*, S. N. Eisenstadt and S. Rokkan (Eds.), Beverly Hills and London: Sage, 73–97.

Rosas, A. (1984): "Notes on the Legal Status on National Red Cross Societies," in *Studies and Essays on International Humanitarian Law and Red Cross Principles*, Ch. Swinarski (Ed.), Genova: Nijhoff, 954–973.

Salamon, L. M. and A. J. Abramson (1982): *The Federal Budget and the Nonprofit Sector*, Washington, D.C.: The Urban Institute Press.

Schmitter, Ph. C. and G. Lehmbruch (Eds.) (1979): *Trends Toward Corporatist Intermediation*, Beverly Hills and London: Sage.

Seibel, W. (1989): "The Function of Mellow Weakness. Nonprofit Organizations as Problem Non-Solvers in Germany," in *The Nonprofit Sector in International Perspective. Studies in Comparative Culture and Policy*, Estelle James (Ed.), New York and Oxford: Oxford University Press, 177–192.

Wilensky, H. (1981): "Foreword," *Voluntary Agencies in the Welfare State*, R. M. Kramer (Ed.), Berkeley (etc.): University of California Press, xiv–xxii.

Williamson, O. E. (1975): *Markets and Hierarchies. Analysis and Anti-Trust Implications. A Study in the Economics of Internal Organization*, New York and London: Free Press (USA) and Cassell & Collier Macmillan (GB).

Biographical Notes

Helmut K. Anheier is Assistant Professor of Sociology at Rutgers University. His research interests are structural analysis, organizational and economic sociology, and the sociology of art. He has published in all these areas, and is currently working on a comparative study of organizational forms located between the market and the state, and on a structural analysis of structural failures in organizational fields. He is founding co-editor of VOLUNTAS.

Edith Archambault is an economist and professor at the University of Poitiers, and holds a research position at the Laboratoire d'Economie Sociale of the University of Paris I (Sorbonne). Current research deals with the accounting of non-market items, such as environment, domestic production, voluntary work, underground economy, and the economics of culture. She has published numerous books and articles.

Christoph Badelt is professor of economics and social policy at the Vienna University of Economics and Business Administration. Areas of publication: economics of the nonprofit sector, volunteer labor, social policy (particularly social services, family policy), public finance (particularly public sector administration), and institutional economics.

Bart F. M. Bakker studied sociology at the University of Amsterdam. Since 1980 he has done research on educational and occupational attainment, income attainment, quality of life and social stratification. Since 1982 he has worked at the Netherlands' Central Bureau of Statistics, and developed a new classification of social classes.

Rudolph Bauer is Professor of Social Policy and Social Work at the University of Bremen, Federal Republic of Germany. He is author of *"Wohlfahrtsverbände in der Bundesrepublik"* (= Welfare Associations in the Federal Republic) and co-editor of *"Organisierte Nächstenliebe"* (= Organized Charity) and *"Verbandliche Wohlfahrtspflege im internationalen Vergleich"* (= Welfare by Associations in International Comparison). In 1989, he was a Senior Fellow in Philanthropy at Johns Hopkins University, Institute for Policy Studies, USA.

Jaap Dronkers studied sociology at the Free University of Amsterdam, and obtained his doctor's degree in the Department of Social Sciences at the same university with a thesis on the selection of students in Dutch universities.

He is active in research on educational and occupational attainment, social mobility and stratification, elites and macro-relations between education and society. Currently, he is associate professor at the Department of Sociology at Tilburg University.

Juan Rovira Forns is senior lecturer in economics, at the Department of Economic Theories of the University of Barcelona, Spain. His current research interests are in the fields of health economics and social policy. He is the current president of the Spanish Health Economics Association.

Henry Hansmann is Professor of Law at Yale University. He is the author of a number of articles on the law and economics of nonprofit and cooperative organizations, and is interested generally in the economic analysis of legal rules and institutions.

Christopher Hood was Professor of Government and Public Administration, University of Sydney. Principal published works: *The Limits of Administration* (1976) *Big Government in Hard Times* (ed. with M. Wright 1981), *Bureaumetrics* (with A. Dunsire 1981), *The Tools of Government* (1983), *Administrative Analysis* (1986), *Delivering Public Services in Western Europe* (ed. with G. F. Schuppert 1988). He know teaches at the London School of Economics.

Estelle James is Professor of Economics at the State University of New York, Stony Brook. She is the editor of *The Nonprofit Sector in International Perspective: Studies in Comparative Culture and Policy* (Oxford University Press) and the co-author of *Public Policy and Private Education in Japan* (Macmillan), *The Nonprofit Enterprise in Market Economies* (Harwood) and *Hoffa and the Teamsters: A Study in Union Power* (Van Nostrand). She has written numerous articles on the economics of education and nonprofit organizations.

Dr. Martin Knapp is Professor of economics and social policy and Deputy Director, Personal Social Services Research Unit, University of Kent at Canterbury. His research activities center around the economic analysis of health, social welfare and criminal justice services, with a particular interest in the comparative performance of non-profit, for-profit and public sector organizations. He is founding co-editor of VOLUNTAS.

Ralph M. Kramer is Professor in the School of Social Welfare, University of California, Berkeley. His teaching and research focus on social policy and management aspects of the voluntary sector. His books include: *Voluntary*

Agencies and the Welfare State, Participation of the Poor, and *Community Development in Israel and the Netherlands.*

Peter J. B. M. Van Laarhoven studied sociology at the University of Utrecht. Since 1982 he has been active in research on educational attainment with an emphasis on secondary education and the transition from school to work. Currently, he is a research fellow at the Institute of Research in Education of Groningen University (RION).

Diana Leat has taught at Swansea University and at the City University London. As Senior Research Fellow at the Policy Studies Institute and at Warwick University her research interests focussed around volunteers, voluntary organisations and broadcast fundraising. She is currently teaching at University of Wales College Cardiff.

Peter C. Lloyd is Professor of Social Anthropology at the University of Sussex, United Kingdom. Twenty years teaching and research in Nigeria were followed by the study of a Peruvian shanty town. He is now engaged in studies of community action in Britain, with special reference to care for the elderly.

Miklos Marschall holds a doctorate in economics from Karl Marx University in Budapest, Hungary, and is a Research Fellow at the Research Institute for Culture in Budapest. In 1988/89 he was a visiting Fulbright Scholar at Yale University's Program on Nonprofit Organizations. He has published numerous articles on public finance, the economics of culture and nonprofit activities in centrally planned economies. Recently, his research has focused on the revival of "third sector" organizations in Hungary.

Victor A. Pestoff, Ph. D., is Senior Research Fellow at the Department of Business Administration, University of Stockholm, Sweden and Adjunct Professor at the Department of Political Science, University of Helsinki, Finland. Author of *Voluntary Associations & Nordic Party Systems* (1977), *Between Markets & Politics or Beyond? – Co-operatives in Sweden* (1990) and *Organizations and the Political Economy of the Nordic Welfare States* (1991).

Eileen Robertson is Research Fellow in The Health Economics Consortium at the University of York, providing research and consultancy services to Health Authorities. Previously she was Research Fellow in the Personal Social Services Research Unit at the University of Kent at Canterbury, working mainly on the evaluation of services for children and young offenders.

Susan Rose-Ackerman is Ely Professor of Law and Political Economy in the Law School and the Department of Political Science, Yale University. She has also taught at the University of Pennsylvania and Columbia University. Professor Rose-Ackerman is the author of *Corruption: A Study in Political Economy* (Academic Press 1978), the editor of *The Economics of Nonprofit Institutions* (Oxford 1978), and the co-author (with Estelle James) of *The Nonprofit Enterprise in Market Economies* (Harwood 1986). Her current work involves the relationship between administrative law and social science.

Lester M. Salamon ist Director of the Institute for Policy Studies at Johns Hopkins University in the United States. He formerly served as director of The Nonprofit Sector Project at The Urban Institute in Washington, D.C., as Deputy Associate Director of the U.S. Office of Management and Budget, and as Professor of Policy Sciences at Duke University. Dr. Salamon has written widely on the nonprofit sector and on policy and governance issues more generally. His most recent books are: *Beyond Privatization: The Tools of Government Action* (Urban Institute Press, 1989); *Managing Foundation Assets* (Foundation Center, 1989); *The Nonprofit Sector and the New Federal Budget* (The Urban Institute Press, 1986).

Susan Saxon-Harrold is Research Manager at the Charities Aid Foundation in London. At CAF she runs the research program on philanthropy and the voluntary sector. Annual publications include: 'Charity Trends', the 'Charity Household Survey' and 'Company Community Involvement'. Prior to joining CAF she was attached to the 'Markets and Voluntary Action' project at the Management Centre, University of Bradford. She obtained her Doctorate in Management and Administration in 1986. She has recently been involved in setting up VOLUNTAS, the new international journal of voluntary sector research.

Huibert Schijf studied political science at the University of Amsterdam. Since 1975 he has been associate professor in methodology at the Department of Sociology there. He has done research on elites, social networks and education.

Dr. Gunnar Folke Schuppert is Professor (Ordinarius) for public law at the University of Augsburg, West Germany. He has previousely taught at the universities of Göttingen and Hamburg. He has published numerous articles on administrative law and legal aspects of governance and public service delivery in modern societies. His books include *Casebook Verfassungsrecht*, and *Delivering Public Services in Western Europe* (with Christopher Hood).

Dr. Wolfgang Seibel is Professor of Political Science at the University of Konstanz, Federal Republic of Germany. Earlier he was Assistant Professor

(Hochschulassistent) at the University of Kassel, FRG. Recent affiliations include a guest scholarship at the Max-Planck-Institut für Gesellschafts-forschung, Cologne, and a membership at the Institute for Advanced Study, Princeton. Seibel is the author of three books and numerous articles on issues of governability, and administrative science and the political sociology of the 'third sector'. His current research focuses on a comparative analysis of the third sector's role in West Germany, France, and the United States.

John G. Simon is August Lines Professor of Law and deputy dean, Yale Law School, and founding director of the Program on Nonprofit Organizations at Yale. He has been engaged in teaching and research on philanthropy and the nonprofit sector since the early 1960's. He has written many articles and book chapters on various topics in law, philanthropy and education.

Corinne Thomason is Research Fellow in the Personal Social Services Research Unit, University of Kent at Canterbury. Her current research interests center around dehospitalization programs, community care and the role of non-profit organizations in the provision of public welfare services. Previously she gained management experience in local government and the health service.

Anna Maria Thränhardt is lecturer at the department of Political Science at the University of Münster. After a year of studying Japanese at International Christian University/Mitaka in Japan she studied Far Eastern Sciences at the University of Bonn, Free University Berlin and Bochum University, where she completed her Ph. D. on "Script Reform-Discussion in Early Meiji Japan — An analysis of its linguistic and political-sociological aspects." She participated in a research project on: "Communal Democracy in Crisis? — Centralization and Decentralization as Challenges to Local Democracy in Japan and the Federal Republic of Germany" and is currently engaged in research on the Japanese Welfare System.

Antonin Wagner was born in Lucerne (Switzerland). After completing his studies in Belgium and Switzerland, he was a Research Scholar at the Center for Research on Economic Development, University of Michigan, USA, in 1973 – 1974. Since 1975, he has been Dean of the School of Social Work in Zurich, Switzerland, and, since 1976 Adjunct Professor at the Department of Economics of the University of Zurich. In 1987, he was a Visiting Professor at the Florence Heller Graduate School for Advanced Studies in Social Welfare, Brandeis University, USA. He has published widely in the area of public finance and social policy.

Name Index

Subject Index

Social policy, 232, 261, 272, 296 – 298, 379
Social problems, 50, 115, 117, 230 – 232, 273, 357
Social Security Act, 226
Social security system,
France 295 – 298
Japan, 348
in a socialist economy, 279, 288
Spain, 273, 333 – 337, 340
in Switzerland, 307, 309, 311
in West-Germany, 11
Social service agencies, 220 – 221, 255 – 267, 290
Social services,
provision at local level, 241 – 253
Socialism, 8, 272, 366
state socialism, 285 – 286, 288
socialist government, 11
Socialist economy, 271, 277 – 291
economic crisis in the, 286
social security system 279, 288
Socialist society,
associations, 277, 287, 290
civic autonomy, 286
Socio-cultural background, 347, 354 – 356
Solidarity, 8, 12 – 13, 116 – 117, 148, 242, 381
Soviet Union, 1, 277
Spain, 2, 271, 273, 328, 333 – 344
health care insurance market, 333 – 344
Specialization, 200 – 204, 262
State, see also government
agencies, 9, 131, 242 – 252, 374, 384
enterprises, 242, 277
regulation of health insurance market, 334 – 338
relationship with the church, 313, 316 – 317
relationship with the third sector, 65 – 74, 77 – 88, 219 – 240, 241 – 252, 277 – 279, 293 – 301, 313 – 329, 347 – 358, 379
state failure, 13 – 14, 48, 329, 340, see also government failure

State-planned economy, see socialist economy
State-Socialism, 285 – 286, 288
economy, see also socialism
Statutory agencies, 133, 135, 206, 255, 258, 264
Strategy of voluntary organizations, 123, 137
Subsidiarity, 94, 274, 316
principle, 99, 101, 316, 328, 383
subsidiarity problems approach, see transaction costs approach
Subzidization, see government funding
Substituting, 204, 228, 256 – 259, compare complementing
Supplementing, see complementing
Supply,
-side aspects of nonprofit organizations, 111, 183 – 185, 200 – 202, 370
undersupply, 56 – 57, 62
Sweden, 2, 35, 47, 77 – 91, 255
government funding, 81, 84 – 85
Conservative Party, 89
Liberal Party, 89
National Board for Consumer Policies, 83 – 87
social democratic government, 49, 84 – 90
Switzerland, 3, 255, 271, 303 – 312
government funding, 304, 306
Systems of National Accounts, 303 – 304, 307
System d'Identification pour le Répertoire des Entreprises et de leurs Établissements (SIRENE), 10, 298 – 299

Tangled web, of funding, 51, 136
Task-contingency theory, 50
Taste, differentiated, 23, 202, 260, 379
Tax,
advantages for charities, 183, 205, 300
authorities, 36, 186, 320
exemption of nonprofit organizations, 21, 66, 185, 196, 202 – 203, 220, 261, 290

de Gruyter Studies in Organization

An international series by internationally known
authors presenting current research in organization

Vol. 15

Boards of Directors Under Public Ownership:
A Comparative Perspective

By *Miriam Dornstein*
1988. 15.5 x 23 cm. X, 166 pages. Cloth. ISBN 3 11 011740 1; 0-89925-496-9 (U.S.)

Vol. 16

The State, Trade Unions and Self-Management
Issues of Competence and Control
Edited by *György Széll, Paul Blyton* and *Chris Cornforth*
1989. 15.5 x 23 cm. X, 362 pages. Cloth. ISBN 3 11 011667 7; 0-89925-475-7 (U.S.)

Vol. 17

Organization Theory and Class Analysis
New Approaches and New Issues
Edited by *Stewart R. Clegg*
1990. 15.5 x 23 cm. XIV, 529 pages. Cloth. ISBN 3 11 012003 8; 0-89925-567-1 (U.S.)

Vol. 18

Strategies for Retrenchment and Turnaround:
the Politics of Survival

by *Cynthia Hardy*
1989. 15.5 x 23 cm. XII, 222 pages. Cloth. ISBN 3 11 011612 X; 0-89925-452-7 (U.S.)

Vol. 19

Organizational Symbolism

Edited by *Barry A. Turner*
1989. 15.5 x 23 cm. XII, 315 pages. Cloth. ISBN 3 11 011051 2; 0-89925-635-X (U.S.)

Vol. 20

Capitalism in Contrasting Cultures

Edited by *Stewart R. Clegg, S. Gordon Redding,* assisted by Monica Cartner
1990. 15.5 x 23 cm. VIII, 451 pages. Cloth. ISBN 3 11 011857 2; 0-89925-525-6 (U.S.)

WALTER DE GRUYTER · BERLIN · NEW YORK

Genthiner Strasse 13, D-1000 Berlin 30, Phone (0 30) 2 60 05-0, Telex 1 83 027
200 Saw Mill River Road, Hawthorne, N.Y. 10532, Phone (914) 747-0110, Telex 64 66 77